The Best American Political Writing 2004

The Best American Political Writing 2004

Edited by Royce Flippin

Thunder's Mouth Press
New York

THE BEST AMERICAN POLITICAL WRITING 2004

Published by
Thunder's Mouth Press
An Imprint of Avalon Publishing Group Inc.
245 West 17th St., 11th Floor
New York, NY 10011

AVALON
publishing group incorporated

Copyright © 2004 by Royce N. Flippin, III
& Avalon Publishing Group Incorporated

Library of Congress Cataloging-in-Publication Data is available.

ISBN 1-56025-613-3

9 8 7 6 5 4 3 2 1

Book design by Sue Canavan
Printed in the United States of America
Distributed by Publishers Group West

This book is dedicated to my parents,
Louise and Royce Flippin,
with many thanks for their ongoing love and support

CONTENTS

National Conversation: Bush vs. Kerry

Part Three: The State of the Union

National Conversation: Gay Marriage

Part Four: (Not) Politics as Usual

Acknowledgments

I would like express my appreciation to all the writers who contributed to this anthology, and to their publishers, for allowing their work to be reprinted. I'd also like to thank everyone who helped shape this collection—particularly Dan O'Connor and Michael O'Connor of Avalon Publishers, whose input and collaboration has been invaluable, as always. Thanks, too, to publisher Neil Ortenberg, marketing director Karen Auerbach, and the Avalon production team, and to Taylor Smith, who acquired the permissions rights for the articles herein. Finally, I want to say a special thank-you to my wife, Alexis Lipsitz Flippin, for her love and good humor as she lived with this project day in and day out for the past several months.

Preface
Royce Flippin

Welcome to *The Best American Political Writing 2004*—the third edition of our anthology. The selections in this special election year volume cover the period from June 2003 through June 2004, including the Democratic primary campaign and the opening rounds of the main event between incumbent president George Bush and challenger John Kerry. As always, we've brought together an eclectic collection of in-depth articles and column-length pieces, offering a variety of thoughtful perspectives on the most pressing political issues of the past year.

The selections in this book range from straightforward reportage—such as Nicholas Lemann's fascinating profile of presidential advisor Karl Rove ("The Controller," p. 32), Lisa DePaulo's hilariously revealing portrait of the California gubernatorial recall election ("Californication," p. 268), and Philip Gourevitch's account of John Kerry's emergence from the pack in the Democratic presidential primary election ("The Shakeout," p. 106)—to investigative pieces like Michael Crowley's look at the troubled Homeland Security Department ("Playing Defense," p. 202), David Rieff's report on where the U.S. occupation of Iraq went off track ("Blueprint for a Mess," p. 359), and Christopher Schmitt and Edward Pound's report on the Bush administration's unprecedented penchant for withholding information from the public ("Keeping Secrets," p. 65). Readers will be especially interested in the unique look inside the workings of the Bush White House provided by two book excerpts—one from Ron Suskind's *The Price of Loyalty* (p. 3), and the other from Bob Woodward's latest bestseller, *Plan of Attack* (p. 317).

Other selections fall more into the category of political analysis. Some of them more or less nonpartisan—such as Jeffrey Toobin's explanation of why Congress is becoming ever more polarized ("The Great Election Grab," p. 165), Ryan Lizza's assessment of John Kerry's decision to keep a low public profile and concentrate on fund-raising after securing the Democratic nomination in early March ("Rope-a-Dope," p. 121), and Joshua Green's breakdown of the states that will most likely decide the presidential election in November ("In Search of the Elusive Swing Voter," p. 177). Other analyses clearly come with a pointed view—including Paul Krugman's scathing critique of the

Republicans' tax-cutting strategy ("The Tax-Cut Con," p. 186), Robert Kagan and William Kristol's carefully reasoned rebuttal of Democrats and others who opposed the invasion of Iraq ("The Right War for the Right Reasons," p. 341), Christopher Hitchens' biting review of Ralph Nader's latest run for the presidency ("Unsafe on Any Ballot," p. 125), and Robert Kennedy Jr.'s sweeping indictment of the Bush administration's environmental record "Crimes Against Nature" p. 213).

Like the selections themselves, the venues where they first appeared run the gamut from news magazines like *Time, Newsweek,* and *U.S. News & World Report* to newspapers like the *New York Times, Washington Post, Boston Globe,* and *San Francisco Chronicle,* to politically oriented magazines such as *The New Republic, The Weekly Standard,* and *The Progressive,* to general-interest publications, including *The New Yorker, GQ, Harper's,* and *Vanity Fair.* Online sources such as *Slate.com, National Review Online,* and *WorldNetDaily.com* are also well-represented.

Besides being well-written, what all of the pieces in this anthology have in common is that each provides a particular, reasoned insight into the complex political issues facing our country. In a year marked by ambiguity—from Iraq's uncertain future to the fight over the national agenda here at home—these selections all attempt to uncover some sort of truth, rather than indulge in polemics. Even when the criticism gets personal—as when David Brooks mocks Kerry for his attempts to have it both ways on any given issue ("The Boston Fog Machine," p. 152), or Jonathan Chait confesses his visceral dislike for President Bush ("Mad About You," p. 259)—these are writers who value clarity over cant, reason over hype, and honest debate over manipulative hectoring. Whether you agree or disagree with their individual views, we think you will respect where each author is coming from.

As in previous editions, this year's anthology is divided into a number of main sections, each containing relatively lengthy pieces: Part One, "More Politics in the Bush Era," focuses on the Bush administration; Part Two, "The 2004 Presidential Campaign," is self-explanatory; Part Three, "The State of the Union," addresses broad political issues effecting the country as a whole; Part Four, "(Not) Politics as Usual," features political subjects that are a bit off the beaten track; and Part Five, "Iraq and the War on Terror," concentrates on U.S. foreign policy, particularly in the Mideast. Sandwiched between each of these sections are segments titled "National Conversation." Each segment contains short columns offering differing views on a controversial topic. This year's subjects are the American economy, the Bush-Kerry presidential face-off, the politics of same-sex marriage, and the debate over the continuing U.S. presence in Iraq.

The world of politics never stops, of course, and events are continuing to unfold as this is being written: After bottoming out at close to 40 percent, George Bush's approval ratings appear to be rebounding slightly—pushed up in part by the so-far, so-good handover of sovereignty in Iraq—and John Kerry has annointed fellow senator John Edwards of North Carolina as his running mate. The economic recovery is struggling to maintain its momentum and the polls have Bush and Kerry in a virtual dead heat, with all signs pointing to another nail-biter of an election on November 2, 2004. As that pivotal election draws closer, we hope you'll find this book to be an enlightening and entertaining guide, both to the events of the recent past and to the unknown terrain that lies just ahead.

The Best American Political Writing 2004

Part One:
More Politics in the Bush Era

From: *The Price of Loyalty*

Ron Suskind

During his two-year tenure as President George W. Bush's treasury secretary, former Alcoa chairman Paul O'Neill proved once more that corporate America and Washington, D.C., are very different arenas. At Alcoa, O'Neill gained fame for turning a struggling company into the world's leading producer of aluminum. In his new post, however, he quickly became known for off-the-cuff remarks that were either politically inept, such as when he credited Enron's collapse to "the genius of capitalism," or economically ill-advised, as when he disparaged Brazil's government and sent its currency into a tailspin.

Touring Africa with Bono, the lead singer for the rock band U2, only added to O'Neill's image as a maverick. When he resisted the third round of Bush tax cuts, ("It reduces our fiscal flexibility to fix Social Security," he later explained, "which we desperately need to do."), that was the last straw. No one was surprised when, in December 2002, O'Neill got the axe in a phone call from his old friend Dick Cheney, the man who'd brought him on board in the first place.

Few imagined, however, that one short year later he would again be generating headlines—this time by going public with an insider's view of the Bush administration, as told to author Ron Suskind. In his book The Price of Loyalty, *Suskind employs a variety of sources, but the book's narrative rests mainly on his extensive interviews with O'Neill—backed up by some 19,000 Treasury documents that the ex-secretary passed along to him. (Some of these original documents can actually be viewed online by going to www.ronsuskind.com and clicking on "The Bush Files.")*

O'Neill's rare look into the famously leak-proof Bush White House turns up some familiar elements: a policy apparatus driven largely by politics and ideology and dominated by Cheney and Karl Rove; a strong interest in unseating Saddam Hussein dating back to well before 9/11; and a tendency to spin intelligence to fit a desired outcome. More interesting—and shocking, to some—was his depiction of George W. Bush as a leader so opaque that aides were often reduced to guessing his intentions, and so non-detail-oriented that at times he seemed to barely follow (or care about) the policy discussion at hand.

O'Neill has gone on record since as saying that he believes his portrait of Bush is actually a flattering one. Administration officials, meanwhile, have painted O'Neill as a disgruntled ex-Cabinet member who was never really in the loop. You can draw your own conclusions from the following two excerpts. The first describes O'Neill's initial

sit-down with his new boss; the second is a blow-by-blow of a meeting held shortly
after the 2002 midterm elections, in which the third round of Bush tax cuts was for-
mally approved. . . .

"Pablo?"

"Mr. President."

"Let's get comfortable," George Bush said as O'Neill entered the Oval Office.

The president moved toward the wing chair near the fireplace, tucked between one of two sofa-and-chair clusters in the thirty-nine-by-twenty-two-foot oval. Bush sat in the wing chair facing the clock, where presidents always sit—and O'Neill sat on the near end of the small adjacent mustard-colored couch, where someone sits if he or she is the only visitor. As O'Neill navigated all this—he'd been here many times and knew the complex seating rules—his mind raced back to a conversation with George W. Bush just before the mid-December press conference in Austin, where the President-elect had announced his nomination . . . yes, there may have been a "Pablo" thrown in among the "Paul"s. O'Neill didn't think anything of it. He didn't know, back then, about Bush's odd enthusiasm for nicknames.

He knew now and settled into the couch . . . and his new identity: a sixty-five-year-old man named Pablo.

"So, whatta ya got?" the president barked, all business.

It was the afternoon of Wednesday, January 24, [2001,] the third day of the Bush administration. The president calls the meetings. It is traditional protocol. One might suggest the need for a meeting to an Andy Card or Cheney, who would then pass it along, but the president issues the summons.

Bush had O'Neill's memo—Paul figured they'd talk about that—and then they'd discuss whatever came up. Cheney had said to him at one point that it might be valuable for Bush at the start of his presidency to have these meetings. To range around a bit.

O'Neill, as treasury secretary, institutionally designated to be the president's leading voice on the economy, offered a fifteen-minute interview on what he considered the informed opinion (that is, his and Greenspan's) and said that they were in the early stages of either an apparently mild recession or a pronounced inventory correction. The key was to remain sober. To watch the numbers. If we look concerned and talk up recession too much, he said, it will depress spending and encourage a downturn. O'Neill explained that the major problem was not the "encumbrances on capital"—there was plenty of low-cost capital out there, unable to find a profitable home. The problem was on the consumption side. The real numbers, he assured the president, did not support the bleakness of some "economic theorists."

O'Neill referred to items of his memo. Marginal rate cuts, if they were affordable, should be the priority. He said the tax cut plan, under almost any permutation thus far proposed, wouldn't provide measurable stimulus in the short term; what would create positive economic effects is "a sense that fiscal discipline has been preserved"—something that should boost equities markets and keep long-term bond rates in check. All that left the economy well suited to respond to a rate cut from the Fed.

There were a dozen questions that O'Neill had expected Bush to ask. He was ready with the answers. How large did O'Neill consider the surplus, and how real? How might the tax cut be structured? What about reforming Social Security and Medicare, the budget busters? How will we know if the economy has turned?

Bush didn't ask anything. He looked at O'Neill, not changing his expression, not letting on that he had any reactions—either positive or negative.

O'Neill decided therefore to move from the economy to a related matter. Steel tariffs. It was a simmering issue—the U.S. steel industry was hurting and pushing for protections. He said to the president, "You were admirably clear during the campaign about your stance in support of free trade—it's the only stance to take—and there's no way it can be squared with tariffs." He suggested that, as treasury secretary, he round up all the world's major producers and create a structure of shared incentives and sacrifices that would avoid tariff wars. He'd already tried some of this to good effect with the aluminum industry in 1993.

The president said nothing. No change in expression. Next subject.

Certainly, each president's style is different. But O'Neill had a basis for comparison. Nixon, Ford, Bush 41, and Clinton, with whom he had visited four or five times during the nineties for long sessions on policy matters. In each case, he'd arrived prepared to mix it up, ready for engagement. You'd hash it out. That was what he was known for. It was the reason you got called to the office. You met with the president to answer questions.

"I wondered, from the first, if the president didn't know the questions to ask," O'Neill recalled, "or did he know and just not want to know the answers? Or did his strategy somehow involve never showing what he thought? But you can ask questions, gather information, and not necessarily show your hand. It was strange."

With steel tariffs left hanging, O'Neill shrugged—if this was to be a monologue, he'd better make it sing.

They'd both been at that education conference five years before, so he went with that. "No Child Left Behind, I like that," O'Neill said, "but the idea that really moves us forward—a real action plan—is One Child at a Time."

It was an idea he'd road-tested with educators for years—that we need "an individualized mandate, where children would be constantly assessed, *one child at a time*, in order to help create a little strategic plan for each student," a personalized learning strategy to fill gaps and develop latent potential. "It's a rethinking of what's possible, Mr. President. There's nothing more important than nurturing our human potential as a nation—our future depends on it."

Bush shifted in the wing-back chair. "Right, that's the concept of disaggregation"—a term used by educational statisticians to break down test scores—"I have that covered."

O'Neill wondered if he should point out that the president might be misusing that term but thought again. Instead, he spoke of the need to rigorously assess how federal money is spent in key areas and how to get more value for each dollar and apply it "to the trillions we've spent in foreign aid over the years . . . what were the goals underlying those expenditures and what were the outcomes." Once that evidence is gathered, O'Neill said, it would be appropriate to examine whether institutions like the World Bank and the International Monetary Fund needed restructuring.

The president seemed to nod in affirmation. O'Neill couldn't be sure.

Using the same model, O'Neill proffered a structure to assess the value of America's role in international economic crises—such as Mexico in 1995 or Indonesia in 1997. O'Neill was no longer expecting a response. He discussed ways to apply "value analysis" to the reform of health care and shrink federal expenditures, an area where he is considered by many as one of the country's most original thinkers. Then he offered a similar analytical framework to approach Japan's economic woes and craft an appropriate role for the United Sates.

O'Neill took a breath. The Oval Office's eighteenth-century grandfather clock—eight feet ten inches of mahogany with satin-wood inlays—was to his back. He glanced at his watch. He'd been talking for just fifty minutes. The meeting was scheduled for an hour.

"All right, Mr. President, maybe to finish up we could talk about global climate change . . . " Along with his memo on the tax cut strategy, O'Neill had sent over a booklet Alcoa had produced in 1998 with the text of an extensive speech he had given—a thorough analysis of the issue, what was known and as yet unknown, and principles to guide future actions. Bush seemed to indicate with a tilt of his head that he'd read it. But, again, O'Neill wasn't certain.

He pushed forward, adding his current thoughts on what the president might do on the issue—a flash point for environmental policy. He assessed the flaws of the Kyoto treaty and offered thoughts about how they might be remedied.

Both men are precise. And the hour was up. They stood at the same moment to shake hands.

"Get me a plan on global warming."

O'Neill nodded, a bit surprised.

Bush said it again. "Get me a plan on it."

Yes, fine, he'd create a plan, O'Neill said. Then he slipped out of the Oval Office, wondering whether that meant he was supposed to call EPA administrator Christie Whitman—the person designated to handle that area—or to *not* call her.

• • •

On November 26, [2002], O'Neill arrived at his office jet-lagged from the two-week tour. He had his list of "deliverables"—he'd met with Musharraf, tried to work out logistics for building the K-to-K road across Afghanistan, dined with the sultan of Oman, and toured various European cities.

It was good to get away from Washington, away from the day-to-day routine of internecine combat and public posturing with little to show.

But as he walked into the Roosevelt Room on the first floor of the White House on November 26, it was clear he had stumbled back into the main arena of U.S. domestic policy.

It was a big crowd for a working session—a rare coming together of the economic and political/communications staff. Even Hughes was here—and her presence, ever since she'd left the White House, indicated a special occasion.

Everyone arrived at 11 A.M. and stood at their assigned places at the long mahogany table: O'Neill at the center, with Hubbard and Keith Hennessy, Lindsey's deputy director at the NEC, to his right; on his left was Lindsey, then Evans and Daniels. Directly across the table from O'Neill was a chair for the president, with Bolten, Rove, and Bartlett to his left; Card, Hughes, and Fleischer to his right. At the end of the table was a video screen. O'Neill looked over and squinted. Dick Cheney was gazing at them from an undisclosed location.

The president entered from the northwest door, in a blue pinstriped suit, blue shirt, red tie, American flag lapel pin; he was looking a bit tired. He sat down, cueing the rest of them to sit, and put on his reading glasses.

"All right, how are we doing?"

Lindsey began. "I'm reminded, looking at the table, of a joke I heard from Prime Minister Koizumi of Japan, that he gets two opinions from each economist, and since, Mr. President, you have five economic advisers—"

"What are you talking about?" snapped Bush.

"Yes, sir. Your economic team agrees on the key elements of an economic growth and jobs package: reduce the double taxation of dividends, accelerate the rate cuts, and provide more expensing of investment losses. Let me now turn to Secretary O'Neill."

O'Neill shuffled some papers—thinking maybe Larry and the president weren't getting on so well after all. But now that he knew about Cheney's posture, it didn't much matter where Larry was.

"I'm just back last night from my trip to India, Pakistan, and the United Kingdom," O'Neill began, giving Bush a thirty-second summary, and then described his view of the current conditions. "On balance, I am more optimistic about the U.S. economy than the group, and I remind you that I was right last year, and we've mostly been right this year in our real-time forecasts. And that leads me to believe that we don't need a major, expensive stimulus package. But this is all beside the point. I think you have made up your mind, so we should get on with discussing the package. I am concerned that what we do now not tie our hands on major tax reform or on creating Social Security private accounts. And when I look at what we have got here, in this package of proposals, I am dubious that we can get anything enacted in time to do much good."

Bush looked at him quizzically. "What is your point about Social Security private accounts?"

"There will be a transition cost, Mr. President," O'Neill explained, surprised. "Perhaps a trillion dollars over many years. This will be more difficult to do with large budget deficits. It will also be difficult to keep Congress in check."

"We have had some success on the spending side, but also some setbacks," Bush said.

Gazing down the row, Bush now looked at Hubbard, a cue that it was his turn.

"I don't think of this as a stimulus package, but a growth package," Hubbard said. "The economy is facing headwinds from increased risk aversion. The third-quarter numbers were strong, but they borrowed from the fourth quarter. . . . "

"Do we have to give it back?" Bush quipped, getting off a good one to big laughs.

Then to Keith Hennessey: "The priority should be eliminating double taxation of dividends. I think that the revenue loss will be much smaller than the static estimate," Hennessy said, referring to the supply-side methodology of using growth projections to boost estimates of tax revenues. "We should also include more expensing of investments and accelerating the rate cuts. I think of this as an insurance policy, not against a double dip back into recession, but against 1 percent slower growth in each of the next two years, when there could be a rise in unemployment to 6.5 percent. I am not saying this is likely, but it certainly is a downside scenario."

The president nodded and looked at Evans. This was the way most meetings went. The president looks at you. You deliver. He moves on.

The commerce secretary echoed much of what had been said. "I think we need an insurance policy. Accelerating the rate cuts and eliminating double taxation of dividends is good policy. I think expensing of capital losses is less important. We should also consider an investor package, where capital losses can offset ordinary income, and expanded tax breaks on IRAs. . . . "

As usual, not a real discussion, O'Neill thought as he looked over at Daniels, next up. He'd had many discussions with the OMB chief; O'Neill knew that terrain intimately—he'd been trying to talk Daniels through the ideals of fiscal probity. He knew Daniels was focused on the perils of rising deficits, but it would take gumption to air those concerns in a room full of tax cut ideologues.

"I think we need to balance concerns," Daniels said, sounding as if he'd rehearsed his opening. "You need to be out front on the economy, but I am concerned that this package may not do it. The budget hole is getting deeper, it will be at least $225 billion next year, and we are projecting deficits all the way to the end of your second term."

From across the table came glares from the entire Bush political team.

Daniels paused, as though he'd been struck. "Umm. On balance, then, I think we need to do a package that makes"—he paused—"long-run sense: accelerate the rate cuts and the double taxation of dividends. You need to occupy the space and propose a complete package before State of the Union."

O'Neill looked with astonishment at Daniels. He had seemed to turn 180 degrees in midsentence.

Lindsey jumped in. "Mr. President, *this is* an insurance policy, and it's a bad time to go uninsured. With the world economy as it is, the United States is the only game in town."

Bush looked with disdain at Lindsey and went in another direction. "We are slowing from third to fourth quarter, but O'Neill hasn't been wrong yet. Why have nominal wages stopped growing?"

The answer was complex—about the underside of the continuing productivity miracle, that GDP growth could occur without traditional pressure to lift wages—the kind of academic discussion the president generally abhorred.

But maybe not today. Bush seemed to be encouraging unscripted exchanges, prepared to search for an answer on his own, in a crowded room. For O'Neill, that was both exciting and unsettling. This discussion could go in a lot of directions. Maybe, in fact, Bush hadn't decided on this second huge tax cut package, and he was finally asking a few pointed, now-hold-on-one-minute questions. Or, O'Neill mused, it could be a devil's advocate exercise such as he'd seen the president attempt a few times—a way for him to collect succinct responses to anticipated attacks. Either way, it was good enough to make O'Neill snap to attention.

Same for Lindsey. "What we are proposing is good long-run tax policy," Lindsey said in a non sequitur, trying to get the president back on track.

Bush acted as if he hadn't heard him. "Are you proposing that we accelerate all the tax cuts, or just for those in the middle? Won't the top-rate people benefit the most from eliminating the double taxation of dividends? Didn't we already give them a break at the top?"

The 2001 tax cut had been criticized for the disproportionate boost it gave to the top 5 percent of earners; it wasn't literally regressive, but it surely departed from progressive ideals that had long defined the tax policies of both parties. The White House's response, that those who pay the most in taxes get the largest reductions, was now echoed by Hubbard: "Mr. President, remember the high earners are where the entrepreneurs are." This was the mantra that had guided much of the administration's stimulus-through-tax-cuts policy. Giving incentives to those with money would drive investment, and that would drive job growth, and newly salaried employees would buy and boost demand. Some economists contended that that is a long way to travel to reach stimulus.

Bush seized on it. "This is about demand," he said. "I want this to work."

"It's also about the supply side," Lindsey said.

"Eliminating the double taxation of dividends is a game changer," Hubbard added. "Game changer" is one of Bush's favorite phrases.

Rove finally spoke up, a rare event in a meeting of this size. "You should be basing the package on principle—if double taxation of dividends is wrong, why do we want to settle for just eliminating 50 percent of the tax for individuals?" "Stick to principle" is another phrase that has a tonic effect on Bush.

A 50 percent cut was the consensus recommendation, owing to steep revenue shortfalls brought about by the dividend change. Rove was pushing for 100 percent.

Josh Bolten leapt into the fray. "This burns a big hole in the budget."

Rove seemed surprised. The ramparts of conservative economic theology—reduce taxes as far as possible, starve the beast of the federal government—were under siege.

Daniels, having changed direction only a few minutes back, now spoke as an ardent supply-sider. "Yes, but we get a lot back."

Without cues from Bush as to when to speak, it had become a free-for-all. They were all on the edges of their seats. Hubbard pushed to protect his prize proposal. "It has to be permanent to work," he said emphatically.

Lindsey also went on the offensive, answering unasked questions. "To get the votes we need, Mr. President, we shouldn't peel back things that work, but add more items as necessary."

"But this is a harder problem, Mr. President . . . ," O'Neill began.

Bush waved him silent. Something was on his mind. It was the class issue again. "I am not in favor of excluding people," he said, almost to himself.

O'Neill picked up his unfinished sentence. " . . . The trouble with the double taxation is that it could have near-term effects, boosting the market and providing some stimulus, but there's a strong chance it will all be dissipated by the middle of next year. With the economy already improving, this could cause an unnecessary boost—that's how you get a bubble—and it could pop in '03 and '04." He put forward an alternative: the permanent expensing of capital expenditures, which lightens the tax burden for small businesses (and is a step toward abolishing corporate taxes, an O'Neill favorite) and prompts expenditures on capital goods that benefit the wider economy. He looked across the table and saw the president was befuddled. He quickly moved to hold the floor by reviving the earlier political argument that the double dividend cut could create a bubble. "We don't want to slam the door on our toes in the fourth quarter of 2004 after the current provisions expire."

Bush picked up on that last dangling reference to the date: "Just as long as we don't slam the door in the third quarter of 2004."

But Rove seemed intrigued by O'Neill's idea of expensing capital expenditures. "On the Hill, there is talk of a plan to change all the depreciable lives," he said, and then ticked off the newly proposed intervals of thirty years, ten years, five years, and three years—in an I-know-this-stuff-too reference to the way businesses depreciate capital equipment based on its useful life. House Republicans wanted to make the useful life shorter, effectively raising the amount you could write off.

The president was now thoroughly lost. "What are you talking about?" he barked at Rove.

Hubbard moved to smooth things: "This should wait for a time when we do major tax reform."

"Glenn thinks that a deficit of $200 billion pushes up interest rates by just three basis points [or .03 percent]," Josh Bolten interjected, bringing things back to the key issue of whether the dividend tax cut was affordable.

"That's right," Hubbard said. Sitting next to him, O'Neill shook his head. Greenspan and he had been running tables on the effects of deficits for years; that figure was wildly low.

Bush waved his arm dismissively.

"Hold on. We're betting that revenue streams come back with growth and that we can hold the line on spending," he said, edging toward the core issue of supply-side growth versus deep deficits. Then he stopped and went in a new direction. "This focus on the top rate, is it a high priority? Again, won't the high end benefit most from the double-taxation elimination?"

No one seemed to want to reply. Eliminating the double taxation is a benefit heavily weighted to those who hold stock; the more stock held, the greater the benefit. A total elimination of the dividend tax was already being estimated to cost nearly $400 billion over ten years.

Of course, the "high end" was the "base"—the income distribution of the proposed cuts was largely a political calculation searching for an economic rationale. Those justifications had already been offered.

After a noticeable, pregnant pause, Dan Bartlett moved back to politics. "We are hearing from governors about state budgets."

Andy Card said, "We need a quick payoff, Mr. President."

Hubbard was intent that they not forget what had brought them here: "Elimination of the double taxation will boost stock prices and repair balance sheets."

Card jerked things back: "There is excess capacity, so why do we want to boost investment?"

O'Neill was pleasantly surprised. "Mr. President, the Business Round Table of the country's leading CEOs says the focus should be on boosting consumption demand. Their warehouses are full. They need a boost in demand to clear away inventories. I'm not sure that a tax cut that benefits mostly wealthy investors, many of whom will just push these gains into savings, will do much for demand."

Bush nodded. He was in a cul-de-sac. The ideology of ongoing tax cuts seemed to make less sense when certain economic realities were considered. Finally he spoke, haltingly. "The dividend tax cut could repair corporate balance sheets," he said, feeling his way, "and that's a kind of growth package, isn't it?" O'Neill was thinking that this is true only if you believe that companies will increase their spending on capital goods, even if demand remains sluggish, because their stock has risen. You also have to be certain the proposal would have that effect on the markets, a very long string of imponderables.

Hubbard rushed to the president's aid. "Households who desire to save more can do so through higher stock prices."

Bolten attempted closure: "I think we have agreement on the components. Now, how big should the package be? How much extra should we allow for so we have something to give back in the legislative process?"

The president didn't seem quite ready to close. "Didn't we do the investment package already? What would you rather have? We went through this last year, are you telling me we did it wrong?" The "investment package" was what they often called the 2001 tax cut, which had investment incentives for small business and rate cuts for the high-end "investment class."

"There are headwinds," Hubbard said.

"Not additional headwinds," Bush countered. "They can say, 'They did it twice and it didn't work.' Why do we play our hand now, negotiate against ourselves? I want to stay with principle."

This seemed to be a cue to Rove. Trying to discuss the basics of fiscal policy had left the room in tatters. Karl moved to tactics. "We want to dictate the debate, Mr. President. Not be too specific out of the box. That is a prescription for piling on; we have to have something to trade."

Daniels, still looking to redeem himself for his earlier deficit hawk comments, jumped to support Rove: "I suggest a $50 billion package—$50 billion a year—and that we go on the offensive, including accelerating the rate cuts, and expensing, and dividends."

The president seemed relieved, as though the key issues had been considered. "Thank you for all the briefing materials, this was good research. So when do we roll this out?"

"You are speaking in Chicago on December 10," Lindsey said.

Bush looked surprised. "That's news to me."

Rove leaned toward the president. "Sir, that's not scheduled yet, but it is important to move earlier rather than later. The Democrats are coming out with a plan."

Then Ari Fleischer, seeing that matters had moved safely from the *whys* to the *hows*, summoned an overall precept, one of the administration's guiding principles. "Perception lags reality," he said importantly.

O'Neill looked on astonished. Rove and Fleischer and the others rarely spoke this way around the centrist treasury secretary. Maybe this meant they didn't care anymore what he heard. Not a great sign.

"Democrats will say we don't care about the middle and bottom, but these class arguments work less and less," Fleischer added. "We should do the right package and roll out in early December."

Throughout the meeting, Hughes had sat back, observing. She was now a consultant, traveling every few weeks from Austin to Washington, and not in on the White House's day-to-day workings. But she still carried clout, as the only one with weight equal to Rove's. She eased in: "Will the announcement of a package boost Christmas spending?"

"Yes, this could be important for consumer confidence," Hubbard said.

O'Neill shook his head. "The truth is nobody knows."

The president was absently watching the back-and-forth. He was thinking of something else.

"What are we doing on compassion?" Bush asked.

No one answered.

The president seemed agitated. "Well, you know . . . do you know what the unemployment rate is?" he said, raising his voice. "It is 5.7 percent! There are a lot of presidents who have had to confront much higher unemployment. This argument that the economy is bad does not resonate with voters. This is all posturing . . . that is why we did so well in the midterm elections. . . . "

Rove laughed. It was coming together—it was as if the president had caught a strong wind, his sails now filled. Another massive tax cut proposal was ahead. "So, we should accelerate the rate cuts and not tax dividends twice? . . . " Rove said.

Then, it was just the two of them, talking to each other. Bush was emboldened. "I can figure this out! We did well in the elections because the economy isn't so bad. What are the optics of this? How specific do we need to be on this proposal?"

Hughes, whose July departure to spend more time with her family was also due to exhaustion from her role as pragmatic counterweight to the ideological Rove, stopped the proceedings. "But there is uncertainty in the economy," she said with her usual bull's-eye candor. "Real uncertainty that this won't solve."

She didn't even have to say the word: Iraq. The administration's drive to justify a war in Iraq had cast a pall over the economy since the previous summer. The lines had crossed. It was something no one wanted to talk about. Businesses were frozen, capital investments had flatlined, people were tightening belts and storing their cash like canned goods in the bomb shelter. The two cherished ideologies of the administration—ongoing tax cuts on the domestic front, and the doctrine of "preemption" in foreign affairs—"were both big, sweeping ideas that were in collision with reality," O'Neill recalled thinking. Now they were also in collision with each other.

Bush stopped in midstride and looked hard at Hughes. He was silent for a moment. "The economic uncertainty is because of SEC overreach," he said pointedly. Directly across the table. O'Neill couldn't quite believe what he was hearing—SEC overreach? No wonder the White House had backed off from the toughest medicine for crooked executives and eventually ceded the corporate governance debate to Congress. How, though, could the president believe that the largely overwhelmed SEC had any significant effect on the vast U.S. economy?

But Bush wasn't finished.

"And look," he said after a moment. "Until we get rid of Saddam Hussein, we won't get rid of uncertainty."

Everyone was quiet. The president looked up and down the table, and then at Cheney, gazing at them from the screen in the breakfront from an undisclosed location.

"Good, what I am hearing is that we roll out in mid-December," President Bush said as he began to stand.

Rove looked at the president with pride. "Stick to principle," he said.

On O'Neill's left, Daniels was still of two minds. "Not a typical Republican package," he muttered. "Definitely not."

• • •

Over the coming week, O'Neill thought often of that extraordinary meeting in the Roosevelt Room, its haphazard, improvised quality, the way portentous issues had been raised and spun and tossed about, untethered from the weight of their consequences. "That's what you get without Brandeis briefs," he thought, "without the hard factual analysis that allows you to make informed judgments about the worth of various proposals, about what you can reasonably expect, about what is known. You can't just balance the competing ideas of how to govern a country this size without that. Do we need stimulus, and will this provide it? How much does it cost? How much can we afford? What are our goals? What are the best-case—and worst-case—scenarios? I think of a meeting like that, with so much at stake. . . . It's like June bugs hopping around on a lake."

The Radical

Franklin Foer and Spencer Ackerman

The New Republic | Dec. 1, 2003

When the history of the Bush administration is written, Vice President Dick Cheney is certain to loom large. His legend is impressive: After serving as chief of staff for President Gerald Ford at the tender age of thirty-four, he went back home to his native Wyoming and was elected to six terms as that state's lone representative to Congress, where he carved out a staunchly conservative voting record. In 1989, Cheney returned to Washington as the elder George Bush's secretary of defense—a stint that included overseeing the invasion of Panama and the first Gulf War—then spent the 1990s in the private sector, running the behemoth Halliburton Corporation. In his current role as the younger President Bush's senior adviser (at sixty-three, he's five years older than George W.), the veep has gained a reputation as a bureaucratic force to be reckoned with, a tough questioner who reserves his true feelings for the boss's ears only—perhaps to be shared during one of their weekly private lunches.

Cheney's frequent post-9/11 stints in an "undisclosed location" (which Time magazine recently revealed to be an underground bunker on the Maryland-Pennsylvania border) have only enhanced his reputation as a power behind the scenes. He's already being called the most influential vice president in history, and his office has been an active participant in shaping and implementing the administration's domestic and *foreign policies. President Bush, for his part, has been quoted as saying he sleeps better at night knowing that Cheney is on the job.*

Nowhere has Cheney's influence been felt more than in the decision to invade Iraq. In the runup to war, writes Bob Woodward in his book Plan of Attack, *"Cheney was a powerful, steamrolling force." The following article gives special attention to the part played by the vice president's office in marshaling pre-war intelligence on Iraq to build the case for an invasion—including its close ties with a secret intelligence unit in the Pentagon called the Office for Special Plans (OSP), which was set up early in 2002 to help funnel Iraq intelligence to top officials. (For a more detailed look at the OSP, see "The Lie Factory," in the Jan.-Feb. 2004 issue of* Mother Jones *magazine.)*

Franklin Foer and Spencer Ackerman's article also takes a retrospective look at Cheney's career, and suggests that both his hardline approach to foreign policy and his lack of confidence in the U.S. intelligence agencies are nothing new, but instead can be traced back some twenty-five years, to the waning days of the cold war. . . .

In early 2002, Vice President Dick Cheney spoke to President George W. Bush from the heart. The war in Afghanistan had been an astonishing display of U.S. strength. Instead of the bloody quagmire many predicted, CIA paramilitary agents, Special Forces, and U.S. air power had teamed with Northern Alliance guerrillas to run the Taliban and Al Qaeda out of their strongholds. As a new interim government took power in Kabul, Cheney was telling Bush that the next phase in the war on terrorism was toppling Saddam Hussein.

Bush was well aware that several of his senior aides wanted to take the battle to Iraq. When his advisers had convened at Camp David the weekend after the September 11 attacks, Deputy Defense Secretary Paul Wolfowitz argued on three separate occasions that the United States should immediately target Iraq instead of the more difficult Afghanistan. Bush had settled the matter by instructing his chief of staff, Andrew Card, to quiet Wolfowitz—a moment humiliatingly enshrined by Bob Woodward in his book *Bush at War*. But, in early 2002, Cheney dispensed with the policy arguments for taking down Saddam in favor of a far more personal appeal. He said simply that he had been part of the team that created what he now saw as a flawed policy—leaving Saddam in power at the end of the Gulf War—and now Bush had a chance to correct it.

His plea was enormously successful. "The reason that Cheney was able to sell Bush the policy is that he was able to say, 'I've changed,'" says a senior administration official. " 'I used to have the same position as [James] Baker, [Brent] Scowcroft, *and your father*—and here's why it's wrong.' " By February, observes a since-departed senior National Security Council (NSC) staffer, "my sense was the decision was taken." The next month, Bush interrupted a meeting between National Security Adviser Condoleezza Rice and three senators to boast, "Fuck Saddam. We're taking him out."

That Cheney had become the decisive foreign policy player in the White House is hardly surprising. Bush had, after all, added him to the ticket precisely for his national security heft. What was astonishing—even to those who thought they knew Cheney well—was that Cheney had seemingly swung so strongly against the policies of the administration he loyally served as defense secretary, an administration that valued stability above democracy-building and crisis management above grand strategy. "Look," confesses someone who has worked with Cheney in the past, "I am baffled."

It's easy to understand this bafflement. When Cheney signed on as Bush's running mate in 2000, many people expected him to bring George H.W. Bush's realist foreign policy instincts with him. *U.S. News & World Report* quickly dubbed him BUSH'S BACK-TO-THE-FUTURE VEEP PICK. After all, Cheney had spent the latter half of the 1990s as CEO of one of the world's largest oil-services companies, where he argued against economic sanctions and for engagement with tyrannies like Iran. And Cheney had *not* spent the '90s—as his longtime ally Wolfowitz had—publicly agonizing over the decision to leave Saddam's regime intact.

But imparting George H.W. Bush's cautiousness to his former defense secretary misreads Cheney entirely. Far from fitting into 41's foreign policy team, Cheney was its ideological outlier. On the greatest issue of the day—what to do about a declining Soviet Union and America's place in a unipolar world— Cheney dissented vigorously. His Pentagon argued, again and again, that the only true guarantee of U.S. security lay in transforming threatening nations into democratic ones—a radical notion to the realists in the first Bush White House. Cheney's policy allies were not National Security Adviser Scowcroft and Secretary of State Baker but rather a set of intellectuals on the Pentagon policy staff who shared and helped him refine his alternative vision of U.S. power and purpose. In the '90s, this worldview came to be known as neo-conservatism. Cheney was there first.

As he fought an uphill ideological battle in the first Bush administration, Cheney's foreign policy vision was paired with a tendency that would prove key to understanding his performance in W.'s White House: a willingness to circumvent the typical bureaucratic channels to gain advantage over his rivals. In particular, Cheney came to see the intelligence establishment as flawed and corrupted by political biases hopelessly at odds with his goals. By 2001, when Cheney became the most powerful adviser to the president of the United States, his vision of global democracy and his mistrust of the CIA had reached full maturity. Both convictions would be brought to bear when the vice president turned his full attention to Iraq.

Similar Wavelengths

When Dick Cheney arrived at the Pentagon in 1989, he created a brain trust in his own image, cultivating young staffers with academic backgrounds like his own. These brainy types congregated in the highest ranks of the policy directorate run by then-Undersecretary Wolfowitz. In most administrations, the policy directorate largely deals with mundane tasks, such as the negotiation of basing rights and arms sales. Those issues held little interest for Wolfowitz and his team. "They focused on geostrategic issues," says one of his Pentagon aides. "They considered themselves conceptual." Wolfowitz and his protégés prided themselves on their willingness to reexamine entire precepts of U.S. foreign policy. In Cheney, they found a like-minded patron. Wolfowitz, in 1991, described his relationship with his boss to the *New York Times*: "Intellectually, we're very much on similar wavelengths." Nowhere was this intellectual synergy more evident than on the Soviet Union.

At the time Cheney took office, Mikhail Gorbachev had been in power for four years. By then, the Soviet premier had charmed the American media and foreign policy establishment with his ebullient style. Like many hardliners, Cheney thought he saw through these atmospherics and publicly intimated his skepticism of perestroika. Appearing on CNN in April 1989—only one month into his term as defense secretary—he glumly announced that Gorbachev would "ultimately fail" and a leader "far more hostile" to the West would follow. Such dourness put Cheney well outside the administration mainstream. Baker, Scowcroft, and President George H.W. Bush—as well as the NSC's leading Russia hand, Condoleezza Rice—had committed themselves to Gorbachev's (and the USSR's) preservation. But Cheney believed that, with a gust of aggressive support for alternatives to Gorbachev, the United States could dismember its principal adversary once and for all.

To craft an alternative strategy, Cheney turned to alternative experts. On Saturday mornings, Wolfowitz's deputies convened seminars in a small conference room in the Pentagon's E ring, where they sat Cheney in front of a parade of Sovietologists. Many were mavericks who believed the Soviet Union was on the brink of collapse. Out of these Saturday seminars, Cheney's Soviet position emerged—with concepts and rhetoric that perfectly echo the current Bush administration's Iraq policy. They would push regime change in the Soviet Union, transforming it into a democracy. Support for rebellious Ukraine would challenge the regime from its periphery; and support for Boris Yeltsin, the elected president of the Russian Republic, would confront the regime at its core. "[Yeltsin] represents a set of principles and values that are synonymous with those that we hold for the Soviet Union—democratization, demilitarization," Cheney announced in a 1991 appearance on NBC's *Meet the Press*. Bush père and Scowcroft fretted about instability, but Cheney retorted, if the demolition of the Soviet Union required a little short-term disruption, such as a nuclear-armed Ukraine, then so be it. After all, as he observed in a 1992 speech to the Economics Club of Indianapolis, true security depended on the expansion of "the community of peaceful democratic nations."

Cheney was unsuccessful in pushing the White House away from Gorbachev. After he mused aloud about Gorbachev's shortcomings in a 1989 TV interview, Baker called Scowcroft and told him, "Dump on Dick with all possible alacrity." When the "Gang of Eight"—Bush's senior advisers—met to decide policy in the final days of the Soviet Union, the meetings featured, as CIA chief Robert Gates has recalled, "Cheney against the field." The Soviet collapse ultimately settled the issue. But Cheney's battle against realism had only begun.

There was, however, a moment of détente in that battle: the Gulf War. Cheney accepted ending the war with Iraqi dictator Saddam Hussein still in power, as did all of Poppy's other senior advisers. (Not even Wolfowitz—now so associated with Saddam's toppling—dissented at the time.) The lasting effect of the war on Cheney, however, was less strategic and more bureaucratic: It shattered his faith in the CIA's ability to produce reliable intelligence.

When Saddam first began amassing troops on the Kuwaiti border in mid-1990, conventional wisdom in the U.S. intelligence community held that he was attempting to gain leverage in OPEC talks and, at the most, might seize a Kuwaiti oil field. The analysis made little sense—Saddam was moving his elite Republican Guard units, the very guarantors of his rule, from their Baghdad positions—yet only a few analysts issued starker warnings of an all-out invasion. Worse still, a National Intelligence Estimate released just before Christmas that year concluded that Saddam would withdraw from Kuwait to avert a war with the United States. In a paper for a 1994 conference on intelligence policy, Wolfowitz reflected, "[W]hen the signs started to turn up that the projected scenario regarding Iraqi behavior was not unfolding as we wished, . . . somebody within the [intelligence] community should have said, 'Wait a minute, here are facts that we ought to take some account of.' "

Cheney saw little option at the time but to request thorough briefings from intelligence analysts and subject their judgments to as much scrutiny as he could muster. Before the Gulf War, one former analyst remembers being "whisked into a room, there's Dick Cheney, he's right in front of you, he starts firing questions at you, half an hour later and thirty questions later, I'm whisked out of the room, and I'm like, 'What the hell just happened?' " Yet analysts can distinguish between thorough questioning and contempt—or pressure. Cheney showed none of it. "He would ask you factual questions like, 'OK, about this thing you said. Do I understand you correctly that such-and-such is true? And are you sure about this, and how do you know that?' " recalls Patrick Lang, the Defense Intelligence Agency's (DIA) Middle East expert during the Gulf War and one of the few analysts to predict the invasion of Kuwait. "And I regard that as a legitimate question. . . . He wasn't hostile or nasty about it; he just wanted to know how you knew. And I didn't mind that in the least."

But, as Cheney and his aides watched, the intelligence failures kept on mounting. In the fall of 1992, UN inspectors uncovered an Iraqi nuclear weapons program far more advanced than the intelligence community had suspected. More disturbingly, the CIA admitted to having no clue about the Soviet Union's massive clandestine biological weapons program, which Yeltsin had spontaneously acknowledged in 1992—and this was an enemy the Agency had studied carefully for decades. Gradually, Cheney and his staff came to consider the CIA not only inept but lazy, unimaginative, and arrogant—"a high priesthood," in their derisive terminology. With uncharacteristic vitriol, Wolfowitz's 1994 paper argued that the Agency's style "allows [analysts] to conceal ignorance of facts, policy bias or any number of things that may lie behind the personal opinions that are presented as sanctified intelligence judgments."

By the time Cheney arrived at Halliburton in the mid-'90s, he felt he could no longer rely on his old Langley connections to provide him the information he needed to do business in the former Soviet Union. So, according to one ex-CIA operative, Cheney hired a team of retired intelligence agents to collect information independently. The ex-agent says, "Cheney would just bitch and moan about the CIA and various parts of the world that they didn't know shit [about]. . . . He was terribly frustrated."

• • •

But, while the decision to leave Saddam in power at the end of the Gulf War would reverberate through neocon circles for the next decade, a policy initiative devised by Cheney's Pentagon in 1992 would be arguably more important, laying the foundation for every major theme of George W. Bush's post–September 11 foreign policy. Under Wolfowitz's direction, the Pentagon produced a strategy paper called the Defense Planning Guidance (DPG). At a moment of strategic uncertainty—the Soviet Union had formally collapsed just months before—the document offered a vision of unbridled U.S. dominance and proposed democratization as the only true guarantor of U.S. security.

Without a Soviet Union to contain, there was no longer any obvious reason for the United States to retain its outsized presence on the world stage. To meet domestic expectations for a "peace dividend," Cheney implemented force reductions across all the armed services. But the defense secretary and his planning staff also saw danger in these cuts. It was impossible to predict the next global rival to the United States, and, without the forward presence to encourage and cement democratization in newly freed nations, the gains of a unipolar world could be short-lived. A new conceptual framework to justify U.S. leadership was necessary.

DPGs typically explain how the Pentagon plans to implement defense requirements. They traffic in the minutiae of weapons systems and force structures, not reconceived notions of global leadership. But, just as Wolfowitz had used a modest policy office for grander ambitions, in February 1992 his staff drafted a DPG, advocating a value-driven security policy. It would be a U.S. priority to "encourage the spread of democratic forms of government." The stakes, they said, were extremely high. Everywhere the DPG authors looked, they saw the prospects for rivalry: in Russia, where there was "the possibility that democracy will fail"; in "Indian hegemonic aspiration"; in communist Asia, "with fundamental values, governance and policies decidedly at variance with our own"; even in allied Europe.

Instead of passively accepting the emergence of such rivals, the DPG proposed snuffing them out. Washington needed to convince other countries that "they need not aspire to a greater [global] role," whether through "account[ing] sufficiently for the interests of the advanced industrial nations" or through traditional deterrence. By preventing the emergence of a rival, U.S. strategy could recreate itself for a unipolar world, where U.S. power could be used more freely. "We have the opportunity to meet threats at lower levels and lower costs," the document read. Chief among those threats was the proliferation of weapons of mass destruction (WMD). A full decade before George

W. Bush enshrined preemption as state policy in his National Security Strategy, the DPG raised the prospect of "whether to take military steps to prevent the development or use of weapons of mass destruction."

It was uncharted territory for the United States, and it alarmed certain Pentagon officials, who leaked drafts of the DPG to the *New York Times*. Cheney, Wolfowitz, and their staffs awoke on March 8, 1992, to the headline U.S. STRATEGY PLAN CALLS FOR ENSURING NO RIVALS DEVELOP. A horrified Senator Joseph Biden said the DPG led the way to "literally a Pax Americana." George H. W. Bush immediately disassociated himself from the document, begging the press corps, "Please do not put too much emphasis on leaked reports, particularly ones that I haven't seen." The White House strongly indicated its displeasure to the defense secretary.

Cheney was forced to revise the document, sanding down its edges considerably, but he did not let its ideas perish. In January 1993, as they were about to leave office, Wolfowitz's planning staff recycled all the controversial ideas in the DPG and published them in a document called the Regional Defense Strategy. Again, the strategy was based on the concept of "a democratic 'zone of peace,' " defined as "a community of democratic nations bound together in a web of political, economic and security ties." It remained the task of American leadership "to build an international environment conducive to our values." The fact that the DPG vision didn't die a quiet, bureaucratic death wasn't just a tribute to the tenacity of Wolfowitz and his staff; it was a reflection of how deeply Cheney believed in it.

To this day, his closest aides point to the document as the moment when Cheney's foreign policy coalesced. The attacks of September 11 may have given Cheney a new sense of urgency, but the framework was already there. As one former staffer puts it, "It wasn't an epiphany, it wasn't a sudden eureka moment; it was an evolution, but it was one that was primed by what he had done and seen in the period during the end of the cold war."

All The Vice President's Men

Cheney's ideology hardly made a dent in the first Bush White House. But, in the second, George W. Bush tasked him with a robust foreign policy portfolio. To ensure his ideas won out, the new vice president reassembled the intellectuals he had relied on in Wolfowitz's policy operation. Stephen Hadley, who had worked on arms control for the Wolfowitz policy staff, became deputy national security adviser. Zalmay Khalilzad, another policy aide, took over the NSC's Middle East portfolio. Others Cheney kept for his own staff.

I. Lewis "Scooter" Libby, Wolfowitz's deputy, particularly rose in influence. In addition to becoming the vice president's chief of staff, he became Cheney's national security adviser and an adviser to the president himself. For his White House deputy, Libby tapped Eric Edelman, the Pentagon's top Sovietologist and organizer of the Saturday seminars. They brought in John Hannah, who had championed the anti-Gorbachev case at the Bush 41 State Department, to handle Middle East affairs. With a nod from Wolfowitz, they recruited a Navy officer, William Luti—who had advised former House Speaker Newt Gingrich—to work with Hannah.

Cheney didn't reconvene the group out of nostalgia. During the transition to the new administration, the NSC had been stocked with wonks from State and the CIA, and hawks felt ideologically frozen out of the new president's foreign policy staff. Other neocons—including Wolfowitz and Undersecretary of State John Bolton—were stuck a rung lower on the bureaucracy than their comrades felt they deserved. "A lot of people didn't end up at State and NSC and DOD [Department of Defense]," one senior administration hawk says. "Scooter tried to find a home for them." Cheney's office came to be viewed as the administration's neocon sanctuary.

The Office of the Vice President (OVP) was more than a consolation prize. Cheney gave his national security staff far greater responsibilities than had traditionally been accorded the vice president's team. His regional specialists wouldn't be involved only in issues relevant to the vice president—they would participate fully in the policymaking process and attend almost every interagency meeting. When Cheney first created this new structure, some Bushies openly described the operation as a "shadow" NSC. For those in the NSC itself, it often seemed like the "shadow" had more power than the real deal. One former Bush official says, "In this case, it's often the vice president's office that's driving the policy, leading the debate, leading the arguments, instead of just hanging back and recognizing that the vice president is not supposed to be driving the policy."

Not only was the OVP staff familiar, so were their ideas. Even before September 11, 2001, Cheney's staff was convinced Iraq could be a democratic outpost in the region—much as they had hoped Ukraine would become—albeit through a U.S.-funded insurgency, not an invasion. According to his aides, Cheney had grown more convinced throughout the '90s of the futility of containing Saddam. In the early '90s, while Cheney was holed up at the American Enterprise Institute, his think-tank colleagues say he met Ahmed Chalabi and increasingly lent the Iraqi National Congress (INC) leader a sympathetic ear. In July 2000, Chalabi delighted over Cheney's vice-presidential nomination, boasting, "Cheney is good for us." He was right. Within two weeks of Bush's inauguration, Cheney helped free U.S. INC funding that had been bottlenecked during the Clinton administration. At the senior staff meetings, which considered Iraq policy almost every week during the first few months of the administration, Cheney's office supported efforts to topple Saddam through empowering the INC even further. According to former Assistant Secretary of State for Near Eastern Affairs Edward Walker, a regular attendee at those meetings, Cheney seemed increasingly exasperated with his options. "Everything that had been tried before didn't work. By a system of elimination—sanctions won't stop him, bombing won't stop him, and so on—you come down to the last resort: Then we'll have to take him out."

The attacks of September 11 violently accelerated Cheney's nascent vision of a democratic Middle East. As the ruins of the Twin Towers smoldered, Cheney decided the administration needed to change the strategic framework that had left the nation vulnerable to mass murder. He unveiled his thinking at the first NSC meeting after the attack. "To the extent we define our task broadly, including those who support terrorism, then we get at states," Cheney said, according to Bob Woodward's account of the meeting. The night before, Bush had told the nation he would make "no distinction" between Al Qaeda and its state sponsors. Cheney was pushing the president's reasoning to its next stage. As a friend recollects, Cheney now understood that "what you had to do was transform the Middle East."

But, if Cheney realized that the Middle East needed to be recast, he also believed that one of the nation's most important instruments for doing so—its intelligence community—was badly broken. An intelligence failure on the scale of September 11, in the view of the vice president and his staff, merely confirmed the OVP's already dim estimation of the CIA. Before the attacks, Cheney had mused about the centrality of intelligence to national security, telling *The New Yorker*'s Nicholas Lemann in May 2001, "You need to have very robust intelligence capability if you're going to uncover threats to the U.S., and hopefully thwart them before they can be launched." Now there could be no confidence in the predictive capabilities of the country's intelligence services. Both lessons—the need to force a strategic realignment in the Middle East and the unreliability of normal intelligence channels—had deep roots in Cheney's Pentagon experience.

• • •

In mid-2002, Cheney made at least two visits to the CIA's Langley headquarters to talk with the analysts on the intelligence assembly line, who warned that they had no evidence showing that Saddam was reconstituting his nuclear program. These visits have been chewed over in the press, decried by retired Agency officials, and condemned as attempts to pressure the CIA into producing more damning intel. But they only begin to capture the depth of the vice president's personal involvement in shaping Iraq intelligence. In addition to trekking to Langley, his former aides say, Cheney paid calls to analysts at the DIA, the National Security Agency, and even the National Intelligence Mapping Agency. "He visited every element of the intelligence community," says a former Cheney staffer. When he wasn't visiting these agencies, his staff snowed them with questions. According to one former CIA analyst, "The Agency [would write] something on WMD, and it would come back from the vice president with a thousand questions: 'What's this sentence mean?' 'What's your source for this line?' 'Why are you disregarding sources that are saying the opposite?' "

Among Cheney's aides, resentment of the CIA went far beyond a healthy skepticism of fallible intelligence analysts and an Agency with a decidedly mixed record. Whereas Cheney's questioning of intelligence during the Gulf war had been probing but respectful, now his staff belittled the intelligence community's findings, irrespective of their merits. For years, Libby and Hannah in particular had believed the Agency harbored a politically motivated animus against the INC and irresponsibly discounted intelligence reports from defectors the INC had brought forward. "This had been a fight for such a long period of time, where people were so dug in," reflects a friend of one of Cheney's senior staffers. The OVP had been studying issues like Iraq for so many years that it often simply did not accept that contrary information provided by intelligence analysts—especially CIA analysts—could be correct. As one former colleague of many OVP officials puts it, "They so believed that the CIA were wrong, they were like, 'We want to *show* these fuckers that they are wrong.' "

Intelligence analysts saw little difference between Cheney and his staffers. The vice president's aides may have made more trips to Langley and signed more memoranda asking for further information, but, as the CIA saw it, the OVP was a coordinated machine working for its engineer. "When I heard complaints from people, it was, 'Man, you wouldn't believe this shit that Libby and [Undersecretary of Defense Douglas J.] Feith and Wolfowitz do to us.' They were all lumped together," says an ex-analyst close to his former colleagues. "I would hear them say, 'Goddamn, that fucking John Hannah, you wouldn't believe.' And the next day it would be, 'That fucking Bill Luti.' For all these guys, they're interchangeable." Adds another, "They had power. Authority. They had the vice president behind them. . . . What Scooter did, Cheney made possible. Feith, Wolfowitz—Cheney made it all possible. He's the fulcrum. He's the one."

From the OVP's perspective, the CIA—with its caveat-riddled position on Iraqi WMD and its refusal to connect Saddam and Al Qaeda—was an outright obstacle to the invasion of Iraq. And, as Cheney and his staff remembered so vividly from their Pentagon days, the CIA was often wrong on the biggest security questions. So Cheney reverted to the intelligence-gathering method he had perfected at Halliburton: He outsourced. Even before September 11, 2001, Cheney had given his staff clear instructions to go beyond the typical information channels in the bureaucracy. "He very, very much did not want to be trapped inside the government bubble and only see intelligence reports and State Department cables and Department of Defense memos," an ex-staffer recounts. Escaping the bubble was often innocuous and intellectually healthy. The OVP arranged meetings for Cheney with Middle East experts, such as the University of Haifa's Amatzia Baram, Princeton's Bernard Lewis, and Johns Hopkins's Fouad Ajami, and it gave him documents, such as the UN's 2002 Arab Human Development Report, which pointed to tyranny as the source of the region's problems.

But Cheney's office didn't escape the government bubble so much as create a new one. Any doubts expressed by the intelligence community about the OVP's sources, especially Chalabi, were ignored. During his stint as an adviser to Secretary of State Warren Christopher, Hannah had been one of the Clinton administration's most fervent INC supporters. Working for Cheney, he stayed in regular contact with the exile group. "He relied on Ahmed Chalabi for insights and advice," says a former Bush administration official. Cheney himself became an increasingly vocal Chalabi advocate. At an NSC meeting in the fall of 2002, the State Department and Pentagon feuded over releasing even more funding to the INC. In a rare burst of open influence, Cheney "weighed in, in a really big way," according to a former NSC staffer. "He said, 'We're getting ready to go to war, and we're nickel-and-diming the INC at a time when they're providing us with unique intelligence on Iraqi WMD.' " To the OVP, the CIA's hostility to such "unique" INC intelligence was evidence of the Agency's political corruption. Before long, "there was something of a willingness to give [INC-provided intelligence] greater weight" than that offered by the intelligence community, says the former administration official.

Chalabi was not the only source Hannah used to get alternative information to Cheney. In 2001, Luti had moved from the OVP to across the Potomac
to become Feith's deputy for Near East and South Asia (NESA). By late 2002,
Luti's Iraq desk became the Office of Special Plans (OSP), tasked with working
on issues related to the war effort. In addition to actual planning, the OSP provided memoranda to Pentagon officials recycling the most damaging—and often
the most spurious—intelligence about Iraq's Al Qaeda connections and the most
hopeful predictions about liberated Iraq. In the fall of 2002, one of the memos
stated as fact that September 11 hijacker Mohamed Atta had met in Prague
with an Iraqi intelligence agent months before the attacks—a claim the FBI
and CIA had debunked months earlier after an exhaustive investigation. And
the OSP didn't just comb through old intelligence for new information. It had
its own sources. For example, one of Luti's aides, a Navy lieutenant commander
named Youssef Aboul-Enein, was tasked with scouring Arabic-language websites and magazines to come up with what Aboul-Enein would call "something
really useful"—statements by Saddam praising the September 11 attacks, Palestinian suicide bombings, or any act of terrorism.

According to those who worked in NESA, Luti's efforts had a specific cus-
tomer: Cheney. "Cheney's the one with the burr under his saddle about Iraq,"
says retired Air Force Lieutenant Colonel Karen Kwiatkowski, who worked
for Luti from May 2002 until the eve of the war. During that time, Luti held
only about six or seven staff meetings, she says, and "I heard Scooter Libby's
name mentioned in half those meetings." Discussing Iraq, Luti would say
"things like, 'Did you give something to Scooter?' 'Scooter called; hey, call
him back,' . . . [or] 'Oh, well, did you talk to Scooter about that?' " And Luti
would make trips across the Potomac to see his old colleagues at the OVP.
White House officials would often see Luti disappearing into Hannah's office
before going on to Libby's.

The OVP didn't just generate this information for themselves. They tried
to pump it back into the intelligence pipeline on visits to Langley. "Scooter
and the vice president come out there loaded with crap from OSP, reams of
information from Chalabi's people" on both terrorism and WMD, according
to an ex-CIA analyst. One of the OVP's principal interlocutors was Alan Foley,
director of the CIA's Nonproliferation Center. Cheney's office pelted Foley with
questions about Iraq's nuclear weapons program—especially about Saddam's
alleged attempts to purchase uranium from Niger. According to a colleague,
Foley "pushed back" by "stressing the implausibility of it." Months earlier,
after all, former Ambassador Joseph Wilson had gone to Niger at the behest

of the CIA—a visit that had itself been instigated by questions raised by Cheney in an Agency briefing—and concluded that the sale almost certainly did not occur. But Cheney kept pressing, and it took its toll on Foley. "He was bullied and intimidated," says a friend of Foley.

In the view of many at Langley, the OVP wasn't simply highlighting what it considered weaknesses in CIA analysis. Rather, it was trying to stifle information that it considered counterproductive to the case for war. The tone of the questioning, some analysts felt, was less inquisitive than hostile. "It was done along the lines of: 'What's wrong with you bunch of assholes? You don't know what's going on, you're horribly biased, you're a bunch of pinkos,'" says a retired analyst close to his active-duty colleagues. Some analysts saw the questioning as a method of diverting overtaxed CIA analysts from producing undesired intelligence product. On one occasion, officials asked analysts hard at work on Iraq to produce a paper on the history of the British occupation of Mesopotamia following World War I. The request might seem reasonable on the surface—after all, an occupation ought to be informed by precedent. But policymakers in the OVP and the DOD could just as easily have picked up histories of Iraq from the library and let the CIA go back to work on classified analysis. But, after enduring the questioning for months, an ex-analyst explains, "It gets to the point where you just don't want to fight it anymore."

Eventually the OVP's alternative analyses found their way into the administration's public case for war. The distance between the OVP and the intelligence community was greatest on terrorism, and the OVP was determined to win. Libby wrote a draft of Colin Powell's February speech to the UN Security Council that outlined a far different threat than the secretary of state envisioned. "[The OVP] really wanted to make it a speech mostly about the link to terrorism," says one former NSC official. Although Powell and his staff balked at the most controversial—and poorly substantiated—details, Libby still provided the initial outline for the speech.

Cheney's own public statements went far beyond what the CIA and other intelligence agencies had verified. In an August 2002 speech in Nashville, Cheney asserted, "The Iraqi regime has in fact been very busy enhancing its capabilities in the field of chemical and biological agents, and they continue to pursue the nuclear program they began so many years ago." The intelligence community was in fact deeply divided over whether the nuclear program was again active, and a classified DIA report a month later indicated that the Agency had "no reliable information" about Iraq's chemical weapons program. But these doubts never seeped into Cheney's public statements. Days before the invasion, Cheney told NBC's Tim Russert on *Meet the Press*, "We know [Saddam is] out trying once again to produce nuclear weapons, and we know that he has a long-standing relationship with . . . the Al Qaeda organization." By contrast, the intelligence agencies assessed that, despite some apparently fruitless contact between Saddam's henchmen and Al Qaeda terrorists in Sudan in the mid-'90s, Iraq and Osama bin Laden were two unrelated threats.

The OVP never considered that it could be wrong, despite the fact that none of its senior members had intelligence training. The CIA, on the other hand, rather than behaving as a rigid and unshakable bastion of unquestionable truth, subjected its judgments to rigorous criticism. On Iraq, the CIA had what is known as the "red cell," a team of four highly regarded retired analysts who conducted alternative assessments of Iraq's ties to terrorism. The OVP, by contrast, put its judgments through no comparable wringer. Perhaps that is why so much of what they embraced was wrong. On the ground in Iraq today, there is no evidence that Saddam reconstituted his nuclear weapons program; according to chief American arms-hunter David Kay's interim report, the evidence of any ongoing chemical or biological weapons programs is fragmentary at best. A classified study prepared by the National Intelligence Council in early 2003 found that only one of Chalabi's defectors could be considered credible, *The New Republic* has learned. A more recent investigation undertaken by the DIA has found that practically all the intelligence provided by the INC was worthless.

September 14 [,2003] was a difficult moment for the occupation of Iraq. In Falluja, a seat of unrest, Iraqis had finished burying ten security officers accidentally killed when soldiers from the 3rd Armored Cavalry Regiment mistook them for guerrillas. One of their comrades, Ali Jassim, told a *New York Times* reporter that the United States was "training their guns on us. . . . They came here to apply the occupier way—just like Saddam." That morning, Cheney returned to *Meet The Press* for his first TV interview since the war began. Despite repeated CIA warnings of postwar chaos, Cheney had insisted that the Iraqis would welcome American troops with open arms, and Russert reminded him that, on March 16, Cheney had flatly declared, "We will, in fact, be greeted as liberators." Instead, it seemed, Iraqis had decidedly mixed feelings about the occupation. A report by former Deputy Defense Secretary John Hamre, initiated at the behest of Defense Secretary Donald Rumsfeld and Iraq administrator L. Paul Bremer, had warned two months earlier, "The Iraqi population has exceedingly high expectations, and the window for cooperation may close rapidly."

Cheney was unfazed. "If you go out and look at what's happening on the ground, you'll find that there is widespread support," he responded. As evidence, he cited a poll conducted by John Zogby. "That's got very positive news in it in terms of the numbers it shows with respect to the attitudes to what Americans have done," he said. "One of the questions it asked is: 'If you could have any model for the kind of government you'd like to have'—and they were given five choices—'which would it be?' The U.S. wins hands down. If you want to ask them, do they want an Islamic government established, by two-to-one margins they say no, including the Shia population. If you ask how long they want Americans to stay, over sixty percent of the people polled said they want the U.S. to stay for at least another year."

Practically nothing Cheney said in his description of the poll—and the situation in Iraq—withstands scrutiny. When Iraqis were asked what model government they wanted, a breakaway plurality of 49 percent desired a democracy guided by Islamic law. The next closest contender, with 24 percent, was a clerical-dominated Islamic state. A secular, democratic Iraq—the closest choice to the U.S. model—garnered only 21 percent support. Over 60 percent of Iraqis wanted the United States and Britain to *leave* Iraq in a year; among Sunnis, the figure rose to 70 percent. Worse, fully half of Iraqis said they expected the United States to hurt their country over the next five years. Only 36 percent voiced faith that it would help. "One thing is clear," Zogby wrote in the *Los Angeles Times*, "the predicted euphoria of Iraqis has not materialized."

Cheney's dubious pronouncements on Iraq didn't end there. When asked if Iraq was involved in the September 11 attacks, Cheney said, "We don't know." He trotted out once more the canard that Atta met in Prague with an Iraqi intelligence agent—the same charge the OSP had continued to circulate even after the intelligence community debunked it. (Cheney's remark was so embarrassing to the administration that, three days later, Bush declared, "We've had no evidence that Saddam Hussein was involved with September 11.")

In short, nothing that has happened in Iraq over the last six months—the missing WMD, the mounting violence, the massive price tag—seems to have prompted any introspection among Cheney or his staff. They continue to carp about the hopelessly dovish bent of the CIA. "Some of these people—do they not have a political view on this?" exclaims a former Cheney staffer. "Did they support or oppose the war? Shouldn't that be factored into how they ended up judging [intelligence]?" In September, Cheney hired David Wurmser from the office of Bolton, the undersecretary of state for arms control. Recruiting Wurmser indicates Cheney's confidence in the approach to intelligence the OVP has taken from the start. After the September 11 attacks, Wurmser and his colleague Michael Maloof had been tasked by Feith to cull the intelligence community's amassed data on Iraq and Al Qaeda to find evidence of cooperation.

With Bush repeatedly affirming Cheney's place on the 2004 ticket, there is no evidence the vice president has reconsidered either the ideological vision that has taken him this far or the process he has used to implement it. And, of course, there are enormous foreign policy challenges remaining on the U.S. agenda: the nuclear crises in North Korea and Iran, America's estrangement from the rest of the world, and above all the unfinished war on terrorism. Anyone who thinks the Bush administration will take a softer line on these questions than it did on Iraq is probably kidding himself. Cheney will continue to push the agenda he set out 15 years ago: aggressive promotion of democracy through military power. This is no mere intoxication with ideas of the moment, spurred by a zealous staff or the pain of September 11. This is who Dick Cheney—the most powerful vice president in history—is.

The Controller

Nicholas Lemann

The New Yorker | May 12, 2003

If Dick Cheney is the éminence grise behind the Bush administration's world view, Karl Rove represents a second, equally powerful force in the White House. A brilliant political operative who got his start in direct-mail campaigning, he was already widely sought after as a consultant when he managed George W. Bush's successful first run for the Texas governorship in 1994. Today, from his adviser's office in the West Wing, Rove's job is to tend to the president's political well-being—a job he does all too well, according to some critics, who complain that many of the administration's policies are designed more to appeal to specific voting blocs (or donor groups—Rove also oversees Bush's fund-raising operation), than to solve existing problems.

So vast is Rove's purported influence that one of the favorite parlor games in Washington, Texas, and elsewhere is to guess at his involvement in various political machinations—what Nicholas Lemann refers to here as "Mark of Rove speculation." This article (published just after Lemann announced he was stepping down as staff writer for The New Yorker *to become dean of the Columbia School of Journalism) doesn't solve any such mysteries, but it does provide a window into why Rove is so effective. As Lemann points out, rarely has any political player ever embodied such a combination of tactical expertise and strategic vision. After all, how many people can devise and implement every detail of a book-length campaign strategy and offer a sophisticated critique of the* Federalist Papers? *No wonder Rove has Democrats scratching their heads. Here, Lemann explores the forces that have shaped the man they call "Bush's Brain"—including his indelible first impression of a young George W., "exuding more charisma than any one individual should be allowed to have".* . . .

Politics is a field with a lot of former practitioners: there is a high failure rate, and success comes tinged with a gnawing nervousness that makes it not worthwhile for everybody. Robert Edgeworth, a Virgil scholar who teaches at Louisiana State University, in Baton Rouge, is in politics purely avocationally these days. Edgeworth is practically a museum-worthy example of what is connoted by the word "professorial": at fifty-six, he has white hair and parchment skin, he wears tweed, and he speaks with great precision. It's hard to imagine him as a budding politico, but, then, his most active period ended nearly thirty years ago, when he placed himself in the onrushing path of Karl Rove, President Bush's chief political adviser. This has never been a smart thing to do, but Edgeworth, as one of the first of many to find that out, had the excuse of not having been as well informed on the subject as people in Washington are now.

The story of Edgeworth and Rove is a well-burnished legend within a very small circle—well burnished enough that just saying "Lake of the Ozarks" is enough to evoke it. The circle is made up of people connected with College Republicans, a group tight enough (it became an independent organization in 1971) that all its significant figures at least know one another's names. Theirs is a subculture that took form in the mid- to late sixties, at a time when what was officially going on in the United States was a great uprising of rebellious youth and a flowering of liberal politics. The College Republicans were young people who believed that the coming thing was a resurgence of the political right. They felt this so strongly, and loved politics so much, that they devoted a ruthless, all-consuming effort to gaining advantage in a small student organization that today seems a little eccentric. The history of College Republicans is like that of a left-wing group, full of coups and counter-coups and intrigue. And the most College Republican of all College Republicans was Karl Rove.

Rove had come out of nowhere—to be specific, Utah, from a nonpolitical and not very well-established family that he didn't talk about much. As a seventeen-year-old, Rove made the leap beyond high-school politics by volunteering in a United States Senate campaign. In 1969, at the University of Utah, he signed up for the College Republicans, and showed enough promise that the organization dispatched him to Illinois the following year to work as a campus organizer in the unsuccessful United States Senate campasign of Ralph Tyler Smith, who had been appointed to the seat of the Senate's Republican leader, Everett McKinley Dirksen, after Dirksen died. This amounted to hitting the big time, because Illinois was the most active College Republican state. In 1971, Rove became a protégé of Joe Abate, the College Republican chairman, who hired him as the organization's national executive director, a position that paid very modestly.

Rove, who is fifty-two, has always appeared to be affable and extroverted—he has a foghorn voice and an innocent face, with pale-blue eyes, a tuft of flyaway blond hair, and light skin that flushes when he's angry—while, at the same time, being very hard to know well. His few close friends knew that in the period preceding his roaring entry into the College Republican world he had been through a tough, even searing, time. His parents' marriage had ended on his nineteenth birthday—Christmas Day, 1969—when his father walked out. Then, shortly afterward, Rove received a second and more unexpected blow. In Illinois, he had dinner with an aunt and uncle, and, during a discussion of his parents' divorce negotiations, they casually mentioned that the man he thought of as his father actually wasn't. "I literally, I think, dropped my soda," Rove told me, in one of three long interviews we had in his office in the West Wing of the White House. In a family of five siblings, he and an older brother were the children of another man, whose connection to his mother had been kept secret, at her insistence, all the time he'd been growing up. Among his friends in College Republicans, the story, to the extent that it circulated, took the form that he had been adopted—which is somehow not quite as upsetting. One person remembers Rove saying to him, "Whose birthday is on Christmas Day? You have to be kidding! They didn't know exactly when I was born, so they just took a guess." But when I asked Rove about it he said the real story is that he was, as it were, half-adopted. I asked him if he'd ever found out who his real father is, and he said that he had, but didn't meet him until many years later, when he was in his forties. He got in touch with the man, arranged to visit him, and was greeted with a chilly reception. Rove spoke of his adoptive father in a tone of fierce admiration, love, and loyalty, for, as he put it, "how selfless his love had been," as shown by his willingness to play, persuasively, the part of a blood parent for two decades. The bond between Rove and his adoptive father became even more important, no doubt, after Rove's mother committed suicide, in Reno, Nevada, in 1981.

Edgeworth was the head of College Republicans in the Midwest, and later the vice-chairman of the organization. Not long ago, he and I had lunch at a quiet restaurant in Baton Rouge. Edgeworth told me that he'd had it in mind that, in 1973, Joe Abate would step down, Edgeworth would become chairman of College Republicans for a two-year term, and Rove would become vice-chairman; then, in 1975, Edgeworth would step down and hand the chairmanship over to Rove. For Rove, as Edgeworth saw it, this would not only be gentlemanly; it would mean that if he was willing to invest two years in being patient he would be rewarded with a coronation as chairman. He wasn't willing. A race for the chairmanship began, between Rove, Edgeworth, and Terry Dolan, who went on to found the National Conservative Political Action Committee. Of the three, Dolan was the most conservative and Rove the least. "If you asked a question like what to do about the United Nations," Edgeworth told me, "Terry would say, 'Withdraw immediately.' I'd say, 'Scale it down and pay less in dues.' Karl would say, 'Leave it alone, the voters won't understand the issue.' He put pragmatic considerations higher than us."

A campaign for the College Republican chairmanship was a serious matter; Rove left his job as executive director in order to spend five months, without pay, campaigning full time. (Rove was consumed with College Republicans for so many years that he didn't spend much time actually going to college; he never graduated.) Rove and his chief assistant, Lee Atwater, later another famous hardball-playing Republican strategist, drove across the South lining up delegate support. Meanwhile, Terry Dolan and Bob Edgeworth decided to form a ticket, with Edgeworth as chair and Dolan as vice-chair. So it became a two-man race: Edgeworth versus Rove.

The national convention was in June, in the mountain resort of Lake of the Ozarks, Missouri. All through the late spring, Edgeworth and Dolan were hearing stories about the Rove forces staging credentials challenges at state and regional conventions, using some technical pretext. Shortly after the Midwest regional convention, for example, according to Edgeworth, the Rove forces, in order to justify the unseating of the Edgeworth delegates on procedural grounds, produced a version of the Midwestern College Republicans' constitution which differed significantly from the constitution that the Edgeworth forces were using. The net result of all the challenges was that a number of states sent two competing delegates to Lake of the Ozarks, one pledged to Edgeworth, the other to Rove, each claiming to be legitimate. Then the meeting of the credentials committee, before the convention itself, turned into a donnybrook. Edgeworth told me that when the southern regional chair of the College Republicans, who was officially uncommitted, cast his first pro-Edgeworth vote in one of the credentials disputes, a Rove person left the room for a minute. After he returned, another Rove person announced that a different person was actually the southern regional chair, and proposed and passed a resolution to have Southern Regional Chair No. 1 thrown out. It went on like that until morning, with the person running Rove's convention operations, John Zemaitis, an ostensibly above-the-fray Republican figure from Illinois, secreted in a room at a Holiday Inn in Jefferson City, thirty miles away. "It was so *raw*," one venerable College Republican figure told me, shaking his head wonderingly at the memory. In the end, there were two votes, conducted by two convention chairs, and two winners—Rove and Edgeworth, each of whom delivered an acceptance speech. After the convention broke up, both Edgeworth and Rove appealed to the Republican National Committee, each contending that he was the new College Republican chairman.

The R.N.C. had a relatively unseasoned chairman: George Herbert Walker Bush, a man thought to be on the downhill slope of a once promising political career. Bush was a former member of the United States House of Representatives who had lost two successive Senate races in Texas, in 1964 and 1970, and then accepted an assignment that did not seem very stature-enhancing, as the public face of the R.N.C. during the Watergate scandal. During the summer of 1973, while Bush's staff was conducting an inquiry into the Lake of the Ozarks affair, Terry Dolan, promoting the Edgeworth cause, leaked to the *Washington Post* a tape recording in which Rove and another College Republican are heard recounting at a training weekend some amusing stories about minor campaign espionage they had engaged in during various campaigns. The *Post* published a story about the tape under the headline "GOP PROBES OFFICIAL AS TEACHER OF TRICKS."

At the end of the summer, Bush wrote Edgeworth a letter saying that he had concluded that Rove had fairly won the vote at the convention and was therefore being installed as the new chairman of the College Republicans.

Edgeworth wrote back, asking on what basis he had ruled. Not long after that, Edgeworth told me, "Bush sent me back the angriest letter I have ever received in my life. I had leaked to the *Washington Post*, and now I was out of the Party forever. That letter is a family heirloom." Edgeworth moved to Australia for several years. And George Bush, evidently impressed with what he had learned about Karl Rove in the course of supervising the Lake of the Ozarks inquiry, gave instructions that Rove be offered a full-time job at the Republican National Committee. The connection has been unbroken ever since.

I asked Rove if he remembered his first impression of the Bushes. "The father was incredibly gentle," he said. "Great character. Very thoughtful. Really generous in his openness and attitude. Clearly pained by Watergate as it unrolled." His first memory of George W. Bush was more precise. "It was the day before Thanksgiving, 1973," Rove said. "Chairman Bush's chief of staff called me and said, 'I've got to be at a meeting on the Hill, the chairman's got to be at a meeting at the White House, the other people in the office have already gone, and the eldest son's going to be coming down from Harvard. He's going to arrive at the train station, early afternoon. He'll call over here when he gets to the train station. Meet him down in the lobby and give him the keys to the family car.' I can literally remember what he was wearing: an Air National Guard flight jacket, cowboy boots, bluejeans, complete with the—in Texas you see it a lot—one of the back pockets will have a circle worn in the pocket from where you carry your tin of snuff, your tin of tobacco. He was exuding more charisma than any one individual should be allowed to have."

Edgeworth told me that one night in 1984, after he'd moved to Baton Rouge, he got a call from John Zemaitis, whom he hadn't heard from in years. During the Lake of the Ozarks affair, Zemaitis had ostensibly been an impartial figure. "I have come to the Lord," Edgeworth remembers Zemaitis saying. "I need to settle my accounts." Then Zemaitis admitted that he had secretly been in league with Rove all along, and he apologized for the conduct of the campaign. Edgeworth's reminiscences of Karl Rove were not without fondness, though. He presented Rove as a smart, funny, supercompetent young man with an obsession with political campaigning and a need to win which trumped social niceties. It was as if Rove's mind were devoted to a permanent, hyperactive search for anything—any contact, any thought, any bit of information—that might serve the cause of political victory. Rove was an autodidact intellectual, and often talked about books. According to Edgeworth, he once told Rove about the dialectic (thesis, antithesis, synthesis), and Rove called him a few days later and said—this was memorable because Rove does not readily admit that somebody else knows something important that he didn't know already—"You know that tripartite deal? Where'd you find that?" (Rove disputes this account, saying that he wrote an elementary-school paper on dialectical materialism and so did not have to be enlightened by Edgeworth.) Rove's favorite book at the time was Eric Foner's *Free Soil, Free Labor, Free Men*, a history of the early days of the Republican Party, which he read less as a dispassionate analysis of the early Republicans' strengths and weaknesses than as a guidebook on how to broaden the appeal of the Party. Another book Rove had read recently was Leonard Lurie's *The King Makers*, a history of the battle between the conservative Robert Taft and the pragmatic Dwight Eisenhower, at the 1952 Republican National Convention. While talking about this, Edgeworth, otherwise serene, suddenly did a double take and slapped the table. "Oh, my God!" he said. "I'm Taft! He's Eisenhower! I never made that connection before. Karl's whole strategy in 1973—it's all in that book."

In his office in the White House, a meticulously neat room with a view of the Washington Monument, pictures of Abraham Lincoln and Theodore Roosevelt, and a framed autograph of James Madison on the walls (as well as a spread from a children's book about American presidents, called *Great Moments in History*, which is the first thing he can remember reading), Rove seems to spend much of his time doing what the people who work for him call "multitasking." This means answering e-mail while simultaneously talking on the phone, conducting a meeting around a big table that occupies most of the empty space in the office, and fielding queries from his assistant, Susan Ralston, and members of the White House staff who poke their heads in. Rove has an omnipresent quality. Everybody seems to have just heard from him— he's a master of the little note or phone call on important occasions. His response to e-mails is often instantaneous. Every White House has a political operative, but Rove has a much bigger charter than his predecessors. He appears to have supervisory authority over the Republican National Committee. Inside the White House, after Karen Hughes, the primary keeper of the Bush image, left, last year, her role was taken over by a protégé and former employee of Rove's, Dan Bartlett. The head of the White House domestic-policy operation, Margaret Spellings, is another Rove associate from Texas. She sees him almost every day, and Rove plays a much heavier role in domestic policy than any previous occupant of his position. (This is not a White House in which the "policy shop" constantly tussles with the "politics shop," as has usually been the case.) He functions as a national personnel director for the Republican Party, hand-selecting candidates for governorships and seats in the Senate and House. His people are widely scattered around the executive departments. He closely supervises political fund-raising. And, of course, the President is someone whose entire political career Rove has masterminded, beginning, if not at that memorable first meeting, then certainly years before Bush's first successful race for office.

As if all this weren't enough, people in politics love to speculate that Rove is up to much more than is apparent. In the same way that prophetic fundamentalists are always on the lookout for emblazonings of the number 666, the Mark of the Beast, in Washington everybody is highly attuned to the possibility that most of what goes on bears the Mark of Karl Rove. There are many cases where Rove is suspected of having engineered a brutal bit of political business without leaving any fingerprints, in the manner of the Lake of the Ozarks affair. In Texas, where Rove was a dominant Republican political consultant, Mark of Rove speculation has filled many an evening in places where politicians and lobbyists hang out. Probably the two leading Texas stories, out of dozens, or even hundreds, are the one that has him bugging his own office on the eve of a crucial campaign debate, so that by "discovering" the dastardly deed he could distract attention from his candidate's poor debating skills, and the one that has him inducing an FBI agent named Greg Rampton to investigate employees of the Texas Department of Agriculture on rather slight grounds, in order to help his candidate for Agriculture Commissioner—Rick Perry, now governor of Texas—defeat the very popular Democratic incumbent, Jim Hightower. (Three of the employees were tried and convicted.) In Washington, Rove gets conversational credit for everything up to and including the war in Iraq, and Democrats, at least, use "Rove" as shorthand for "the Bush administration," as in, "Is Rove going to invade Syria?"

Rove has many times looked people in the eye and stoutly denied the Mark of Rove stories. On the other hand, it doesn't seem to torment him that he's the center of attention and speculation, or that he's thought of as all-powerful. Rove is complicated. His usual mode is one of irony—sometimes there seems to be a twinkle in his eye as he professes outrage over the unfair attribution of enormous influence to him. At the same time, he seems to be genuinely thin-skinned. People who come from backgrounds suffused with love, praise, and security often have the ability to dismiss criticism out of hand; people who don't, especially if they're as smart as Rove, often devote great effort to building structures of refutation. If you mention any possible lacuna or shortcoming, his face reddens and he offers a well-thought-through rebuttal. One day, I mentioned his decision to send Bush to California late in the 2000 campaign, something that in retrospect looks like a costly mistake, since Bush was never going to win California and since the election turned out to be so close. Rove shot back, "Well, the late trip to California is—As long as you're going to drag yourself out to fight for Washington and Oregon, drag yourself all the way out to the West Coast, you might as well stop in California. You can create news there. Out of our hundred-million-dollar campaign, we spent a million and a half in California. The rest of the effort was a gigantic effort funded by the Californians, who raised thirteen million for their victory-committee effort." Sorry!

Also, Rove's pride in his knowledge of politics is so great that he has an evidently irresistible impulse to dispute, correct, or improve upon virtually anything anybody says on the subject, in a tone that's half rehearsed lecture, half teasing one-upmanship. Mention that West Texas is conservative, and Rove will come right back and say no, there are actually four subregions in West Texas, each with its own distinct history and ideology, and then he'll give detailed, decades-old election results in each one from memory. Point to Rove. But, although the No. 1 occupational disease in the field of political consulting is a conversational tendency to run up one's own brilliance while, either subtly or overtly, running down the candidate, Rove manages to combine a manner that has no trace of self-effacement with an attitude toward his boss which appears to be truly worshipful.

I asked Rove if it was true that he had engineered the demise of Trent Lott, of Mississippi, as Senate majority leader, and Lott's replacement by the more Bush-friendly Bill Frist, of Tennessee—it would be hard to find anyone in Washington who believed he hadn't. (In 1990, Lott publicly criticized President George H. W. Bush for raising taxes, and the Bushes have long memories.) "No," Rove said, flatly. Then he mentioned, in what I thought was a less than entirely sombre tone, that on the day the Lott affair reached its dramatic peak, when Lott was scheduled to appear on Black Entertainment Television to defend himself, Rove had got a call from his friend Bill Frist: "Monday morning, Frist calls me and says, 'You know, on Friday we're supposed to take our boys and go hunting in South Texas together—you think we ought to go?' I said, 'I don't know, let me think about it. Can I call you tomorrow?' And the next day"—after Lott's performance on BET, which came across as abjectly liberal, and failed to save him—"I call Frist and say, 'I don't think it's going to be good for you or for me to be seen in South Texas, hunting with our boys.' I think the world of Bill, but I don't take credit." That certainly settles that!

A variant of the Mark of Rove is what might be called the Arabesque of Rove, in which the administration openly makes a political move, but its meaning is presumed to be something else. A policy that looks like an appeal to one group is actually an appeal to another—the locus classicus being Bush's promise to "leave no child behind" in education, which gestures, not disingenuously, toward ghetto kids but drives up Bush's poll numbers with suburban women. (Rove, who salts his conversation with election and poll results, told me, "Remember, in 1996, if education's your No. 1 issue, you vote for Clinton-Gore over Dole-Kemp by 76-16. By 2000, you vote for Gore-Lieberman over Bush-Cheney by 52-44.") Or something will be aimed simultaneously at both "base" voters, on the right, and "swing" voters, in the middle, like the slogan "compassionate conservatism," which moderates hear as "not all that conservative" and fundamentalists hear as "conservative and dedicated to serving Jesus Christ." Or the administration will propose something that receives the universal approbation of respectable opinion and also fails to pass, but that actually has hidden benefits, such as distracting liberal attention from something else, or propitiating an important Republican interest group.

The idea of eliminating taxation on individuals' dividend income, for example, is probably never going to become the subject of some future term paper entitled "How a Bill Becomes Law." But proposing it may help win the hearts of senior citizens, the group most heavily dependent on dividend income, and of the securities industry. "Fifty-two percent of all American households own equities," Rove reminded me. "Nearly two-thirds of all voting households own equities." The recent nomination of Miguel Estrada for a federal appellate judgeship is in trouble, too, but it sends a signal to Latinos, a group the administration is eager to woo, and it soaks up most of the available supply of liberal energy for opposing the administration's judicial nominees. All through the Estrada fight, the Senate has been confirming, on average, six federal Bush judicial nominees a month.

The way Rove talks publicly about these maneuvers is influenced by a desire not to give away trade secrets and by what appears to be a sincere belief (one common, however, in aggressive people) that it is his bad fortune to be up against unusually ruthless, unfair opponents—the likes of Jane Fonda and

Barbra Streisand and the N.A.A.C.P. I asked him if the liberal editorial pages would have liked the dividend-tax cut better if it had been applied to corporations rather than to individuals, as most economists have advocated. "No, they wouldn't!" Rove shot back. "No, they wouldn't! No, it wouldn't! 'Corporate giveaway!' If you're against tax cuts, if you believe that the way for a strong economy is for the government to hold on to every dime it can get its hands on and spend it, then you'll find a way to be against any proposal that ends the double taxation of dividends." When I asked Rove about the Estrada nomination, he said, "In anything but the current hypercharged partisan environment in Washington, Miguel Estrada would be the kind of person that would come out of the United States Senate 98-2, or 98-0. Great American success story. Comes to the country as an immigrant. Doesn't speak English. Graduates from two of America's leading universities and law schools. Serves in the administrations of both Democrats and Republicans. Look, if it wasn't Miguel Estrada that they fought about, they would have fought about somebody else. It's their choice that they picked Miguel Estrada."

Rove is both a fox and a hedgehog. He is the detail man of all detail men, but he also makes a point of doing more long-term strategic planning than other political consultants. For especially important campaigns, he produces written plans far in advance, mapping out the race in its entirety, and he's famous for sticking precisely to the plan no matter what. Rove's main goal over the next year and a half is making George W. Bush what his father wasn't, a reelected president—when I asked if he had mapped out the campaign, he said, "Don't expect me to answer this question"—but he is too ambitious to want only that. The real prize is creating a Republican majority that would be as solid as, say, the Democratic coalition that Franklin Roosevelt created—a majority that would last for a generation and that, as it played itself out over time, would wind up profoundly changing the relationship between citizen and state in this country. "I think we're at a point where the two major parties have sort of exhausted their governing agendas," Rove told me. "We had agendas that were originally formed, for the Democrats, in the New Deal, and, for the Republicans, in opposition to the New Deal—modified by the cold war and further modified by the changes in the sixties, the Great Society and societal and cultural changes. It's sort of like the exhaustion of two boxers fighting it out in the middle of the ring. This periodically happens. This happened in 1896, where the Civil War party system was in decline and the parties were in rough parity and somebody came along and figured it out and helped create a governing coalition that really lasted for the next some-odd years. Similarly, somebody will come along and figure out a new governing scheme through which people could view things and could, conceivably, enjoy a similar period of dominance." Karl Rove clearly wants to be that somebody, and his relentless pressing for every possible specific advantage is in service of the larger goal.

In 1977, Rove moved to Houston to become the second employee of what appeared to be a quixotic enterprise, the Fund for Limited Government, a political-action committee dedicated to making George H. W. Bush president. Rove married a young woman named Valerie Wainright, whose family was in the Bush social circle in Houston. (The marriage didn't last long, and Rove remarried in 1986; he and his wife, Darby, have one son.) Texas was an important Democratic state that Republicans saw as an arena of opportunity, but the opportunity hadn't materialized yet. It had one Republican United States senator, John Tower, but no Republican state officeholders. Jimmy Carter had carried Texas in the 1976 presidential election. James A. Baker III, the future secretary of state, ran a well-financed race for Texas attorney general in 1978, and lost.

Rove left the Bush pre-presidential operation to work in the gubernatorial campaign of Bill Clements, an oilman who in 1978 became Texas's first Republican governor since Reconstruction. Rove was appointed Clements's chief of staff. In 1981, he left to set up a direct-mail business in Austin called Karl Rove + Company. This put him in a position to make more money than you can as a politician's full-time employee, and allowed him to work for many Republican candidates at the same time. Rove had the imprimatur of Texas's Republican aristocracy from the beginning, through his connection to the Bush family and to Clements. An early financier of Karl Rove + Company was Tobin Armstrong, the owner of a Texas ranch (it was on land leased from Armstrong Rove and Bill Frist were planning to go hunting) and the husband of Anne Armstrong, a former Republican Cabinet officer. Becoming chairman of the College Republicans provided Rove with an introduction to such people, which may be one reason that winning mattered so much to him; it also seems that Rove, the self-made man, gets pleasure as well as practical advantage from his association with the Texas upper crust, people who give off the glow of ease, charm, and connection which he detected in George W. Bush the first time they met.

That Rove got his start in the direct-mail business, a technical and unglamorous political subspecialty, is important in understanding the way he thinks and operates today. Television gave birth to political consulting as an organized business, and the royalty of political consulting has been made up of people who create television advertising for candidates. Media consultants tend to think in terms of "message"—they look at poll results and decide what note a short television advertisement should strike so as to affect the voting behavior of a large audience made up of people who are only lightly affiliated with politics.

Direct-mail consultants are trained to think in quite a different way. Their communications medium is a long letter that conveys many points in printed form, rather than a single "message" in visual and aural form. (One media consultant who worked with Rove remembered his counting the number of syllables in a thirty-second spot, and then proposing a rewrite of the spot in which it would make half a dozen additional points using the same number of syllables.) Media consultants tend to think of raising money as somebody else's job, but direct-mail consultants are fund-raisers—there's that little envelope in each letter—and are more closely attuned to where the money is. Most important, direct-mail consultants are in the business of narrowcasting rather than broadcasting. They have to be on perpetual patrol for new groups with intense opinions about politics. James Moore and Wayne Slater, the authors of a new and generally unfavorable Rove biography called *Bush's Brain*, found a memo he wrote Clements in which he suggested renting the subscriber list of *Krugerrand Buyer*, a magazine for investors in the South African gold currency, because they'd be good Republican donor prospects. That's direct-mail thinking. (And, not surprisingly, after Rove read *Bush's Brain* before publication, Slater received a fifteen-page single-spaced letter of refutation from him.)

During Clements's term as governor, Rove expanded his business, from direct mail to general strategic consulting. In 1982, during the Reagan recession, the Democrats had what turned out to be their last great election season in Texas, unseating Clements and sweeping all the state elective offices. In 1984, Rove worked in the campaign of Texas's second modern Republican United States senator, Phil Gramm, who had recently defected from the Democratic Party. In 1986, Clements, an ornery old man, ran again, with Rove advising him, and beat the governor who'd beaten him four years earlier. The apotheosis of Rove really began in 1988, when he orchestrated the election of Texas's chief justice, Tom Phillips, a young judge in Houston who was both very smart and very well connected. Phillips went to see Rove and said he was thinking about running for the state Supreme Court. Shortly afterward, Texas's sitting chief justice had a series of private conversations with Governor Clements, at the end of which he resigned and Clements appointed Phillips as his temporary replacement. Phillips was sworn in at noon on the last day on which Supreme Court candidates could file for election. By this time, he had hired Rove as his consultant and filed his candidacy. "Karl, then as now, was a master of the numbers," Phillips told me not long ago, when I went to see him in his chambers. "He wrote a *book* outlining the campaign: exactly how many votes I needed and where they'd come from. And then how much money it would take and where it would be spent, and how to raise it." Phillips and Rove gave me a copy of this document, which provides a good example of the kind of specificity that Phillips was talking about. It contains a statistical formula for determining the efficiency of campaign spending, which Rove applies to a hundred and seventy-eight Texas counties likely to vote Republican, based on weighted averages of the Republican vote in recent elections. Phillips became the first Republican elected to a statewide office below the governorship, and his victory created an important new issue in Texas politics: "tort reform"; that is, limiting the ability of plaintiffs' lawyers to obtain huge damage awards from the courts. Not all issues that resonate with voters also resonate with interest groups, but tort reform does, and it became a signature issue in Rove campaigns. Today, the Texas Supreme Court, of which Phillips was the first Republican chief justice in the modern era, has no Democratic members—and by the time Rove left for Washington seven of the nine justices were his clients.

After the Phillips race, Rove and George W. Bush gave some thought to Bush's running for governor in 1990. "I met with him a couple times about it," Rove told me. "But he thought it would be awkward as long as his dad was president. He decided this wasn't the time." (In 1992, Bush made an unsuccessful try for the position of commissioner of Major League baseball.) By the time Bush did run for governor, in 1994, Rove had engineered the demise of two of Texas's most promising Democratic politicians, Jim Hightower, the agriculture commissioner, and Lena Guerrero, a young commissioner of a state agency, who, Rove revealed (in a rare fully owned-up-to Mark of Rove incident), had lied about her academic credentials. He had helped Rick Perry, the future governor, win his first state office. And in 1994 he helped get Kay

Bailey Hutchison, a protégée of Anne and Tobin Armstrong whom Rove had known for years, elected to a full term in Texas's other United States Senate seat, even though she had just been indicted and acquitted for misusing state resources. When Bush won, after an extensive training period supervised by Rove that included briefings on policy issues and out-of-town speaking engagements, Texas's final Democratic political star, Governor Ann Richards, was history. Rove clients held Texas's governorship, both its Senate seats, a majority of the seats on its Supreme Court, and most of the other statewide offices.

By the mid-nineties, Rove had got himself into a highly unusual position for a political consultant—functioning more in the manner of an old-fashioned political boss than of a for-hire member of the service sector. Rather than his pitching candidates for their business, candidates pitched him for his commitment. The key to his power was that he had a particularly solid connection to the money side of politics. He carefully cultivated Texas's biggest Republican donors, people like Peter O'Donnell and Louis Beecherl, in Dallas, and Bob Perry and Kenneth Lay (before the fall of Enron), in Houston; they saw him as someone whose clients usually won, and made their decisions about whether or not to invest in a candidate partly on the basis of Rove's decision whether or not to work for the campaign. The Rove operation, at its peak, was like an old-fashioned Hollywood studio, with Rove as the mogul. Rove and his aides, the people behind the camera, were smart, geeky, ruthless, and workaholic; the candidate-clients were handsome, forthright, vigorous, friendly, and easy, with firm jaws and great hair. After they made it through the auditioning process, they'd be sent around the studio lot for buffing and polishing—a stop in Message, a stop in Fund-Raising—before they were given their public debut.

Robert Duncan, a state senator whose victory in 1996 gave the Republican Party the majority in the Texas Senate, described the process. More than a year before his race, Duncan told me, he went to see Rove and successfully pitched him; Rove offered his services if Duncan decided to run. Then Rove arranged for introductions to some of his funding sources, such as Enron and the tort-reform movement, one of whose political-action committees paid for Duncan's first poll. "I was in favor of talking about higher education and judicial selection," Duncan said. "Karl said, 'You may be right, but people don't *care*. It doesn't *compel* people to vote for you. You have to stay with the issues that *compel* people.' " So Duncan, like most Rove candidates, stayed relentlessly "on message," using the same issues Bush had used in 1994. The most nervous moment of the campaign, Duncan said, came when his fund-raising effort seemed to be going poorly. He went to the Governor's office for a meeting with Rove and Bush, at which they expressed concern about the slow pace of his fund-raising, and then, with Rove, he went to a second meeting, with a group of lobbyists. "About twenty people were there," Duncan remembered. "I asked those guys, 'Are you with me or against me?' Would they support me, would they raise the money necessary from their clients? That was a pivotal point." The lobbyists ponied up, Duncan won, and in 2000 he was reelected with no opposition.

As aggressively as Rove played in politics generally, he played even more aggressively inside the particular subculture of Republican political consulting. After a special 1991 election in Pennsylvania, Rove sued Richard Thornburgh, the former governor of Pennsylvania and former attorney general, for not paying his Karl Rove + Company bill after he lost the race—even though the Republican National Committee, worried that the suit would make it hard to recruit good candidates, urged Rove to back off, and, when he wouldn't, hired Kenneth Starr to write an amicus brief on Thornburgh's behalf. Rove put Thornburgh through the humiliation of a trial in Austin, and won the case.

Other Republican consultants in Texas often found themselves in conflict with Rove. An oft-told story involved Rove and a Republican consultant named John Weaver. At one time, Rove and Weaver were so close that they planned to go into business together. Then the plans were dropped, and shortly afterward Rove called Weaver in and accused him of a personal misdeed. Lots of people in Texas heard the story—thanks to Rove, it seemed. The bitterness between the Bush and the John McCain campaigns during the 2000 Republican primary season was in part a continuation of that feud, since Weaver played the same role in McCain's campaign that Rove played in Bush's. After Bush had been badly beaten by McCain in the New Hampshire primary and his campaign moved on to South Carolina, its back against the wall, the McCain people thought they were seeing the Mark of Rove when scurrilous material started circulating—dark suggestions that McCain had committed treason while a prisoner of war, and had fathered a child by a black prostitute. But there were no fingerprints, Bush won the primary, and that was the end of the McCain campaign.

"Karl's relationships with people are based on mutual interest, or mutual use," says John Deardourff, a veteran Republican media consultant whom Rove brought to Texas to work in the 1986 Clements campaign, and who then worked with him in all the Supreme Court races. "You just sort of accept that. If you're useful to him, he'll be perfectly nice to you. But when that mutual interest is no longer there the relationship does not continue." For Deardourff, that point came after Rove brought him in to help do with the Alabama Supreme Court what they had done together with the Texas Supreme Court—change it from a Democratic body friendly to tort claims into a Republican one unfriendly to them. Deardourff, an old-fashioned good-government liberal Republican, began to feel uncomfortable when, at Rove's request, he accompanied Rove to a meeting at the Washington headquarters of the American Council of Life Insurance. At the meeting, there was a discussion of the national insurance-industry lobby making contributions, in the form of "soft money" donations, to the Republican National Committee, with the presumption that the money would be passed on to the Alabama Republican Party and then used to support candidates in judicial races there—a technique that was legal but was designed to evade campaign-spending limits. Later, Deardourff recalled, "Karl said, 'I want you to sign on now for three more races, but we don't know who two of the candidates are yet.' I said, 'Karl, I can't do that. You're telling me to sign up before I know who the candidate is.' He said, 'John, this is easy money. What do you mean, you can't do it?' We had an odd conversation where, at the end, he seemed to be congratulating me for saying no. I don't think I've ever heard from Karl since then."

The premier achievement of Rove's Texas years, of course, was George W. Bush's presidential race. It may not have occurred to Bush himself that his first race for the governorship was merely a prelude to something much bigger, but, according to people in Austin, it had certainly occurred to Rove. One consultant told me that he'd mentioned to Rove early in the Bush governorship that he wasn't so sure Bush was going to run for president. Rove blew up at him. "He intimated that I didn't know what I was talking about," the man said. "What the fuck was I thinking? I was making people unhappy by being stupid."

Years before the 2000 campaign was under way, Rove began orchestrating a procession of politicians, lobbyists, intellectuals, journalists, and organizers to Austin to meet Bush—a stratagem that echoed the "front-porch campaign" in Canton, Ohio, that the supposedly reluctant William McKinley, one of Rove's favorite historical figures, ran before the 1896 presidential election. Rove helped design the enormous fund-raising effort that enabled Bush to announce, well in advance, that he would forgo federal funding because of the spending limits it entailed—an announcement that dissuaded several potential opponents from running. Rove had the wit to lock up the support of most of the key figures on the religious right, such as Ralph Reed, whom Rove arranged to be put on retainer by Enron. And the campaign itself bore Rove's stamp in every particular.

Karl Rove is not a man to whose lips the words "I made a mistake" spring easily, and, as regards the 2000 election, he has often pointed out (and did to me) that his candidate far outperformed all those predictive models that posited Al Gore, as the nominee of the party in power during peaceful and prosperous times, as unbeatable. Still, Rove was heard during the last month of the campaign saying that Bush was going to win by six points. That the election was, instead, a tie seems to have come as a surprise to him. "I don't know what we were going to win by," he said, when I asked him about it. "I mean, toward the end it was bravado. But particularly after that last, after the D.U.I."—the revelation during the campaign's last week that Bush had been arrested in Maine for drunk driving years earlier—"it was closing, as these things tend to anyway, and then that just accelerated it." He added that the Republicans had been "grossly outspent" by groups affiliated with the Democratic Party.

The Democrats believe that the reason for their late close was an unusually intense and effective get-out-the-vote effort, and there is evidence that Rove agrees. Ten days after the election, Morton Blackwell, a former national executive director of the College Republicans, who had been out of touch with Rove for years, picked up the phone and heard that familiar booming voice on the other end of the line: "Morton, how does it feel to have advocated something for decades and have it come true?" What Blackwell had been advocating for decades, ever since he trained the teen-age Karl Rove to be a field organizer, was that people in politics should pay less attention to consultants, television advertising, polls, and "message," and more attention to the old-fashioned side of the business: registering voters, organizing volunteers, making face-to-face contact during the last days of a campaign, and getting people to the polls on election day. Soon, Rove had launched a project called the 72-Hour Task Force, which conducted scientific experiments in grassroots political organizing during the three days before election day in five geographically scattered races in 2001.

For Democrats who spend a good deal of their time looking for the Mark of Rove, an exciting moment came in June 2002, when a backup computer disk was found in Lafayette Park, across from the White House, containing two PowerPoint presentations, one by Kenneth Mehlman, Rove's deputy and the White House political director, called "The 2002 Challenge," and the other by Rove himself, called "The Strategic Landscape." (Inevitably, speculation has begun over whether the Lafayette Park PowerPoint, as it has been referred to, is the Rosetta stone to the mind of Karl Rove or a piece of deliberate disinformation designed to throw the Democrats off the scent.)

Since that discovery, an even more interesting PowerPoint presentation has fallen into Democratic hands, and from there into mine. This one outlines, in ninety slides, the work of the 72-Hour Task Force. It acknowledges, much more freely than Rove does in conversation, that in the 2000 Presidential election the Democrats outperformed the final opinion-poll predictions in state after state, and attributes this to their superior organizing. In 2001, the presentation says, the Republicans conducted more than fifty separate tests, in New Jersey, Virginia, Pennsylvania, South Carolina, and Arkansas, often using paired venues, one for experimenting, the other as a control. The over-all finding was that grassroots efforts work, and that grassroots efforts by local volunteers work especially well.

The 2002 elections, which represented a high-water mark of Rove's career, in that he pulled off the feat of picking up seats in Congress for the party in the White House during an off-year election, were treated in the press as having turned on Rove's making all congressional races into referenda on Bush's handling of the war on terrorism. But people in politics think it was the 72-Hour Task Force's work paying off—that is, the Republicans had moved ahead of the Democrats in last-minute organizing skills. In politics now, everybody is trying to figure out twenty-first-century means of achieving the nineteenth-century goal of establishing face-to-face relationships between political parties and voters. Turnout, which was falling for decades, is now rising slightly. Television advertising has reached the saturation point. (Rove said that voters have become so media-aware that television advertising is losing effectiveness: "I can remember focus groups in 2000 where you thought you had a room full of directors. People were talking about the production values of the spot.")

Meanwhile, technological developments—in general, the personal computer, the Internet, and e-mail, and in particular a data technology called XML—have made it possible for political organizations to have much richer information about individual voters. It used to be that you could find registered Republicans and registered Democrats, or heavily Democratic and heavily Republican precincts, but that was about it; now, because XML cross-references previously incompatible databases, you can easily blend electoral and commercial information (gleaned, for example, from mail-in product-warranty cards) and identify the people in Republican precincts who are most likely to vote Democratic, or Republican voters who can be moved by a specific appeal on one issue but not by the Party's main over-all TV-ad pitch. (In the 2002 Georgia governor's race, the Republicans were able to use pro-Confederate flag material with rural voters without the major media markets noticing.) Both in Rove's shop in the White House and in the Democratic National Committee and A.F.L.-C.I.O. offices, the air is thick with buzzwords like "niche marketing," "micro-modelling," "targeting," and "granular information." National politics, in other words, is turning into a very large version of the direct-mail business.

That development is good news for Karl Rove. Most of the reliable indicia of what he's up to involve his cultivating close political relations with specific groups, in particular locales, that know exactly what they want from government. If you have an idea involving a hitherto undiscovered but distinct group of voters that the Republican Party might be able to attract, chances are that you have heard from Rove. Deal Hudson, for example, is the editor and publisher of a small-circulation Catholic magazine called *Crisis*. In 1998, he published an article called "The Catholic Vote," in which he said that Catholic voters who attend Mass once a week or more—thirteen and a half million people—have more conservative political views than other Catholics and represent an incipiently Republican voting group. A few weeks after the article came out, Hudson got a call from Rove, who invited him to Austin for a long talk, which was followed by a meeting with Governor Bush, and then a lengthy visit by Rove to Hudson's office in Washington. Rove and Hudson remained in frequent touch through election day 2000, and after the election Hudson got something he cared about tremendously and the general public didn't notice—the nomination (unsuccessful, it turned out) of a devoutly Catholic abortion opponent, John Klink, as the head of the State Department's Bureau of Population, Refugees, and Migration. Rove's attentiveness to emerging voter blocs caused a minor embarrassment not long ago, when it turned out that Sami al-Arian, a Kuwaiti living in Florida who was recently indicted for terrorist activities, had been to the White House as part of a Muslim group and met with him. Rove is interested in courting the Arab vote, especially in Michigan, the state with the biggest percentage of Arabs.

Everybody in politics thinks of Rove as an expert pursuer of interest groups, but whenever I asked him about this he resisted. I got the sense that this aspect of his reputation wounds his vanity, because it implies that he is engaged merely in, as he put it, "stringing together a group of associations that you found in the Washington Yellow Pages," rather than something more imaginative. Also, one of the rules with Rove is that anything he's been criticized for must be denied. He was widely condemned last year when the Bush administration granted trade protection to the steel industry (which was thought to be an attempt to carry Pennsylvania in 2004) and big subsidies to farmers (to carry Iowa). Late last year, *Esquire* quoted from a long, indiscreet e-mail that John DiIulio, the short-tenured head of the White House effort to launch faith-based anti-poverty initiatives, had sent to Ron Suskind, a writer profiling Rove. DiIulio complained bitterly about the lack of "meaningful, substantive policy discussions" in the Bush White House. Therefore Rove is highly invested in countering the charge that he puts politics ahead of policy.

Every time I interviewed someone close to Rove, that person first checked with him to make sure it was O.K. to talk to me, and then, in the interview, made a point of offering a testimonial to Rove's deep and sincere interest in public policy. It's true that Rove is far more knowledgeable about the details of government than most other political consultants. But the idea that he performs Brookings Institution–style policy evaluations, never sullying himself with considerations of the politics of an issue, is probably a stretch; it would perhaps be better to say that Rove is unusually adept at using government policy as a political tool—in the same way that he is unusually adept at using books as a political tool. A friend of mine happened to be talking to Rove during the presidential transition when Andrew Card, soon to be the White House chief of staff, looked in to say that the Associated Press was reporting that a New Jersey Republican congresswoman named Marge Roukema had been given the obscure position of treasurer of the United States. Card noted that Dennis Hastert, the Speaker of the House, had suggested the appointment because he wanted to avoid Roukema's becoming chairman of a committee. This news provoked an outburst from Rove: absolutely not. (And, if you take a look at the lower-left-hand corner of a dollar bill, you'll see that the signature is not Marge Roukema's.) I asked Rove about it, and he said, "It's not an important job, but she had been of no help to us on the campaign and had been a net negative, and what they were attempting to do was give her a chance to leave Congress so they could fill her seat with somebody else, and solve a committee-chairman problem. But we had people. Rosario Morin, who is the treasurer of the United States, had been a loyal warrior for Bush." Is that policy, or politics? I asked one of Rove's associates, Maria Cino, an assistant secretary of commerce, for an example of his interest in policy, and she said that the Bush education slogan "Leave no child behind" "cuts across every demographic of race and sex." Exactly.

I asked Rove why he thought George H. W. Bush had lost the 1992 election. "If you go back and read President Bush's State of the Union address in 1992, it is a fabulous speech," he said. "But where was the government, where was the administration, where were the people to execute it? This great man was let down by a campaign and an administration that simply didn't measure up to what was needed to help him." Rove, obviously, is going to be riding herd on this Bush administration to make sure that kind of thing doesn't happen again. It's also obvious, though, that Rove knows better than to allow the reelection campaign to come across as the sum of a million hectoring telephone calls and group-outreach efforts. In another interview, Rove offered this formula for winning elections: "Have a robust domestic and foreign agenda. Don't trim your sails. Be bold. People want to hear big, significant changes. They don't want to be fed small micro-policy." The reelection effort will position Bush as the steward of the war on terrorism. (Last year, Rove wrote a fan letter to a junior academic who had published a book pointing out that during the Civil War the Republican Party developed a "tendency to conflate Republicanism with loyalty and Democracy with treason.") While the war in Iraq—which probably wasn't Rove's idea, but which he has been skillful at playing for maximum political advantage—was still going on, I asked him how voters might see the war during the 2004 campaign. "They will see the battle for Iraq as a chapter in a longer, bigger struggle," he said. "As a part of the war on terrorism." To assist people in seeing it that way, the 2004 Republican National Convention has been planned so as to recall the September 11th attacks to the maximum possible extent: the location is New York City, and the time is unusually late for a convention, extending into September.

In one of our interviews, I asked Rove to lay out the basic American political correlation of forces—who's a Republican and who's a Democrat. He started with Republicans. "First of all, there is a huge gap among people of faith," he said. "You saw it in the 2000 exit polling, where people who went to church on a frequent and regular basis voted overwhelmingly for Bush. They form an important part of the Republican base. It's easy to caricature them, but they're essentially your neighbors who go to church on a regular basis and whose life is a community of their faith and who are concerned about values. Another part of the coalition is the growing entrepreneurial class, which is increasingly nonwhite. A majority of new businesses in California last year were created by African-Americans, Latinos, and women. More women formed new small businesses in California last year than did men. I'm not sure exactly why, but if you're married and with kids you are far more likely to be a Republican than to be a Democrat."

He moved on to the Democratic base: "Somebody with a doctorate." This he said with perhaps a suggestion of a smirk. "What was Daniel Bell's phrase? The information class. Some elements of labor, particularly those that are in government-employee unions or those that are in the hospitality industry, but not the traditional trades. The traditional trades and crafts are increasingly independent—I wouldn't say Republican, but independent and willing to vote for a Republican. And people who are socially and economically liberal, who imbibed the values of the sixties and seventies and stuck with them. In some instances, inherited them from their parents." And then, besides the Democrats and the Republicans, there are the swing voters, the people in the middle—except that Rove hates that frame of reference, with its implication that politics entails persuading wishy-washy centrists by offering them broad, vague, moderate sentiments. "There is no middle!" Rove told me once; his mind is engaged in looking for groups that other consultants haven't discovered yet, and then figuring out what their particular passions are. In another conversation, he said, " 'Middle' is the wrong word. 'The unattached' is a better way of putting it. Because to say 'the middle' implies that they are philosophically centrist in outlook, and they aren't. Some of the people who are unaffiliated are on the left. Some of the people who are unattached are on the right. Some of the people who are unattached are hard to characterize philosophically at all on the traditional left-right continuum."

This makes for a much more complicated picture than the old one of better-off Republicans and worse-off Democrats. There is, however, still a brutally simple division between the parties, concerning government. Bigger government strengthens the Democratic Party. It generates federal employees who will mostly vote Democratic and government programs whose beneficiaries will have reason to feel grateful and protective toward a large central government.

(There are nearly fifty thousand fewer federal postal workers today than in 1999.) Conversely, smaller government helps the Republicans. The more taxes are cut, the more programs are privatized, the fewer strictures there are on economic activity, the more people feel that their security and well-being depend on markets and not government or unions, the more the fundamental rationale of the Democratic Party erodes. This year's Economic Report of the President even toyed with the idea of eliminating the income tax. One of Rove's signature moves is to be unusually nonconfrontational, for a Republican, on some things—no Draconian budget cuts in programs for the poor in this administration—so as to be better positioned to accomplish a much more important thing: fundamentally changing the social compact in order to enthrone the Republican Party as firmly as possible for as long as possible.

Karl Rove reads mostly American history, but that doesn't tell you much—everybody in Washington who reads reads American history. It's possible, though, to derive from the specifics of his reading preferences a sense of his over-all ideas about politics. He often mentions a book edited by Michael Novak, the Catholic theologian and conservative intellectual, called *Democracy and Mediating Structures: A Theological Inquiry*. In conversations with me, Rove cited with great enthusiasm the work of Robert H. Wiebe, a historian at Northwestern who died not long ago. Ken Mehlman, Rove's deputy, mentioned Wiebe, too, and also a book called *Populism and Elitism: Politics in the Age of Equality*, by Jeffrey Bell, a conservative who ran for the United States Senate from New Jersey in 1978. Rove is also a big fan of *Our Country*, by Michael Barone, the conservative Washington journalist. All these works fit together. Wiebe's two best-known books, *The Search for Order 1877-1920* (1967) ("Yeah!" Rove said, when I mentioned this one. "There we go, baby! There we go!") and *Self-Rule: A Cultural History of American Democracy* (1995), are attacks on early-twentieth-century Progressivism; Wiebe presents the Progressives' enshrinement of "good government" and "public policy" as replacements for spoils-system party politics as having been a way for an educated elite to take more than its fair share of power. In the Rove schema, the large, centralized, public structures of the modern, regulated welfare state are to be mistrusted, and smaller, more private, more local forms of human organization are to be admired. It's this view that accounts for his conviction—and that of many other Republicans—that their party is anti-elitist: they define elite status in non-economic terms. In a memo about Tom Phillips's first campaign for Texas chief justice, Rove wrote, "No Republican has won by running as an establishment candidate. Our party's candidates have won by appearing as champions of the little man and not the big boys. . . . By nature, Texans are voters with chips on their shoulders. . . . Texans are drawn to candidates who, like them, believe there is a small group of insiders who run things for their personal benefit." One might find it curious that Rove, of all people, would see himself and his party as the dispossessed outsiders, but this identification of government with elitism rather than with democracy lies at the core of Rove's ideology. It explains why Rove's Republican-majority America would be not just pre–Great Society, and not just pre–New Deal, but pre–Progressive era.

Rove's intellectual hero is James Madison; his only child is named Andrew Madison Rove. The first time we spoke, I asked him about Madison's Federalist No. 10, which is about "curing the mischiefs of faction" (by "faction," Madison meant, roughly speaking, what we'd call "interest groups"). "*Very good! Very* good!" Rove boomed out, and then he elaborated, defending interest groups as being supportive of the national interest: "I think this goes back to the definition of 'faction.' I don't think Madison was contemplating, you know, the American Dry Cleaners Association. I think he was thinking about farmers, or tradesmen, or people who lived in the mountains, or planters, or seacoast dwellers, or townspeople, or land speculators, or stock-jobbers. So I think he was thinking of it in a different way, much closer to what I'm suggesting is the proper way to think about it, than in the way that some look at modern American politics. It's not so much that the farmer says, 'I have to have $5.6 billion in drought relief,' as it is 'Do you recognize the importance of animal husbandry and of rural America?' and 'Do you have something that gives me hope for my future and for the future of my children?' The implication that, in No. 10, Madison is saying that groups are driven by their interest and there's only one way in which their interest can be satisfied, I think, is incorrect."

The next time I saw Rove, he had a copy of the Federalist Papers on the table in his office, with scraps of paper marking No. 10 and No. 51, which is also by Madison, and lays out the principle of separation of powers. (It contains the line "If men were angels, no government would be necessary.") In both essays, Madison is concerned with devising structural means to prevent any one force in American society from becoming too powerful. I asked Rove to talk more about the Federalist Papers.

"No. 10 is about how do you avoid the dangers of majority domination," he said, "which Madison characterizes as 'faction.' Which isn't necessarily the

same as 'party,' or even 'interest.' He means, by 'faction' "—here Rove opened
the book and began to read from it—" 'a number of citizens, whether amounting
to a majority or minority of the whole, who are united and actuated by some
common impulse of passion or of interest adverse to the rights of other citizens, or to the permanent and aggregate interests of the community.' And you
can't say that interests are automatically bad. The issue is, is it adverse to the
permanent and aggregate interests of the community? So what he's looking
at is how do you, in a society, keep the majority from dominating?"

Rove flipped forward in the book. "And in No. 51 he says there are two
ways to go about doing this. One is by creating 'a will in the community independent of the majority'—that is, of society itself. Heredity or self-appointed
authority. The other is 'by comprehending in the society so many separate
descriptions of citizens as will render an unjust combination of a majority
of the whole very improbable, if not impracticable.' Again, it's not that he's
against majorities—he says 'an unjust combination of a majority of the whole.'
Well, that means there could be a *just* combination of a majority of the whole.
But how do you guard against permanent, oppressive domination by a group,
a majority, over all others? And he says you can try it two ways. One is by
heredity or self-appointed authority, and that's precarious. The second way
is the federal republic." Here he picked up the book and read aloud again.
"'The society itself will be broken into so many parts, interests, and classes
of citizens that the rights of individuals or of the minority will be in little
danger from interested combinations of the majority.' "

So, I said, Rove was saying that if we had to choose, for our protection
against the perils of democracy, between a benign elite, of the sort that the
Progressives imagined themselves to be, and an intricate Madisonian balancing of groups—Rove cut in: "Groups balancing!" I asked what he thought
of Alexis de Tocqueville. "Tocqueville all the way!" Rove replied. "I think he's
more Madison than Madison, because I do think Madison, to some degree,
views the utility of competing interests as exactly that: competing, and through
their competition they will weaken the drive of anyone for dominant majority
status, oppressive majority status. But I think Tocqueville values the little battalions"—here the ever-ambitious Rove was unconsciously enlarging
Edmund Burke's idea of "the little platoon we belong to in society"—"for the
sake of being little battalions."

Karl Rove presents what would be an interesting theoretical problem, only
it isn't theoretical. What happens when someone who believes that the best
society is one in which many groups compete and counterbalance each other,

to the point of perfect political equipoise, is also in a position to work with tremendous aggressiveness and skill to stitch these groups together in such a way as to create the very thing that Madison most feared: a single, permanent, crushingly powerful majority group, in the form of the Republican Party, which, after all, is where most people who have power already, economically, make their political home? Rove genially dismissed the idea. As important as building a long-lasting, dominant Republican majority is to him in practice, in the abstract he sees one-party domination as a problem that would automatically correct itself. He communicates the feeling that he's having a great time trying to make the Republican Party dominant, and appears to believe that, if he succeeds, some Democratic Karl Rove will probably come along in a few decades and figure out how to undo his handiwork— so, no worries. His project, for now, involves the practical task that he has set for himself, not the abstract concerns that a good Madisonian ought to have about his succeeding at it.

In our last interview, I tried out on Rove a scenario I called "the death of the Democratic Party." The Party has three key funding sources: trial lawyers, Jews, and labor unions. One could systematically disable all three, by passing tort-reform legislation that would cut off the trial lawyers' incomes, by tilting pro-Israel in Middle East policy and thus changing the loyalties of big Jewish contributors, and by trying to shrink the part of the labor force which belongs to the newer, and more Democratic, public-employee unions. And then there are three fundamental services that the Democratic Party is offering to voters: Social Security, Medicare, and public education. Each of these could be peeled away, too: Social Security and Medicare by giving people benefits in the form of individual accounts that they invested in the stock market, and public education by trumping the Democrats on the issue of standards. The Bush administration has pursued every item on that list. Rove didn't offer any specific objection but, rather, a general caveat that the project might be too ambitious. "Well, I think it's a plausible explanation," he said. "I don't think you ever kill any political party. Political parties kill themselves, or are killed, not by the other political party but by their failure to adapt to new circumstances. But do you *weaken* a political party, either by turning what they see as assets into liabilities, and/or by taking issues they consider to be theirs, and raiding them?" The thought brought to his round, unlined, guileless face a boyish look of pure delight. "Absolutely!"

Bush's War Against Wonks
Bruce Reed

Washington Monthly | March 2004

The Washington Monthly *is a favorite publication of political insiders, offering a blend of policy discussion, electoral analysis, political history, book reviews, and assorted commentary from both journalists and political players. Bruce Reed, author of this essay, counts as a player: A former domestic policy adviser in the Clinton administration, he's currently president of the Democratic Leadership Council, home of the so-called "New Democrat Movement," which was established a decade ago to modernize the Democratic Party's policies and programs (in other words, help come up with issues that can win elections).*

Here, for the benefit of all those who toil outside the Beltway, Reed puts partisanship aside (well, almost) to offer a primer on those two great classes of Washingtonian—political hacks and policy wonks. He then goes on to explain why, in his opinion, the Bush administration badly needs a few less of the former, and a lot more of the latter. . . .

Strip away the job titles and party labels, and you will find two kinds of people in Washington: political hacks and policy wonks. Hacks come to Washington because anywhere else they'd be bored to death. Wonks come here because nowhere else could we bore so many to death. These divisions extend far beyond the hack havens of political campaigns and consulting firms and the wonk ghettos of think tanks on Dupont Circle. Some journalists are wonks, but most are hacks. Some columnists are hacks, but most are wonks. All members of Congress pass themselves off as wonks, but many got elected as hacks. Lobbyists are hacks who make money pretending to be wonks. The *Washington Monthly, The New Republic*, and the entire political blogosphere consist largely of wonks pretending to be hacks. *The Hotline* is for hacks; *National Journal* is for wonks. *The West Wing* is for wonks; *K Street* was for hacks.

After two decades in Washington as a wonk working among hacks, I have come to the conclusion that the gap between Republicans and Democrats is as nothing compared to the one between these two tribes. We wonks think we're smarter than hacks. Hacks think that if being smart makes someone a wonk, they'd rather be stupid. Wonks think all hacks are creatures from another planet, like James Carville. Hacks share Paul Begala's view that wonks are all "propeller heads," like Elroy on *The Jetsons*. Wonks think the differences between hacks and wonks are as irreconcilable as the Hutus and the Tutsis. Hacks think it's just like wonks to bring up the Hutus and the Tutsis.

In every administration, wonks and hacks fight it out. The measure of a great president is his ability to make sense of them both. A president must know the real problems on Americans' minds. For that he needs hacks. But ultimately, he needs policies that will actually solve those problems. For that he needs wonks. President Bush has husbanded some big policy changes through Congress—a testament to his considerable political skills. Unfortunately, his policies seem to be better at causing problems than solving them. The economy can't create jobs despite hundreds of billions of dollars in stimulus. The reconstruction in Iraq is going over like a remake of Ishtar. The price tag of the new Medicare law is soaring even faster than prescription-drug costs. With a record $521 billion deficit, Bush has just presented what might be called the Justin Timberlake budget, ripping off the taxpayers and pretending it wasn't on purpose.

Democrats are understandably eager to blame all these epic failures on ideology. To be sure, Bush is running perhaps the most partisan and ideological White House in the modern era. His party's longstanding fondness for tax cuts has evolved into a pathological need to reduce every remaining burden on the wealthy. But the longer I watch this White House, the more convinced I become that ideology is just a convenient rationalization for why the president's agenda isn't working. The real reason is darker and more disturbing: The Bush White House is so obsessed with the politics of its agenda that it never even asks whether it will work.

Hack attack

Journalist Ron Suskind first sounded this warning in January 2003, in an extraordinary *Esquire* interview with John DiIulio, the brilliant academic who had resigned from Bush's faith-based initiative the previous year. DiIulio told Suskind, "There is no precedent in any modern White House for what is going on in this one: a complete lack of a policy apparatus. What you've got is everything—and I mean everything—being run by the political arm." As if to prove the point, the White House got DiIulio to disavow the allegations as soon as they became public.

Suskind's new book about former Treasury Secretary Paul O'Neill, *The Price of Loyalty*, is one long lament on the same theme: the administration's complete disregard for evidence. O'Neill becomes so desperate for an honest broker that he pleads with, of all people, Vice President Cheney: "[We] need to be better about keeping politics out of the policy process. We need fire-walls. The political people are there for presentation and execution, not for creation." By the time he left, O'Neill actually pined for the less political days of the Nixon White House: "The biggest difference between then and now is that our group was mostly about evidence and analysis, and Karl, Dick, Karen, and the gang seemed to be mostly about politics."

Ironically, putting someone so impolitic in charge of Treasury only strength-ened the politicos' advantage. Dick Cheney and Karl Rove could not have found an easier adversary to ignore. O'Neill proved to be a hopelessly inept bureaucratic warrior, firing off random memos about subjects far beyond Treasury's purview, such as an action plan on global environmental policy. He and his old friend Alan Greenspan privately wrung their hands over the long-term fiscal consequences of the 2001 tax cut, but publicly (and in Greenspan's case, disastrously) embraced it anyway. Despite a lifelong rep-utation for blunt candor, O'Neill managed to meet with the president for an hour every week while only once raising the meekest of doubts about the tax cuts. He has famously said of these meetings, "The president is like a blind man in a roomful of deaf people." But what's just as deafening is the apparent silence of those who know better.

Every White House worries too much about politics. What DiIulio and O'Neill most tellingly reveal is how little this White House worries about any-thing else. As DiIulio puts it, "The lack of even basic policy knowledge, and the only casual interest in knowing more, was somewhat breathtaking: dis-cussions by fairly senior people who meant Medicaid but were talking Medicare; near instant shifts from discussing any actual policy pros and cons to discussing political communications, media strategy, etc."

What Rove wove

Rove and Cheney routinely say, and no doubt believe, that "good policy makes for good politics." We said the same thing in the Clinton White House—and over the long haul, it's almost always true. But the real question is much harder and more interesting: What makes for good policy?

The great irony is that the political equilibrium of the nation's capital depends on both wonks and hacks, but the two groups can't even commu-nicate because the hack and wonk dialects have so few words in common. I learned this first as a campaign speechwriter and later as a White House policy geek, when I was sometimes called in to translate. In 1993, I went to a meeting with some of the president's top communications strategists to plan the signing ceremony for a bill that had just passed the Congress. A wonk had to point out that under the Constitution, if the president fails to sign a bill within 10 days while the Congress is adjourned, the bill is pocket vetoed and does not become law.

On the most politically charged issues, like crime and welfare reform, hacks thought wonks were from Pluto and wonks thought hacks were from Uranus. Near the end of Clinton's first year in office, a series of high-profile murders produced a groundswell of public support for our crime bill. One group of wonks, terrified that the public might get what it wanted, formed a violence prevention task force whose sole purpose seemed to be churning out ideas the public would not support. The task force included one of the most ridiculously named subcommittees of all time, the "Subgroup on Place." Hacks still laugh about it.

Wonks were just as quick to sneer at their adversaries. Every time I brought them a message from the hacks, they made me feel like a wonk without a country. When I co-chaired Clinton's welfare reform working group from 1993-94, every time I won a policy argument, a dissenting member would leak to the press that we were driven by political expediency. Harvard professor David Ellwood, one of two assistant secretaries at the Department of Health and Human Services who served as my co-chairs, teased me all the time over how little White House politicos knew about welfare. In *The New York Times'* tick-tock story on our efforts, Ellwood gleefully described my role as "right-wing hack."

Paul O'Neill is naïve to wish for an upstairs-downstairs divide, where wonks make all the decisions and hacks get to spin them. As a wonk, I would be the last to suggest that my fellow propeller heads have all the answers. I spent Clinton's first term across the hall from Ira Magaziner, architect of the administration's health care plan. The road to Ira's office was paved with good intentions.

On the other hand, O'Neill is right to worry about the republic if indeed the hacks are in charge. In 1995, when Clinton brought in Dick Morris to get the White House's politics back on track, I was the wonk assigned to shoot down hack ideas if they didn't pass wonk muster. Every week, Morris had at least one notion crazy enough to get us laughed out of town. I especially liked his proposal to put voluntary warning labels on violent toys, so that parents would know, for example, that a toy gun was actually a toy gun. Morris always reminded me of the Tom Lehrer song about the German rocket scientist,

Wernher von Braun: "Once the rockets are up, who cares where they come down? / That's not my department, says Wernher von Braun." (For all his faults, though, Morris was often a useful spur to the bureaucracy, because he enabled the White House policy team to deploy our own Madman Theory: If the agencies wouldn't go along with our sensible proposals, we warned them that the president might just listen to Dick Morris. Agency productivity soared as a result.)

Karl Rove may not have Morris's eccentricities. But O'Neill's instincts are correct: Any president who lets people like Rove make the key decisions is sure to get the big ones wrong. Even the most gifted hacks, like Rove and Morris, have an insurmountable blind spot: The only results they understand are polling.

Consider perhaps the most telling example of Rove's policy input—Bush's 2002 decision to impose tariffs on imported steel. Bush's economic advisers unanimously opposed the move, on the grounds that it was directly contrary to the president's principles, and would cost more jobs at factories that make products with steel than it would help steelworkers. But Rove insisted that politics should trump principle, and that the steel vote was essential to Bush's hopes in Pennsylvania and West Virginia.

And so Rove got a day of headlines in those states, followed by a week of national stories critical of the administration's cynicism. More important, the results of the policy quickly became clear: An International Trade Commission report found that the tariffs were hurting steel buyers nine times more than they helped steel producers. The move nearly sparked a disastrous trade war with the European Union. In December 2003, the president was forced to reverse himself and abandon the tariffs. The revised political tally sheet shows why Rove is no genius: The president looks unprincipled and foolish, the recovery is slower in key states like Michigan and Florida, and steelworkers are angrier than ever.

As we begin an election year, the paint-by-numbers politics of this White House is wearing thin. The administration threw over conservatives last fall to get a prescription drug bill because elderly voters are crucial in Florida. The result: The bill turns out to cost $134 billion more than the White House told Congress, angry right-wingers have forced Bush to cut other popular programs like Even Start, and even though the drug benefit doesn't take effect until 2006, polls show the bill is already unpopular among seniors.

When hacks rule, policies often drool—and come back to hurt hacks' cause. Bush's proposal to grant temporary legal status to guest workers is another

Rove rifle-shot at Hispanics. Unfortunately, Hispanics quickly figured out that the proposal wouldn't actually lead to citizenship, because the White House had bowed to political pressure from another quarter, the far right. Now most Hispanics don't like the idea and the right wing hates it. That manned mission to Mars, which the White House hoped would lift Bush's appeal for a second term, bombed so badly that the President couldn't even find time to mention it in the State of the Union.

Wonk if you love the issues

The American people are a lot smarter than either the hacks or the wonks give them credit for. For all the talk in both parties about the urgent need to win one constituency or another, most Americans apply the same political yardstick: They vote for what works. There aren't enough hacks, even in Washington, to sell a policy that doesn't.

Hacks and wonks still need each other. In the end, the best leaders are those who can surround themselves with the best advice from both quarters, and synthesize it to find the wisest, straightest course the nation can sustain. As O'Neill puts it, what holds a good administration together is that the president's advisers like "the way the president thinks."

The secret of Bill Clinton's success was that he was the biggest wonk ever to hold the presidency, with political gifts that no hack could equal. He said he would cut the deficit and boost the economy, and he did. He said he would put more cops on the street to lower the crime rate, and he did. He said he would end welfare as we know it in a way that wouldn't hurt those in the system, and he did. (The Census Bureau recently reported that poverty among single mothers had fallen by a stunning one-third from 1993 to 2001, a turnaround the *Washington Post* credited mainly to the work requirements and child support provisions of Clinton's 1996 welfare reform law.) Clinton was his own best policy adviser, by far, yet he also would have been the greatest political consultant in the history of the world's second-oldest profession.

Presidents don't have to be super wonks, and George W. Bush certainly never promised to be one. Long before he expressed any interest in the presidency, he was known as a consummate political hack. He worked on several of his father's campaigns, including as an enforcer in the failed 1992 bid, and even now finds himself dealing with charges that he may have skipped some National Guard duty to work on a Senate campaign.

In the end, Bush's undoing may be that he has planted his flag so firmly on one side of the wonk-hack divide. Sooner or later, the fate of every White House comes down to the way the president thinks.

Keeping Secrets
Christopher Schmitt and Edward Pound

U.S. News & World Report | December 22, 2003

"Democracies die behind closed doors."
—U.S. APPEALS COURT JUDGE DAMON J. KEITH

While the pros and cons of the Bush administration's economic and foreign policies can (and will) be debated endlessly, one fact that cannot be disputed is that the Bush team has guarded information much more closely than any White House in recent memory. Much of this secrecy—including the administration's refusal to name any of the prisoners being held in Guantanamo Bay, the White House's reluctance to hand over classified material to the 9/11 Commission (the commissioners had to threaten to file a subpoena to get the requested information), and the provisions of the Patriot Act that allow for clandestine search warrants to be issued—has been attributed to the heightened security demands of our post-9/11 fight against terrorism. But as this article in U.S. News *makes clear, the White House's penchant for keeping the public in the dark has been evident from the very start of the Bush presidency. "For the past three years," write Christopher Schmitt and Edward Pound, "the Bush administration has quietly but efficiently dropped a shroud of secrecy across many critical operations of the federal government."*

One note of interest: The article mentions a legal action filed by the Sierra Club and Judicial Watch, who jointly sued the executive branch in an attempt to learn exactly who met with Vice President Cheney's energy-policy task force early in 2001. Two lower courts have ordered that the task force's records be turned over—a move that the administration insists would seriously impair the future ability of any president to seek out advice. The White House appealed the decision to the Supreme Court, which heard arguments for the case in April of 2004. In June, by a 7-2 vote, the justices sent the case back down to the U.S. Court of Appeals for further adjudication. No action is expected until after the November election. . . .

At 12:01 P.M. on January 20, 2001, as a bone-chilling rain fell on Washington, George W. Bush took the oath of office as the nation's 43rd president. Later that afternoon, the business of governance officially began. Like other chief executives before him, Bush moved to unravel the efforts of his predecessor. Bush's chief of staff, Andrew Card, directed federal agencies to freeze more than 300 pending regulations issued by the administration of President Bill Clinton. The regulations affected areas ranging from health and safety to the environment and industry. The delay, Card said, would "ensure that the president's appointees have the opportunity to review any new or pending regulations." The process, as it turned out, expressly precluded input from average citizens. Inviting such comments, agency officials concluded, would be "contrary to the public interest."

Ten months later, a former U.S. Army Ranger named Joseph McCormick found out just how hard it was to get information from the new administration. A resident of Floyd County, Virginia, in the heart of the Blue Ridge Mountains, McCormick discovered that two big energy companies planned to run a high-volume natural gas pipeline through the center of his community. He wanted to help organize citizens by identifying residents through whose property the 30-inch pipeline would run. McCormick turned to Washington, seeking a project map from federal regulators. The answer? A pointed "no." Although such information was "previously public," officials of the Federal Energy Regulatory Commission told McCormick, disclosing the route of the new pipeline could provide a road map for terrorists. McCormick was nonplused. Once construction began, he says, the pipeline's location would be obvious to anyone. "I understand about security," the rangy, soft-spoken former business executive says. "But there certainly is a balance—it's about people's right to use the information of an open society to protect their rights."

For the past three years, the Bush administration has quietly but efficiently dropped a shroud of secrecy across many critical operations of the federal government—cloaking its own affairs from scrutiny and removing from the public domain important information on health, safety, and environmental matters. The result has been a reversal of a decades-long trend of openness in government while making increasing amounts of information unavailable to the taxpayers who pay for its collection and analysis. Bush administration officials often cite the September 11 attacks as the reason for the enhanced secrecy. But as the inauguration day directive from Card indicates, the initiative to wall off records and information previously in the public domain began from Day 1.

Steven Garfinkel, a retired government lawyer and expert on classified information, puts it this way: "I think they have an overreliance on the utility of secrecy. They don't seem to realize secrecy is a two-edge sword that cuts you as well as protects you." Even supporters of the administration, many of whom agree that security needed to be bolstered after the attacks, say Bush and his inner circle have been unusually assertive in their commitment to increased government secrecy. "Tightly controlling information, from the White House on down, has been the hallmark of this administration," says Roger Pilon, vice president of legal affairs for the Cato Institute.

Air and water. Some of the Bush administration's initiatives have been well chronicled. Its secret deportation of immigrants suspected as terrorists, its refusal to name detainees at the U.S. base at Guantanamo Bay, Cuba, and the new surveillance powers granted under the post-9/11 U.S.A. Patriot Act have all been debated at length by the administration and its critics. The clandestine workings of an energy task force headed by Vice President Dick Cheney have also been the subject of litigation, now before the Supreme Court.

But the administration's efforts to shield the actions of, and the information obtained by, the executive branch are far more extensive than has been previously documented. A five-month investigation by *U.S. News* detailed a series of initiatives by administration officials to effectively place large amounts of information out of the reach of ordinary citizens. The magazine's inquiry is based on a detailed review of government reports and regulations, federal agency Web sites, and legislation pressed by the White House. *U.S. News* also analyzed information from public interest groups and others that monitor the administration's activities, and interviewed more than 100 people, including many familiar with the new secrecy initiatives. That information was supplemented by a review of materials provided in response to more than 200 Freedom of Information Act requests filed by the magazine seeking details of federal agencies' practices in providing public access to government information.

The principal findings:

Important business and consumer information is increasingly being withheld from the public. The Bush administration is denying access to auto and tire safety information, for instance, that manufacturers are required to provide under a new "early-warning" system created following the Ford-Firestone tire scandal four years ago. The U.S. Consumer Product Safety Commission, meanwhile, is more frequently withholding information that would allow the public to scrutinize its product safety findings and product recall actions.

New administration initiatives have effectively placed off limits critical health and safety information potentially affecting millions of Americans. The information includes data on quality and vulnerability of drinking-water supplies, potential chemical hazards in communities, and safety of airline travel and other forms of transportation. In Aberdeen, Maryland, families who live near an Army weapons base are suing the Army for details of toxic pollution fouling the town's drinking-water supplies. Citing security, the Army has refused to provide information that could help residents locate and track the pollution.

Beyond the well-publicized cases involving terrorism suspects, the administration is aggressively pursuing secrecy claims in the federal courts in ways little understood—even by some in the legal system. The administration is increasingly invoking a "state secrets" privilege that allows government lawyers to request that civil and criminal cases be effectively closed by asserting that national security would be compromised if they proceed. It is impossible to say how often government lawyers have invoked the privilege. But William Weaver, a professor at the University of Texas-El Paso, who recently completed a study of the historical use of the privilege, says the Bush administration is asserting it "with offhanded abandon." In one case, Weaver says, the government invoked the privilege 245 times. In another, involving allegations of racial discrimination, the Central Intelligence Agency demanded, and won, return of information it had provided to a former employee's attorneys—only to later disclose the very information that it claimed would jeopardize national security.

New administration policies have thwarted the ability of Congress to exercise its constitutional authority to monitor the executive branch and, in some cases, even to obtain basic information about its actions. One Republican lawmaker, Representative Dan Burton of Indiana, became so frustrated with the White House's refusal to cooperate in an investigation that he exclaimed, during a hearing: "This is not a monarchy!" Some see a fundamental transformation in the past three years. "What has stunned us so much," says Gary Bass, executive director of OMB Watch, a public interest group in Washington that monitors government activities, "is how rapidly we've moved from a principle of 'right to know' to one edging up to 'need to know.' "

The White House declined repeated requests by *U.S. News* to discuss the new secrecy initiatives with the administration's top policy and legal officials.

Two Bush officials who did comment defended the administration and rejected criticism of what many call its "penchant for secrecy." Dan Bartlett, the White House communications director, says that besides the extraordinary steps the president has taken to protect the nation, Bush and other senior officials must keep private advice given in areas such as intelligence and policymaking, if that advice is to remain candid. Overall, Bartlett says, "the administration is open, and the process in which this administration conducts its business is as transparent as possible." There is, he says, "great respect for the law, and great respect for the American people knowing how their government is operating."

Bartlett says that some administration critics "such as environmentalists . . . want to use [secrecy] as a bogeyman." He adds: "For every series of examples you could find where you could make the claim of a 'penchant for secrecy,' I could probably come up with several that demonstrate the transparency of our process." Asked for examples, the communications director offered none.

There are no precise statistics on how much government information is rendered secret. One measure, though, can be seen in a tally of how many times officials classify records. In the first two years of Bush's term, his administration classified records some 44.5 million times, or about the same number as in President Clinton's last four years, according to the Information Security Oversight Office, an arm of the National Archives and Records Administration. But the picture is more complicated than that. In an executive order issued last March, Bush made it easier to reclassify information that had previously been declassified—allowing executive-branch agencies to drop a cloak of secrecy over reams of information, some of which had been made available to the public.

Bait and switch. In addition, under three other little-noticed executive orders, Bush increased the number of officials who can classify records to include the secretary of agriculture, the secretary of health and human services, and the administrator of the Environmental Protection Agency. Now, all three can label information at the "secret" level, rendering it unavailable for public review. Traditionally, classification authority has resided in federal agencies engaged in national security work. "We don't know yet how frequently the authority is being exercised," says Steven Aftergood, who publishes an authoritative newsletter in Washington on government secrecy. "But it is a sign of the times that these purely domestic agencies have been given national security classification authority. It is another indication of how our government is being transformed under pressure of the perceived terrorist threat." J. William Leonard, director of the information oversight office, estimates that up to half of what the government now classifies needn't be. "You can't have an effective secrecy process," he cautions, "unless you're discerning in how you use it."

From the start, the Bush White House has resisted efforts to disclose information about executive-branch activities and decision making. The energy task force headed by Cheney is just one example. In May 2001, the task force produced a report calling for increased oil and gas drilling, including on public land. The Sierra Club and another activist group, Judicial Watch, sued to get access to task-force records, saying that energy lobbyists unduly influenced the group. Citing the Constitution's separation of powers clause, the administration is arguing that the courts can't compel Cheney to disclose information about his advice to the president. A federal judge ordered the administration to produce the records, prompting an appeal to the Supreme Court.

Energy interests aren't alone in winning a friendly hearing from the Bush administration. Auto and tire manufacturers prevailed in persuading the administration to limit disclosure requirements stemming from one of the highest-profile corporate scandals of recent years. Four years ago, after news broke that failing Firestone tires on Ford SUVs had caused hundreds of deaths and many more accidents, Congress enacted a new auto and tire safety law. A cornerstone was a requirement that manufacturers submit safety data to a government early-warning system, which would provide clues to help prevent another scandal. Lawmakers backing the system wanted the data made available to the public. After the legislation passed, officials at the National Highway Traffic Safety Administration said they didn't expect to create any new categories of secrecy for the information; they indicated that key data would automatically be made public. That sparked protests from automakers, tire manufacturers, and others. After months of pressure, transportation officials decided to make vital information such as warranty claims, field reports from dealers, and consumer complaints—all potentially valuable sources of safety information—secret. "It was more or less a bait and switch," says Laura MacCleery, auto-safety counsel for Public Citizen, a nonprofit consumer group. "You're talking about information that will empower consumers. The manufacturers are not going to give that up easily."

• • •

Get out of jail free. Government officials, unsurprisingly, don't see it that way. Lloyd Guerci, a Transportation Department attorney involved in writing the new regulations, declined to comment. But Ray Tyson, a spokesman for the traffic safety administration, denies the agency caved to industry pressure: "We've listened to all who have opinions and reached a compromise that probably isn't satisfactory to anybody."

Some of the strongest opposition to making the warning-system data public came from the Alliance of Automobile Manufacturers. The organization, whose membership comprises U.S. and international carmakers, argued that releasing the information would harm them competitively. The Bush administration has close ties to the carmakers. Bush Chief of Staff Card has been General Motors' top lobbyist and head of a trade group of major domestic automakers. Jacqueline Glassman, NHTSA's chief counsel, is a former top lawyer for DaimlerChrysler Corp. In the months before the new regulations were released, industry officials met several times with officials from the White House's Office of Management and Budget.

The administration's commitment to increased secrecy measures extends to the area of "critical infrastructure information," or CII. In layman's terms, this refers to transportation, communications, energy, and other systems that make modern society run. The Homeland Security Act allows companies to make voluntary submissions of information about critical infrastructure to the Department of Homeland Security. The idea is to encourage firms to share information crucial to running and protecting those facilities. But under the terms of the law, when a company does this, the information is exempted from public disclosure and cannot be used without the submitting party's permission in any civil proceeding, even a government enforcement action. Some critics see this as a get-out-of-jail-free card, allowing companies worried about potential litigation or regulatory actions to place troublesome information in a convenient "homeland security" vault. "The sweep of it is amazing," says Beryl Howell, former general counsel to the Senate Judiciary Committee. "Savvy businesses will be able to mark every document handed over [to] government officials as 'CII' to ensure their confidentiality." Companies "wanted liability exemption long before 9/11," adds Patrice McDermott, a lobbyist for the American Library Association, which has a tradition of advocacy on right-to-know issues. "Now, they've got it."

Under the administration's plan to implement the Homeland Security Act, some businesses may get even more protection. When Congress passed the law, it said the antidisclosure provision would apply only to information submitted to the Department of Homeland Security. The department recently proposed extending the provision to cover information submitted to any federal agency. A department spokesman did not respond to requests for comment. Business objections were also pivotal when the Environmental Protection Agency recently backed off a plan that would have required some companies to disclose more about chemical stockpiles in communities.

If the administration's secrecy policies have helped business, they have done little for individuals worried about health and safety issues. The residents of the small town of Aberdeen, Maryland, can attest to that. On a chilly fall evening, some 100 people gathered at the Aberdeen firehouse to hear the latest about a toxic substance called perchlorate. An ingredient in rocket fuel, perchlorate has entered the aquifer that feeds the town's drinking-water wells. The culprit is the nearby U.S. Army's Aberdeen Proving Ground, where since World War I, all manner of weapons have been tested.

Trigger finger. After word of the perchlorate contamination broke, a coalition of citizens began working with the Army to try to attack the unseen plume of pollution moving through the ground. But earlier this year, the Army delivered Aberdeen residents a sharp blow. It began censoring maps to eliminate features like street names and building locations—information critical to understanding and tracking where contamination might have occurred or where environmental testing was being done.

The reason? The information, the Army says, could provide clues helpful to terrorists. Arlen Crabb, the head of a citizens' group, doesn't buy it. "It's an abuse of power," says Crabb, a 20-year Army veteran, whose well lies just a mile and a half from the base. His coalition is suing the Army, citing health and safety concerns. "We're not a bunch of radicals. We've got to have the proof. The government has to be transparent."

Aberdeen is but one example of the way enhanced security measures increasingly conflict with the health and safety concerns of ordinary Americans. Two basics—drinking water and airline travel—help illustrate the trend. A public health and bioterrorism law enacted last year requires, among other things, that operators of local water systems study vulnerabilities to attack or other disruptions and draw up plans to address any weaknesses. Republicans and Democrats praised the measure, pushed by the Bush administration, as a prudent response to potential terrorist attacks. But there's a catch. Residents are precluded from obtaining most information about any vulnerabilities.

This wasn't always the case. In 1996, Congress passed several amendments to the Clean Water Act calling for "source water assessments" to be made of water supply systems. The idea was that the assessments, covering such things as sources of contamination, would arm the public with information necessary to push for improvements. Today, the water assessments are still being done, but some citizens' groups say that because of Bush administration policy, the release of information has been so restricted that there is too little specific information to act upon. They blame the Environmental Protection Agency for urging states to limit information provided to the public from the assessments. As a result, the program has been fundamentally reshaped from one that has made information widely available to one that now forces citizens to essentially operate on a need-to-know basis, says Stephen Gasteyer, a Washington specialist on water-quality issues. "People [are] being overly zealous in their enforcement of safety and security, and perhaps a little paranoid," he says. "So you're getting releases of information so ambiguous that it's not terribly useful." Cynthia Dougherty, director of EPA's groundwater and drinking-water office, described her agency's policy as laying out "minimal standards," so that states that had been intending to more fully disclose information "had the opportunity to decide to make a change."

The Federal Aviation Administration has its own security concerns, and supporters say it has addressed them vigorously. In doing so, however, the agency has also made it harder for Americans to obtain the kind of safety information once considered routine. The FAA has eliminated online access to records on enforcement actions taken against airlines, pilots, mechanics, and others. That came shortly after the 9/11 attacks, when it was discovered that information was available on things like breaches of airport security, says Rebecca Trexler, an FAA spokeswoman. Balancing such concerns isn't easy. But rather than cut off access to just that information, the agency pulled back all enforcement records. The FAA has also backed away from providing access to safety information voluntarily submitted by airlines.

As worrisome as the specter of terrorism is for many Americans, many still grumble about being kept in the dark unnecessarily. Under rules the Transportation Security Administration adopted last year—with no public notice or comment—the traveling public no longer has access to key government information on the safety and security of all modes of transportation. The sweeping restrictions go beyond protecting details about security or screening systems to include information on enforcement actions or effectiveness of security measures. The new TSA rules also establish a new, looser standard for denying access to information: Material can be withheld from the public, the rules say, simply if it's "impractical" to release it. The agency did not respond to requests for comment.

This same pattern can be seen in one federal agency after another. As Joseph McCormick, the former Army Ranger trying to learn more about the pipeline planned for Virginia's Shenandoah Valley, learned, the Federal Energy Regulatory Commission now restricts even the most basic information about such projects. The agency says its approach is "balanced," adding that security concerns amply justify the changes.

The Bush administration is pressing the courts to impose more secrecy, too. Jeffrey Sterling, 36, a former CIA operations officer, can testify to that. Sterling, who is black, is suing the CIA for discrimination. In September, with his attorneys in the midst of preparing important filings, a CIA security officer paid them a visit, demanding return of documents the agency had previously provided. A mistake had been made, the officer explained, and the records contained information that if disclosed would gravely damage national security. The officer warned that failure to comply could lead to prison or loss of a security clearance, according to the lawyers. Although vital to Sterling's case, the lawyers reluctantly gave up the records.

What was so important? In a federal courtroom in Alexandria, Virginia, a Justice Department attorney recently explained that the records included a pseudonym given to Sterling for an internal CIA proceeding on his discrimination complaint. In fact, the pseudonym, which Sterling never used in an operation, had already been disclosed through a clerical error. Mark Zaid, one of Sterling's attorneys, says the pseudonym is just a misdirection play by the CIA. The real reason the agency demanded the files back, he says, is that they included information supporting Sterling's discrimination complaint. Zaid says he has never encountered such heavy-handed treatment from the CIA. "When they have an administration that is willing to cater [to secrecy], they go for it," he says, "because they know they can get away with it." A CIA spokesman declined comment.

In this case, which is still pending, the administration is invoking the "state secrets" privilege, in which it asserts that a case can't proceed normally without disclosing information harmful to national security. The Justice Department says it can't provide statistics on how often it invokes the privilege. But Jonathan Turley, a George Washington University law professor active in national security matters, says: "In the past, it was an unusual thing. The Bush administration is faster on the trigger."

• • •

Surveillance. At the same time, the government is opening up a related front. Last spring, the TSA effectively shut down the case of Mohammed Ali Ahmed, an Indian Muslim and naturalized citizen. In September 2001, Ahmed and three of his children were removed from an American Airlines flight. Last year, Ahmed filed a civil rights suit against the airline. But TSA head James Loy intervened, saying that giving Ahmed information about his family's removal would compromise airline security. The government, in other words, was asserting a claim to withhold the very information Ahmed needed to pursue his case, says his attorney, Wayne Krause, of the Texas Civil Rights Project. "You're looking at an almost unprecedented vehicle to suppress information that is vital to the public and the people who want to vindicate their rights," Krause says.

Secret evidence of a different kind comes into play through a little-noticed effect of the U.S.A. Patriot Act. A key provision allows information from surveillance approved for intelligence gathering to be used to convict a defendant in criminal court. But the government's application—which states the case for the snooping—isn't available for defendants to see, as in traditional law enforcement surveillance cases. With government agencies now hoarding all manner of secret information, the growing stockpile represents an opportunity for abusive leaks, critics say. The new law takes note of that, by allowing suits against the federal government. But there's an important catch—in order to seek redress, one must forfeit the right to a jury trial. Instead, the action must be held before a judge; judges, typically, are much more conservative in awarding damages than are juries.

Most Americans appreciate the need for increased security. But with conflicts between safety and civil rights increasing, the need for an arbiter is acute—which is perhaps the key reason why the vast new security powers of many executive-branch agencies are so alarming to citizens' groups and others. A diminished role of congressional oversight is just one area of fallout, but there are others. Some examples:

- It took the threat of a subpoena from the independent commission investigating the 9/11 attacks to force the White House to turn over intelligence reports. Even at that, family members of victims complain, there were too many restrictions on release of the information. In Congress, the administration has rebuffed members on a range of issues often unrelated to security concerns.

- In a huge military spending bill last year, Congress directed President Bush to give it 30 days' notice before initiating certain sensitive defense programs. Bush signed the bill into law but rejected the restraint and said he would ignore the provision if he deemed it necessary.
- Initial contracts to rebuild Iraq, worth billions of dollars, were awarded in secret. Bids were limited to companies invited to participate, and many had close ties to the White House. Members of Congress later pressed for an open bidding process.
- Many public interest groups report that government agencies are more readily denying Freedom of Information Act requests—while also increasing fees, something small-budget groups say they can ill afford. The Sierra Club, for example, has been thwarted in getting information on problems at huge "factory farms" that pollute rivers and groundwater. Says David Bookbinder, senior attorney for the group: "What's different about this administration is their willingness to say, 'We're going to keep everything secret until we're forced to disclose it— no matter what it is.' "

The administration is undeterred by such complaints. "I think what you've seen is a White House that has valued openness," says Daniel Bryant, assistant attorney general for legal policy, and "that knows that openness with the public facilitates confidence in government."

That's not the way Jim Kerrigan sees it. He operates a small market-research firm in Sterling, Virginia, outside Washington. For more than a decade, he has forecast federal spending on information technology. Three months after Bush took office, the Office of Management and Budget issued a memo telling government officials to no longer make available such information so as to "preserve the confidentiality of the deliberations that led to the president's budget decisions."

As a result, Kerrigan says, information began to dry up. Requests were ignored. And the data he did get came with so much information censored out that they were barely usable. The fees Kerrigan paid for a request, which once topped out at $300, jumped to as much as $6,500. "I can't afford that," he says. "This administration's policy is to withhold information as much as possible."

Key Dates: Secrecy and the Bush Administration

Inauguration Day (1/20/01) Administration freezes Clinton-era regulations, without allowing for public comment.

10/12/01 Attorney General John Ashcroft, reversing Clinton policy, encourages agencies to deny Freedom of Information Act requests if a "sound legal basis" exists.

10/26/01 President Bush signs U.S.A. Patriot Act, expanding law enforcement powers and government surveillance.

2/22/02 Congress's General Accounting Office sues Vice President Dick Cheney for refusing to disclose records of his energy task force; the GAO eventually loses its case. A separate private case is pending.

3/19/02 White House Chief of Staff Andrew Card directs federal agencies to protect sensitive security information.

11/25/02 Bush signs Homeland Security Act. Its provisions restrict public access to information filed by companies about "critical infrastructure," among other matters.

01/3/03 Administration asks, in papers filed before the Supreme Court, for significant narrowing of the Freedom of Information Act.

3/25/03 Bush issues standards on classified material, favoring secrecy and reversing provisions on openness.

National Conversation: It's (Still) the Economy, Stupid

Un-American Recovery

Harold Meyerson

The Washington Post | December 24, 2003

As the 2004 presidential campaign headed into the summer backstretch, the U.S. economy remained a huge political question mark. Although the U.S. has technically been out of a recession since the fall of 2001, the recovery has been fairly tepid; 2002 growth was a respectable 3.1 percent overall, but these numbers have been overshadowed by troubling job statistics. Payroll data showed a net loss of some 2.7 million jobs from the time George W. Bush took office through August 2003, leading the Democrats to predict gleefully that he could become the first president since Herbert Hoover to suffer a net job loss on his four-year watch.

Economists have responded by noting that job growth always lags behind GDP— and lately the job front has been looking much better. The U.S. Department of Labor announced an increase of 353,000 non-farm jobs in March of 2004, followed by 346,000 more new jobs in April and another 248,000 in May—almost a million additional jobs in three months. Between this and a robust 3.9 percent GDP growth in the first quarter of 2004, the Bush administration is now claiming that their tax-cutting strategy is finally paying off.

However, many economy watchers remain doubtful. Pointing to continuing wage stagnation and the growing trend of outsourcing jobs overseas, they question whether U.S. economic expansion has become disconnected from the plight of the average worker. Here, Harold Meyerson takes a closer look at this issue and how our politicians are dealing with it. . . .

Why is the Bush recovery different from all other recoveries? A slump is a slump is a slump, but it's during recoveries that the distinctive features of a changing economy become apparent. And our current recovery differs so radically from every other bounce-back since World War II that you have to wonder whether we're really talking about the same country.

After inching along imperceptibly for quarter after quarter, the economy is, by some measures, roaring back. The annual growth rate last quarter topped 8 percent, while productivity increased by more than 9 percent. To be sure, employment is still down by 2.4 million jobs since Bush took office, but it's finally begun to rise a bit.

And there are some indices that make even the productivity increases pale by comparison. Corporations have been having a bang-up recovery all along, it turns out; they are about to experience their seventh straight quarter of profit growth. The operating earnings of the 500 companies on the Standard and Poor's index, researchers at Thomas First Call in Boston estimate, will rise by 21.9 percent over last year. Who could ask for anything more?

Well, the American people, for one. Since July the average hourly wage increase for the 85 million Americans who work in non-supervisory jobs in offices and factories is a flat 3 cents. Wages are up just 2.1 percent since November 2002—the slowest wage growth we've experienced in 40 years. Economists at the Economic Policy Institute have been comparing recoveries of late, looking into the growth in corporate-sector income in each of the nine recoveries the United States has gone through since the end of World War II. In the preceding eight, the share of the corporate income growth going to profits averaged 26 percent, and never exceeded 32 percent. In the current recovery, however, profits come to 46 percent of the corporations' additional income.

Conversely, labor compensation averaged 61 percent of the total income growth in the preceding recoveries, and was never lower than 55 percent. In the Bush recovery, it's just 29 percent of the new income coming in to the corporations.

Someone with an antiquarian vocabulary might rightly note that this is a recovery for capital, not labor; indeed, that it's a recovery for capital at the expense of labor. But we are none of us antiquarians, so let's just proceed.

There are only a couple of ways to explain how the capacity of U.S. workers to claim their accustomed share of the nation's income has so stunningly collapsed. Outsourcing is certainly a big part of the picture. As Stephen S. Roach, chief economist for Morgan Stanley, has noted, private-sector hiring in the current recovery is roughly 7 million jobs shy of what would have been the norm in previous recoveries, and U.S. corporations, high-tech as well as low-tech, are busily hiring employees from lower-wage nations instead of from our own.

The jobless rate among U.S. software engineers, for instance, has doubled over the past three years. In Bangalore, India, where American companies are on a huge hiring spree for the kind of talent they used to scoop up in Silicon Valley, the starting annual salary for top electrical engineering graduates, says *Business Week*, is $10,000—compared with $80,000 here in the States. Tell that to a software writer in Palo Alto and she's not likely to hit up her boss for a raise.

That software writer certainly doesn't belong to a union, either.

Indeed, the current recovery is not only the first to take place in an economy in which global wage rates are a factor, but the first since before the New Deal to take place in an economy in which the rate of private-sector unionization is in single digits—just 8.5 percent of the workforce.

In short, what we have here resembles a pre-New Deal recovery more than it does any period of prosperity between the presidencies of the second Roosevelt and the second Bush. The great balancing act of the New Deal—the fostering of vibrant unions, the legislation of minimum wages and such, in a conscious effort to spread prosperity and boost consumption—has come undone. (The federal minimum wage has not been raised since 1997.) And the problem with pre-new deal recoveries is that they never created lasting prosperity.

The current administration is not responsible for the broad contours of this miserably misshapen recovery, but its every action merely increases the imbalance of power between America's employers and employees. But the Democrats' prescriptions for more broadly shared prosperity need some tweaking, too. With the globalization of high-end professions, no Democrat can assert quite so confidently the line that Bill Clinton used so often: What you earn is a result of what you learn. This year's crop of presidential candidates is taking more seriously the importance of labor standards in trade accords, and the right of workers to organize. But they've got a way to go to make the issue of stagnating incomes into the kind of battle cry it should be in the campaign against Bush. If they're not up to it, I say we outsource 'em all and bring in some pols from Bangalore.

Where Are The Jobs?

Bruce Nussbaum

BusinessWeek | March 22, 2004

One of the "x factors" in the U.S. economy has been the recent, unprecedented surge in business productivity—which, after years of increasing at an annual rate of 1 to 2 percent, suddenly shot up by 5 percent in 2002, then grew another 4.4 percent in 2003. And with yet another steep rise of 3.8 percent for the first quarter of 2004, it looks like we can expect more of the same this year. But besides being uncertain as to what exactly has caused this spike in productivity (more skillful use of information technology is one likely reason), economists are also hard-pressed to say where our ever-more-efficient business sector is taking us as a country. Here, Bruce Nussbaum makes two key points: First, that increased productivity (not outsourcing) is mainly to blame for the current paucity of U.S. jobs; and second, that the savings generated by these productivity gains are bound to help the American economy and its work force in a big way—sooner or later. . . .

Americans live in a faith-based economy. We believe deeply in education, innovation, risk-taking, and plain hard work as the way to a better life. But that faith is being eroded. The link between strong growth and job creation appears to be broken, and we don't know what's wrong with it. Profits are soaring, yet no one is hiring. Angry voices are blaming Benedict Arnold CEOs who send jobs to India and China. If highly educated "knowledge" workers in Silicon Valley are losing their jobs, who is really safe?

The truth is that we are living through a moment of maximum uncertainty. The economy is at an inflection point as new forces act upon it. Yet the shape and impact of these forces remains unknown. Outsourcing looms large as a potential threat because no one knows how many jobs and which industries are vulnerable. And productivity seems problematic because it's hard to see where the rewards for all the cost-cutting and hard work are going. Meanwhile, the Next Big Thing that is supposed to propel the economy and job growth forward after the Internet boom isn't obvious. As a result, CEOs are reluctant to place big bets on the future. Workers hunker down. And those laid off are at a loss trying to retrain. How can they, when they don't know where the new jobs will be and who will be hiring? It's not even clear what college students should major in anymore. No wonder this feels like a new age of uncertainty.

The Real Culprit

Yet there are things we do know. The real culprit in this jobless recovery is productivity, not offshoring. Unlike most previous business cycles, productivity has continued to grow at a fast pace right through the downturn and into recovery. One percentage point of productivity growth can eliminate up to 1.3 million jobs a year. With productivity growing at an annual rate of 3 percent to 3.5 percent rather than the expected 2 percent to 2.5 percent, the reason for the jobs shortfall becomes clear: Companies are using information technology to cut costs—and that means less labor is needed. Of the 2.7 million jobs lost over the past three years, only 300,000 have been from outsourcing, according to Forrester Research Inc. People rightly fear that jobs in high tech and services will disappear just as manufacturing jobs did. Perhaps so. But odds are it will be productivity rather than outsourcing that does them in.

We know also where the benefits of rising productivity are going: higher profits, lower inflation, rising stocks, and, ultimately, loftier prices for houses. In short, productivity is generating wealth, not employment. Corporate profits as a share of national income are at an all-time high. So is net worth for many individuals. Consumer net worth hit a new peak, at $45 trillion—up 75 percent since 1995—and consumers have more than recouped their losses from the bust.

We know, too, that outsourcing isn't altogether a bad thing. In the '90s, high-tech companies farmed out the manufacture of memory chips, computers, and telecom equipment to Asia. This lowered the cost of tech gear, raising demand and spreading the IT revolution. The same will probably happen with software. Outsourcing will cut prices and make the next generation of IT cheaper and more available. This will generate greater productivity and growth. In fact, as venture capitalists increasingly insist that all IT startups have an offshore component, the cost of innovation should fall sharply, perhaps by half.

We know something about the kinds of jobs that could migrate to Asia and those that will stay home. In the '90s, the making of customized chips and gear that required close contact with clients remained in the U.S., while production of commodity products was outsourced. Today, the Internet and cheaper telecom permit routine service work to be done in Bangalore. But specialized jobs that require close contact with clients, plus an understanding of U.S. culture, will likely remain.

• • •

America has been at economic inflection points many times in the past. These periods of high job anxiety were eventually followed by years of surging job creation. The faith Americans have in innovation, risk-taking, education, and hard work has been sustained again and again by strong economic performance.

There's no question that today's jobless recovery is causing many people real pain. The number of discouraged workers leaving the workforce is unprecedented. Labor-force participation is down among precisely the most vulnerable parts of the workforce—younger and nonwhite workers. Some are going back to school, but many are simply giving up after fruitless searches for decent jobs. If the participation rate were at its March 2001 level, there would be 2.7 million more workers in the labor force looking for jobs. This would push the unemployment rate up to 7.4 percent, not the current 5.6 percent.

History has shown time and again that jobs follow growth, but not necessarily in a simple, linear fashion. America has a dynamic, fast-changing economy that embodies Joseph A. Schumpeter's ideal of creative destruction. We are now experiencing the maximum pain from the wreckage of outmoded jobs while still awaiting the innovations that will generate the work of the future. While America's faith in its innovation economy has often been tested, it has never been betrayed. Given the chance, the economy will deliver the jobs and prosperity that it has in the past.

The Mother of All Big Spenders: Bush Spends Like Carter and Panders Like Clinton
Veronique de Rugy and Tad DeHaven

National Review Online | July 28, 2003

The deficits are back. After four years of surpluses, the U.S. federal budget is firmly in the red again, running shortfalls of $157 billion in fiscal year 2002 and $375 billion in 2003. Meanwhile, the nonpartisan Congressional Budget Office projects a still-larger deficit of $477 billion for 2004.

Since the Republicans control the presidency and both houses of Congress, this red ink can't be pinned on "tax and spend" Democrats. Instead, the White House has blamed the lingering effects of 9/11, the 2001 recession, increased spending on home-land security, and the cost of the Iraq war—while also noting the deficits aren't all that bad by historical standards. Left-wing critics like economist Paul Krugman, on the other hand, attribute the shortfall mainly to the three large tax cuts passed by Congress over the past three years. (See "The Tax-Cut Con," p. 186).

At the same time, some of the loudest grumbling over the deficits has come from conservatives who complain that Bush is "too liberal" in his budgetary policy. In this essay, for example, Veronique de Rugy and Tad DeHaven, who both work for the lib-ertarian Cato Institute, chastise the Bush team for overindulging in non-defense dis-cretionary spending in an effort to ensure the president's reelection. . . .

The Bush administration's newly released budget projections reveal an antic-ipated budget deficit of $450 billion for the current fiscal year, up another $151 billion since February. Supporters and critics of the administration are tripping over themselves to blame the deficit on tax cuts, the war, and a slow economy. But the fact is we have mounting deficits because George W. Bush is the most gratuitous big spender to occupy the White House since Jimmy Carter. One could say that he has become the "Mother of All Big Spenders."

The new estimates show that, under Bush, total outlays will have risen $408 billion in just three years to $2.272 trillion: an enormous increase in federal spending of 22 percent. Administration officials privately admit that spending is too high. Yet they argue that deficits are appropriate in times of war and recession. So, is it true that the war on terrorism has resulted in an increase in defense spending? Yes. And, is it also true that a slow economy has meant a decreased stream of tax revenues to pay for government? Yes again.

But the real truth is that national defense is far from being responsible for all of the spending increases. According to the new numbers, defense spending will have risen by about 34 percent since Bush came into office. But, at the same time, non-defense discretionary spending will have skyrocketed by almost 28 percent. Government agencies that Republicans were calling to be abolished less than 10 years ago, such as education and labor, have enjoyed jaw-dropping spending increases under Bush of 70 percent and 65 percent respectively.

Now, most rational people would cut back on their spending if they knew their income was going to be reduced in the near future. Any smart company would look to cut costs should the business climate take a turn for the worse.

But the administration has been free spending into the face of a recessionary economy from day one without making any serious attempt to reduce costs.

The White House spinmeisters insist that we keep the size of the deficit "in perspective." Sure it's appropriate that the budget deficit should be measured against the relative size of the economy. Today, the projected budget deficit represents 4.2 percent of the nation's GDP. Thus the folks in the Bush administration pat themselves on the back while they remind us that in the 1980s the economy handled deficits of 6 percent. So what? Apparently this administration seems to think that achieving low standards instead of the lowest is supposed to be comforting.

That the nation's budgetary situation continues to deteriorate is because the administration's fiscal policy has been decidedly more about politics than policy. Even the tax cuts, which happened to be good policy, were still political in nature considering their appeal to the Republican's conservative base. At the same time, the politicos running the Bush reelection machine have consistently tried to placate or silence the liberals and special interests by throwing money at their every whim and desire. In mathematical terms, the administration calculates that satiated conservatives plus silenced liberals equals reelection.

How else can one explain the administration publishing a glossy report criticizing farm programs and then proceeding to sign a farm bill that expands those same programs? How else can one explain the administration acknowledging that entitlements are going to bankrupt the nation if left unreformed yet pushing the largest historical expansion in Medicare one year before the election? Such blatant political maneuvering can only be described as Clintonian.

But perhaps we are being unfair to former President Clinton. After all, in inflation-adjusted terms, Clinton had overseen a total spending increase of only 3.5 percent at the same point in his administration. More importantly, after his first three years in office, non-defense discretionary spending actually went down by 0.7 percent. This is contrasted by Bush's three-year total spending increase of 15.6 percent and a 20.8 percent explosion in non-defense discretionary spending.

Sadly, the Bush administration has consistently sacrificed sound policy to the god of political expediency. From farm subsidies to Medicare expansion, purchasing reelection votes has consistently trumped principle. In fact, what we have now is a president who spends like Carter and panders like Clinton. Our only hope is that the exploding deficit will finally cause the administration to get serious about controlling spending.

The Nixon Recovery
Charles Morris

The New York Times | February 7, 2004

In this column, written just as job growth was beginning to take off in early 2004, Charles Morris looks further into the deficit issue and sees two fiscal strategies at play: A short-term plan to use deficit spending to help get the economy up to full speed in time for the presidential election in November, and a long-term plan to cut taxes on business and investment income as much as possible. Morris's worry is that, in implementing this slash-and-spend policy, the administration has "reject[ed]...a half-century's consensus on the proper management of a modern economy." Any dreams Republicans have of cutting entitlements, he suggests, are simply politically unrealistic. As another indicator of a potential fiscal train wreck down the road, Morris notes that the administration is basing its projections of smaller deficits later this decade on the fact that parts of the 2003 tax-cut bill are due to expire between 2005 and 2008—while at the same time it's pushing for legislation to make those tax cuts permanent. . . .

Yesterday's good news on the job front, on top of strong growth in the last half of 2003, may finally signal that President Bush's economic recovery is on solid ground. There is still plenty to worry about. Unused production capacity continues to drag down business profits, and job growth, while finally rebounding, remains slow. Consumers have loaded up on debt and could be devastated by a spike in interest rates. But the economic tea leaves are more positive than they have been for a long time.

If President Bush can maintain the recovery through his reelection campaign, he will be in rarefied company. Richard M. Nixon, in fact, may be the only recent president to accomplish this feat, timing a recovery from a midterm recession to coincide with his 1972 race. The reason this is so hard is that, despite all the bragging about creating jobs or speeding growth, presidents really have few economic tools at their disposal. Most federal spending is outside a president's direct control—locked up in things like retirement programs that chug along pretty much by themselves. The same is true of taxes and interest rates. A president can set the agenda, but taxes are ultimately controlled by Congress. Interest rates fall under the domain of the independent Federal Reserve.

Yet Nixon proved that if a president plays his weak hand ruthlessly—without restraint or regard for long-term consequences—he can make the economy sit up and roll over at his command. In the end, of course, the Nixon "recovery" was short-lived and America soon paid a steep price for it. Unfortunately, Mr. Bush's economic performance so far is eerily similar.

Back in the early 1970s, with both high inflation and slow growth, Nixon's economic challenge may have been even more intractable than Mr. Bush's. So, with his reelection in jeopardy, Nixon and his Treasury secretary, John B. Connally, bludgeoned both the Congress and Federal Reserve into a truly radical experiment. Congress passed wage and price controls and the Federal Reserve simultaneously increased the money supply.

The gamble was that a big jolt of money would rev up the economy while the price controls would suppress inflation. It worked, allowing Nixon to win in 1972. But success came at a huge cost. Once the price controls were removed through 1973 and 1974, all the suppressed inflation came roaring out, hitting the double digits and plaguing the second half of the 1970s. Worse, the resulting collapse of the dollar led to the 1973 OPEC "oil price shock." Altogether, it was one of history's most expensive election campaigns.

Many analysts worry that a Bush-style recovery could be similarly catastrophic. Taking a page from the Nixon playbook, Mr. Bush has wielded his fiscal tools aggressively. Over the last two years, there has been a half-trillion dollar swing in the federal books, from a $100 billion surplus in 2001 to a deficit of about $400 billion in 2003, and an expected $521 trillion in red ink for 2004.

The deficits have been driven by deep tax cuts and unrestrained spending. That includes big increases for domestic security, but other initiatives as well, like a generous new subsidy program for industrial farmers. On the surface, this looks like a standard, if unusually forceful, application of textbook economics. The government is supposed to run deficits in slack times and stash away surpluses during the fat years. So why the worries? Mr. Bush's program, like Nixon's, is not the textbook one-time kick in the pants, but a rejection of a half-century's consensus on the proper management of a modern economy.

The Bush program was not originally intended as a response to the recession. Instead, it was just the opening wedge of an unprecedented 10-year program to eliminate virtually all taxes on businesses and investment income, on the theory that everyone's better off when investors are well fed. The administration, in fact, first justified its program as necessary to head off high federal surpluses, then opportunistically switched the argument when the recession started to bite hard. The tax cuts, moreover, have come at a time when federal taxes, as a share of gross domestic product, are already at their lowest level since 1959.

President Bush's planners claim that budgets will be back in balance within the decade. But a recent Brookings Institution study makes those calculations look like sleight of hand. To keep cost estimates down, for example, the administration has built "sunset" provisions into almost all of its tax cut programs. In theory, when the sunset dates arrive, the tax law will switch back to its pre-Bush status. Fat chance. The administration itself is pushing hard to abolish all the sunset provisions. The Brookings analysts foresee deficits increasing every year for the next decade, with total red ink around $8 trillion.

The consequences of that could be bad enough—higher interest rates and declining competitiveness and growth. But it gets worse. In the coming years, baby boomers will start making their first claims on Social Security and Medicare. There is no way the country can run deficits on the scale of the Brookings forecasts and decent retirement programs at the same time. Boomers do not take rejection with good grace, and their tolerance will not improve as they get older. From the perspective of 2010 or so, citizens may look back on the post-Nixon 1970s as halcyon days.

Fighting Big Pharmacy
Eleanor Clift

Newsweek | August 1, 2003

Health care is emerging as a potent issue in the 2004 presidential election, as medical costs continue to rise, led by escalating drug expenses. In particular, many seniors now find themselves struggling to afford needed medications. Until recently, Medicare was no help: Established in the 1960s, when pharmaceuticals represented a small portion of health-care costs, it has traditionally paid nothing toward prescription drugs.

This changed in December 2003, when President Bush signed legislation adding prescription drug coverage to Medicare. The bill—which takes effect in 2006—requires recipients to pay a $35 monthly premium and a $250 deductible. Medicare then pays for

75 percent of a person's drug costs up to $2,250 per year, plus 95 percent of annual costs above $5,100. Reaction has been mixed: Some seniors dislike the bill's "doughnut hole" (recipients pay $3,600 out of pocket before the high-end coverage kicks in), while policy advocates criticize the fact that it bans Medicare from negotiating with pharmaceutical companies for better prices (a provision Senator John McCain called "outrageous"). Meanwhile, the green-eye-shade types worry that the the bill's ten-year cost will be far higher than the administration's current $530 billion estimate (a number they kept under their hat until the legislation had safely passed; the original figure given to Congress was a more palatable—and patently inaccurate—$400 billion).

In one apparent boon for consumers, the Medicare reform bill also contains language allowing reimportation of drugs from Canada, where medication can often be bought for a fraction of the U.S. cost. Here, Eleanor Clift tells the political tale of the brave congresswoman who made this provision possible. As Clift forewarns, however, the final legislation included a catch: It calls for the FDA to approve the safety of every drug being imported—"all but assuring," in the words of one physician's publication, "that the practice will remain illegal." . . .

The prescription-drug industry is a cash cow for Republicans, and its generosity is normally rewarded with favorable votes on Capitol Hill. That's why it was big news when the Republican-controlled House voted overwhelmingly—hours before leaving for summer recess last week—to give American consumers access to U.S.-made drugs that are sold more cheaply in Canada and elsewhere.

Under current law, it is illegal to bring in these drugs from abroad, forcing cash-strapped Americans to become criminals. For example, the drug Tamoxifen, which is used to combat breast cancer, is available in Canada for a 10th of what it costs in this country.

Missouri Republican Jo Ann Emerson engineered the stunning rebuke to the drug industry and its mighty benefactors. "She's the woman who brought the House to a standstill, and she kicked their a—," says an admiring lobbyist.

Back home in her rural Missouri district, everybody is talking about Emerson's surprise victory and how thrilled they are that relief is in sight. "Don't thank me yet," she says. "The war is yet to be won." The bill to legalize drug reimportation passed by 57 votes as dozens of Republicans opposed their leadership to vote yes. Now the bill moves to a conference committee where it is part of a broader Medicare reform bill and where differences between the House and Senate must be reconciled. The Senate is on record opposing reimportation with 53 senators, including Democrat Ted Kennedy, signing a letter stating their concern that cheap drugs could flood the American market and compromise safety.

The conference committee is appointed by the leadership in both the House and Senate and dominated by friends of the pharmaceutical industry. The betting is that they will find a way to kill the provision. "That's where the pros go to work," says a lobbyist. The wild card is public opinion, and whether Emerson and the bipartisan coalition she helped forge can keep the drug issue front and center. Emerson arrived at her activism through personal experience. After her husband, former representative Bill Emerson, died in 1996 and she took over his seat, she had the responsibility of looking after his aged mother, who was in assisted living and on a fixed income.

Her mother-in-law's prescription drugs cost $1,000 a month. Through generics and wise shopping, Emerson pared that down to $600. But she was shocked to learn that prescription-drug prices are increasing at the rate of 10 percent to 15 percent a year, even for drugs that have been on the market for years. "You would think the opposite would occur," she says. "People are getting angry, and that's a good thing if they understand they can make a difference by contacting their legislator."

Emerson voted against her party's Medicare reform bill because she thought $400 billion for prescription drug expenses over 10 years fell far short of the $1.8 trillion seniors are projected to spend on their medication during that period, and the bill did nothing to curb rising drug prices. The night of the vote in late June, GOP leaders discovered they were one vote short and Emerson traded her support for a promise to bring drug reimportation to the floor for a vote and to strip so-called "poison pill" language from the Medicare bill that would block drug reimportation if it passed. "There's nothing worse than having people heckle you as you walk down the aisle to vote," Emerson recalls. With her colleagues chanting "Don't do it," Emerson filled out her green card for yes, reversing her earlier no vote. New York Democrat Nita Lowey, an advocate of drug reimportation, hugged Emerson in a display of emotion that erased party lines.

It was 3:30 in the morning when Emerson got home, heady with success and determined to hold the big boys to their promises. She took a nap, got up at 7 A.M. and typed up her understanding of the deal they'd struck. She sent an e-mail to each of the House leaders and committee chairmen involved asking for their commitment in writing. The floor vote that took place before dawn on Friday, June 25, would never have happened if she had not pressed the case. Now she's watching the conference committee to see if the promise is kept to remove six lines requiring the secretary of Health and Human Services to certify the absolute safety of reimported drugs, the language that is the poison pill.

Emerson believes there are ways to write safety standards that are reasonable, and the bill as written requires drug companies to use anticounterfeit packaging. In fact, 40 percent of drugs on the market are already imported from FDA-approved plants in foreign countries, including Nive, a small island nation off the coast of New Zealand. "We had to look it up in the [CIA's] World Fact Book," says Emerson's press secretary, Jeffrey Connor.

Emerson's slogan is, "Putting people before politics." She represents the ninth-poorest district in the nation, and has a reputation for working across partisan lines and being willing to stand up to the Republican leadership. "I was sent to Washington by the people I represent and not the drug companies," she says. "The night of the vote, drug lobbyists were everywhere. I never saw so many suits in the halls of Congress." According to Public Citizen's Congress Watch, the pharmaceutical industry has 623 hired guns, more than one for every member of Congress. Twenty-three former members of Congress with special access to their colleagues lobby for the industry.

Betting on the little guy, or gal, against a massive industry is risky. But heavy-handed tactics have a way of backfiring. When the Coalition for Traditional Values, allied with the pharmaceuticals, blitzed two dozen conservative members saying drug reimportation would allow women to get the anti-abortion pill RU-486 over the Internet, which is not true, Emerson's coalition picked up two or three votes from members who were offended. "I don't mind a fair fight, but lying and distorting the truth is not a fair fight," says Emerson. Neither is what happens behind closed doors—but that's where this issue will be resolved.

Part Two:
The 2004 Presidential Campaign

How to Build a Better Democrat

Joe Klein

Time | May 19, 2003

When the following story ran on the cover of Time *in the late spring of 2003 (accompanied by a photo of a smiling Franklin Roosevelt, complete with fedora and uptilted cigarette holder), the Democrats had good reason to be gloomy. In the wake of the swift and successful invasion of Iraq, President Bush's approval rating—which had soared above 90 percent after 9/11—was still hovering in the 60 to 70 percent range. At the same time, none of the nine Democrats who'd declared themselves as candidates for the presidency were generating much enthusiasm, with the exception of the unpredictable (and, many party veterans fretted, unelectable) ex-governor of Vermont, Howard Dean.*

It was the perfect time for Joe Klein to weigh in with some sage advice for the nine would-be chief executives. Besides being a seasoned political analyst, Klein is also a terrific stylist and a consistently entertaining storyteller—as anyone who's read his novels Primary Colors *and* The Running Mate *can tell you. Looking back on this essay a year later, the Kerry campaign seems to have taken at least some of Klein's advice to heart. . . .*

Two days after George W. Bush strutted across the deck of the U.S.S. Abraham Lincoln in full fighter-pilot regalia—an image we may see from time to time between now and election day—the nine Democrats running for president of the U.S. held their first debate of the 2004 campaign. No more than 10 minutes into it, two of those Democrats, John Kerry of Massachusetts and Howard Dean of Vermont, had entangled themselves in a ridiculous scuffle over the issue of gay rights. Not that they disagreed. Both are staunch advocates of equal rights and "civil unions." But Kerry believed that Dean had accused him of a lack of courage on this topic. "I don't need any lectures in courage from Howard Dean," said Kerry, a Vietnam War hero who probably should have saved that line for a more crucial evening.

Dean insisted that he had been misquoted by a San Francisco newspaper; the paper had printed a correction. This seemed a classic Democratic Party moment—woolly liberals taking time from crucial issues like war and peace and prosperity to argue over who could offer the most extravagant pander to a narrow, controversial interest group. Happily for both Kerry and Dean, practically no one was watching. The debate was aired by a smattering of ABC affiliates at 11:30 on Saturday night and by CSPAN the next day.

There are futility metaphors aplenty here: The contrast between the swaggering president and the squabbling Dems. The nonargument over periphera. The absence of an audience. But then, the Democrats have excelled at futility for more than 30 years. They have elected two presidents during that time, Jimmy Carter and Bill Clinton. Both were governors of southern states. Neither was a well-known party leader. Neither ran on what many Democrats would consider a traditional—that is, liberal—agenda. Carter was the first born-again Christian president; Clinton once owned a pickup truck with AstroTurf carpeting in the back. Carter won because he seemed a simple, honorable antidote to the excessive dishonesty of the Nixon era. Clinton won because he was far more talented than his opponents—George H. W. Bush and Bob Dole—but also because he rejected his party's orthodoxy on crime (especially the death penalty), welfare reform, free trade and fiscal conservatism. One could argue that the only winning strategy for Democrats in the past nine presidential campaigns has been camouflage.

Which brings us to 2004, another election the Democrats should lose. They are facing a popular incumbent who has just won a war. George W. Bush is everything Democrats have not been—bold, decisive, uncomplicated, a man of real convictions who has not been afraid to take unpopular positions. Furthermore, unlike his father, this Bush is a political animal. He has a clever team. If the Democrats do happen to find a winning issue, you can be sure that Karl Rove, the president's strategist, will figure out a way to trump or co-opt it (as he did with education and Medicare prescription-drug benefits in the election of 2000). And the Democrats enter the fray with all the shape and substance of fog. "People have no idea what we stand for," says Stan Greenberg, a Democratic pollster. "They have a vague sense that we were against the war in Iraq and a vaguer sense that things were somehow better economically when we were in power. Beyond that, nothing."

For these reasons and others, some Republicans are quietly predicting that 2004 will be not just a Bush landslide but also a transformational election—an election that creates a new Republican majority, just as the 1936 election created an enduring Democratic majority for Franklin D. Roosevelt. There is a problem with this notion, though. The last transformational election was not 1936 but 1968—the year that Richard Nixon created a new political reality by exploiting Southern white resentment of the civil rights movement (and of Vietnam War protesters). The solid Democratic South became the solid Republican South, a truly momentous event in American political history, and the pendulum has been swinging right ever since. The laws of politics, to say nothing of physics, would indicate that a second conservative transformation, an election that moves the center of gravity even further to the right, is unlikely.

In fact, despite the hot Republican rhetoric, it's difficult to imagine what else conservatives can conserve on the federal level (although the world would be a better place if monstrosities like last year's farm-subsidies act were repealed). The past two years have shown a renewed public appetite for a stronger federal presence—not merely in the pursuit of terrorists but also in the regulation of Wall Street and corporate boardrooms, and perhaps in the stimulation of an economy that the Federal Reserve Bank has indicated may be approaching a deflationary contraction. The brutal cutbacks looming on the state and local levels may also have an impact on the political climate. There will be fewer police, fire fighters and teachers. There will be more potholes. Civilians may remember how valuable government can be. We could be on the cusp of an era where government is regarded once more with mere skepticism, rather than the out-and-out disdain of recent years.

And so, yes, the Democrats do have a chance in 2004. A chance, but they will have to become something different from the Democrats we have come to know and ridicule. They face challenges on three different fronts: patriotism, optimism and confidence. They will have to convince the public that they are as committed to national defense, and to the judicious use of military force, as the Republicans are. They will have to shed their congenital pessimism. They can't just rant against the administration and hope for bad news to confirm their prejudices. They will have to propose firm, reasonable policy alternatives that are easy to understand and defend. If they oppose the Bush tax cuts, they will have to lay out, in some detail, what they would do instead.

Finally, they will have to change the mingy, defensive, consultant-driven style of recent campaigns. They will need a candidate who is easy in his skin, who sounds different from other politicians—freer, perhaps; funnier, certainly—and who is confident enough to risk broad, bold themes that capture the national imagination rather than parsing the special yearnings of enough demographic slivers to win the election. Camouflage will not be enough this time.

Step One: Recapture the Flag

There are plenty of Democrats who nominally supported the war in Iraq—five of the six credible presidential candidates did, but only Joe Lieberman supported the president's policies without reservation. Most Democrats were dragged along on this adventure, carrying suspicions that it was, at bottom, equal parts political enterprise concocted by Rove, ideological enterprise concocted by utopian neoconservatives, and family psychodrama—young Bush avenging and one-upping his old man. There was, as always, a congenital distrust of all things martial among the "Democratic wing of the Democratic Party," as Howard Dean would say. And it was Dean who made himself into a semi-plausible contender by voicing these suspicions and by excoriating his fellow candidates for not standing up to Bush on Iraq.

Throughout the winter, Republicans could point to Dean's candid and bracing performances on the stump and say, This is what the Democrats are really all about. They are the party of peaceniks; they mistrust the military; they are not tough enough to protect America. This analysis was both right and wrong. In February, Dean did set the Democratic National Committee's winter meeting afire, but the reaction of the party faithful to Dean was no different from the Republican faithful's wild enthusiasm for red-meat orators like Alan Keyes and Pat Buchanan in years past. Most Democrats do not have a death wish. Ever since the George McGovern disaster in 1972, the party has routinely chosen technocratic moderates as standard-bearers. This doesn't bode well for Dean, especially now that the war is over. He has been making some real Iraq-related blunders in recent weeks, saying of the removal of Saddam, "I suppose that's a good thing," and raising the possibility that "we won't always have the strongest military."

The Democrats may never be able to outdo the Republicans on patriotism and national defense, but they do have to be credible in those areas. "This is the threshold question," says Donna Brazile, a longtime Democratic Party activist. "We have to be able to close the leadership gap with Bush. We can't do that if we don't field a candidate who is strong on defense." In the South Carolina debate, Lieberman made good sense with this formulation: "I am the one Democrat who can match George Bush in the areas where many think he's strong—defense and moral values—and beat him where he is weak, on the economy and his divisive right-wing social agenda."

In the wake of Bush's flying stunt, a new and unfair test was proposed by journalists—the aircraft-carrier primary: Which of the Democrats could have duplicated Bush's photo op without seeming foolish? Not Lieberman, and certainly not Dean. John Edwards and Dick Gephardt are plausible flyboys, and Bob Graham might have been at one time. No, Kerry wins this contest hands down. His military record is his ticket to this dance. On the day before the debate, Kerry did something no other Democrat in the race could do. He gave a moving tribute, surrounded by Vietnam combat veterans, at the Vietnam memorial in Columbia, S.C. He introduced the gunner on his swift boat in the Mekong Delta, a local African-American minister named David Alston, and talked about the bond they shared. "We are brothers who love each other today because of our shared experiences," he said, "and that is a gift we veterans can give to the rest of the country. We can remind people of the importance of service like David Alston's—his sense of duty, of mission, of obligation, which are the definition of patriotism."

As the man said, Kerry doesn't need any lectures in courage. In fact, Kerry has already effectively questioned Bush's military policy in Afghanistan from the right. He argued that a more aggressive use of American troops might have trapped Osama bin Laden and the Al Qaeda leadership at Tora Bora. But Kerry's performance on Iraq raises a question. He voted for the war, but reluctantly. One almost senses that it was a political vote, intended to neuter his opposition to the first Gulf War. He was not a happy warrior. He said he could support the war only if the U.S. exhausted all diplomatic efforts—and then supported the war anyway when Bush abandoned the diplomatic process. Kerry has continued to criticize the Bush administration's clumsy, arrogant behavior in the world, its myopic willingness to offend friend and foe alike. He believes that the administration's intention to go it alone on the reconstruction of Iraq is a mistake as well. These are not startling criticisms. They are common among both Democrats and Republican traditionalists. The members of Bush the Elder's foreign policy team have expressed these very sentiments privately, and sometimes publicly. But Kerry has been criticized by Dean and Lieberman, and by much of the press, for seeming wishy-washy. The question is, Are the Democrats' qualms about Bush's foreign policy too technical, too complicated to work as a political issue? In a battle of bumper stickers, STRONG DEFENSE beats YOUR FAMILY IS SAFER IN A WORLD WHERE AMERICA IS LOOKED UP TO, NOT IN A WORLD WHERE WE ARE HATED, which is Edwards' elegant formulation of the problem.

This is a chronic Democratic woe: lousy bumper stickers. The Republicans can trot out three two-word killers—STRONG DEFENSE, LOWER TAXES and TRADITIONAL VALUES. Democrats are more likely to offer impenetrable position papers. In 1992, Clinton chose to fight the Republicans on their own ground. He used three one-word slogans and won with "Opportunity, Responsibility and Community." The moderate Democratic Leadership Council cleverly revised the slogan at its annual meeting last summer: "Opportunity, Responsibility and Security." Several of the Democratic contenders have fixed on security as a theme this year. Not just national security but homeland security, financial security, health-care security and so forth. It seems likely that this one word will be as prominent in 2004 as the image of George Bush in his jump suit. But on the real security issue—national security—the Democrats will fail if they merely agree with the President.

They will have to risk complexity. They will have to argue that foreign policy involves more than just the threat of force, more than just bullying friends and clobbering foes. Indeed, the greatest threats today involve a new kind of power that is neither hard (military) nor soft (economic and cultural) but viral. These new threats attack the global community insidiously. Terrorism is one virus, obviously; but there are also crime syndicates, environmental problems, and businesses that operate beyond the reach of international law (not to forget actual viruses like SARS and AIDS). In an age of viral power, Democrats might argue, the U.S. has to be more than a hammer looking for nails. We have to find a way to act as a vaccine. But the Democrats can make that sort of broad argument only if they are unassailable in their support for military strength.

Step Two: Lose the Frown

There are times when Richard Gephardt, a truly decent man, seems the embodiment of all that is clunky about the Democratic Party. His 1988 presidential campaign was militantly dismal. At one point, he criticized Ronald Reagan's 1984 "Morning in America" advertising theme: "It's closer to midnight," Gephardt insisted, "and getting darker all the time." This is another inveterate Democratic problem: every silver lining comes equipped not just with a cloud, but often with a full-fledged hurricane and heavy coastal flooding. Who would want to spend four years with such spoilsports whining away on TVs in the kitchens and family rooms of America? The economy is on the brink of collapse. The health-care system is on the brink of collapse. The schools are literally collapsing. Every war is Vietnam. In reality, it is never, ever midnight, or even twilight, in America, the most hopeful country in all of history. Even Gephardt seems intent on running a sunnier campaign this time.

He has offered a handful of big ideas, some of them quite good. But the centerpiece of Gephardt's candidacy—his universal health-care plan—is immense and anachronistic. It offers huge subsidies to large corporations that already offer health insurance to their workers. It mandates that small companies offer health insurance as well. This is a classic Old Democratic plan, pegged to a constituency that is shriveling: the Big America of Rust Belt manufacturing and trade unions. Entrepreneurial America—the immigrant grocers, the hi-tech start-ups in Sun Belt garages, the source of most economic growth—doesn't need the additional burden of finding and securing health plans for its workers. The notion of offering "health security" to the 41 million Americans who don't have insurance—an idea that every Democrat is likely to endorse in one form or another—can be done more simply (and for about one-third of Gephardt's $247 billion a year) by offering tax credits and subsidies to individuals who don't have health insurance.

Gephardt is right about one thing: the Democrats have to offer a clear alternative to Bush domestically—and opposition to any but the most targeted tax cuts is the place to start. This is less risky than it might seem. The public hasn't been hot for tax cuts for quite some time. (In 1998 Clinton managed to stop congressional Republicans on this issue with four words: "Save Social Security First.") But if Democrats are going to oppose tax cuts—which are pretty much the entirety of Bush's domestic policy—they are going to have provide a compelling and comprehensive alternative.

That is not easy. Privately, most leading Democrats—especially those who are economists—agree on only two principles: there is no One Big Dramatic Thing you can do to fix the economy, but you probably have to do something to nudge the country out of the current rut. The "security" theme might work nicely here. Universal health insurance is a form of security. Spending more to protect Americans from terrorism is another. Spending more on highways and communications can be seen as a form of national security as well. Eisenhower was able to fund the creation of the interstate highway system in the 1950s by calling it the National Defense Highway Act.

All the above would create jobs, unlike Bush's rather indirect and speculative tax cuts, and they would have some social "security" benefits as well. But none are ideas to stir the soul. Democrats haven't done much soul stirring since the Kennedy era—and they haven't spent much time courting young people since then, either. (Their fixations on prescription drugs for the elderly and leaving Social Security alone are utter losers with nongraybeards.) If the Democrats want to think romantic as well as big, the obvious area is the environment. Several of the candidates have proposed dour, incremental "energy-independence" schemes that feature many of the worthy, ho-hum notions of years past—conservation, fuel-efficiency standards and the like. But the fun part of the environment is gizmos. The president, a gizmo kind of guy, embraced the hydrogen car. The Democrats could do that and more— nuclear fusion, wind power, digital interstate highways (a computer chip in your car locks you in at 70 m.p.h. a safe distance from the cars in front of and behind you). Whatever. The key is to have at least one issue on which the candidate is free to dream, think big, tap the national spirit of adventure in a way that doesn't involve Abrams tanks. My guess is that enthusiasm is contagious. A candidate who sounds stoked about the environment will have an easier time selling less inspirational issues like health insurance.

There wasn't much romance in campaign-finance reform, either, but John McCain managed to make it into a rollicking adventure in 2000. McCain was a brash, confident, unfettered candidate. The Democrats have been too frightened—scared that their belief in government, in larger public purposes, could be twisted into public perversity by the Republicans—to even attempt fizziness, to say nothing of brashitude. This lack of confidence has shriveled the Democrats. They run for office in shackles of their own making.

Step Three: Kill the Consultants

In the spring of 2000, Al Gore hired a new—it seemed his umpteenth—team of political consultants. They asked him what he cared about most, as consultants always do. He said the environment. They told him the environment was nice, but it wouldn't win him any more electoral votes than he already had. They gave him a list of issues that might win a few crucial states. Gore followed their advice. "They ran about 26 different Senate races rather than a presidential campaign," says John Podesta, Clinton's former chief of staff. "They won more votes than the Republicans, but they lost something too. They gave up having Gore look like a president."

The Democrats did the opposite in 2002. They ran 34 separate Senate races as a national campaign. It was a disaster. The unified campaign was run by consultants and pollsters working for the Democrats' House and Senate campaign committees, which disbursed money and political advice. The advice was not to talk about the most important issues on everyone's mind—the war in Iraq and national security. And not to talk about Bush's tax cuts. Instead, the Democrats ran on three issues: they blamed Bush for the recession, without offering an alternative; they tried to scare senior citizens about the privatization of Social Security; they offered a wildly expensive prescription-drug plan for the elderly without proposing any reform of the Medicare system. This was not only ineffective and uninspiring, it was disgraceful.

Look, some of my best friends are political consultants. And campaign strategy is ultimately the candidate's responsibility. Gore had the power to tell his consultants to go jump in a lake. Republican consultants aren't much different. But Republican candidates simply seem to have more faith in their message—smaller government is better, except when it comes to the military—than Democrats do. And so Democratic candidates pay more attention to small-bore political-issue evasions and tactical finesses than Republicans do. There is immense voodoo power attached to the man or woman who comes to the candidate and says, You can't do that because the polls say the public doesn't like it, or the focus group didn't buy it. Politicians are suckers for almost anyone who tells them what not to do, especially if there are numbers that appear to support the contention.

But there are reasons, mechanical and spiritual, why this sterile, straitened form of politics may have finally outlived its usefulness. Polling is not much of a science when only 5 percent of people contacted by phone—that's the current average—actually agree to answer questions. One wonders if that 5 percent is a certain type of citizen—a lonely one, perhaps. One wonders about the 19 in 20 who hang up the phone. What do they believe? Focus groups are more reliable, but they are poison to spontaneity. They can tell a candidate a lot about what the public thinks it wants to hear but nothing at all about how to lead. And the public has begun to catch on. "People understand what shrink-wrapped language sounds like," says Bob Shrum, who was Gore's consultant in 2000 and is Kerry's for 2004. "They want to feel that politicians are speaking directly to them, without marketing or intermediaries. This was a real strength Bush and McCain had in 2000. They didn't talk like the usual Republicans. Bush talked about compassionate conservatism and passionately about education. And we all know about the freshness McCain brought to the campaign."

But it is the pedestrian application of Shrum's art that has created a generation of strait-jacketed Democrats who think small, who sound as if they were animatronic, who are willing to bend themselves into pretzels for the love of frenzied, myopic special interests, who think that smart politics means complaining about the cost of Bush's trip to the U.S.S. *Abraham Lincoln* rather than finding some alternative and more inspirational way to capture the public's attention. If the Democrats want to transcend their perpetual pickiness, their inability to rise above the bite-size, they are going to have to find a candidate talented and fearless enough to meet the public without having to consult a focus group first. In the end, talent can make the most carefully massaged message sound fresh, as Clinton almost always could.

There is much that we don't know about this election. There may be another terrorist attack, or not. The economy may sag, or not. The president may try one too many cowboy tricks, or he may simply be seen as the guy who got us through a tough time. The country post–September. 11 may be entirely different from the country before the outrage occurred. It may be a more serious electorate, less tolerant of political boilerplate, more favorably disposed toward serious governance and ready to make sacrifices for the common good. Or not. If the world stays quiet and the economy picks up, the Democrats may face an unbeatable incumbent in 2004, no matter how hard they try. All the more reason to act as Democrats haven't in quite a while: Speak your minds, dream a little, tell people some truths they don't want to hear. Get angry. Be funny. But, above all, provide a real alternative. The Republicans offer smaller government. The Democrats, at their best, offer serious government. A direct clash on those principles would be an argument worth having, and one the country badly needs.

The Shakeout
Philip Gourevitch

The New Yorker | February 9, 2004

If it's true, as former British prime minister Harold Wilson once said, that "a week is a long time in politics," than a month constitutes an eternity—as both Howard Dean and Richard Gephardt know all too well. In December, 2003, polls had Dean leading John Kerry by a whopping 42–17 margin among likely voters in the crucial January 27 New Hampshire primary, and also showed him running neck-and-neck with Gephardt in the January 19 contest for Iowa caucus delegates, with Kerry and John Edwards lagging far behind.

On January 6, thirteen days before the Iowa contest, the New York Times *reported that Kerry was hoping for, at best, a second- or third-place finish there, as part of a "bankshot" strategy. On January 12,* Time *magazine reported that "Howard Dean leads the eight other Democrats by every measure that matters (at least until people start voting): in polls, money, organization and enthusiasm." By then, however, the races had already started to tighten. As of January 16, polls were depicting a four-way contest in Iowa, with Kerry and Edwards drawing ever-larger crowds. Kerry, who had been written off for dead just weeks earlier, was increasingly ebullient. "Do you feel the surge?" he screamed to cheering supporters.*

Still, the Iowa results were a shocker. When the dust cleared, Kerry had 38 percent of the delegates, followed by Edwards (buoyed by a surprise endorsement from the Des Moines Register) with 32. Dean was a distant third at 18 percent, while Gephardt pulled only a meager 11 percent—prompting him to quit the race two days later.

Then came the infamous Dean scream, and another thumping Kerry victory in New Hampshire, and suddenly the writing was on the wall. In this post–New Hampshire article, The New Yorker's Philip Gourevitch explores where Dean went wrong, and how Kerry emerged virtually overnight as the man who would take on George Bush in the fall. . . .

John Kerry's long, angular face has something of the abstraction of a tribal mask. The features are at once stark and exaggerated, and, with the exception of his mouth, none of the parts appear to move. The eyes are astonishingly small and, because they are also deep-set and heavily hooded, it is hard to find a direct line of sight into them. You have to draw very near Kerry to discover that his face is animated by a range of intense feeling. Of course, now that he is leading the race for the Democratic presidential nomination, it won't be as easy to get near him as it was in Iowa and New Hampshire, where he wooed voters one by one, with a patience that bordered on the stoical. And, even at close range, there is an aura of distance about him, which the deep, oratorical pitch of his voice reinforces. Even in a tête-a-tête, the rumbling formality of his diction can make him sound as if he were giving a speech. Occasionally, on the stump, during a sustained eruption of applause from his audience, a smile full of lightness and joy will break his grave composure. But his default look is unyieldingly earnest—an expression that suggests a man "seized," as a commission of inquiry might say, by matters of consequence.

Kerry, a high-toned Brahmin, is the stiffest candidate in a generally humorless Democratic-primary field. Yet his campaign rallies consistently muster a fuller and more complex emotional charge than those of his rivals. Kerry achieves the unlikely mix of coolness and passion by packing the rostrum with surrogates—friends, family members, former comrades in arms, and political pals—to whom he surrenders a good deal of his own speaking time. Kerry's rivals all have access to one or two nerve endings in their stump repertoire: Howard Dean does righteous outrage; Wesley Clark does patriotism; Richard Gephardt did working-class solidarity; John Edwards, the Party's spellbinding, stem-winding new superstar speech-maker, does the sting of injustice coupled with exuberant optimism so well you can taste the opportunity in the air. But a Kerry rally is something of a variety show: a raucous Teddy Kennedy whips up the crowd, and cracks wise about being the in-law of an Austrian bodybuilder turned Republican governor of California; Kerry's stepson, Chris Heinz, may do his Arnold impersonation, or he may express surprise at how the family has been drawn more closely together by the stresses of the campaign; Kerry's wife, Teresa Heinz Kerry, and daughters, Alexandra and Vanessa, chat easily about his presence in their lives, intimating his affectionate nature by displaying their own; and Vietnam veterans tell of their time under Kerry's command, and his continuing support long after the shooting stopped.

The high point of the Kerry road show came in Iowa, two days before the caucuses, when a man named Jim Rassmann flew into Des Moines from his home in Oregon and identified himself as a special forces veteran who had been blown off a swift boat under Kerry's command in Vietnam during "a hellacious firefight." He had survived only because Kerry, who was himself wounded, turned back under fire and pulled him out of the water. The two men had not seen each other since that brief encounter in the war, but Rassmann, a registered Republican, had suddenly decided that his savior was a good thing for the country and volunteered for his campaign. Rassmann appeared in Des Moines just before the caucuses, and at a rally there, he told the story of his rescue. Then Kerry reclaimed the mike and said, "there isn't a person in this room who wouldn't have gone back under those conditions to get a fellow American." There were a thousand people in the room, but Kerry's words made one wonder about the other candidates, and about President Bush.

Even after his upset victory in Iowa over the longtime front-runner, Howard Dean, Kerry refused to portray himself as the new man to beat. "I feel like a guy who's been on the catch-up road for a while and who's coming from behind," he told me on his campaign bus, the Real Deal Express, shortly after dusk on the eve of the New Hampshire primary. But the next night New Hampshire, too, was his. The results in these first two contests upended expectations and dramatically transformed the Democratic race. Just three weeks earlier, before any votes had been cast, Dean's lead had appeared virtually unassailable, and Kerry's candidacy seemed moribund. It is impossible to say if this abrupt shakeout was more a function of Kerry's success in winning the confidence of voters or of Dean's failure to retain it. Democrats say that what they are seeking above all this year is a candidate who can beat Bush, and while Dean, campaigning as an antiwar, anti-establishment, outsider maverick, tapped the leaderless Party's hot anger, the stolid war hero Kerry, with twenty years of experience in the foreign and domestic policy debates of the Senate, better fit the cold calculus of electability. A popular lapel button describes the scenario for many voters in Iowa and New Hampshire: "Dated Dean—Married Kerry."

Howard Dean spent much of the week between his humiliating defeat in the Iowa caucuses and his crushing rejection in New Hampshire attempting to act mild-mannered and chastened. He told *USA Today* that he had decided to go back to being himself, which made one wonder when he'd stopped and who he'd been in the meantime—on caucus night in Iowa, for instance, when he stalked the stage of the Val Air ballroom in West Des Moines, in shirt sleeves, assuring a howling throng of about a thousand followers, "We will not give up. . . . We will not quit, now or ever. We want our country back for ordinary Americans," then belting out the names of all the states he vowed to conquer on his way to the White House and letting loose his now canonical scream. He looked berserk, and sounded worse—like a man being stabbed. The incessant cycles of audio and video replay that ensued created the impression that Dean had lost Iowa because he screamed, when it was the other way around: he screamed because he lost. And what one really felt inside the Val Air ballroom that night was that the candidate and his followers—who whooped right along with him—were in shock and had not really registered the ferocity of the blow they had received.

The speed and extremity of Dean's reversal of fortune is attributable chiefly to self-inflicted wounds. At the peak of his popularity, in December and early January, Dean made a series of missteps and intemperate or impolitic statements that required retraction or clarification and repelled voters seeking the sort of plain-spoken, steady, and reliable man he professed to be. The relentless press scrutiny that comes with front-runner status also proved withering. By mid-January, with the Iowa caucuses a few days off, Joe Trippi, who was then Dean's campaign manager, complained that reporters and rival campaigns had set a tone of "Here's the attack, what's the response, here's the attack, what's the response," and, he said, "our message got lost." In fact, when it came to attack politics in Iowa, Dean gave every bit as good as he got. After all, the premise of his crusading campaign was to taunt "Washington insiders" like Kerry—and also Congressman Gephardt and Senator Edwards—as spineless, and co-opted by association with "special interests." Yet, even as Dean hammered away at this theme, he solicited establishment grandees (members of Congress, labor leaders, and figureheads such as Jimmy Carter and Al Gore) to stand beside him and smile while he scolded Washington and its fat cats.

Dean likes to call his grass-roots support base a movement to change American politics, and he clearly considers it to be something bigger and grander than a mere presidential campaign. (His ambition, in this respect, is apparently boundless: in New Hampshire, two days before the primary, I saw him address a gathering sponsored by Women for Dean where, instead of concluding his remarks as he normally does, by saying, "We want our country back," he said, "The most important thing is the human soul and we want that back.") His following, forged largely in cyberspace through online communities, had the quality of a political Internet bubble: insular and sustained by collective belief rather than by any objective external reality.

For all his invocation of Harry Truman's blunt pragmatism, Dean—with his plump Rotarian looks, and his oddly impish Dennis the Menace smile—presented himself on the stump in distinctly messianic tones. To hear the Dean team tell it, he was the only American in public life who had the guts to disagree with George Bush, the only one who criticized the war, the only one with a national health-care plan, the only one who talked about the need to cleanse Washington of the corrupting influence of special interests. "This campaign is about power," he said, and claimed that a vote for him was a vote for "the people," to whom he proposed to return that power. Lifting a line from Ralph Nader's playbook from 2000, he said, "The way to beat George Bush is to reach out to the fifty percent of Americans who quit voting because they can't tell the parties apart." Dean let stand the notion that the two parties are the same, labelling his rivals with Washington on their résumés "Bush Lite."

Joe Trippi, who was responsible for many of the most successful tactical and fund-raising innovations of the Dean campaign, as well as for many of Dean's best lines, said to me, "George Bush's view is either you're with us or you're against us. The other Democrats have said, 'O.K., let's meet partway and work with you.' We're saying, 'No, you don't get it. They say if you're not with us you're against us. They don't give you a choice. So we say, O.K., let's make this really clear: we're against you.' " Yet, in their zeal to run a revolutionary "movement to take back America" by animating the disenfranchised Democratic base rather than playing to swing voters in the center, Dean and his followers adopted the same with-us-or-against-us posture that they found so objectionable in Republicans.

Ultimately, it was not the tone so much as the substance of Dean's message that turned off his erstwhile supporters. The steep decline of his popularity in the run-up to the Iowa caucuses and the New Hampshire primary corresponded to the rise of "electability" as a chief consideration in determining Democrats' choice of a candidate. Dean's desire to reinstate all the taxes Bush has cut, including those on the middle class, might make sense, but as a campaign plank it is probably suicidal. (The other major Democratic contenders seek to repeal only the tax breaks that the Bush administration has bestowed on those who make more than $200 thousand a year.) Dean's vaunted antiwar message also failed to mobilize voters. Though he harangued Kerry, Edwards, and Gephardt for supporting the congressional resolution in October, 2002, that authorized Bush to go to war against Saddam Hussein, his claim that they "voted for the war" was effectively neutralized by their powerful critiques of the administration's unilateral invasion of Iraq. Democrats who wondered how Dean's inexperienced and at times incoherent approach to foreign policy might play if he were the Party's nominee could not help noticing that Republican Party bosses and pundits considered him easily defeatable. The editors of *The National Review* ran Dean's face on the cover of the magazine with the headline "Please Nominate This Man."

Democrats who never took to Dean celebrated his defeat as a liberation from doom. But many who dreaded the prospect of Dean as the presidential nominee also acknowledged that he had liberated the party and given it spine after the protracted period of cowed complacency following September 11, 2001. "Before Dean did his thing, the Party, the press—everyone—had this idea that it was impossible to confront Bush without looking unpatriotic," James Rubin, a former assistant secretary of state in the Clinton administration, who is now General Clark's senior foreign-policy adviser, said to me. "I give the guy full credit for restoring political opposition—well, that is, restoring normal politics—in America." And a veteran Democratic strategist who worked closely with Kerry for a time said, "I think what Dean has done is tapped into a notion of an opposition party. But no candidate yet has really created an opposition identity to stand up ideologically to the Republican Party. You haven't seen anyone out there announcing their New Deal, their New Frontier."

What Democrats who speak this way are grappling with is the fact that their party lacks cohesion, discipline, and direction. Its identity is entirely dependent on its leader, and, ever since Gore conceded the election to Bush in 2000, that means it has been a party up for grabs. As the Party chairman, Terry McAuliffe, told CNN on the morning of the Iowa caucuses, "Whoever the nominee of the Democratic Party is," that person "will become the messenger . . . and that will become the message as we head forth."

John Kerry said much the same thing. "We don't really have an opposition party in this country except during the brief period, every four years, between the nomination and the election," he told me. Richard Holbrooke, who represented the Clinton administration at the United Nations, agrees: "The primaries provide an opportunity for opposition parties to get their act together." This is especially significant when a single party controls the White House and both houses of Congress, as the Republicans do now. The Democrats, without any means to set the agenda, are not so much in opposition as in exile. So, while policy differences do matter in a primary, Kerry said, "I think people are really measuring who has shown leadership, whose vision is consistent with the fights he's picked in a lifetime, and whose vision connects to his life and to their gut." An aide to one of Kerry's rivals put it more bluntly: "The way people elect presidents is very different from how they elect other officeholders. If it was smarts or experience people are looking for, Gore would've won in a landslide. But with presidents they vote a feeling. They don't give a crap whether they like their senators. But they care whether they like their presidents. They're going to watch him on television for four years and have feelings about him every time, and they vote for someone they like and want to keep liking."

The power of personality over the fate of the Party is precisely what makes some Democrats nervous about Kerry, whose sepulchral demeanor and patrician locutions proved such an obstacle to connecting with voters until the prospect of a Dean candidacy started losing its lustre. He is plainly tougher than Gore, more sure of himself, less wooden. But outside of V.F.W. lodges he is hard-pressed to pass himself off as a man of the people, particularly in the South, a region whose support—or lack of it—has long been decisive for Democratic presidential hopefuls. "On that level, Kerry's the same as Dean, a typical Democratic implosion device: Northeast liberals, they'll just get slaughtered," a former Clinton administration adviser fretted. He believes that the Party's hope lies with Wesley Clark or John Edwards, the two southerners in the race. (An Edwards volunteer from Tennessee told me that Clark, Arkansas roots notwithstanding, wouldn't play well in the South. "We haven't had good luck with generals as President," the Tennessean said. When I remarked that in the past century that could mean only Eisenhower, he said, "Yeah, but we remember Ulysses S. Grant. Traditions in the South kind of die hard.")

Like Dean, Clark is an insurgent candidate—and, unlike Dean, he is a true outsider to both the Party, which he joined only last year, and domestic politics. When Clark declared his candidacy, last fall, he had no political experience at all. Nevertheless, he was running on his résumé as the former Supreme Allied Commander of NATO. Clark had star power, and the fundraising advantages that accompany it, but although he developed into a compelling campaign orator, when it came to spelling out his policies he was often erratic, and not infrequently seemed simply to be winging his positions as he went along. He is running as an international-affairs man, but the strongest parts of his stump speech are his riffs on faith, in which he accuses Bush of failing to practice the religion he preaches and denounces as a form of apostasy the Republican Party's exploitation of God-talk.

Clark came on the scene when Kerry appeared to be a lost cause and Dean was in his ascendancy. He presented himself as a fierce critic of the Iraq war, with the patriotic and military credentials that Dean lacks. Having entered the race late, he skipped Iowa to make his name in New Hampshire, where he assumed that he would be running as an alternative to Dean, and he was thrown off kilter when Kerry emerged as the front-runner. In the days after the New Hampshire primary, as the nomination race moved south and west, several members of Clark's staff said that they did not expect the campaign to last much longer.

Then again, one of John Edwards's advisers had told me in early January that Edwards would not survive Iowa. But, a week before the caucuses, he won the endorsement of the Des Moines *Register*, a newspaper that for several crucial weeks every four years becomes among the most influential publications on earth. All at once, after languishing near the bottom of the polls for months on end, Edwards was the candidate to reconsider in Iowa, and, as his crowds swelled from dozens to scores and then hundreds, the word went out that he was the best Democratic stump speaker anyone could remember—"better even than Clinton," James Carville declared.

Edwards's boyish ease, his smooth good looks, and his astonishing verbal agility create an aura of sunny youth that is not entirely accurate. He is, after all, a successful trial lawyer, and he is anything but happy-go-lucky. All that polished charm is in the service of a message of political reform and social justice. "We have so much work to do in this country," he begins his standard speech, and, having thus enlisted the audience as his partner, he describes an America divided by economic and racial inequality and lays out a program to fix it: education reform, a national healthcare program, economic policies to spur job growth. These are the issues all the other Democrats speak about, but Edwards seems to be talking about the lives of the people gathered around him, not just about policy. He never tires of reminding people that he is the son of a millworker, and although he went around in a suit and tie in Iowa and New Hampshire, he seemed to be at home everywhere. At town-hall meetings, Dean delivered his responses to the TV cameras; Edwards never broke eye contact with the person who had addressed him.

During a ten-minute meet-and-greet at Willy Woodburn's diner, in Cedar Rapids, Iowa, on the morning of caucus day, which was also Martin Luther King Day, Edwards hopped onto a chair, and, after speaking about the wages of segregation in the South during his boyhood, he shifted to "another issue that we don't talk about enough these days—the issue of thirty-five million Americans who are living in poverty." Edwards speaks of poverty, and the public silence that surrounds it, at every opportunity. "I know that most of these folks don't vote," he said, "but we should talk about Americans living in poverty because it is wrong. . . . In a country of our wealth it is wrong for children to go to bed hungry, for children not to have the clothes to keep them warm. It is wrong in a country of our wealth to have folks who are working full time every day, trying to provide for their families, working for minimum wage, and living in poverty. This is not the country that we want to live in." Then he said, "It's time for me and you to lift up this country again, to make the American people believe again in what is possible." He invoked the examples of Franklin Roosevelt and John Kennedy, who had come to office in times of great divisions. "I don't believe I can change this country alone," he said. "But I believe that you and I can do it together."

A few minutes later, aboard his campaign bus, Edwards told me that the issues Iowans cared most about were jobs, health care, and the American predicament in Iraq. He hadn't mentioned any of these things to the crowd at Willy Woodburn's. "I think the way for the Democratic Party to be strong and to reach out to people who feel disenfranchised, and also to bring others into the Party, is to spend more time talking about what's right and what is wrong," he said. "I started doing this awhile back just because I felt the need to do it, and there's been an enormous response to it."

Edwards has held public office for only five years, and his relative lack of experience in foreign policy—despite a seat on the Senate Intelligence Committee—is often seen as his biggest handicap in the first presidential race since September 11th. But he speaks of Iraq with as much fluency and confidence as the other candidates, advocating a Kosovo-like model, with the UN overseeing the civilian authority, and NATO providing security along the borders with Saudi Arabia and Iran, so that American forces "can concentrate on the Sunni triangle where most of the violence has occurred." Without naming any of his rivals, Edwards repudiates the isolationist sentiment that is widespread among antiwar Democrats. "I think it's a mistake for America not, first of all, to be out there addressing the threat of terrorism, the threat of the spread of weapons of mass destruction, and addressing democracy," he said. "I think America should lead. When we don't lead, there's a huge vacuum in the world. I don't agree with the way this president leads, but I think it is important for us to lead."

Edwards doesn't apologize for supporting the Iraq war resolution. Like Kerry, he understands that vote to be an essential credential for mounting an effective challenge to Bush's handling of Iraq. It allows the candidate to say: I voted to give you the authority a Commander-in-Chief needs, because that was the right and responsible thing to do in order to confront a dictator who was flouting international law, but you squandered my trust by failing to honor your own responsibility, and by rushing to war without provocation, on the basis of misleading evidence, without the support of our allies, without a proper plan for the aftermath, at a great expense of American lives, treasure, and international reputation, and now you must answer for that.

"I'm prepared to fight in the toughest way possible against George Bush," Edwards said. "I think you must be tough and make the case and hold him accountable for what he has done across multiple fronts, because he is out of touch with what's going on with the American people. But you also have to have a specific alternative about where the country needs to go. Without the second part, you're just running against him." No wonder the Bush-Cheney campaign, which has announced a strategy of depicting Democrats as carping pessimists and naysayers, is reported to be unhappy with the prospect of Edwards winding up on the ticket, even as another candidate's running mate. Some of the loudest applause for his stump speech always comes when he says, "My campaign is not based on the politics of cynicism. My campaign is based on the politics of hope."

To judge by the State of the Union address this year, President Bush must have been very nearly as surprised as Dean was by Kerry's win and Edwards's strong second-place showing in Iowa. The speech, which the White House had scheduled for the night after the caucuses, was conceived as the opening salvo of Bush's reelection campaign, and it read almost like a point-by-point dismissal of the Dean stump speech. (The Republican National Committee swiftly redirected its attention to Kerry's legislative record, and, upon finding that he has a higher approval rating than Ted Kennedy from the liberal organization Americans for Democratic Action, the RNC chairman, Ed Gillespie, quipped, "Who would have guessed it? Ted Kennedy is the conservative senator from Massachusetts.")

But if the voters of Iowa and New Hampshire are any indication of the broader national mood, the president's premature focus on Dean as his challenger may be part of a greater strategic miscalculation. While the Bush-Cheney camp wants the "war on terror" and issues of national and international security to dominate the agenda and determine the outcome of November's election, one of the clear messages of the nominating contests is that many Democratic voters are still upset with the President Bush they remember from September 10, 2001. John Kerry lists the chief concern of the voters he's met in the same order that John Edwards does, with domestic economic, social, and health issues foremost. "To get to those issues, we have to have a nominee who can address the security issue, meet the test, and get past it," Kerry said to me. "And then you can get to the critical issues regarding the quality of life, and that's where I think the election will be decided."

Of course, Kerry was talking about the presidential election. If a Democrat does win the White House in November, he may not be able to do everything he's now telling voters he means to do. After all, a Democratic strategist said to me over drinks recently, "There are five—five!—Democratic seats in the Senate up for grabs in the South. We could lose four. I think we will. And the Republicans could have a majority for thirty to forty years. Do you understand what's at stake? George Bush with no concern about reelection, a filibuster-proof Senate, a GOP able to raise a billion dollars a year, packed courts, government shrunk to whatever level they like, gerrymandered districts." A colleague of the strategist, who was a bit soberer, agreed. "This has the potential to be one of those periods in the country's history when a single party dominates for a very long time—unless we nominate the right guy."

Judy, Judy, Judy
Katha Pollitt

The Nation | February 16, 2004

Presidential candidates spend an inordinate amount of time trying to appear like average men and women—flipping pancakes, swallowing hot dogs and beer, donning hard hats, and so on. But in truth, Americans expect their candidates and their spouses to be something other than normal: The voters, and especially the media, want them to be presidential—and woe to those who don't fit the image.

Dr. Judith Steinberg, the longtime spouse of Howard Dean, is a case in point. While her husband was busy stumping for the presidency from coast to coast, she had the nerve to stay home in Vermont, caring for her patients and tending to her teenage son. In other words, living a normal life. But as The Nation's *Katha Pollitt notes, there is nothing the media scorns more than a political wife who refuses to play the role assigned to her. . . .*

I used to think we should get rid of first ladies. Plenty of countries manage without a national wife: Cherie Blair aside (and how long would Britain's answer to Hillary have lasted over here?), can you name the spouse of the man who leads France, Germany, China, Canada or Russia? And no, "Mrs. Putin" doesn't count as a correct answer. Is Lula married? What about Ariel Sharon? Is there a Mrs. General Musharraf ready with a nice cup of tea when her man comes home after walking the nuclear weapons? Do you care? The ongoing public inquest into Dr. Judith Steinberg makes me see, however, that we need first ladies: Without them, American women might actually believe that they are liberated, that modern marriage is an equal partnership, that the work they are trained for and paid to do is important whether or not they are married, and that it is socially acceptable for adult women in the year 2004 to possess distinct personalities—even quirks! Without first ladies, a woman might imagine that whether she keeps or changes her name is a private, personal choice, the way the young post-post-feminists always insist it is when they write those annoying articles explaining why they are now calling themselves Mrs. My Husband.

The attack on Dr. Judy began on the front page of the *New York Times* (you know, the ultraliberal paper) with a January 13 feature by Jodi Wilgoren, full of catty remarks about her "sensible slipper flats and no makeup or earrings" and fatuous observations from such academic eminences as Myra Gutin, "who has taught a course on first ladies at Rider University in New Jersey for 20 years." It seems that Dr. Steinberg "fits nowhere" in Professor Gutin's categorizations. Given that she counts Pat Nixon as an "emerging spokeswoman," maybe that's not such a bad thing. "The doctors Dean seem to be in need of some tips on togetherness and building a healthy political marriage," opined Maureen Dowd, a single woman who, even if she weds tomorrow, will be in a nursing home by the time she's been married for twenty-three years like the Deans. Tina Brown, another goddess of the hearth, compared Dr. Judy to mad Mrs. Rochester in *Jane Eyre*. On ABC News's *Primetime*, Diane Sawyer put both Deans on the grill, with, according to Alexander Stille, who counted for the *LA Times*, ninety negative questions out of a total of ninety-six. Blinking and nodding like a kindly nurse coaxing a lunatic off a window ledge, Sawyer acted as if she wanted to understand Dr. Judy's bizarre behavior: She keeps her maiden name professionally (just like, um, Diane Sawyer, *a k a* Mrs. Mike Nichols); she doesn't follow the day-to-day of politics (like, what, 90 percent of Americans?); she *enjoyed* getting a rhododendron from Howard for her birthday. Throughout this sexist inquisition, Dr. Steinberg remained as gentle as a fawn, polite and unassuming—herself. "I'm not a very 'thing' person," she said when Sawyer pressed too close on that all-important rhododendron. She allowed as how she was not too interested in clothes—whereupon Sawyer cut to a photo of Laura Bush, smiling placidly in a red ball gown.

I don't think Dr. Judy is weird at all. She's leading a normal, modern, middle-class-professional life. She has been married forever. She has two children. She likes camping and bike riding and picnics. She volunteers. She has work she loves, as a community physician—not, you'll note, as a cold-hearted status-obsessed selfish careerist user, as professional women are always accused of being. (Let's also note that she is not someone who was ever, even once, during her husband's twelve-year stint as governor of Vermont, accused of using her marriage to advance a friend or enrich herself or obtain special perks and privileges.) And here's another secret: Not too many women in long marriages want to spend their lives gazing rapturously at their husband for the benefit of the camera every time he opens his mouth. Vermonters liked Judy Dean—they had no problem with her low-key, independent style. But, then, if you listen to the press, you know Vermonters—they're weird, too.

I have no idea why Judith Steinberg hasn't slogged through the snow for her husband. Maybe she's nervous in public. Maybe she's busy. ("It's not something I can say, 'Oh, you take over for a month,' " she explained to Diane Sawyer. Imagine that, Tina, Diane, Maureen—a job where if you don't show up, it matters!) Maybe, like lots of Democrats, she's waiting to see if the Dean campaign has legs. It's possible she and her husband didn't understand they had left the real world for Mediaville, where it's always 1955, and thought it was no big deal if she kept working in Shelburne instead of being marched around Iowa in a power suit with a big bottle of Valium in her purse. Here's something I do know, though: Every day, this woman, about whom nobody who knows her has a mean word to say, gets up and does one of the most valuable things a human being can do on this earth: She takes care of sick people. Ordinary local people, not media princesses and princes. Is that the problem? If Judy Steinberg were a cosmetic surgeon or a diet doctor or held Botox parties after office hours, if her patients were famous, or the friends of the famous, if she could dish on the phone about Arnold Schwarzenegger and Martha Stewart, would the media cat pack think Judy Steinberg was cool?

Granted, rightly or wrongly, the media are going to take a look at the wives of the candidates, so you can argue that the Deans should have been prepared, especially given the media's dislike of Howard. This, after all, is the same media that managed to make a major scandal out of the Scream, a moment of campaign exuberance of zero importance (especially when compared with—for example!—Bush's inability to speak two consecutive unscripted sentences that are not gibberish, his refusal to read newspapers, and the fact that much of the world thinks he's a dangerous moron). But actually, it's only when a wife has her own identity that her choices are scrutinized. If Dr. Judith Steinberg was simply Judy Dean, if she spent her life doing nothing so important it couldn't be dropped to follow her husband as he followed his star, no one would question her priorities. No one thought less of Barbara Bush because she dropped out of college to get married, like those Wellesley girls in *Mona Lisa Smile*. No one reprimands Laura Bush for abandoning her career as a librarian and spending her life as her husband's den mother. No one asks

Hadassah Lieberman or Elizabeth Edwards or Gertie Clark how come they have so much free time on their hands that they can saddle up with their husbands' campaign for months, or why, if they care so much about politics, they aren't running for office themselves.

Don't you wish, just once, the questioners and pontificators would turn it around? After all, if a woman were running for president, would they expect her doctor husband to abandon his ailing patients and his high-school-age son to soften her image? *Au contraire*, they would regard such a man as a pussy-whipped wimp, a loser, very possibly even . . . weird. When Bob Dole said he'd give money to John McCain, his wife Elizabeth's rival in her brief presidential campaign in 2000, nobody called him a self-centered, disengaged, mean husband, or made much of the fact that his wife had knocked herself out for him when he ran in 1996.

What if the media tried on for size the notion that having an independent wife says something *good* about a candidate? For example, maybe, if his wife is not at his beck and call, he won't assume the sun rises because he wants to get up; maybe, if his wife has her own goals in life, her own path to tread, he won't think women were put on earth to further his ambitions; maybe, if he and his wife are true partners—which is not the same as her pouring herself into his career and his being genuinely grateful, the best-case scenario of the traditional political marriage—he may even see women as equals. Why isn't it the candidates who use their wives to further their careers with plastic smiles and cheery waves who have to squirm on *Primetime*?

Dean's poor showing in Iowa and second-place finish in New Hampshire suggest that media mud sticks. In a race with many candidates, in which the top contenders each have their pluses and minuses but are also rather close to one another politically, perception matters. Dean too "angry"? Something off about the marriage? Mrs. Dean a fruitcake? Oh, you heard that too? A lot of Democratic primary voters are looking not for the candidate they themselves like best but for the one with the best shot at beating Bush. If a candidate starts looking wounded, however unfair the attack, forget him—on to the next. The process feels a bit like rifling through the sale racks at Bloomingdale's when you have to find a fancy dress for a party given by strangers—no, no, maybe, hmmm, oh all right—but who knows, maybe out of all this second-guessing the strongest candidate, with the broadest appeal and the best organization, will ultimately emerge.

Right now, John Kerry may look like that man. But consider this: Before Dr. Judy, it was Teresa Heinz Kerry in the headlights of the *New York Times* front page. She was, John Tierney suggested, too opinionated, not fixated enough on her husband, unable to connect with the voters, off in her own world. You know, weird. There was that pesky name problem, too: Teresa Heinz? Teresa Kerry? Such a puzzle.

Rope-a-Dope
Ryan Lizza

The New Republic | May 3, 2004

Following his come-from-behind wins in Iowa and New Hampshire, Democratic presidential contender John Kerry proved to be unstoppable. Within a month, he'd sewn up the nomination—beginning on February 3, when he scored decisive victories in five out of seven states, and culminating in the Super Tuesday primaries of March 2, when Kerry racked up wins in nine out of ten states, including New York and California. That night, his last remaining rival, fellow Senator John Edwards, withdrew from the race.

Over the next two months, Kerry stayed largely out of sight as he concentrated his energy on fund-raising—pulling in $43 million in March and another $31 million in April, in part through an agressive Internet campaign. Meanwhile, the Bush team, well on its way to its own $200-million fund-raising goal, was pouring some $75 million into an unprecedented springtime ad campaign attacking the presumptive Democratic nominee. Their aim was to define Kerry early on as a flip-flopping liberal, but there was an added incentive: President Bush's approval rating had slipped below 50 percent in the polls, driven down by the steady drip of bad news from Iraq and the months of pummeling he'd taken from the Democratic candidates; and no sitting president with sub-50 percent approval ratings has ever been reelected.

In the short run, the strategy worked. Despite continuing negative news, including ex-counterterrorism advisor Richard Clarke's public trashing of the administration's anti-terror efforts, a CNN-USA Today-Gallup Poll showed Bush leading Kerry by 49 to 46 percent among registered voters at the end of March, wiping out the 50–45 edge Kerry had held after Super Tuesday. Kerry's unfavorable ratings also rose from 26 to 36 percent during this period. In this column, Ryan Lizza, campaign analyst for The New Republic, *ponders Kerry's decision to lay low while the Bush forces attacked. . . .*

When John Kerry was a swift-boat commander in Vietnam, his job was to steer his small, noisy vessel down the Mekong Delta in an attempt to draw enemy fire. As the *Boston Globe* explained in its excellent series about the candidate last June, "Kerry's mission was to wait until hidden Vietcong guerrillas started shooting, then order his men to return fire." Not surprisingly, swift-boat crewmembers were frequently shot. The commander of these operations once estimated that his men had a 75 percent chance of being killed or wounded. Kerry himself was injured three times.

Kerry's presidential campaign strategy echoes his days on that swift boat: He has spent the last eight weeks drawing enemy fire and taking hits. Consider the numbers: The Bush campaign has raised $184 million and spent $100 million of it, half of that on TV ads. "It's the most expensive and concentrated political advertising campaign we've ever seen in American politics," says Tony Corrado, a campaign finance expert at the Brookings Institution. Kerry stumbled out of his primary victory and into President Bush's sights, as vulnerable as he was in his flimsy boat taking incoming fire from the Vietcong. He had little money, and his campaign wasn't yet staffed for the general election.

Worse, the little money Kerry did have, or the money spent on his behalf by so-called 527s, did not fund what would have been the most effective commercials—those making an affirmative case for him. "Attack ads against Kerry and positive ads from Kerry should be the most powerful ads," says Mandy Grunwald, who made Bill Clinton's spots in 1992, "because Bush's positive case is known and the case against him is known." Yet the 527s have spent at least $28 million in the last two months on ads attacking Bush. And, instead of a biographical ad or positive spot in which the senator articulates his plans for the country, the gist of the Kerry campaign's advertising has been to defend him from Bush's tax-raising charge. "They are basically doing defense on taxes so far," says a top Democratic strategist.

All of which has prompted concern among Democratic strategists outside the Kerry campaign. Some blame the strained relationship between Kerry's ad-makers that led to the recent departure of former adman Jim Margolis. Others blame the memory of the last Massachusetts Democrat to win his party's nomination. "One theory is that the Kerry people are obsessed with [Michael] Dukakis," says the strategist. "They are fighting the last war—rapid response above all else."

But, whatever the explanation, the Kerry strategy may not be so bizarre. Indeed, after absorbing the full brunt of Bush's most concentrated attack for eight weeks, the race is essentially tied. And that is before Kerry has really started to return his fire. When I asked one of Kerry's most influential advisers about the criticism of the campaign's decision to lay low through March and April, he sharply dismissed the complaints and pointed out that just because Kerry has been almost invisible over the last eight weeks doesn't mean the campaign hasn't been doing anything. He pointed to the Iowa caucuses, where the campaign quietly laid the groundwork for victory even as the press dismissed Kerry as a goner and hinted at a similar effort this time around. "I'm not paying attention to you guys anymore," he said.

So what has Kerry been doing in the weeks since clinching the nomination? Raising money—more money than any presidential candidate, Democrat or Republican, has ever raised in a single quarter. While Bush burned through over $50 million in the last two months, almost one-third of the total he has raised, Kerry banked $55 million.

The Bush strategy was to use the ad blitz to put the race away by the end of April. But Kerry's money has exposed several flaws in the Bush campaign's assumptions about the race. First of all, the White House originally assumed that a bloody Democratic primary would force the eventual nominee to spend so much money that he would be hemmed in by restrictive spending caps that come with taking federal dollars. But, following Howard Dean's lead, Kerry opted out of that system and its rules for the primaries.

More important, the White House assumed the Democratic nominee would simply have no money to spend. But, within 48 hours of Super Tuesday, March 2, Kerry raised $4.6 million online. The money never stopped pouring in. Kerry raised $42.8 million in March alone, fueled by 200,000 individual online donations. "That allowed us to bridge the gap as we got into the traditional fund-raising," says Michael Meehan, a senior Kerry aide. On March 29, Kerry pivoted to wealthier donors and embarked on a monthlong fund-raising tour to hit up $2,000-check-writers in 20 cities. As Tad Devine, a senior Kerry strategist, pointed out in an April 21 call with reporters, Al Gore had just $9 million to spend from Super Tuesday to the convention. John Kerry will have about $100 million.

But, instead of spending this money as it came in, the Kerry campaign made a decision to absorb Bush's blows and to rely on the effects of the 527s and the negative news from Richard Clarke, Iraq, and the 9/11 Commission. This decision may be remembered as the most brilliant move of the campaign or the one that cost Kerry the presidency. It is a large-scale version of rope-a-dope—allow your opponent to unload with his most powerful punches as you hunker down and bide your time, waiting to unload in the next round, once the other guy has spent himself. If it works, it will partly be because Bush was hit with a blizzard of bad news that overlapped precisely with his anti-Kerry advertising schedule. "[Bob] Shrum was lucky, not good," says one Democratic strategist, speaking of Kerry's senior adviser. "I wouldn't want to plan my presidential election strategy around the machinations of some wacko Iraqi cleric and the Simon and Schuster publication schedule, but those are the only things keeping this 'don't shoot until you see the whites of their eyes' gambit plausible."

Still, the implications of Kerry's decision to sit on his fund-raising haul are profound. Most important, Bush's greatest mechanical advantage—his war chest—is no longer a top concern for Kerry. On March 1, Kerry had $2.4 million in the bank and Bush had $110 million. By the end of April, a rough educated guess, based on how both candidates are raising and spending money, would put Kerry's cash on hand at about $60 million and Bush's at about $75 million. But Bush may actually be at a disadvantage. First of all, Kerry will continue to be supplemented by the millions of dollars the 527s will still be spending for him. And Bush's money has to last a month longer than Kerry's. Once each candidate is officially nominated at his respective convention, he can no longer use the money he has been raising for the last year. Bush and Kerry plan on abiding by the federal financing rules and will run their general election campaigns with the $75 million check the government will hand over on the fourth night of each convention. Kerry gets his check on July 29. But, because Bush scheduled the Republican Convention in late August and early September, partly to push it closer to the third anniversary of September 11, the president doesn't get his money until September 2. It is conceivable that, in the three months before the Democratic Convention in Boston, Kerry will spend more on advertising than Bush. "In May, June, and July, Kerry should be spending about $4.4 million a week," says a Democratic strategist. "That's what Bush is spending now. And that doesn't include the outside groups." Compounding the problem for Bush is the fact that during the Olympics, in August, advertising prices across the TV spectrum will rise dramatically. (The flip side of this, of course, is that Bush will have just two months to spend his $75 million after the convention, while Kerry will have to stretch the same amount over three months.)

On Wednesday, Kerry finally began his counterattack and released two new ads. One shows him standing in a formal living room in front of an American flag, speaking directly into the camera while patriotic music plays softly. He talks about his "clear national priorities for America," security, jobs, health care, and education. In a second, similar ad, he talks about Iraq. Aides say the ads are mostly an attempt to make Kerry look "presidential," which Mike Donilon, the partner in Shrum's firm who made the ads, says "is typically a very high hurdle for challengers to get over." The Bush campaign immediately responded with its toughest spot of the campaign, an ad called "Doublespeak" that features quotes from biting newspaper editorials criticizing Kerry. The basic strategies are simple and unlikely to change for a long time. Bush knows he is vulnerable to defeat, so he must disqualify Kerry as an acceptable alternative to the majority of voters who want a change. Kerry must finally define himself as a potential president for those same voters.

The old conventional wisdom was that all this had to be done in the early spring. Kerry has bet his campaign on the fact that it can be done this summer. "We made a decision to parry," says Devine, speaking of Kerry's March and April lull, "and now we have begun our thrust." Of course, it could be too late.

Unsafe on Any Ballot
Christopher Hitchens

Vanity Fair | May 2004

On February 22, 2004, consumer activist Ralph Nader drew condemnation from across the liberal-to-moderate political spectrum by announcing that he was once again running for president. Many Democrats are convinced that the 97,000 votes Nader got in Florida in 2000 were responsible for George Bush's 537-vote win over Al Gore in that state—this based on poll data showing that Nader took twice as many votes from Gore as he did from Bush.

Kerry supporters are banking on the expectation that Nader will receive far less support this November than the 2,880,000 votes (2.7 percent of the total) he got in 2000. For one thing, he won't be on the Green Party's ballot line in this election. Also, many progressives who backed Nader in 2000 have vocally opposed his decision to run again. Stung by three years of Bush policies, the political left has made electing a Democrat their top priority; many liberals are angry and disappointed in Nader's continuing

insistence that there's little difference between the two major parties, and in his will-
ingness to play the spoiler role again.

In this essay, Christopher Hitchens offers his own take on what's driving Nader to
run again, and reports on the strange bedfellows he's keeping company with this time
around. . . .

For me, it was all over as soon as it began. The day after he announced himself as a candidate for president on *Meet the Press*, Ralph Nader held a press
conference at which he said, "I think this may be the only candidacy in our
memory that is opposed overwhelmingly by people who agree with us on the
issues."

Hold it right there, Ralph. First, don't you realize that politicians who start
to refer to themselves in the plural, as in the royal "we," are often manifesting
an alarming symptom? (Mrs. Margaret Thatcher started to employ this dis-
tressing locution shortly before the members of her own Cabinet began to stir
nervously and finally decided to call for the men in white coats.) Second, if by
"we" and "us" you really meant to say yourself and your allies in this enterprise,
then you should not complain if it's pointed out who those allies actually turn
out to be. Third, by stating that your campaign is "opposed overwhelmingly by
people who agree with us on the issues," do you mean to imply the corollary,
which is that you will appeal to those who *don't* agree with you on the issues?

Nader's answer to that third question, astonishingly enough, does appear
to be in the affirmative, since he had told Tim Russert just the day before that
he expected to reap votes from "conservatives who are furious with Bush over
the deficit," as well as "liberal Republicans who see their party taken away
from them." The job of reconciling these opposed factions of the GOP will
be hard enough for Bush himself. But the idea that either group would rally
to a Nader banner, this year or any other, is a non sequitur of hallucinatory
proportions.

The psychedelic effect is only intensified when one examines the forces that
might allow Nader to speak in the plural. A short while before announcing his
candidacy, he had been the featured attraction at a conference of third-party
"independents" in Bedford, New Hampshire. The word "independent" can conceal more than it reveals, as anyone with any savvy in American "alternative"
politics can tell you, but in this case it only barely masked the influence of Fred

Newman, Leonora Fulani, and the former New Alliance Party (NAP), whose latest front organized the New Hampshire hootenanny.

Not to mince words, the Newman-Fulani group is a fascistic zombie cult outfit, based on the eternal principle that it is a finer and nobler thing for the members to transfer their liquid assets to the leadership. It's where you would turn when you had exhausted all the possibilities of a better life with Lyndon LaRouche, or Jim Jones, or any of the other alliterative crackpot or quasi-redemptive formations (KKK, AA . . .).

The Newman-Fulani faction is protean and sinister in one way, and pathetically obvious and transparent in another. In New York City, for example, it sometimes calls itself the Independence Party, which also controlled the rump and letterhead of the Reform Party—Ross Perot's gift to American pluralism. Indeed, Leonora Fulani, a black woman who, like her mentor Fred Newman, professes to be a shrink of some sort, was a prominent co-chair of Pat Buchanan's Reform Party candidacy in 2000. That must have made a soothing change from being a Louis Farrakhan fan in her two presidential election bids. "Try anything once" would seem to be the motto here. And now she's endorsing Ralph Nader. "I think it's pretty cool," she breathes. "I think Nader is a distinguished independent and he needs to be supported." A fabulous detail about Fulani, incidentally, is the hold that she seems to exert on the cast of *The Sopranos*. Dominic Chianese, who plays Uncle Junior, is a regular at the All Star Project, co-founded by Fulani and Newman, which puts on Newman's unwatchable dramas, and has taken along other members of the team, including James Gandolfini, for photo ops. Analyze *that*, if you dare.

Am I asserting guilt by association here? After all, a candidate needn't necessarily be judged by his disciples. And at "third party" events in previous campaigns there was certainly a fair sprinkling of people with propeller beanies, the fillings in their teeth wired for instant Martian dial up access. (You get these people at mainstream gatherings, also; be in no doubt of it.) No, the difference in this case is that the Newman-Fulani cult more or less is the Nader campaign. Through its network of shell organizations and front groups, and given its batteries of living-dead petition-drive robot-artists, it has arrived at the point where it can at least guarantee ballot access in many, many states. All you have to do is agree to run on its ballot line. Even Michael Bloomberg, princeling of opportunists, was willing to take out this Newman-Fulani insurance in his campaign for mayor. This, you may say, is partly the fault of restrictive ballot access laws, riveted into place by the Democratic-Republican duopoly in many jurisdictions—an offense to the spirit and letter of the United States Constitution. But Nader kept people guessing, in a rather irritating way, about whether he would run at all or whether he might deign again to accept the Green Party nomination (which he has suddenly decided he won't anymore). So, having come down from his Sinai, he finds it's the loonies or nothing. Is this politics? And if it is, is it clean politics? Does it "empower" the average voter, who is so often taken for a ride by the party machines, or does it empower clusters of well-financed, marginal nut-bags with whom, behind closed doors, the party machines can and do frequently make deals?

Nothing is more difficult to write than a "more in sorrow than in anger" letter. Sentimentality swirls around your feet like a swamp, tempting you to become even more moist and runny yourself. But if this were an open letter to Ralph Nader, it would begin by being genuinely soft. We don't have enough heroes. (We have replaced them with "role models" and don't even know what we have lost.) We do not have many candidates of whom it could be said that, if they were caught on video seeming to accept a bribe or kickback, we would automatically assume that the video had been faked. Washington, as a community, and Washington, as a federal city, would be a very much worse place without Ralph Nader. He stood up against the rotten bureaucracy and mayoralty of the town itself, while unsettling the folks who live on Capitol Hill. Some of the story is known by everyone, including people who have never heard Nader's name. The exploding car that the manufacturers lied about; the lead in the water; the nonregulation of the meat and mining industries. It really wouldn't be too much to say that there are many people now living who would be dead without Ralph. It certainly wouldn't be too much to say that successive generations of reforming lawyers and legislators got their start and their continuing encouragement from him.

In writing, about him, therefore, one need not declare an interest. "Sea-green incorruptible" was Carlyle's sardonic description of Robespierre, but it recurs to my mind as an almost frighteningly apt phrase, in this case. Why frightening? Well, I first met Nader 22 years ago, when he took me to lunch on my arrival as a columnist in Washington. We had what I thought was a great time, and he later telephoned to say that he was worried, about my smoking. He would, he said with perfect gravity, pay me the oddly exact figure of four and a half thousand dollars, and cover any therapy bills I might incur, if I would quit the habit and thus save myself for the nation (or *The Nation*, as he may possibly have thought of it). On every occasion that we have met since, he has renewed this offer, adjusted for inflation and other variables. I once really needed the money, and considered calling him up and claiming to have sworn off, before realizing that the very idea of exploiting his innocence and concern was profane.

Of course, there is something paternalistic in such a gesture (if he could be the father I never had, I could be among the many, many children that he never had). Indeed, his whole crusade for greater "safety" and regulation could be described as paternal in character. And a slight secret about Ralph Nader is the extent of his conservatism. The last time I saw him up close, he was the guest at Grover Norquist's now famous "Wednesday Morning" gathering, where Washington's disparate conservative groups meet—by invitation only, and off the record—under one ceiling. He gave them a sincere talking-to, pointing out that their favorite system—free-market capitalism—was undermining their professedly favorite values. I remember particularly how he listed the businessmen who make money by piping cable porn into hotel rooms. (He rolled this out again on *Meet the Press*.) Nader was the only serious candidate in the last presidential election who had favored the impeachment, on moral and ethical grounds, of Bill Clinton. When asked about his stand on gay and transgender rights and all that, he responds gruffly that he isn't much interested in "gonadal politics." He has often made a united front with conservatives like Norquist, and even more right-wing individuals like Paul Weyrich, on matters such as term limits and congressional pay raises. When I asked Grover about Ralph's prospects of attracting Republicans, incidentally, he told me that he thought a Nader campaign just might appeal to some of the former Buchanan wing—anti-trade and anti-interventionist (not to forget anti-immigrant). So Nader and Buchanan might as well run for each other's votes, or skip all that and just take in each other's washing.

Nader's Puritanism and austerity—he lives in a rooming house with a shared pay phone in the hall and doesn't own a car—have been his shield since 1966, when the clever people at General Motors admitted to putting private dicks on their most scathing critic. Nader was followed, and his friends were questioned, on the assumption that an unmarried guy of Lebanese parentage must be up to something. But no: no drinks and no drugs and no carnality and no terrorism. Nader testified, a congressional subcommittee saw Bobby Kennedy trashing G.M.'s president, and an all-American star was born, one who rejected the affluent part of the American Dream.

Ralph could have gone on being an uneasy conscience for Washington, as he was all through the Nixon and Carter and Reagan years (after all, you don't need to campaign for office to do that), but he seems finally to have found a temptation he cannot resist. By running for president in 2000 and accidentally changing history, he has at last imbibed a draft of something addictive. Someone should tell him that the next bender will bring diminishing returns. In 2000, no matter how much he claimed to be above such distinctions, Nader clearly ran from the left. He also repudiated one of the center left's favorite mantras, concerning the "lesser evil," scornfully pointing out that this meant giving in to evil without a fight. In most of his speeches he maintained that he didn't care which of the two main candidates won, because it made no difference. But when pressed, he would sometimes try to have this both ways, saying that his candidacy energized liberal Democrats and even helped get out their vote. His less conspicuously intellectual supporters, such as Michael Moore, assured the faithful crowds that Bush couldn't get elected anyway, so there was no need to worry.

At that point, a certain intellectual corruption crept in. You must accept the logical and probable consequences of what you propose. Nader could not quite be honest and admit that, given the national arithmetic, he was very much more likely to help Bush than Gore. There are 10 toss-up states, with 106 electoral votes among them (and everybody now knows about the electoral college). They are Florida, Iowa, Minnesota, Missouri, Nevada, New Hampshire, Ohio, Oregon, New Mexico, and Wisconsin.

Once you understand the arithmetic, you cannot really claim that any consequences are unintended. For example, we have it on Gore's own word that if he had been elected, Saddam Hussein would still be in power. Nader is currently the only recognizable candidate who wants the United States to withdraw from Iraq. This discrepancy is not exactly a detail. It is, in fact, too big a contradiction to be explained away. But could it explain why Nader this time seems to be running from the right? He is spouting the rhetoric of social and fiscal conservatism, and pitching for allegedly disillusioned Republicans who would have nothing to be disillusioned about if he hadn't helped squeak their man past the post in the first place.

The NAP could also probably be described as a right-wing force even if, as befitted a party run by a couple of shrinks, it suffered from chronic schizophrenia. It began as a Maoist splinter group and mutated through LaRoucheism to Buchananism. Guru Fred Newman characterizes Jews as "storm troopers," and Fulani calls them "mass murderers of people of color," positions which have a nice, demented ring to them. Nader seems, to his credit, a touch sensitive on the point. When Doug Ireland, one of the country's toughest and brightest radical columnists (and a two-time Nader endorser), called attention to the unholy alliance he got a call from Ralph, who shouted at him for being "a McCarthyite bully" and repeatedly asked, about Newman, "Has he committed any *crime*?"

I had better luck when Ralph called me back late one night and nearly persuaded me to argue against myself. It's a pleasure to debate with him. But he told me, when I asked about the NAP, that "I never saw Fulani at the meeting," which I suppose could be technically true as long as he was looking away. (She was a prominent member of the platform committee.) He maintained that the Newmanites were no different, in principle, than, say, the Mountain Party in West Virginia: "They're recognized as 'on the ballot' by the Federal Election Commission, so you can 'jump on.'" He said that the Green Party wasn't going to decide until its June convention, and that it still might vote not to campaign in swing states, so there was no purpose in delaying. In the very rational and seductive tone of voice that he can bring to bear, Ralph insisted that there is no bad time at which to challenge the gerrymandering of one-party districts, the fixing and front-loading of primaries, the rigging of party conventions, and the exclusion of third-party candidates from the "presidential debates." The liberal intellectuals who take these deformities for granted and then turn on him are, as he put it, "incarnate autocrats."

And whose fault is Gore's defeat? "He slipped on 18 banana peels, of which I was only one. Anyway, he won the election, didn't he?" This is quite funny and also quite shrewd, as regards Democratic self-pity, but it shows again that tendency to have everything both ways. "I'm going to take more votes from Bush this time—no doubt about it." (By the way, at least one exit poll suggests that this was true in 2000, if only in New Hampshire.) But on the other hand, and only moments later, he says, "I'll show Kerry how to take Bush down; we'll be a free consulting firm for the Democrats; be our guest—take our issues."

Since one of the main "issues" is the pressing need to demolish the Democratic Party, my head began to swim a little, and I told him as much. He made a friendly inquiry, renewing his smoke-ending offer. We chatted about a heroic Israeli dissident we had both known. He recommended a good comrade of his who was deeply involved in the rebuilding of Afghanistan. There are not enough people like Nader running for office, even at the local level, let alone the national one. I hung up with a truly bad case of the blues.

When Nader says "corporate" he really *means* corporate, and not just Halliburton. When he says that politics should not be a "zero-sum" game, he articulates a truth. When he says that Americans ought to be able to vote "No," rather than being compelled to say "Yes," he asserts something morally important. But when he proposes to help elect a corporate Democrat by outbidding a conservative Republican, he is building a bridge from the middle of the river, and ends up not by combating the many absurdities of our electoral system but rather by illustrating them.

A Fistful of Peanuts
David Samuels

Harper's Magazine | March 2004

Did we mention that it takes a lot of money to run for president? By the end of May 2004, President Bush's reelection campaign had raised some $215 million, while John Kerry—who just five months earlier had been forced to take out a $6 million mortgage on his home to keep his campaign afloat—had banked $149 million, breaking the record for a non-incumbent set by George W. back in 2000. (All that is in addition, of course, to the $75 million in federal funds each candidate will receive at the time of their nominating conventions.) According to campaign finance laws, $2,000 is the maximum donation anyone can make to a candidate. Obviously, then, we're talking about a lot of people coughing up checks. For this article, David Samuels traveled to Houston, Texas to see how the Bush campaign gets the job done. . . .

Above the enameled plain of truck stops and diners and focus-group mills rises the latest dazed version of the quadrennial American lament: What happened?

Is George W. Bush a hero or a flop? For the one third of the American electorate that regularly votes Republican, the answer is hero. For the Democratic one third, the answer is flop. All that can be said for certain in this age
of politically motivated confusion is that the stable party structures that once
provided presidential candidates with money and votes are gone. What remains
of the old-time American electoral process is the institution of the campaign,
paid for in cash—the stage-managed process of public appearances by the candidates, and the ever more sophisticated sloganeering, the stray words or
phrases that emerge from focus groups and stick to voters' minds like lint after
being endlessly repeated on television, in phone-bank calls and direct-mail
solicitations, in what has become a more or less fully interactive process, the
thousand-and-one-fingered massage of the opinion-polled collective.

The process of reelecting a president of the United States can be understood as a single-player game like Pac-Man, the old Reagan-era arcade favorite
in which a smiley face devours a trail of luminescent yellow dots—each dot
in this case representing a bundle of $3 million or $4 million assembled by
a team of fund-raisers in a hotel banquet hall near an airport. The circuit of
fund-raising events having been set up in advance by the President's finance
team, the goal is for the bundlers to pack the rooms with $2,000 donors while
the candidate gobbles up enough campaign-funding dots to placate the pollsters and the phone-bank gods and to keep the image-makers happy while
avoiding Inky, Pinky, Blinky, and Clyde. Last year, George Bush's total of 130
million campaign dollars was more than the combined scores for Howard
Dean, John Kerry, John Edwards, Wesley Clark, and the rest of the president's
Democratic opponents, totals so puny by comparison that Democrats can
be said to have been playing Jr. Pac-Man. Individuals who write checks, out
of conviction or simply for sport, are largely irrelevant to the campaigns. We
are only pixels—fractions of a dot.

The Houston Galleria is a perfect place for the president to run up his score.
It's the best shopping mall south of Los Angeles. Actually, the Galleria is four
malls in one. The old Galleria, Houston's original luxury indoor shopping mall,
has a year-round ice-skating rink, so you can shop and skate in the middle
of July, when the temperature climbs over a hundred degrees and the humidity
is so bad that the outdoor parking offered at inferior area malls can be haz-
ardous to your breathing. In addition to the ice-skating rink and multilevel
indoor parking, the Galleria features more than 2.4 million square feet of retail
space and more than 350 fine retail establishments, including Neiman Marcus,

Macy's, Tiffany & Co., The Sharper Image, Ralph Lauren Collection, Lord & Taylor, Houston's only Nordstrom, Church's English Shoes, Gucci, Louis Vuitton for luggage, Jacadi Paris for nursery clothes, Baccarat for crystal, and a jewel-like Prada boutique, nestled inside the cashmere-soft womb of Saks Fifth Avenue.

With the new wing that opened in March 2003, the Houston Galleria became the fifth-largest mall in the nation, a temple to America's thriving addiction to shopping. The new wing employs nine types of stone and several more of wood, suspended glass balconies, plush leather seating, skylights, a Starbuck's, three premium office towers, and two Westin hotels—the Westin Oaks and the Westin Galleria—which are popular destinations for luxury-brand shoppers from Mexico City as well as for wealthy Houstonians, nearly 700 of whom have gathered this afternoon in the Westin Galleria banquet room to pay tribute to the forty-third president of the United States, George W. Bush. Houston is a city that belongs more to the president's father, George H. W. Bush, the forty-first president, who represented Houston's Seventh Congressional District between 1967 and 1971. After losing the 1992 election to Bill Clinton, Bush 41 retired to Houston, where the local airport was renamed in his honor.

"On the boats and on the planes, they're coming to America!" Neil Diamond's stentorian voice rings out.

"Today! Today! Today!"

"Oh, wow," a pretty girl in a party dress exclaims. The music is turned up so loud that most of the Sunday-afternoon crowd has no choice but to drink pretty heavily in preparation for the president's arrival, still more than an hour away. In the middle of the windowless function room, which suggests a cross between a casino floor and a concrete bunker, are three round tables decorated with an electric-lit Lone Star boot set in the middle of the canapés. The vegetable platter on each table includes a selection of freezer-burnt carrots and cauliflower, while the cheese plate offers supermarket-sliced sticks of smoked gouda and cheddar. Deep-fried items that look like egg rolls appear on closer inspection to be quesadillas; the breaded heart-attack chicken fingers are unaccompanied by dip or sauce. The high, round cocktail tables scattered around the room boast finger bowls filled with peanuts and pretzels, to alleviate the rigors of the open bar. Altogether, a dedicated scavenger working these tables might be able to put together the equivalent of the in-flight meal on a commuter flight to Phoenix. After almost an hour's worth of the open bar, barely any of the food has been touched.

• • •

Chad Sweet is a perfect candidate to be raising money for George Bush in Houston. A handsome, dark-haired young banker who works for Goldman Sachs, Chad looks like a grown-up version of one of the rich-but-decent preppy characters on Fox's nighttime teen drama *The O.C.* One thing that makes Chad a likely fund-raiser for George Bush is that his boss at Goldman, Peter Coneway, was a big Bush fundraiser in 2000. There is also the fact of Chad Sweet's name, which is almost too good to be true. The pretty girl in the party dress is Chad's sister. She is here to help Chad meet his fundraising quota. A friendly, peaceful-seeming young woman, she is wearing a maternal but sexy halter dress; she supports the war in Iraq, she says, "regardless if there were any weapons of mass destruction or not." What matters, Chad's sister explains, is that the president did something. He acted, and acted decisively, in defense of America's children and Sunday afternoons at the mall.

By the nearest pretzel table, I meet two young lawyers, Jesse and David, who work for a powerful Houston firm that represents clients in the oil and gas business. We agree that Chicago, New York, and Boston are good cities in which to watch a baseball game. I tell them that I am writing a movie about baseball, which is more or less true.

"You should try to go to a game here in Houston then," Jesse says. "The stadium is great."

"There's a retractable roof," David adds. "It's kind of cool. It can retract in five to seven minutes."

Jesse calls out to his friend Patrick Hughes, a tall, dark-haired attorney in his mid-thirties, who walks over and shakes everyone's hand.

"I'm glad I'm not the only one who wrote a check," Patrick says. "It seems like everyone I talk to says, 'Hell, no, I didn't write a check.'"

"I didn't have a choice," Jesse says. "There's a lot of muscle in my office."

"Yes, sir. We all wrote a check," David says. "I'm really getting tired of it, too."

Jesse and David don't give their last names, because the senior partner in their law firm is a major donor to the Bush reelection campaign who yearns to represent the United States as an ambassador to a foreign country. ("I think any country will do," David says.) In keeping with customary practice in recent Republican and Democratic administrations, nearly two dozen of Bush's biggest contributors, many of them only casual acquaintances of the candidate himself, received the keys to U.S. ambassadors' mansions in return for their prowess in helping the president eat more dots; Robert Jordan, senior partner in the

Houston-based law firm of Baker Botts, is the current U.S. ambassador to Saudi Arabia. The necessity for these rituals to take place in banquet halls is dictated by three decades' worth of "reform laws" that prohibit any individual from donating more than $2,000 to the political candidate of his or her choice. The result is a system in which ambassadorial hopefuls must round up bushels of checks from friends, relatives, vendors, contractors, and young attorneys who hope to make partner. In the 2000 presidential campaign, nearly 60 percent of the money that George W. Bush received came from 59,279 donations of what was then the maximum legal amount of $1,000—more than triple the number of maximum donations compiled by any competitor.

One symptom of the easier availability of $2,000 checks to the Bush campaign this time around is that fundraisers no longer receive credit for donations gathered by those they recruited, as they would in any decent incentive-based network marketing system, like Amway; they get credit only for checks that they hoover up themselves. Fund-raisers pledge to meet target amounts and are assigned a tracking number, which appears on every check they bring in to the campaign. Those seeking the campaign's highest fundraising designation, that of "Ranger," must come up with the equivalent of a hundred personal checks for $2,000 made out to "Bush-Cheney '04." Those who bring in $100,000 worth of checks are "Pioneers." There are performance incentives along the way. Those who raised at least $50,000 for the Bush campaign's kickoff dinner in Manhattan on June 23, 2003, were treated to a special off-the-record "leadership luncheon" with Karl Rove, the president's chief political strategist. By recruiting his sister, her husband, and another eight friends, co-workers, and business contacts to buy ten $2,000 tickets to this afternoon's event, Chad Sweet has earned himself a photograph with the president and the first lady in a smaller ballroom upstairs, where he is marking time right now along with the other fifty or so bundlers whose big-money contributions are represented in the ballroom below in human form.

"It's not like it was back in the eighties," explains Patrick Hughes, who works for Haynes and Boone, a Dallas-based firm with what is reputed to be the largest white-collar-defense practice in Texas. "There's been some oil and gas fallout," he adds, when I ask for signs of economic damage from the terrorist attacks, recession, and war. "Oil traders, every twenty years they go bankrupt." A fan of George Bush, he is accustomed to his lowly status as a pixel, a serf on the campaign-finance farm. "This is more than I expected," he says, when I complain about the paucity of my $2,000-a-plate spread. "I'm going to get myself a piece of that chicken."

Mixing with the plebes by the bar is Joe B. Allen III, the politically wired former senior partner of the Houston super law firm Vinson and Elkins. He left the firm after the Enron debacle. A Bush Pioneer in the last election, he is standing with a spidery, desiccated-looking lobbyist in a blue-and-white seersucker suit, a Dust Bowl vision of Uncle Sam.

"This isn't exactly our second rodeo," Allen confirms. Vinson and Elkins provided more money for George Bush during the last election cycle than any other corporate entity in Texas. "There are very few people in Houston you can point to and say these are the Bush people," he confides, over the blare of "Living in America," the James Brown number. "The key people are mostly in Midland and Dallas."

A Vinson and Elkins secretary is lurking nearby, dressed all in pink. "I do love Laura Bush," she confirms, when I ask her if she enjoys dressing like the first lady. Together we scan a small knot of ladies in pink silk suits and Hermès scarves, representatives of a spooky subterranean world where everyone loves George W. Bush, or is eager at least to score points with the boss. The secretary is understandably reluctant to give me her name. She works for partner Thomas Marinis, another lawyer for Enron.

The next donor I meet is more forthcoming. Willie Carl of Beeville, Texas, is a pleasant, moonfaced man who proudly claims to be the owner of two ranches in addition to a hunting spread and an office building downtown.

"Well, good for you!" he exclaims with real pleasure, when I tell him that I'm from New York. When I mention the effects of the summer humidity in Houston, he claps a friendly hand on my shoulder. "We have air-conditioning," he explains.

A History Channel buff, he also enjoys watching programs about current events. "I'm a Tony Blair fan," he says. "Did you get to hear that Tony Blair speech on Fox? I thought he was Patrick Henry—'Give me liberty or give me death!' " Willie Carl chuckles. "I've had two British friends, they're both dead, one died of cancer and the other flew a plane into the ground," he says in a speculative voice, as if wondering what conclusions a man in late middle age might rightfully draw about the transience of all flesh. When I ask about the absence of Stetson hats in the room, he gives me a doubtful glance.

"I've got an uncle here, he might have on his Stetson," he says. "He was probably the last guy in Houston to take off his open-road hat." He looks mournfully out at the trickle of well-dressed men and women who are now joining the crowd by the bar. "You remember LBJ's hat? Well, that's the same one. The open-road hat. There's a lot of different Stetson hats and they all have different names. I wear my Stetson when I go check on the ranch, where we have exactly two cows, which is really about all you want."

All in all, he says, George W. Bush has done America proud in the years since he was elected president.

"This kid, he's a real person. I'd give him my last dollar so he could be president for the next four years," he says. When I ask him why he isn't upstairs with the president and the first lady right now, he sighs, loud enough to make me feel bad for asking.

"I've had all I need," Willie Carl says, with maybe a touch of defiance, tucking his thumbs in his hand-tooled black leather belt. "Enough to pay for my $2,000 egg roll and live in a million-and-a-half-dollar house, paid for, and enjoy my 3,000-acre rice farm. I just don't have any money, that's all."

"Well, gang, we are doing well in Texas," says the tall, silver-haired man at the podium, Fred Meyer. His sunburnt skin glowing against his white shirt, dark suit, and blue tie, Meyer stands with an easy, aw-shucks manner before a patriotic backdrop in which the flags of the United States of America and the Lone Star Republic of Texas are given equal billing.

"In the 2000 election, it was Texas that led the nation in financial contributions to the GWB campaign," Meyer says with an easy grin. "Ladies and gentlemen, we're going to do it again in 2004."

A former captain of the Purdue Boilermakers' marching band, where he played the piccolo, Meyer is a natural master of ceremonies. His ecumenical demeanor hides the true face of one of America's most terrifyingly successful political fund-raisers, the man who transformed the Texas Republican Party from the sleepy, relatively impoverished back-office operation it was in 1988, when he took it over, to the triumphant financial and electoral juggernaut it is today, with Republicans in all twenty-nine statewide offices, including two senators, the governor and lieutenant governor, and speakers of the house and the senate. As chairman of George W. Bush's Victory 2000 campaign, Meyer directed Republican fund-raising throughout the fifty states, then he served as fund-raiser in chief for the presidential inaugural. Over the last six weeks, Meyer explains, the Bush-Cheney '04 campaign has raised more than half of the total raised during the entire eighteen months of the 2000 campaign. To Meyer's right, a sign-language interpreter spells out the symbol for financial contributions with a wide gesture of her hands, indicating the size of the Bush campaign's recent haul.

"Your money goes first and your heart goes afterwards," Meyer says, in a soothing voice. "But they're both together once your money's in the till."

Now that he has explained the facts of life to any doubtful hearts in the crowd, the former state party chair goes on the offensive, attacking "the media, trial lawyers, and various extremist groups that are constantly harassing the president and the programs that the majority of the American people support." Having tossed some red meat to the one or two die-hards in the crowd, for old time's sake, he nods benignly, looking out over the audience of secretaries, lawyers, contractors, subcontractors, and big-money fundraisers, still glowing from their $20,000 photo ops with the president and the first lady.

"Our president has integrity beyond question," he intones. "Our president does what is best for all Americans. Our president will stay the course, and he has the courage to do that. And he will again demonstrate to this country the great, strong leader that he is."

The big-money donors in the crowd this afternoon have reason to applaud. To date, 43 of the 538 known Pioneers from the 2000 campaign have been rewarded with federal appointments, including ambassadorships to France, Spain, Switzerland, the Netherlands, Portugal, New Zealand, and more than a dozen other countries, as well as positions with various government boards and commissions. Two of the 2000 Pioneers have made it into the president's Cabinet: Labor Secretary Elaine L. Chao and former Governor Tom Ridge of Pennsylvania, director of Homeland Security. Still, it would be wrong to characterize the sponsors of tonight's event as being interested merely in accumulating fancy letterhead and second and third vacation homes at taxpayer expense. They are here after bigger game. John W. Johnson of Permian Mud Service, Inc., is interested in tax laws and the regulatory structure that governs the energy business. Pat Oxford works for Bracewell and Patterson, a large Texas law firm that represents banks. Stephen Payne, a lobbyist, has plenty of clients who are interested in contracts with Halliburton or its local subsidiary, the construction firm of Kellogg, Brown and Root—lifelong backers of the last Texan president, Lyndon B. Johnson, and the recent recipient of U.S. Army contracts for services in Iraq worth a potential $7 billion. Tom Loeffler, head of the law firm of Loeffler, Jonas and Tuggey, another sponsor of today's event, knows the ins and outs of such arrangements better than anyone else in the room. As the congressman serving George W. Bush's hometown of Midland, Texas, he made friends with the president early on, sharing his interest in hunting, football, baseball, and politics. As a lobbyist, he came to represent Tom Hicks, who made George W. Bush rich by buying his shares in the Texas Rangers baseball team, a transaction that allowed Mr. Bush to run for governor. Loeffler has represented the Monsanto Company, the American Gaming Association, and the Nuclear Energy Institute, a corporate umbrella group whose members stand to profit greatly from the Bush administration's energy policies.

That the presidential photo-op crowd has come downstairs to mingle is a clear signal that the president himself will soon be on his way. As bundlers and small-time donors alike crowd the stage, I find myself next to a tall, blond, fit-looking man named Steve Papermaster, who was just upstairs with the president and who says he spent "plenty of time" at the governor's mansion in Austin.

"We love the Bushes," says Papermaster's pretty blonde wife, Kathy. "They're incredibly warm, wonderful, gracious people. I don't think that being in Washington has changed them one bit."

Once mentioned as a possible Cabinet member in Bush's administration, Papermaster never made it to Washington. Instead, as the head of Agillion, Papermaster became one of the most visible symbols of the late 1990s' tech-stock madness in Austin, spending $3 million on a 30-second advertising spot to promote his Internet company during the 2000 Super Bowl. According to a recent lawsuit filed against Agillion and Papermaster, the company succeeded in attracting only "a few dozen" customers for its services; revenues were so inconsequential, the lawsuit states, "that management never recorded a single dollar in revenue in their internal bookkeeping." Nevertheless, Papermaster spent half a million dollars to take Agillion's employees on a trip to Cabo San Lucas, Mexico, where he donned a sombrero and addressed his staff through a wireless microphone while cantering his horse along the beach. In 2001, Agillion bought another Super Bowl ad. Six months later the company filed for bankruptcy.

If Steve Papermaster is in the market for lessons about how to spend his shareholders' money, he could do worse than to look to Michael Dell, one of the sponsors of this afternoon's event. After contributing $250,000 to the Republican National Committee in 2002, Dell received a seat on the president's Export Council, as well as a $500 million contract to provide computers to the Pentagon—a two-thousand-fold return on the Austin tech entrepreneur's initial investment, for less than one tenth the cost of one of Papermaster's Super Bowl ads. Equally instructive is the story of Rich Kinder, the former president of Enron. Healthy and tan, he stands near his wife in a privileged corner by the stage, having suffered no apparent damage from his former employer's implosion—he left the company in 1996 with a $200 Swiss Army watch on his wrist and a $30 million severance package. He also took Ken Lay's personal secretary, a woman named Nancy McNeil. After divorcing his wife Anne and marrying McNeil, Kinder started buying up Enron's tangible assets, parlaying his golden parachute into three companies with a combined market capitalization of $13.5 billion.

To the high-society gossips in the crowd, this afternoon's successful fundraiser for the president is the second leg of a social trifecta that began with Nancy Kinder's successful fund-raising ball for the Houston Museum of Fine Arts last year and will conclude with the completion of the $12 million house the Kinders are building on Houston's Lazy Lane. Those with more earthy interests will note that Rich's company, Kinder Morgan, is the largest publicly traded oil- and gas-pipeline limited partnership in the United States. With 25,000 miles of pipeline and 80 terminals, Kinder Morgan moves 2 million barrels of gasoline and other petroleum products per day, and up to 7.8 billion cubic feet per day of natural gas. In a June 11, 2003, conference call with analysts and investors, Kinder laid out the current state of his business.

"The Texas pipelines have been experiencing pretty good load, that's of course a lot of hot weather in Texas," Kinder explained. "And our Rocky Mountain pipelines have been running pretty full, too."

Earlier that day, Kinder Morgan announced that it would increase its dividend 167 percent, from $.60 to $1.60 per year. The increase in the dividend made sound business sense, Kinder assured David Fleischer, an analyst at Goldman Sachs, thanks to the current occupant of the White House, who would continue to serve for the next four and a half years.

"We would expect continuous increases in the dividend on a going-forward basis," Kinder informed his fellow corporate contributor to the president's reelection campaign. "Assuming that this tax regime is in effect, and it will be, I'm sure, through 2008."

After a short intermission, Fred Meyer returns to the stage, accompanied by white-haired Houston banker Ben Love, the former chairman of Texas Commerce Bancshares (now part of J. P. Morgan Chase), and the state's governor, Rick Perry.

"It's my great honor to introduce our great friend, a strong leader, a great Texan. He's led America with a strong hand and a clear vision," Meyer says, gesturing broadly at the man to his right. Having raised $4 million the previous evening in Dallas, and then spent the night on his ranch, the president of the United States looks calm and relaxed in a dark navy suit. He's a healthy athlete at the top of his game, standing in a patch of empty space in front of the American flag. His wife, Laura, stands beside him.

"He's shown the world his commitment to—to values, and freedom," the fund-raiser offers. "Ladies and gentlemen, the president of the United States."

"First let me say, it's great to see so many familiar faces," George Bush begins, nodding at the crowd. "A couple of them scolded me when I was a kid." Nodding his head like a schoolboy at the applause, he continues with the traditional invocation. "A lot of the people in this room worked hard to see to it that I became the governor, and I want to thank you all for your continued friendship and your support," he says, allowing a little Texas grit to filter into his voice. "I want to thank you for your loyalty to our country, and I want to thank you for comin' tonight."

Editorialists don't like the president. His blunt talk, the way he stands with his legs apart, his very political DNA, inspire a fevered hatred in the one third of the electorate that can be counted on to vote Democratic, a hatred that in turn inspires a reflexive support of the president in the reliably Republican third of the electorate. Like Bill Clinton before him, his aim is to capitalize on the hatred of his foes and the support of his friends in order to win over the remaining third of the electorate. With the hatred of the left assured, and his party's core voters safely in the bank, he operates in a gravity-free state, discarding his stated dislike of nation-building and foreign adventures, his opposition to affirmative action, his preference for balanced budgets, his opposition to increased immigration, and other keystones of his carefully focus-grouped persona from the 2000 campaign. Freed from the laws of gravity, the president can decapitate unfriendly regimes, occupy foreign countries, rewrite the tax code, send astronauts to the moon and Mars if he likes, while turning a $200 billion surplus into a $500 billion deficit, buying the favor of the uncommitted middle at zero cost to his political base.

Bush makes an after-dinner joke about a recent encounter with a pair of mating elephants in Botswana. "Learned a lot more about our party's mascot," he says. As he speaks, it is possible to hear the father's clipped, East Coast Yankee accent beneath the son's Dust Bowl drawl. The president gets a laugh.

"We're going to need your help at a grass-roots level," he says, rehearsing the lines of the stump speech he will deliver another ten dozen times before the election next fall. "We're going to need you to talk to your neighbors and to send out the flyers and put up the SIGNS and turn out the VOTE."

He tunes up the Texas in his voice another notch. "And I'm gettin' ready," he says, flexing his shoulders to an appreciative laugh. "And I'm loosenin' up." The crowd laughs again. "It's a funny time for politics," the president reflects. "Right now, I'm focused on the PEOPLE's business in Washington, D.C."

Hitting the word "people" a bit too hard, the president has thrown off his rhythm. He looks mad. "We will continue to work hard to earn the confidence of all Americans by keeping this nation secure, and strong, and prosperous, and free," he recites, with a slight scowl. Her head tilted to the side, Laura Bush focuses her attention on a point somewhere out there in middle space. She has complemented her pink suit this afternoon with a silver necklace.

"I'm glad Laura is here tonight," her husband says, with an appreciative nod. "I love her a lot, and I hope she loves me a lot for dragging her out of Texas." The crowd hollers at the phony gallantry, but one look at Laura Bush's face during such moments is enough to convince even the most hardened observer of political spouses that her husband is serious—the first lady couldn't care less about healthcare policy or haute-couture dresses. Laura Bush hides in plain sight, projecting a steady beam of approval that doesn't disguise the fact that she would rather not be up here on the stage. What the first couple have in common isn't politics but rather the fact that they grew up in Midland, where their early lives were marked by death and by the excessive consumption of liquor. George W. Bush lost his sister and grew up to become an alcoholic. Laura Bush killed a high school friend in a head-on collision. Now she's the first lady and he's the president—a pair of privileged people who suffered and then cleaned up their act, a born-again Tom and Daisy Buchanan who have learned that they are no better than the lowest wretch.

The president is duly grateful. He praises Rick Perry, the tall, boyish-looking Republican standing to the president's right, as "the right guy to be governor of Texas," because he "watches the people's money very closely," and he thanks Nancy Kinder for "puttin' on this party tonight," as well as everyone else who worked so hard. Then the president turns to his left, searching out a familiar face in the crowd.

"I want to thank my friend Tom DeLay for being here," the president says, acknowledging the old Republican dragon from Sugarland, Texas. A sallow-faced former pest exterminator known as "the Hammer," DeLay is the majority leader of the U.S. House of Representatives. His latest contribution to the national debate is something called STOMP—the Strategic Task Force for the Organization and Mobilization of People, a group of specialized volunteers who, according to the congressman's website, will be deployed across the country in time for next fall's elections.

"Congressman DeLay is a leader . . . ," Bush says, his voice trailing off. What more is there to say? Tom DeLay is a nasty piece of work, the type of friend who is best kept under wraps.

"Lieutenant Governor David Dewhurst is here," Bush says, adding insult to injury by ungratefully lumping the majority leader in with a procession of state and local officials, including the Speaker of the Texas House of Representatives and Joe Nixon, a patsy for the health-care industry who was named one of the worst legislators in the state in the July 2003 issue of *Texas Monthly*.

"I came to this office to solve problems," he announces, "not to pass them on to future presidents and future generations."

Invigorated by the declarative strength of his lines, the president stands up straight behind the podium.

"Terrorists declared war on the United States of America, and war is what they got," he pronounces. "We have captured or killed many key leaders of Al Qaeda. And the rest of them know we're on their trail. . . . Those regimes chose defiance," he says, manfully resisting the urge to squint, "and those regimes ARE NO MORE."

The president nods his head in self-assent, then presses on. At the words "morale was beginning to suffer," the sign-language lady makes a sad, sinking motion with her hands.

"Fifty million people . . . once lived under tyranny. Today they live in freedom," the president proclaims, in a measured voice, leading up to the clincher. "We acted."

He leans back a bit from the podium, satisfied. In two words, he has summed up an entire political philosophy. He is the anti-Hamlet. His role is to act.

"We have twice led the United States Congress to pass historic tax relief for the American people," he says, falling back into his folksy accent. "It is not the government's money. It is the people's money. We're returning the money to the people—help 'em raise their families." His next line needs no folksy accent to go over with the crowd: "We're reducing taxes on dividends and capital gains to encourage investment." If the president's 2,600-word stump speech has earned him a record $2,700 per word over the last twenty-four hours, these are no doubt the most profitable words of the day.

"We are challenging the soft bigotry of low expectations," he says. The applause-getting line from his last campaign lands with a thud. He squints out at the crowd. Clearly no one out there gives a hoot about dismantling affirmative action anymore. "The days of acute thinking are over," he promises. Or did he say "excuse making"? Waving his hands, he summons forth "new markets for America's entrepreneurs and farmers and ranchers." Then he essays a fib so large that not even the friendliest hometown audience can possibly believe him.

"We passed a budget agreement that is helping to maintain spending discipline in Washington, D.C.," he says, bouncing on his heels for extra emphasis. The crowd is silent. Even some of the less acute thinkers in the room are aware that the budget is fundamentally out of whack. The Bush administration enacted a 6 percent increase in nonmilitary, non-homeland-defense-related government spending in 2002 and an almost 5 percent increase in 2003. By 2008 the country will be another $1.9 trillion in hock, whether we are still in Afghanistan and Iraq or not.

"Our country has had no finer vice president than Dick Cheney," the president says. The applause for the former Halliburton chief is just barely respectable, as many of the people in the audience study their shoes. No one in this room wants to end up like Dick Cheney, an angioplasty man locked away in a bunker somewhere.

"Mother may have a different thought," Bush says, after a pause, completing the punch line to the joke. Relieved, the audience gives the president his biggest laugh of the day.

"On the continent of Africa, America is now bringing the healing power of medicine to millions of men, women, and children now suffering with AIDS," he assures his friends. Shazam! It's happened again, right there on the stage. In a flash, just like Bill Clinton, the man who defeated his father, then balanced the budget, slashed welfare, and used U.S. government jets to fly business executives to China, Bush has used the opening supplied by the anger of his political enemies to morph into the opposite of the man who ran for office, busting the budget, adopting a starry-eyed program of nation-building, and saving African children from AIDS. At moments like this, when the president hits his rhetorical stride, it is interesting to contemplate the conceivable limits on his actions. A moment later the answer becomes apparent. The man can say and do whatever he wants.

"We need to cut down on the frivolous lawsuits that increase the cost of medicine," Bush offers. Pursing his lips as he lashes out against lawyers "fishing for rich settlements," the president of the United States seems weirdly angry. Putting his hand to his brow, it takes the president a moment or two to calm down. "We must be less dependent on foreign sources of energy," he suggests. It's not a bad suggestion. Then again, the Zamboni driver on the skating rink upstairs might lose his job. In the "ownership society" of the future, the president promises, every American will be "empowered" to own his or her own home, health-care plan, and personal-retirement account. What Americans must understand, the president explains, is that we alone are responsible for the decisions that we make in life.

"Absolutely," someone calls out. Encouraged by the response, Bush warms to his theme.

"It is you who is responsible for lovin' your child!

"If you're concerned about the quality of the education in the community in which you live, you're responsible for doin' somethin' about it!

"If you're a CEO in America, you have the responsibility to tell the truth to your shareholders and your employees!"

The president's voice drops like Elvis Presley's in the talking parts of "Love Me Tender."

"In responsibility society, each of us . . . ," he says, turning all heavy-lipped and pouty, "responsible for lovin' our neighbor . . . jus' like we'd like to be loved ourselves."

The message is clear: In the new America, there will be no more government sugar tit to suck on—except, of course, for the fortunate few in the audience. A young couple near the Papermasters are making out. The girl—brown-skinned, with high cheekbones, bare-shouldered in a black dress with embroidered tulips—is kissing her boyfriend, a blond, bleary-eyed preppy in a white shirt and navy linen suit, as the president praises "the vibrancy of many of the faith-based organizations and neighborhood healers that are concerned about saving lives." Although the phrase "neighborhood healers" might be unfamiliar to the well-heeled crowd at the Westin, it will surely resonate later this year with those of the president's supporters who believe in snake handlers and voodoo charms, as well as with the increasing number of Americans who lack affordable health care.

"All the tests of the last two and a half years have come to the right nation," the president says, his head up and chest thrust forward in a pigeon-toed stance, like a runner crossing the finish line.

"Abroad, we seek to lift whole nations by spreading freedom. At home, we seek to lift up lives by spreading opportunity to every corner of America," the president says. The crucial element of his pitch is the word "we." George

Bush and America are a single character, ready for action. "May God bless America," the president says.

For those not wealthy or powerful enough to merit a photograph with the president upstairs, there is always the rope line after his speech. The art of the rope-line campaign photo op requires the balance of a halfback to make it through the scrum, as well as the participation of a willing accomplice whose shutter-finger reflex is fast enough to capture the grinning donor in the two- or three-second window before the president moves on to shake the next hand. As President Bush walks the rope line, donors hurl themselves forward, grabbing for a golden handshake with the Man. "Stop pushing, stop pushing," someone says. Grinning broadly, his hair plastered across his forehead, an Indian gentleman leans over the rope at a 45-degree angle as a coworker photographs the president clasping his forearm. "Good work," the Indian man says, as he shakes the president's hand.

Halfway down the rope line, the president whips out his Sharpie. Like everything else that happens at these events, the move has been choreographed in advance by the president's handlers. In the time it takes to pose a single photograph, he can sign three or four items, suitable for framing.

Emerging from the hectic scene, those who succeeded are naturally elated. "I did feel his animal magnetism, yes," says the secretary from Vinson and Elkins. A younger black man in the crowd is also pleased. "I'm a homebuilder. I'm trying to do a little modeling and acting on the side," he explains, as we compare our experiences shaking hands with the president. I found his handshake firm and dry, with a well-timed squeeze at the end. From what I could tell, in the second and a half that I shook his hand, the president is a man in peak physical condition. He has an athlete's grip. It's a terrific handshake, the homebuilder agrees.

A middle-aged ethnic Chinese man named Morgan Lin pops out of the pile; he has brought with him a delegation from Sugarland. "I supported him as governor," he says of the president. "No better man than him."

"Look here," I say, showing him the back of my invitation to the event, on which the president has signed his name with bona fide celebrity flair.

I find Chad Sweet in a quiet corner, away from the bar. "9/11 changed everything," he says. "I was pretty active, but a moderate Democrat. Socially, I felt stronger on the Democratic side. I was pro-choice. Republicans, for the most part, they're fiscally more sound, and national-security-wise, you can't beat the

Republican Party." And yet there are things about the Republicans that puzzle him still. "Historically, the Republican Party is the party of Abraham Lincoln," Chad says. "I don't think we need Kevlar-coated bullets or automatic weapons, I'm in favor of safety locks, but people ought to be able to own a gun."

Ideologically, what Chad Sweet has in common with his newfound friends in the Republican Party is that nothing he says makes much sense. But politics isn't about coherence anymore. That the George W. Bush who exercises power today with the support of a clear majority of the American people is so radically different from the candidate who was narrowly rejected by a majority of the American electorate three years ago has a number of obvious causes—the bombing of the World Trade Center, the evil of the radical Muslim fanatics, the belligerence of the president's advisers, the inept diplomacy of Colin Powell, and the president's own obvious skill at the political game. But the bottom line, as always, is us. The pursuit of moderation and humility has never really been the American way, and, as Bush learned in 2000, it makes a poor slogan at election time. Americans are in no mood to stop driving SUVs or to give up skating at the mall in July. Chad Sweet sticks out his hand. The banquet room is almost empty. It's time to say goodbye.

Upstairs, by the skating rink, local kids in Ecko Unlimited and Phat Farm gear are watching the Zamboni circle the ice. Skating at the Polar Ice concession costs $6 if you bring your own skates, $9 if you don't. The electric bills here must be incredible. I peek into the nearby Abercrombie & Fitch, a riot of gravel-ground authentic vintage camouflage fatigues with jump straps hanging out everywhere. It's military chic, the dread-locked clerk explains. Beneath the Starbuck's is a music store called FYE, which means "For Your Entertainment." There are racks and racks of CDs by the Byrds, the Butthole Surfers, Da Brat, DJ Screw, Del Tha Funky Homosapien, and hundreds of other artists—a fact worth mentioning only because I'd never heard of FYE before I set foot in the Galleria. I ask Susan, a pretty, blonde-haired clerk who is walking the aisles, how many FYE outlets there are in America.

"I couldn't even tell you," she says, her blue eyes glazing over at having to contemplate something so vast. "I can't tell you how many there are in Texas." Behind her is a cutout of a G.I. in combat fatigues standing next to a cutout of George W. Bush. I ask her if she knew that the president was here at the Galleria today. She shakes her head no. I show her the president's signature on the back of my invitation to the $2,000-a-plate event.

She stares curiously at the back of the card.

"What does it say?"

The question catches me off guard. I look more closely at the president's signature. It comes in three distinct parts, I notice—a bold "G," the last half of the letter "W," which looks a bit like a "U," and the last two letters of Bush.

"It says 'Gush,' " I say. "Or 'Guze.' "

"Gus," she says, peering over my shoulder. "It says 'Gus.' "

"You're right," I tell her, examining my presidential souvenir in the unblinking twilight of the Galleria. "It's Gus."

National Conversation: Bush vs. Kerry

The Boston Fog Machine

David Brooks

The New York Times | March 13, 2004

One obstacle facing John Kerry is the fact that it isn't easy to get elected president from the Senate. (John Kennedy was the last sitting senator to do so, back in 1960). In part this is because senators have to cast many nuanced votes for large, complicated pieces of legislation—producing a voting record that can be readily attacked by an opponent. A perfect example is Kerry's October 2003 vote against a bill authorizing $87 billion in new funding for the Iraq conflict. Kerry favored (and had cast an early vote for) a different version of the bill that would have used a tax surcharge on the wealthy to pay for the additional cost. His "no" vote on the final bill, however, left him open to the charge that he wasn't supporting our troops. Kerry made matters worse when he was tape-recorded explaining to a veteran's group, "I actually did vote for the $87 billion, before I voted against it"—a line that the Bush campaign now uses in their campaign ads to illustrate what they feel is Kerry's biggest weakness: An over-fondness for complexity, which can give the appearance that he's trying to have it both ways on any given issue.

A related problem has been Kerry's brand of oratory, which often tends toward the kind of long-winded pontificating that senators are used to inflicting on each other. In this piece, conservative columnist David Brooks takes aim at both the style and the substance of Kerry's years in the Senate—a career that, Brooks argues, has been characterized by chronic ambiguity. . . .

The 1990s were a confusing decade. The certainties of the cold war were gone and new threats appeared. It fell to one man, John Kerry, the Human Nebula, to bring fog out of the darkness, opacity out of the confusion, bewilderment out of the void.

Kerry established himself early as the senator most likely to pierce through the superficial clarity and embrace the miasma. The Gulf War had just ended. It was time to look back for lessons learned. "There are those trying to say somehow that Democrats should be admitting they were wrong" in opposing the Gulf War resolution, Kerry noted in one Senate floor speech. But he added, "There is not a right or wrong here. There was a correctness in the president's judgment about timing. But that does not mean there was an incorrectness in the judgment other people made about timing."

For you see, Kerry continued, "Again and again and again in the debate, it was made clear that the vote of the U.S. Senate and the House on the authorization of immediate use of force on January 12 [1991] was not a vote as to whether or not force should be used."

In laying out the Kerry Doctrine—that in voting on a use-of-force resolution that is not a use-of-force resolution, the opposite of the correct answer is also the correct answer—Kerry was venturing off into the realm of Post-Cartesian Multivariate Co-Directionality that would mark so many of his major foreign policy statements.

The next crisis occurred in Somalia. Again, the U.S. Senate faced what appeared to lesser minds as a clear choice: to withdraw in the wake of U.S. casualties or not to withdraw. The oxymoronically gifted junior senator from Massachusetts perceived an equivocation between the modalities: "The choice for the United States of America is not between two alternatives only: staying in or getting out. There are many other choices in between which better reflect the aspirations and hopes of our country."

Kerry backed a policy of interventionist withdrawal, which jibed with the "third way" option embraced by President Bill Clinton himself. As Kerry noted, "I think that the president today made the right decision to try to establish a process which will maintain the capacity of our forces, protect them, and to disengage while simultaneously upholding the mission we have set out to accomplish."

The Balkan crisis emerged, and again the Congress seemed to face a tough decision, whether to authorize the use of American force. But then the Boston Fog Machine rolled in: "It is important to remember that this resolution does not authorize the use of American ground troops in Bosnia, nor does it specifically authorize the use of air or naval power. It simply associates the U.S. Senate with the current policies of this administration and of the Security Council." The vote, Kerry concluded, was over whether to associate with a process that would determine certain necessary conditions involving uncertain modalities, which must be explored, in order to reach certain desirable ends.

The Iraq problem returned in 1998, and Kerry proved again that there is no world crisis so grave it can't be addressed with a fusillade of subordinate clauses. Teams of highly trained spelunkers have descended into the darkness of the floor speech he gave on October 10, 1998, searching for meaning, though none have returned alive.

In a characteristic sentence, which admittedly sounds better in the original French, Kerry exclaimed: "We know from our largely unsuccessful attempts to enlist the cooperation of other nations, especially industrialized trading nations, in efforts to impose and enforce somewhat more ambitious standards on nations such as Iran, China, Burma and Syria, that the willingness of most other nations—including a number who are joined in the sanctions to isolate Iraq—is neither wide nor deep to join in imposing sanctions on a sovereign nation to spur it to 'clean up its act' and comport its actions with accepted international norms."

Can anyone say Churchillian?

Kerry has made clear that if he is elected president, the nation will never face a caveat shortage. He has established the foragainst method, which has enabled him to be foragainst the war in Iraq, foragainst the Patriot Act and foragainst No Child Left Behind. If you decide to vote for him this year, there would be a correctness in that judgment, but if you decide to vote for George Bush, that would also be correct.

Up Is Down
Daniel Drezner

The New Republic Online | April 28, 2004

Most pundits agree that if things improve in Iraq by this November—if the handover of sovereignty goes smoothly and the security situation takes a turn for the better—it will help George W. Bush's chances of reelection, and hurt John Kerry. In this essay, Daniel Drezner, an assistant professor of political science at the University of Chicago (he also has his own "blog" at danieldrezner.com), suggests that the exact opposite may actually be true. As long as attention is focused on Iraq rather than the economy, he reasons, voters will feel compelled to support Bush and our troops. Kerry, on the other hand, has the near-impossible task of finding a way to oppose Bush's war policy without opposing the war itself. Drezner's conclusion: "It would be in [Kerry's] political interest for the entire situation to fade from the spotlight". . . .

Most people believe that the state of Iraq come November will largely determine whether George W. Bush is reelected. A stable Iraq, this reasoning goes, helps Bush, while a chaotic, violent Iraq could doom his chances. But that bit of conventional wisdom has looked shaky in recent weeks, as Iraq has gotten worse and Bush's poll numbers have gotten better. The latest Gallup poll has Bush widening his lead over John Kerry from 4 to 6 points. A *Washington Post*/ABC News poll shows a 1-point increase in Bush's approval ratings over the past six weeks. On the question of which candidate can be trusted to handle the situation in Iraq, Bush went from being 1 point down in early March (before the Iraqi insurgency began) to being 11 points up in late April.

At this point, Kerry has to wonder whether he's in a parallel political universe. It seems neither logical nor fair that problems in Iraq should boost the president who sent U.S. troops there in the first place, while imperiling the challenger who voiced qualms about the invasion before it happened. But odd as this will sound, it's worth considering the possibility that failure in Iraq is helping Bush's reelection chances—and that immediate U.S. success in Iraq is Kerry's only chance to win.

This apparent paradox has more to do with Kerry than Bush. The *Post*/ABC poll showed that Bush's disapproval numbers on Iraq (54 percent) and terrorism (35 percent) have been climbing for the last four months, and are currently at their highest levels ever. The problem is not that Bush is unbeatable; the problem is that he seems unbeatable when compared to Kerry.

This is because Kerry is in an impossible box on Iraq. Mainstream Democrats like Kerry may have opposed going into Iraq last year, but now they're stuck with the proof of purchase. Few Democrats want to see the U.S. pull out of the country. It's worth remembering that even Howard Dean, the most vocal of the antiwar candidates, said last summer that he wanted to increase the number of U.S. troops in Iraq. Kerry's conundrum is that the politically coherent position of opposing the war both before and after the invasion is substantively unappealing. On a normal issue, if a challenger disagrees with an incumbent—and, moreover, if the incumbent's initiatives are both objectively failing and increasingly unpopular—then the challenger can simply advocate taking the opposite approach. But Iraq isn't a normal issue; there is no opposite approach (or, at least, no responsible opposite approach). There are also political considerations—Kerry is fighting a decades-old perception that the Democrats are soft on national security issues. So Kerry needs to find a way to oppose Bush on Iraq without advocating a pullout of U.S. troops. Simply reminding everyone about his prewar qualms is not doing the trick.

Kerry's response over the past month has been to try to marry his criticism on Iraq to a broader point about Bush alienating U.S. allies. For example, on *Meet the Press* last week, Kerry said in response to a question about how he would handle Iraq: "I will immediately reach out to other nations in a very different way from this administration. Within weeks of being inaugurated, I will return to the UN and I will literally, formally rejoin the community of nations and turn over a proud new chapter in America's relationship with the world." This position sounds faintly familiar—and it should, because it was the Clinton administration's policy in Somalia after Mogadishu: internationalize the problem to the United Nations as a way to reduce U.S. commitments over the long run. In 1993, the Clinton team thought that staying in Somalia another six months was sufficient to show resolve. A decade later, everyone agrees that the pullout was a mistake—even Richard Clarke pointed this out in *Against All Enemies*. As a result, this tack isn't likely to get Kerry very far.

The senator's remaining option is to run to Bush's right by demanding that more U.S. troops and firepower be dispatched to Iraq. Andrew Sullivan has suggested that this could be Kerry's Sister Souljah moment vis-à-vis the antiwar left. The senator has hinted at this position, but can't make it his full-throated battle cry without enraging segments of his Democratic base, something he can ill afford to do. Put simply: Kerry has no good political options on Iraq; it would be in his political interest for the entire situation to fade from the spotlight. The only way for that to happen is for the situation to improve.

If you think Kerry's political position is weird, consider the Bush administration's situation. Ordinarily, presidents are rewarded for doing their jobs well. In Bush's case, however, quiet in Iraq would allow Americans to focus on their pocketbooks. While the economy—and Bush's approval numbers on the issue—have rebounded from lows, the president remains far weaker on domestic issues than on international affairs. Democrats can still claim that Bush is the first president since Herbert Hoover to preside over a decline in the number of jobs. The latest Gallup poll shows a 54 percent disapproval rating on Bush's handling of the economy. Bush's best hope for reelection is for the electorate to focus on his leadership abilities—and one way for that to happen is for there to be trouble in Iraq.

Now, before conspiracy theorists start squealing with delight, this does not mean that it's in Bush's interest to purposely fail in Iraq. It's important to remember that Bush's best strategy for reelection remains to succeed both in Iraq and on the economy. That's still a possibility. But just as successes have unintended consequences, so do failures. And it seems more and more likely that one unintended consequence of a failure in Iraq could be a boost for Bush. If so, the conventional wisdom would end up being half right and dead wrong at the same time: Bush's chances for reelection might very well depend on the state of Iraq come November. Just not in the way everyone thinks.

Taking the GOP Bait, Hook, Line, and Stinker
Tina Brown

The Washington Post | April 29, 2004

As the Kerry-Bush contest began to crystallize in the spring of 2004, Democrats continued to be plagued by a general sense of worry, brought on by the underlying fear that, even if the economy and Iraq broke in their favor, Kerry and his team were neither nimble nor tough enough to counter the hardball, swing voter savvy tactics of Karl Rove and the Bush reelection machine. In this installment of her weekly Washington Post *column, Tina Brown—who is best known for her storied career as a magazine editor-in-chief, beginning at Britain's* Tatler *at age 25, and followed by high-profile stints at* Vanity Fair, The New Yorker, *and her own startup* Talk—*serves up this liberal anxiety in a handful of coconut cake. . . .*

There was a surreal moment at a serious Manhattan dinner party Tuesday night when twelve power players who had all been talking at once about the mess in Iraq suddenly fell silent to listen to the waiter. He dove in shortly after he had served the coconut cake with lemon dessert—perhaps to give moral support to the only Republican present, who was beginning to flag. Or perhaps he just thought it might be helpful for the guests to hear from one of the Ordinary Americans whose unhappiness with the status quo they are in the habit of earnestly invoking.

"I'm from the suburbs," he announced, "and I'm voting for Bush."

All eyes turned to him. "It might seem odd that a savvy New Yorker like me is voting for a guy in a cowboy hat," he went on, as he recklessly doled out ice cream to a network anchor, "but what we want is stability. This Kerry guy—he's all over the place."

Huh? Stability? What about all the mayhem in Iraq? His intervention immediately brought the table back from a troubled analysis of American options in Iraq to how the medals debacle is affecting perceptions of Kerry. It was as if the waiter was a plant from the Bush campaign, diverting attention at a critical moment, just as he was supposed to.

The Republican attack machine—again—has made the right calculation: Hit 'em with trivia. Bait the hook with the absurd "issue" of whether it was medals or ribbons that Kerry hurled over the wall when he was a 27-year-old hothead. Then watch the media bite—they'll do it every time—and let Kerry rise to it and blow it. Presto, a thrice-wounded, decorated war hero running against a president who went missing from the National Guard is suddenly muddying up his own record on the morning talk shows. Shades of 2000, when Bush jokily bowled oranges down the aisle of his campaign plane while Gore argued about whether he did or didn't say he invented the Internet.

The blueprint for what's happening now is all up there on the screen in the unapologetically partisan documentary *Bush's Brain*, about the president's political strategist Karl Rove, which opens at the Tribeca Film Festival next week. It tracks the techniques of Rove from his earliest days running Republican campaigns in Texas, using interviews on camera and off by two Texas journalists, Wayne Slater, senior political writer for the *Dallas Morning News*, and James Moore, TV reporter and producer.

"When I watch Kerry trying to swat away the issue of ribbons and medals I see Karl as the Oz figure all over again," Slater told me on the phone. "Rove's technique is always to go for a candidate's strength, not his weakness. In Texas, when Bush was running against Governor Ann Richards, her strength was her tolerance, her inclusiveness. She had brought a lot of women and minorities into government. So suddenly in conservative East Texas there was a whispering campaign about why she had hired so many lesbians and homosexuals. It's the same with Kerry. The war record is his strength—so instead of leaving it alone, Rove just goes right at it."

It's spooky to see it working, both in the polls and anecdotally. In the past 10 days, Democrats in New York have been distracted for the first time from focusing their wrath on Bush to dumping it on Kerry. Even among heavy donors there has been a wave of buyer's remorse.

"You don't have to fall in love," Hillary Rodham Clinton reportedly reproved a top Democratic fundraiser who was recently moaning about Kerry's lackluster performance as a candidate. "You just have to fall in line."

New York Dems, having raised a staggering $9 million for Kerry on his last swing through town, now want to see their money in motion. They're vexed with the campaign's sluggish response to attack. They want Kerry to quit being his own surrogate on the talk shows. They want Max Cleland, John Glenn, and Bob Kerrey to do the talking about the medals—like how he earned them in the first place. Get his old Vietnam buddies to do a commando raid on the Bush-Cheney mud machine! Get those guys to travel with him all the time in a pack in sweaty old uniforms! Democrats long to bring on a new attack dog with unimpeachable Q ratings. Unleash the scimitar chin of Eliot Spitzer!

Insiders ask whether Kerry was right to turn down an invitation to meet with Tony Blair (a real foreign leader in a real New York restaurant) in favor of trolling for swing votes in Pennsylvania. By missing the Blair photo op, Kerry booted away a presidential moment with a global player.

Micropolitics vs. macroimagery: That's the Kerry dilemma. There's a terror among the macroschool that Kerry will choose a running mate for reasons of geography rather than imagery and wind up in dullsville. A veep groundswell is building again for John Edwards. So what if he doesn't deliver a state? He has charisma. He's a jury-pleaser. He'll stay cool under fire. Choose him right now to change the subject!

Most of all there is a sense in New York that what Democrats need is someone as dark and devilish as Karl Rove to go after Bush. It's a nostalgic experience for some to dip into George Stephanopoulos's 1999 memoir of his Clinton years, *All Too Human*. There's not just a sentimental longing for George in the war room but for the villain of the book—brilliant, conniving, unscrupulous Dick Morris.

" 'This is the moment to strike and watch the poll numbers go UP!' " Stephanopoulos quotes Morris. "On that last phrase, Morris threw his hands high above his head while wiggling his fingers and standing on the tips of his toes—a political shaman casting a spell, enraptured by his own ecstatic dance." Bring back Morris?

Don't Discount the Middle

E. J. Dionne Jr.

The Washington Post | May 14, 2004

In the final column of this section, pundit E. J. Dionne takes a mid-May snapshot of the Bush-Kerry race and concludes that, contrary to the popular image of a completely polarized American electorate, there's actually a very large group of uncommitted voters—including independents and moderates of both parties—who could conceivably swing in the direction of either candidate this November. Dionne's parsing of the poll numbers also suggests that a majority of these swing votes are currently poised to break Kerry's way. . . .

The conventional wisdom on this presidential election is wrong.

It's frequently said that John Kerry is the man in trouble. Yes, Kerry does have a gift for getting in his own way. But President Bush is the candidate with big problems.

It's also said that the country is so polarized there is no moderate vote that matters. On the contrary, there is a very big middle that has shifted back and forth between Kerry and Bush over the past several months. That middle will decide this election.

That does not mean the election will be about who can successfully mouth centrist mush. The middle will move on the basis of events and also on judgments about which of these candidates can solve the problems these voters care about—Iraq, health care, education costs, jobs, and wages. The issue is problem solving, not positioning.

The polls over the past week portray a president in trouble. The most recent, the Pew Research Center survey released Wednesday, found that only 44 percent of Americans approved of Bush's handling of his job, down 14 points since early January. In a two-way contest, Kerry led Bush by 50 percent to 45 percent. Even when Ralph Nader was included as a choice, it was Kerry 46 percent, Bush 43 percent.

But the poll's details are what should trouble Bush. While Kerry and Bush have overwhelming support among their own partisans, Kerry led Bush among independents by seven points. Many other polls have shown independents moving away from Bush and holding pessimistic views of administration policy.

It's a long way to November, so it's useful to look at voters who say they are sure of where they stand. The Pew poll found 42 percent of registered voters saying they were certain they would vote for Kerry and 36 percent who were certain they'd vote for Bush. The hard core on each side is committed. Among conservative Republicans, 85 percent said they were certain for Bush. Among liberal Democrats, 90 percent were certain for Kerry.

But look at the middle. Among moderate and liberal Republicans, only 59 percent were certain for Bush. By contrast, 73 percent of moderate and conservative Democrats were certain for Kerry. And again, independents are a problem for Bush: 40 percent of them were sure for Kerry, only 32 percent sure for Bush.

Bush thus faces the prospect of substantial defections among moderate Republicans and has huge work to do among independents.

The central truth about presidential elections is that when an incumbent is on the ballot, the incumbent is the issue unless the challenger is utterly discredited. The Bush campaign has been spending its vast treasury not on making the case for the president but on trying to turn Kerry into an unacceptable alternative. While the Bush side has made some progress in denting Kerry's image, it has not been enough. Hostility to the president is such that, for now, voters are willing to take a chance on Kerry.

Bush's weakness in the middle reflects not only the failures in Iraq but also the president's abandonment of his "compassionate conservative" agenda in favor of a martial presidency that gambled all on the current war. He thereby made himself hostage to events far away.

David Winston, a Republican pollster, is passionate in arguing that up to 30 percent of voters are in play this year and that the incessant focus on each party's political base reflects a misunderstanding of who will decide this election. The uncertainties about Bush among independents and moderate Republicans and the big shifts between Bush and Kerry over the past six months suggest he's right.

As Winston notes, there is time between now and election day for the economy to grow and for the situation in Iraq to improve. And Kerry could keep playing into the stereotype the Bush campaign is creating for him. If Kerry seems to be moving toward the political center in an entirely mechanical way, the very middle to which he's appealing could come to mistrust him.

But on the current numbers, Kerry will win if he's simply good enough. Bush's task is harder: to seem a whole lot better than he does now to voters who already know him well.

Part Three:
The State of the Union

The Great Election Grab

Jeffrey Toobin

The New Yorker | December 8, 2003

Back in the spring of 2003, fifty-one Democratic members of the Texas State Assembly made national headlines when they fled en masse to Oklahoma to prevent the legislature from convening. They were attempting to stop their Republican colleagues from redrawing the state's congressional districts in their favor—something that had never before been done in mid-decade. Here, New Yorker legal correspondent Jeffrey Toobin examines the evolution of redistricting into a computerized (and highly politicized) science, and how this has led to less competitive congressional elections and a more polarized U.S. House of Representatives. One note: On May 7, 2004, the Supreme Court case on Pennsylvania gerrymandering tactics discussed below was decided in favor of the Republican defendants by a 5-4 margin. . . .

With his West Texas twang, loping swagger, and ever-present cowboy boots, Charlie Stenholm doesn't much look like or sound like anybody's idea of a victim. Since 1979, he has been the congressman for a sprawling district west of Dallas, and his votes have reflected the conservative values of the cattle, cotton, and oil country back home. He opposes abortion, fights for balanced budgets, and voted for the impeachment of President Clinton. His Web site features photographs of him carrying or firing guns. Through it all, though, Stenholm has remained a member of the Democratic Party, and for that offense he appears likely to lose his job after the next election.

Stenholm was a principal target in one of the more bizarre political dramas of recent years—the Texas redistricting struggle of 2003. Following the 2000 census, all states were obligated to redraw the boundaries of their congressional districts in line with the new population figures. In 2001, that process produced a standoff in Texas, with the Republican State Senate and the Democratic State House of Representatives unable to reach an agreement. As a result, a panel of federal judges formulated a compromise plan, which more or less replicated the current partisan balance in the state's congressional delegation: seventeen Democrats and thirteen Republicans. Then, in the 2002 elections, Republicans took control of the state house, and Tom DeLay, the Houston-area congressman who serves as House majority leader in Washington, decided to reopen the redistricting question. DeLay said that the current makeup of the congressional delegation did not reflect the state's true political orientation, so he set out to insure that it did.

"This was a fundamental change in the rules of the game," Heather Gerken, a professor at Harvard Law School, said. "The rules were, Fight it out once a decade but then let it lie for ten years. The norm was very useful, because they couldn't afford to fight this much about redistricting. Given the opportunity, that is all they will do, because it's their survival at stake. DeLay's tactic was so shocking because it got rid of this old, informal agreement." But Texas law contained no explicit prohibition on mid-decade redistricting, so the leadership of the state government, now unified in Republican hands, tried during the summer of 2003 to push through a new plan. Democrats attempted novel forms of resistance. In May, fifty-one House members fled to Oklahoma, to deprive the new leadership of a quorum; in July, a dozen senators decamped to New Mexico, for the same purpose. But defections and the passage of time weakened Democratic resolve, and, on October 13th, the plan sponsored by DeLay was passed.

"They did everything they could to bust up my political base," Stenholm told me. "They drew my farm and where I grew up into the Amarillo district, and they drew Abilene, where I live now, into the Lubbock district." As a result, Stenholm will be forced to run in one of these districts if he wants to remain in the House. The new map creates similar problems for half a dozen other incumbent Texas Democrats, so the reapportionment may add as many as seven new Republicans to the GOP majority in the House of Representatives and shift the state's delegation to 22-10 in favor of the Republicans. "Politics is a contact sport," Stenholm said. "I've been in this business twenty-five years. I will play the hand I was dealt."

In Texas and elsewhere, redistricting has transformed American politics. The framers of the Constitution created the House of Representatives to be the branch of government most responsive to changes in the public mood, but gerrymandered districts mean that most of the four hundred and thirty-five members of Congress never face seriously contested general elections. In 2002, eighty-one incumbents ran unopposed by a major party candidate. "There are now about four hundred safe seats in Congress," Richard Pildes, a professor of law at New York University, said. "The level of competitiveness has plummeted to the point where it is hard to describe the House as involving competitive elections at all these days." The House isn't just ossified; it's polarized, too. Members of the House now effectively answer only to primary voters, who represent the extreme partisan edge of both parties. As a result, collaboration and compromise between the parties have almost disappeared. The Republican advantage in the House is modest—just two hundred and twenty-nine seats to two hundred and six—but gerrymandering has made the lead close to insurmountable for the foreseeable future.

There is, it appears, just one chance to change the cycle. On December 10, the United States Supreme Court will hear arguments in a case that could alter the nature of redistricting—and, with it, modern American electoral politics. The court has long held that legislators may not discriminate on the basis of race in redistricting, but the question now before the court is whether, or to what extent, they may consider politics in defining congressional boundaries. "There is a sense of embarrassment about what has happened in American politics," Samuel Issacharoff, a professor at Columbia Law School, said. "The rules of decorum have fallen apart. Voters no longer choose members of the House; the people who draw the lines do. The court seems to think that something has to be done." The case could well become the court's most important foray into the political process since *Bush v. Gore*. As Ronald Klain, a Democratic lawyer in election-law cases, puts it, "At stake in this case is control of Congress—nothing more, nothing less."

The off-cycle timing of the Texas redistricting fight, as well as the farcical drama of the fleeing Democratic legislators, made the saga look like a colorful aberration. But the results of that altercation merely replicated what happened, after the 2000 census, in several other states where Republicans controlled the governorship and the legislature. Even in states where voters were evenly divided, the Republicans used their advantage in the state capitals to transform their congressional delegations. In Florida, the paradigmatically deadlocked state, the new district lines sent eighteen Republicans and seven Democrats to the House. In the Gore state of Michigan, which lost a seat in redistricting, the delegation went from 9-7 in favor of the Democrats to 9-6 in favor of the Republicans—even though Democratic congressional candidates received thirty-five thousand more votes than their Republican opponents in 2002. (The Michigan plan was approved on September 11, 2001, so it received little publicity.) Pennsylvania, which also went to Gore, had one of the most ruthless Republican gerrymanders, and it is the one being challenged before the Supreme Court.

After 2000, Pennsylvania lost two seats in Congress, and its legislature had to establish new district lines. Republican legislative leaders there engaged in no subterfuge; they candidly admitted that they intended to draw the lines to favor their party as much as possible. In the midst of the battle over the Pennsylvania plan, DeLay and Dennis Hastert, the Speaker of the House, sent a letter to the Pennsylvania legislators, saying, "We wish to encourage you in these efforts, as they play a crucial role in maintaining a Republican majority in the United States House of Representatives." The Republicans in Harrisburg used venerable techniques in redistricting, like "packing," "cracking," and "kidnapping." Packing concentrates one group's voters in the fewest possible districts, so they cannot influence the outcome of races in others; cracking divides a group's voters into other districts, where they will be ineffective minorities; and kidnapping places two incumbents from the same party in the same district.

Frank Mascara was kidnapped. A Democrat first elected to Congress in 1994, Mascara represented a district in the rugged industrial country south of Pittsburgh. "My district had been more or less the same for about a hundred years," Mascara told me on the porch of his house in Charleroi, which overlooks a glass-making plant on the banks of the Monongahela River. The son of a steelworker and the first member of his family to go to college, Mascara worked his way through county politics until he won his seat in the House. "A lot of people couldn't believe that a congressman lived in a house like mine," he said, noting its aluminum siding and probable resale value of about thirty-five thousand dollars. "But that's the kind of guy I am," he said. "I go to church down the street. I represent the average person."

With the Republicans in charge in Harrisburg, Mascara knew he would be little more than a spectator to the redistricting process. "I still thought my district would for the most part remain intact," he said. "That didn't occur." Mascara had met me at a McDonald's in Charleroi's ragged downtown, and then led me to his home on a quiet street called Lincoln Avenue, where we parked because he has no garage. From his porch, he pointed to our cars. "The cars are in the twelfth congressional district, and my house is in the eighteenth," he explained. "When they drew the new lines, they started in Allegheny County, which is north of here, and made, like, a finger out of that district, and the finger went down the middle of the street where I live. The line came down to my house and stopped." The Republicans' meticulous line-drawing through Charleroi was designed to force Mascara into a primary battle with his fellow-Democrat John Murtha, which it did. Murtha defeated Mascara, ending his congressional career and reducing the Democratic presence in the House by one.

The Republicans carved up Pennsylvania into many strangely shaped districts, which won monikers like the "supine seahorse" and the "upside-down Chinese dragon." Such nicknames for gerrymandered districts go back to the origin of the term, which was coined as an epithet to mock Massachusetts Governor Elbridge Gerry, who in 1811 approved an election district that was said to resemble a salamander. Like most gerrymanders throughout history, the Republicans' creation in Pennsylvania produced the desired results. Even though a Democrat, Ed Rendell, won the governorship in 2002, Republicans in that election took control of twelve of the nineteen House seats.

Democrats accomplished less in the 2000 redistricting cycle only because they controlled fewer states and thus could do less to protect their interests. DeLay's mid-cycle reapportionment may be without precedent, but Democrats have their own inglorious history of gerrymandering. Before the Texas coup this year, the most notorious redistricting operation in recent years was the one run by Representative Philip Burton, following the 1980 census in California, which transformed the Democrats' advantage in House seats there from 22-21 to 27-18. In 2002, a Democratic plan in Maryland turned that delegation from being evenly divided to a 6-2 Democratic advantage, and Georgia Democrats gained two seats in the House even though in the same election voters rejected a Democratic governor and a Democratic United States senator. In California, where Democrats also controlled the process, they settled for protecting incumbents of both parties. There, in 2002, not one of fifty general-election House challengers won even forty per cent of the total vote.

There is no doubt, though, that on balance the 2000 redistricting cycle amounted to a major victory for Republicans. Even though Al Gore and George W. Bush split the combined vote in Florida, Pennsylvania, Ohio, and Michigan, Republican control of the process meant that, after redistricting, the GOP now holds fifty-one of those states' seventy-seven House seats. "The important thing to realize was in 1991 the Republicans had control of line-drawing in a total of five congressional districts," one GOP redistricting expert told me. "In 2001, it was almost a hundred seats. Both parties made the most of it."

• • •

The transformation of congressional redistricting began long before the 2000 census, and the crucial issue was race. In the early nineteen-sixties, the Supreme Court, under Chief Justice Earl Warren, transformed American politics by enforcing the principle of one man, one vote, and requiring that all legislative districts contain the same number of people. Before these decisions, which started with the famous case of Baker v. Carr, in 1962, southern (and some northern) states had designed districts so that black voters had no meaningful say in Congress. Later in the decade, the Voting Rights Act established the principle that not only did blacks have the right to vote but they had to be placed in districts where black candidates stood a good chance of winning. The act, which was one of Lyndon B. Johnson's most important civil-rights initiatives, led to the election of many more black members of Congress—and was a classic demonstration of the law of unintended consequences.

"When the civil-rights movement started, you had a lot of white Democrats in power in the South," Bobby Scott, a congressman from Virginia who was first elected in 1992, said. "And, when these white Democrats started redistricting, they wanted to keep African-American percentages at around thirty-five or forty per cent. That was enough for the white Democrats to keep winning in these districts, but not enough to elect any black Democrats. The white Democrats called these 'influence' districts, where we could have a say in who won." But Republicans sensed an opportunity. "They came to us and said, We want these districts to be sixty percent black," Scott, who is African-American, said. "And blacks liked that idea, because it meant we elected some of our own for the first time. That's where the 'unholy alliance' came in."

The unholy alliance—between black Democrats and white Republicans—shaped redistricting during the '80s and '90s. Republicans recognized the value of concentrating black voters, who are reliable Democrats, in single districts, which are known in voting-rights parlance as "majority-minority." As Gerald Hebert, a Democratic redistricting operative and former Justice Department lawyer, puts it, "What you had was the Republicans who were in charge for every redistricting cycle at the Justice Department—'81, '91, '01. And there was a kind of thinking in the eighties and in the early nineties that if you could create a majority-minority district anywhere in the state, regardless of how it looked and what its impact was on surrounding districts, then you simply had to do it. What ended up happening was that they went out of their way to divide and conquer the Democrats." The real story of the Republican congressional landslide of 1994, many redistricting experts believe, is the disappearance of white Democratic congressmen, whose black constituents were largely absorbed into majority-minority districts.

It was a version of the unholy alliance which may doom Charlie Stenholm and his fellow Texas Democrats. All the congressmen who are likely to lose their jobs in the new DeLay plan are white. Many of their black constituents have been transferred to safe Democratic seats, where they can't harm Republicans. The unholy alliance has had the additional side effect, especially in the South, of making the Democrats the party of blacks and the Republicans the party of whites—which presents daunting long-term political problems for the Democratic Party. Many Democrats can't help but express a perverse admiration for the cleverness of the strategy. Benjamin Ginsberg, a Republican redistricting operative who helped to construct the unholy alliance during the 1990 cycle, referred to the initiative as "Project Ratfuck."

Since the 2000 cycle, these Republican gains have locked in and even expanded. To see how this was done, I asked Nathaniel Persily, a genial assistant professor of law and political science at the University of Pennsylvania, to visit my office and bring his laptop. Persily, who is thirty-three, has built a reputation as a nonpartisan expert and occasional practitioner in the field of redistricting.

Before 1990, most state legislators did their redistricting by taking off their shoes and tiptoeing with Magic Markers around large maps on the floor, marking the boundaries on overlaid acetate sheets. Use of computers in redistricting began in the nineties, and, as Persily demonstrated, it has now become a science. When Persily opened his computer, he showed me a map of Houston, detailed to the last census block. (The population of each block usually ranges from fewer than a dozen to about a thousand.) "This is the same map that DeLay's people used to redistrict," Persily said. Indeed, DeLay's political operation purchased ten copies of the software, which is called Caliper's Maptitude for Redistricting and costs about four thousand dollars per copy. The software permits mapmakers to analyze an enormous amount of data—party registration, voting patterns, ethnic makeup from census data, property-tax records, roads, railways, old district lines. "There's only one limit to the kind of information you can use in redistricting—its availability," Persily said. (In Pennsylvania, Republicans used Carnegie-Mellon University's mainframe computer, which would have allowed them to add even more data, such as real-estate transactions.)

With a few clicks, Persily changed the map from one that showed party registration in each census block to one that revealed voting results in each block. The colors ranged from dark red, for heavily Democratic votes, to dark blue, for strongly Republican. He showed voting results in about two dozen races, from president to governor and from congressman to local offices. "The whole process has got much more sophisticated," Persily went on. "Party-registration data are not the only kind of data you want to use. You want to use real election results. That's a big change from ten years ago. We have become very good at predicting how people are going to vote. People's partisanship is at a thirty-year high. If I know you voted for Gore, I am better able to predict that you are going to vote for any given Democrat in a future election."

I asked Persily to give me a demonstration of how to draw district lines. He moved his mouse to the border between two congressional districts. A ledger on the top half of the screen showed that one of the districts, as currently configured, had about forty thousand more people than the other one. "The Supreme Court has said that the requirement of one man, one vote means that each district must have exactly—exactly—the same number of people," Persily explained. An early version of the Pennsylvania plan was rejected by the courts because the districts were just nineteen voters apart, in districts of about a half million people. Requirements for that sort of precision virtually mandate the use of computers for redistricting.

Persily zeroed in even more closely, and a little donkey popped up inside one of the census blocks. "That's where the local congressman lives, a Democrat," he explained. "We have little elephants for the Republican incumbents." The program seemed easy to use, justifying the boast, on the software company's Web site, that you could "start building plans thirty minutes after opening the box." Persily chuckled. "At a certain point, you admire the video-game appeal of all this.

"There used to be a theory that gerrymandering was self-regulating," Persily explained. "The idea was that the more greedy you are in maximizing the number of districts your party can control, the more likely it is that a small shift of votes will lead you to lose a lot of districts. But it's not self-regulating anymore. The software is too good, and the partisanship is too strong."

The effects of partisan gerrymandering go well beyond the protection of incumbents and the guarantee of continued Republican control. It has also changed the kind of people who win seats in Congress and the way they behave once they arrive. Jim Leach, a moderate Republican and fourteen-term congressman from Iowa, has watched the transformation. Leach agrees with Richard Pildes on the numbers: "A little less than four hundred seats are totally safe, which means that there is competition between Democrats and Republicans only in about ten or fifteen per cent of the seats.

"So the important question is who controls the safe seats," Leach said. "Currently, about a third of the over-all population is Democrat, a third is Republican, and a third is no party. If you ask yourself some mathematical questions, what is half of a third?—one-sixth. That's who decides the nominee in each district. But only a fourth participates in primaries. What is a fourth of a sixth? A twenty-fourth. So it's one twenty-fourth of the population that controls the seat in each party.

"Then you have to ask who are those people who vote in primaries," Leach went on. "They are the real partisans, the activists, on both sides. A district that is solidly Republican is a district that is more likely to go to the more conservative side of the Republican part of the Party for candidates and platforms. Presidential candidates go to the left or the right in the primaries and then try to get back in the center. In House politics, if your district is solidly one party, your only challenge is from within that party, so you have every incentive for staying to the more extreme side of your party. If you are Republican in an all-Republican district, there is no reason to move to the center. You want to protect your base. You hear that in Congress all the time, in both parties—'We've got to appeal to our base.' It's much more likely that an incumbent will lose a primary than he will a general election. So redistricting has made Congress a more partisan, more polarized place. The American political system today is structurally geared against the center, which means that the great majority of Americans feel left out of the decision-making process."

Scholarly research gives some support to Leach's impressions. "Partisan gerrymandering skews not only the positions congressmen take but also who the candidates are in the first place," Issacharoff, of Columbia, said. "You get more ideological candidates, the people who can arouse the base of the party, because they don't have to worry about electability. It's becoming harder to get things done, whether in Congress or in state legislatures, because partisan redistricting goes on at the state level, too." Among members of the House, partisan redistricting has also bred an almost comic sense of entitlement to landslides. In a hearing on the post-2000 reapportionment in New York, Representative Benjamin Gilman, an upstate Republican, said that during the 1982 redistricting he was promised by the majority leader of the State Senate that "if I accepted that challenge of a fair-fight district, I would never again be asked or forced by the state to face that prospect of a fair fight once again. . . . I think it would be unfair not only to myself and my district to face that divisive prospect once again."

With partisan gerrymandering, House members in effect pay a penalty if they reach out too much to members of the other party. "What is laughable is the basic premise of what is going on," Charlie Stenholm, the endangered Texan, said. "The great sin I committed is that I won the last election 51-47 in a district that went 71-28 for President Bush. But I am a conservative Democrat, and that's why these people vote for me. There shouldn't be a penalty for reaching out across party lines." If Stenholm and his ilk disappear, they will be replaced by reliable Republicans—who won't have to worry about their own chances for reelection.

The question before the Supreme Court later this month is not whether partisan gerrymandering is wise but whether it is constitutional. The issues are strikingly similar to those faced by the Warren Court in the early sixties—and the stakes may be as large as well. The framers of the Constitution designed the House of Representatives to reflect the popular will. James Madison, in the Federalist Papers, said the House was meant to be a "numerous and changeable body," where the members would have "an habitual recollection of their dependence on the people." While the House was supposed to be impetuous, the Senate was intended to be stable. Madison said that senators would serve six-year terms as a defense against "the impulse of sudden and violent passions" of the House, and the members of the Senate were to be elected by state legislators, providing a further level of insulation from the popular will. (The Constitution was amended to require direct election of senators in 1913.) The Senate had to remain stable, Madison wrote, because "every new election in the states is found to change one half of the representatives."

Today, the House and the Senate have precisely flipped roles. Senate races, which are not subject to redistricting, are decided by actual voters, who do indeed change their minds with some regularity. Control of the Senate has shifted five times since the 1980s. The House, by contrast, has changed hands just once in the same period, in the Republican takeover of 1994. In 2002, only one out of twelve House elections was decided by ten or fewer percentage points, while half of the governors' and Senate races were that close. In 2002, only four House challengers defeated incumbents in the general election—

a record low in the modern era. In a real sense, the voters no longer select the members of the House of Representatives; the state legislators who design the districts do.

The question, then, is what, if anything, is unlawful about that? The legal debate on that question is especially stark. In the case now before the Supreme Court, Pennsylvania Democrats argued that the Republican gerrymander denied them equal protection of the laws, asserting in their brief that it is "unconstitutional to give a State's million Republicans control over ten seats while leaving a million Democrats with control over five." The Republican response is to say, in effect, "Welcome to the big leagues. State legislatures have always played this kind of hardball, the courts ought to stay out of the game altogether, and there's no such thing as a nonpartisan solution." Justice Sandra Day O'Connor, a former Arizona state senator herself, may have put the argument best when, in the mid-eighties, the Supreme Court last considered a political-gerrymandering case. According to Justice William Brennan's notes of the court's internal debate, O'Connor said that any legislative leader who failed to protect his party's interest in redistricting "ought to be impeached."

In that case, a challenge to the congressional-reapportionment plan in Indiana following the 1980 census, a plurality of the justices said for the first time that a partisan gerrymander might, in theory, violate the equal-protection clause. But in the 1986 decision the court ruled that the Indiana plan did not violate the Constitution. Indeed, the court said that the Constitution was not violated unless one political party was "essentially shut out of the political process." According to Heather Gerken, of Harvard, "The court set the bar so high for constitutional violations that no one has ever successfully fought a partisan gerrymander anywhere since 1986. Political parties are never totally 'shut out' of the process—they raise funds, put up candidates, make speeches. So these challenges have always lost. By taking the Pennsylvania case, the court seems to be saying that it's time to get back in the process."

The best argument for Republicans in the Pennsylvania case, it seems, is that it's simply not the court's business to scrutinize legislative maps for partisan gerrymandering. "Redistricting deals with inherently political questions," J. Bart DeLone, the senior deputy state attorney general who will argue for the case for Pennsylvania, said, "and those questions should be left to the political branches of government, where they belong, not to the courts. Then you are trying to measure things that have no standards unless you are making political judgments." Still, this is a Supreme Court that has not hesitated to tell politicians what to do. "It's an extremely confident court," Gerken said. "They second-guess Congress, states, state judges all the time. They are deeply engaged in the democratic process. I can't imagine that this is anything but an effort to pull in the reins of partisan gerrymandering."

But how? The Democrats propose a rule based, in part, on the Court's race jurisprudence. In a series of cases in the nineties which challenged some of the majority-minority districts, the Court held that it violated the Constitution for states to gerrymander congressional districts exclusively for racial reasons. "The rule now is, You can't draw ugly districts if it's purely for race," Sam Hirsch, one of the lawyers for the Pennsylvania Democrats, said. "The rule should be, You can't draw ugly districts if it's purely for politics, either." But Hirsch's adversary, DeLone, pointed out, "There is a fundamental difference between race and politics. Racial classifications are inherently suspect. If you are doing something specifically because of race, we are always going to take a hard look at it. Not only are political judgments O.K. but we expect them." Since it's been so long since the Supreme Court addressed the issue, most election-law experts see the Pennsylvania case as difficult to handicap, and the key factor may simply be how bad the justices believe the problem of partisan gerrymandering to be.

In any case, the situation appears to be getting worse, even as the Pennsylvania case has been pending. While Texas was shifting its districts, the governing Republicans in Colorado did their own mid-cycle reapportionment, to solidify their hold on the one House seat in the state that produced a close election in 2002. (Legal challenges to the new Texas and Colorado districts are now pending.) At one point, the Democrats who control Oklahoma and New Mexico threatened retaliation, but the Party lacks a DeLay-like figure to press the issue. One state that has gone its own way is Iowa, which turned redistricting over to a nonpartisan civil-service commission after the 2000 census. Consequently, four of Iowa's five House races in 2002 were competitive, so a state with one percent of the seats in the House produced ten percent of the nation's close elections. The rest of the country will follow only, it seems, if the Supreme Court requires it.

When it comes to drawing political boundaries, there never was a golden age of statesmanship. "When we Democrats controlled the legislature, sure we protected Democrats," Charlie Stenholm said. "But we didn't do harm to the Republicans who were in office. This thing today is a whole different order of magnitude." On his porch in Charleroi, Frank Mascara said the issue is a lot bigger than he is. "I'm through, I'm done, out of politics," he said. "It won't affect me one way or the other. But the system is now totally out of whack, and that matters to a lot of people. It's not about me, it's about power on a national scale."

In Search of the Elusive Swing Voter
Joshua Green

The Atlantic Monthly | January/February 2004

As of June 2003, both the Bush and Kerry campaigns had already spent tens of millions running political advertisements in key markets across the nation. One odd aspect of the 2004 presidential campaign—or any presidential campaign, for that matter— is that this advertising battle has been largely invisible to people living in uncontested states like New York, which is sure to go to Kerry this fall, or solid-for-Bush Texas. The candidates' media advisers simply don't want to waste precious ad money on a state whose electoral college votes are a foregone conclusion. If, on the other hand, you're a television viewer residing in Columbus, Ohio (one of the most heavily-contested cities in one of the most evenly-split states in the nation), you had the dubious privilege of being bombarded with an estimated 3,000 political advertisements between March and the end of June. That's an average of twenty-five per day.

In this essay, Atlantic Monthly *senior editor Joshua Green reports on the fifteen, or so, swing states that are likely to decide the outcome in November, and what the two major parties are doing to woo their undecided voters. . . .*

During the primary season we are accustomed to focusing on the drama and intrigue in a few important states such as New Hampshire and Iowa. A candidate who can win these, it is believed, is all but certain to carry the nomination. Suddenly that's less true than in years past. Because so many candidates are running, and because the contests are not winner-take-all, formerly inconsequential states such as Oklahoma, New Mexico, and even Delaware could be critical in determining who finally emerges as the next Democratic nominee. In contrast, we tend to view the general election as wide open, when in fact fewer and fewer states have determined the outcome in recent presidential elections. The reason for this is the growing polarization of the American electorate.

In fact, there is empirical evidence to suggest that this year's contest may be the most partisan in history. In the 2000 election less than 10 percent of Democrats voted for George W. Bush, and a similarly small percentage of Republicans voted for Al Gore—the lowest voter crossover ever documented. The Supreme Court's decision in *Bush v. Gore*, the Bush administration's hard-nosed tactics, and the war in Iraq have only widened this divide.

As the American electorate becomes ever more polarized, the number of undecided voters and the number of states in which the two parties will truly compete have diminished considerably. Two decades ago as much as a third of the electorate was deemed to be in play, and there were grand debates, particularly in the Democratic Party, about whether the best way to win "swing" voters was to pursue a southern strategy or to target the Rocky Mountains. "A basic postulate of American politics today," says the political demographer Mark Gersh, a Democratic strategist, "is that the swing vote is much, much smaller than it used to be." Strategists in both parties have narrowed their focus to no more than 10 percent of the electorate (some have narrowed it even further), and both parties plan to seriously contest only about fifteen states in November. This shrunken playing field, along with hardening lines in the electorate, all but guarantees a close race. That in turn limits the strategic possibilities for both parties to the point where it is possible to predict in considerable detail what the next campaign will look like—even without knowing the identity of the Democratic nominee.

There is a widespread misperception that the course of a presidential campaign flows directly from the candidate's persona. Naturally, a Howard Dean campaign would differ in style and atmospherics from one featuring Wesley Clark or John Kerry or Richard Gephardt. But with so little room to maneuver, the Democratic formula for victory will depend less than ever on the identity of the nominee. Instead it will be dictated by geographic and demographic necessity—how best to cobble together the necessary 270 electoral votes. The candidate must carry a sufficient number of swing states, and success in each one will depend on highly specific combinations of constituencies and issues—many of which can already be identified. In other words, just as the genetic blueprint for human beings and chimpanzees is 95 percent identical, the campaign blueprint for the Democratic candidates will be nearly the same, regardless of which becomes the party's nominee.

• • •

The unprecedented closeness of the 2000 presidential election has had dramatic effects on the political world, from the news media's hesitancy to call election results to the parties' renewed emphasis on voter turnout to the newfound superstition among speechwriters that they must prepare *three* versions of a candidate's election-night remarks: the dignified victory speech, the gracious concession, and a third in case the election is too close to call. To political demographers, who digest ungodly amounts of data in an effort to understand and predict the behavior of the American electorate, the 2000 contest provided a sort of Rosetta stone: a demographic snapshot of a nation in perfect balance, which has become the starting point for strategy in 2004.

All told, twelve states in the previous presidential election were decided by fewer than five percentage points. Along with two or three other states where demographic changes portend a similar closeness, they make up the battleground this year. The most significant states are scattered across the Pacific Northwest (Oregon, Washington), the Southwest (Arizona, Nevada, New Mexico), and the Rust Belt (Ohio, Pennsylvania, West Virginia), with outliers on the East Coast (Florida and New Hampshire) and others along a lengthy stretch of the Mississippi River, from Minnesota and Wisconsin down to Arkansas and Missouri. The next Democratic campaign will closely follow this map.

The Northwest

In numerical terms the most striking aspect of the 2000 election remains the number of votes Al Gore lost to Ralph Nader. "Democrats created an opening for Nader in 2000 by not taking the Green Party seriously enough until it was too late," says Doug Sosnik, a White House political director under Bill Clinton. To head off a similar catastrophe the Democratic nominee will probably begin his campaign with an early pilgrimage to the Pacific Northwest, where Green Party support is strongest, to quell a potential challenge. Such a move would not only strengthen the candidate's standing in Oregon and Washington, two states Gore won narrowly, but also provide a platform for talking about the environment—one of the few "wedge issues" available to Democrats, and an issue pollsters believe is the primary motivator for six percent of voters.

• • •

The South

The other great political truth revealed in 2000—and reinforced in 2002—is the Republicans' consolidation of the South. The long-standing axiom that the Democrats must carry southern states to win the presidency still holds sway among many political consultants, and at least partially accounts for the premium placed on southern candidates such as Wesley Clark and John Edwards. But Democratic strategists are increasingly aware that that goal has become nearly unattainable. With the exception of Florida, the South has trended away from the party. Bill Clinton's success in the 1990s was not indicative of a southern Democratic resurgence—rather, it masked this erosion. Georgia, which Clinton carried in 1992, went Republican in 1996. Arkansas, Kentucky, Louisiana, and Tennessee, which Clinton carried in both his elections, all followed suit in 2000. Thomas F. Schaller, a professor of political science at the University of Maryland, Baltimore County, warns, "Pursuing a southern strategy in 2004, instead of looking ahead to other areas, could relegate the party to minority status for years to come." Indeed, the futility of a southern strategy is tacitly acknowledged in the list of swing states that Democratic groups are planning to contest this year. Of the seventeen states targeted by America Coming Together, a coalition of liberal interest groups aimed at mobilizing Democratic voters, only Florida and Arkansas are in the South.

The Southwest

The Democrats' new area of opportunity is a swath of formerly Republican territory where an influx of Latinos and transplanted white Democrats is changing the demographic profile. Gore's lone win in this region was New Mexico, where his margin of victory was even narrower than his margin of defeat in Florida. But newly elected Democratic governors in Arizona and New Mexico and booming Hispanic populations there (25 percent and 42 percent, respectively) should persuade this year's nominee to spend considerable time and effort in the region. Nevada, too, has become a case study for Democratic optimism: although Bush carried the state in 2000, the Latino population surged by 15 percent in just the next two years; Clark County, which leans Democratic, is among the nation's fastest-growing counties; and Las Vegas, in that county, is rapidly unionizing. Furthermore, Nevada presents an enticing opportunity to raise the issue of Yucca Mountain, where President Bush recently decided to dump nuclear waste after vowing during his campaign not to do so.

Florida

Latinos, who have historically been identified with the Democratic Party, now represent an important swing vote. As it became clear in the closing weeks of the 2000 campaign that several battleground states would go down to the wire, the Republicans spent an unprecedented amount of money on Spanish-language television advertising; overall, they ended up spending more than twice as much as the Democrats. According to Adam J. Segal, the director of the Hispanic Voter Project, at Johns Hopkins University, the Bush campaign poured money into Florida media markets in particular, stoking Hispanic anger over the Clinton administration's handling of the Elián González affair—and ultimately helping to deprive Gore of the state and the election. (In contrast, Gore outspent Bush nearly three to one in New Mexico, and won.) And with some strategists believing that the 2004 election, too, could hinge on Florida—and that Florida could hinge on the heavily Hispanic I-4 corridor between Tampa and Orlando—the Democrats are sure to avoid making the same mistake again.

The Upper Midwest

The culturally cautious Rust Belt states that were a key to Bush's win have been particularly hard hit by the net loss of three million jobs since Bush took office, 2.4 million of them in the manufacturing sector. As the Democratic contenders delight in pointing out, Bush stands to become the first president since Herbert Hoover to see the country lose more jobs than it gained on his watch. Even if the economy improves, a critical component of the Democrats' regional rhetoric will be reminding voters exactly how many manufacturing jobs have been lost in states such as Michigan (127,000), Pennsylvania (132,500), and Ohio (151,800).

The Mississippi Basin

Finally, for all the ribbing it drew, Gore's four-day riverboat tour along the Mississippi after the Democratic convention is likely to be repeated in some fashion by the next Democratic nominee. Though Bush's campaign manager, Karl Rove, dismissed it at the time as a corny gimmick, he later changed his mind. By floating down the river Gore hit small, difficult-to-reach media markets in such key midwestern swing states as Minnesota, Wisconsin, Illinois, Iowa, and Missouri. (He won all but Missouri.) When Rove later sought to target some of these same areas, he discovered that no airport nearby was large enough to land the Boeing 757 that served as Bush's campaign plane. "We never got Bush there," Rove lamented afterward, and he laid the blame for Gore's narrow win in Iowa on that fact.

If the 2000 election supplied the road map for the next campaign, the 2002 midterm elections gave both parties an urgent mandate to reach swing voters. Democratic campaigns mostly outperformed their Republican counterparts in the elections of 1996, 1998, and 2000. (Gore did, after all, win more votes than any U.S. president except Reagan.) This was thanks largely to election day voter-turnout efforts, which got Democrats to the polls and often proved decisive. But in 2002 the Republicans shocked the Democrats by besting them on this front, nullifying an important edge. This has set off a pitched battle to capture the narrowing sliver of what pollsters call "persuadables"—the undecided voters who will make the difference in any close election.

In fact, it has sparked a kind of demographic arms race. For the first time, both parties are embracing sophisticated and costly demographic technology that until recently was the province of consumer market-research companies. The Democratic National Committee has acquired a database of 158 million voters it has dubbed the "DataMart." Appended to every name are as many as 306 "lifestyle variables" gleaned from voter files, consumer databases, and other sources. From these, candidates can find out a citizen's voting record, number of children, kind of car, favorite television shows and magazines, and even number of pets. Not to be outdone, the Republican National Committee has its own Orwellian construct, called the "Voter Vault," which contains records on 165 million people.

By drawing samples from the DataMart, the thinking goes, Democratic pollsters and interest groups can create intricate predictive models of where the most sought-after voters will be found. "In a crowded marketplace," the pollster Geoff Garin explains, "it's about being able to know the architecture of the people most likely to be supportive of you and seeking them out."

It is no longer enough to posit that a broad notional category such as "soccer moms" will decide an election. Advances in computer and database technology now offer infinitely more detail, promising campaign staffs the capacity to learn not only which issues matter most to a *particular* soccer mom but also her home address, the phrasing likeliest to persuade her, and when, how, and by whom she might prefer to be approached. Karen White, the political director for the pro-choice women's group Emily's List, which is working with Data-

Mart information, says, "In the past we've always tried to bring voters to us on our issues. This time we're getting so much insight into their personal lives that we can actually bring what they need to hear to them, on their terms."

The New Democrat Network, a centrist political organization, was among the first in this election cycle to use polling to sketch out a profile of the latest generation of swing voters. Data shared with each of the Democratic candidates (and provided to *The Atlantic*) describes them as mainly white and also younger, less likely to vote, and more likely than self-identified Democrats or Republicans to characterize themselves as "workaholics." They are most heavily concentrated in suburbs and small cities, and though they disapprove of many Bush administration policies, they tend to be more religious and to admire military service more than most Democrats do. "On many issues their attitudes correspond strongly with the Democratic Party even though demographically they are closer to Republican voters," says Peter Brodnitz, of the firm Penn, Schoen and Berland, which conducted the poll. The New Democrat Network identified civil liberties and the environment as the two issues on which independents and Republicans most strongly disagree—and, indeed, many of the Democratic candidates have sounded precisely these themes. (Buried in the report's "tactical recommendations" is information that both sides in the next campaign may find useful: independents listen to a disproportionate amount of country radio, and they watch *SportsCenter* more often than other Americans—a taste, the poll reveals, that corresponds more closely with Democrats' than Republicans'.)

Other organizations, including Emily's List, have conducted broader studies to sort independents into smaller "lifestyle clusters," the better to target them in the fall. Emily's List has identified four basic groups: disengaged "Bystanders," who when motivated to vote lean Democratic; "Senior Health Care" voters, whose gender (predominantly female) suggests an inclination to support Democrats; "Education First" voters, 64 percent female and 66 percent pro-choice but currently more supportive of Bush and the Iraq War than the typical Democrat; and the "Young Economically Pressured," many of whom work more than forty hours a week and may care for an elderly parent. Though this last group tends to support the Democratic position on funding public schools and other issues, its members live predominantly in small towns or rural areas and are culturally conservative.

The challenge for the next Democratic candidate will be reaching all these independents, many of whom live in small cities and suburbs that are gradually abandoning the Democratic Party. The suburban vote, which Bush won narrowly in 2000, continues to grow. Suburban women already tend to vote Democratic, so the nominee must make a special effort to appeal to men, whose vote fluctuates more than women's in presidential elections and who have lately deserted the party in large numbers: men now prefer Republicans over Democrats by 19 percentage points. Efforts to do this are under way on gun control and other issues. Gore was widely thought to have lost blue-collar swing voters in West Virginia and Ohio because of his position on guns and—pollsters argue—how he spoke about it: gun owners believed that Gore would take away their weapons, and voted accordingly. But pollsters discovered that if the discussion had simply been reframed to acknowledge the Second Amendment right to bear arms (as in the phrase "with rights come responsibilities"), 20 percent of gun owners—seven percent of the electorate—would have been inclined to vote Democratic. It's probably no accident that none of the leading Democratic candidates have echoed Gore.

One early lesson that ought to figure in the Democratic campaign is the importance of values, which have replaced income as the best indicator of voting behavior. In the past income corresponded strongly to party preference: voters supported the Democratic Party when they were poor and grew increasingly Republican as they moved up the income scale. That's no longer true. The exodus of white working-class voters from the Democratic Party has been well documented ever since the Republican revolution of 1994. A similar migration away from the Republican Party by affluent suburbanites alienated by the party's social conservatism has received less notice. Just as white working-class voters swung Georgia and other once Democratic states to the Republican Party, affluent suburbanites turned formerly Republican states such as Illinois and New Jersey into Democratic strongholds. The Democratic nominee will have to hold on to these upscale voters while winning back working-class voters.

"We're a party that prefers to talk about issues, not values," says Bruce Reed, who was Bill Clinton's domestic-policy chief. "Clinton demonstrated that if we want to expand our reach, we have to talk in terms of values." Clinton successfully rewrote the language of values to fit his own policies—family and medical leave, the V-chip, school uniforms—rather than those of the social conservatives who popularized it. In fact, both Clinton and Bush set an example for the next Democratic nominee by rising above party stereotype to attract independents: Clinton by endorsing fiscal conservatism, fighting crime, and opposing welfare dependency; Bush by using enough compassionate rhetoric to persuade independents that he wasn't another meanspirited Republican like Newt Gingrich.

. . .

It is a rare point of agreement among Democrats that the party owes its win in the 2000 popular vote to an unprecedented mobilization of minority and union voters. Any serious discussion of another close election must be premised on a similar performance. The strong Republican turnout efforts in the 2002 and 2003 elections have only increased the pressure on the next Democratic campaign to keep pace.

One way Democrats hope to do so is by improving their methods of reaching voters. Party bosses once relied on local precinct captains to impart a measure of personalization to even the largest campaigns. In the 1970s and 1980s, however, television developed into a more efficient medium; direct human contact waned, eventually giving rise to the maddening wall-to-wall carpet-bombing of TV attack ads that are the hallmark of modern campaigns. Today, in light of the proven benefits of voter-turnout efforts, strategists in both parties are hoping to combine demographic information with political research in order to repersonalize campaigns and lure back dropout voters who are disillusioned with politics. Emily's List has even asked voters in certain elections to keep a diary of every political contact they received, recording each instance in which a television ad, phone call, or direct-mail brochure caught their attention.

Perhaps most striking about the Democratic effort to shape the next campaign is its urgency. The McCain-Feingold campaign-finance-reform laws have had the effect of directing much of the available campaign money away from the Democratic National Committee and toward a broad range of liberal interest groups. Within these groups there is a palpable sense of desperation about the party's predicament and a corresponding willingness to experiment that the hidebound DNC rarely displayed. There is also the stinging example of Karl Rove, who brilliantly understood that rigorously pursuing a patchwork of distinct constituencies could add up to an unlikely electoral victory. But above all there is the pervasive fear that the next Democratic candidate will once again be a hairsbreadth from victory—and once again manage to lose.

The Tax-Cut Con

Paul Krugman

The New York Times Magazine | September 14, 2003

There's a reason why tax cuts are such a political bone of contention: As Princeton economics professor and New York Times op-ed columnist Paul Krugman makes clear below, the debate over taxation is really a battle over the shape and substance of our government—something that different political groups have very different ideas about.

In this article, Krugman traces the current Republican tax-cutting agenda back to its earlier incarnation as Reagonomics. He then goes on to question the alleged connection between lower taxes and economic growth, and to examine how the Bush administration packaged a tax-cut windfall for the rich as a populist movement. In Krugman's view, the current federal budget deficits are actually a "planned crisis," designed to force major reductions in our nation's safety-net programs: Social Security, Medicare, Medicaid, and unemployment insurance. How we respond politically to this agenda, he argues, will largely determine what kind of country the United States will be in the twenty-first century. . . .

1. The Cartoon and the Reality

Bruce Tinsley's comic strip, "Mallard Fillmore," is, he says, "for the average person out there: the forgotten American taxpayer who's sick of the liberal media." In June, that forgotten taxpayer made an appearance in the strip, attacking his TV set with a baseball bat and yelling: "I can't afford to send my kids to college, or even take 'em out of their substandard public school, because the federal, state and local governments take more than 50 percent of my income in taxes. And then the guy on the news asks with a straight face whether or not we can 'afford' tax cuts."

But that's just a cartoon. Meanwhile, Bob Riley has to face the reality.

Riley knows all about substandard public schools. He's the governor of Alabama, which ranks near the bottom of the nation in both spending per pupil and educational achievement. The state has also neglected other public services—for example, 28,000 inmates are held in a prison system built for 12,000. And thanks in part to a lack of health care, it has the second-highest infant mortality in the nation.

When he was a member of Congress, Riley, a Republican, was a staunch supporter of tax cuts. Faced with a fiscal crisis in his state, however, he seems to have had an epiphany. He decided that it was impossible to balance Alabama's budget without a significant tax increase. And that, apparently, led him to reconsider everything. "The largest tax increase in state history just to maintain the status quo?" he asked. "I don't think so." Instead, Riley proposed a wholesale restructuring of the state's tax system: reducing taxes on the poor and middle class while raising them on corporations and the rich and increasing overall tax receipts enough to pay for a big increase in education spending. You might call it a New Deal for Alabama.

Nobody likes paying taxes, and no doubt some Americans are as angry about their taxes as Tinsley's imaginary character. But most Americans also care a lot about the things taxes pay for. All politicians say they're for public education; almost all of them also say they support a strong national defense, maintaining Social Security and, if anything, expanding the coverage of Medicare. When the "guy on the news" asks whether we can afford a tax cut, he's asking whether, after yet another tax cut goes through, there will be enough money to pay for those things. And the answer is no.

But it's very difficult to get that answer across in modern American politics, which has been dominated for 25 years by a crusade against taxes.

I don't use the word "crusade" lightly. The advocates of tax cuts are relentless, even fanatical. An indication of the movement's fervor—and of its political power—came during the Iraq War. War is expensive and is almost always accompanied by tax increases. But not in 2003. "Nothing is more important in the face of a war," declared Tom DeLay, the House majority leader, "than cutting taxes." And sure enough, taxes were cut, not just in a time of war but also in the face of record budget deficits. Nor will it be easy to reverse those tax cuts: the tax-cut movement has convinced many Americans—like Tinsley—that everybody still pays far too much in taxes.

A result of the tax-cut crusade is that there is now a fundamental mismatch between the benefits Americans expect to receive from the government and the revenues government collect. This mismatch is already having profound effects at the state and local levels: teachers and policemen are being laid off and children are being denied health insurance. The federal government can mask its problems for a while, by running huge budget deficits, but it, too, will eventually have to decide whether to cut services or raise taxes. And we are not talking about minor policy adjustments. If taxes stay as low as they are now, government as we know it cannot be maintained. In particular, Social

Security will have to become far less generous; Medicare will no longer be able to guarantee comprehensive medical care to older Americans; Medicaid will no longer provide basic medical care to the poor.

How did we reach this point? What are the origins of the antitax crusade? And where is it taking us? To answer these questions, we will have to look both at who the antitax crusaders are and at the evidence on what tax cuts do to the budget and the economy. But first, let's set the stage by taking a look at the current state of taxation in America.

2. How High Are Our Taxes?

The reason Tinsley's comic strip about the angry taxpayer caught my eye was, of course, that the numbers were all wrong. Very few Americans pay as much as 50 percent of their income in taxes; on average, families near the middle of the income distribution pay only about half that percentage in federal, state and local taxes combined.

In fact, though most Americans feel that they pay too much in taxes, they get off quite lightly compared with the citizens of other advanced countries. Furthermore, for most Americans tax rates probably haven't risen for a generation. And a few Americans—namely those with high incomes—face much lower taxes than they did a generation ago.

To assess trends in the overall level of taxes and to compare taxation across countries, economists usually look first at the ratio of taxes to gross domestic product, the total value of output produced in the country. In the United States, all taxes—federal, state and local—reached a peak of 29.6 percent of GDP in 2000. That number was, however, swollen by taxes on capital gains during the stock-market bubble.

By 2002, the tax take was down to 26.3 percent of GDP, and all indications are that it will be lower still this year and next.

This is a low number compared with almost every other advanced country. In 1999, Canada collected 38.2 percent of GDP in taxes, France collected 45.8 percent, and Sweden, 52.2 percent.

Still, aren't taxes much higher than they used to be? Not if we're looking back over the past 30 years. As a share of GDP, federal taxes are currently at their lowest point since the Eisenhower administration. State and local taxes rose substantially between 1960 and the early 1970s, but have been roughly stable since then. Aside from the capital gains taxes paid during the bubble years, the share of income Americans pay in taxes has been flat since Richard Nixon was president.

Of course, overall levels of taxation don't necessarily tell you how heavily particular individuals and families are taxed. As it turns out, however, middle-income Americans, like the country as a whole, haven't seen much change in their overall taxes over the past 30 years. On average, families in the middle of the income distribution find themselves paying about 26 percent of their income in taxes today. This number hasn't changed significantly since 1989, and though hard data are lacking, it probably hasn't changed much since 1970.

Meanwhile, wealthy Americans have seen a sharp drop in their tax burden. The top tax rate—the income-tax rate on the highest bracket—is now 35 percent, half what it was in the 1970s. With the exception of a brief period between 1988 and 1993, that's the lowest rate since 1932. Other taxes that, directly or indirectly, bear mainly on the very affluent have also been cut sharply. The effective tax rate on corporate profits has been cut in half since the 1960s. The 2001 tax cut phases out the inheritance tax, which is overwhelmingly a tax on the very wealthy: in 1999, only 2 percent of estates paid any tax, and half the tax was paid by only 3,300 estates worth more than $5 million. The 2003 tax act sharply cuts taxes on dividend income, another boon to the very well off. By the time the Bush tax cuts have taken full effect, people with really high incomes will face their lowest average tax rate since the Hoover administration.

So here's the picture: Americans pay low taxes by international standards. Most people's taxes haven't gone up in the past generation; the wealthy have had their taxes cut to levels not seen since before the New Deal. Even before the latest round of tax cuts, when compared with citizens of other advanced nations or compared with Americans a generation ago, we had nothing to complain about—and those with high incomes now have a lot to celebrate. Yet a significant number of Americans rage against taxes, and the party that controls all three branches of the federal government has made tax cuts its supreme priority. Why?

3. Supply-Siders, Starve-the-Beasters and Lucky Duckies

It is often hard to pin down what antitax crusaders are trying to achieve. The reason is not, or not only, that they are disingenuous about their motives—though as we will see, disingenuity has become a hallmark of the movement in recent years. Rather, the fuzziness comes from the fact that today's antitax movement moves back and forth between two doctrines. Both doctrines favor the same thing: big tax cuts for people with high incomes. But they favor it for different reasons.

One of those doctrines has become famous under the name "supply-side economics." It's the view that the government can cut taxes without severe cuts in public spending. The other doctrine is often referred to as "starving the beast," a phrase coined by David Stockman, Ronald Reagan's budget director. It's the view that taxes should be cut precisely *in order* to force severe cuts in public spending. Supply-side economics is the friendly, attractive face of the tax-cut movement. But starve-the-beast is where the power lies.

The starting point of supply-side economics is an assertion that no economist would dispute: taxes reduce the incentive to work, save, and invest. A businessman who knows that 70 cents of every extra dollar he makes will go to the IRS is less willing to make the effort to earn that extra dollar than if he knows that the IRS will take only 35 cents. So reducing tax rates will, other things being the same, spur the economy.

This much isn't controversial. But the government must pay its bills. So the standard view of economists is that if you want to reduce the burden of taxes, you must explain what government programs you want to cut as part of the deal. There's no free lunch.

What the supply-siders argued, however, was that there *was* a free lunch. Cutting marginal rates, they insisted, would lead to such a large increase in gross domestic product that it wouldn't be necessary to come up with off-setting spending cuts. What supply-side economists say, in other words, is, "Don't worry, be happy and cut taxes." And when they say cut taxes, they mean taxes on the affluent: reducing the top marginal rate means that the biggest tax cuts go to people in the highest tax brackets.

The other camp in the tax-cut crusade actually welcomes the revenue losses from tax cuts. Its most visible spokesman today is Grover Norquist, president of Americans for Tax Reform, who once told National Public Radio: "I don't want to abolish government. I simply want to reduce it to the size where I can drag it into the bathroom and drown it in the bathtub." And the way to get it down to that size is to starve it of revenue. "The goal is reducing the size and scope of government by draining its lifeblood," Norquist told *U.S. News & World Report*.

What does "reducing the size and scope of government" mean? Tax-cut proponents are usually vague about the details. But the Heritage Foundation, ideological headquarters for the movement, has made it pretty clear. Edwin Feulner, the foundation's president, uses "New Deal" and "Great Society" as terms of abuse, implying that he and his organization want to do away with the institutions Franklin Roosevelt and Lyndon Johnson created.

That means Social Security, Medicare, Medicaid—most of what gives citizens of the United States a safety net against economic misfortune.

The starve-the-beast doctrine is now firmly within the conservative mainstream. George W. Bush himself seemed to endorse the doctrine as the budget surplus evaporated: in August 2001 he called the disappearing surplus "incredibly positive news" because it would put Congress in a "fiscal straitjacket."

Like supply-siders, starve-the-beasters favor tax cuts mainly for people with high incomes. That is partly because, like supply-siders, they emphasize the incentive effects of cutting the top marginal rate; they just don't believe that those incentive effects are big enough that tax cuts pay for themselves. But they have another reason for cutting taxes mainly on the rich, which has become known as the "lucky ducky" argument.

Here's how the argument runs: to starve the beast, you must not only deny funds to the government; you must make voters hate the government. There's a danger that working-class families might see government as their friend: because their incomes are low, they don't pay much in taxes, while they benefit from public spending. So in starving the beast, you must take care *not* to cut taxes on these "lucky duckies." (Yes, that's what *The Wall Street Journal* called them in a famous editorial.) In fact, if possible, you must *raise* taxes on working-class Americans in order, as the *Journal* said, to get their "blood boiling with tax rage."

So the tax-cut crusade has two faces. Smiling supply-siders say that tax cuts are all gain, no pain; scowling starve-the-beasters believe that inflicting pain is not just necessary but also desirable. Is the alliance between these two groups a marriage of convenience? Not exactly. It would be more accurate to say that the starve-the-beasters hired the supply-siders—indeed, created them—because they found their naive optimism useful.

A look at who the supply-siders are and how they came to prominence tells the story.

The supply-side movement likes to present itself as a school of economic thought like Keynesianism or monetarism—that is, as a set of scholarly ideas that made their way, as such ideas do, into political discussion. But the reality is quite different. Supply-side economics was a political doctrine from Day One; it emerged in the pages of political magazines, not professional economics journals.

That is not to deny that many professional economists favor tax cuts. But they almost always turn out to be starve-the-beasters, not supply-siders. And they often secretly—or sometimes not so secretly—hold supply-siders in contempt. N. Gregory Mankiw, now chairman of George W. Bush's Council of Economic Advisers, is definitely a friend to tax cuts; but in the first edition of his economic-principles textbook, he described Ronald Reagan's supply-side advisers as "charlatans and cranks."

It is not that the professionals refuse to consider supply-side ideas; rather, they have looked at them and found them wanting. A conspicuous example came earlier this year when the Congressional Budget Office tried to evaluate the growth effects of the Bush administration's proposed tax cuts. The budget office's new head, Douglas Holtz-Eakin, is a conservative economist who was handpicked for his job by the administration. But his conclusion was that unless the revenue losses from the proposed tax cuts were offset by spending cuts, the resulting deficits would be a drag on growth, quite likely to outweigh any supply-side effects.

But if the professionals regard the supply-siders with disdain, who employs these people? The answer is that since the 1970s almost all of the prominent supply-siders have been aides to conservative politicians, writers at conservative publications like *National Review*, fellows at conservative policy centers like Heritage, or economists at private companies with strong Republican connections. Loosely speaking, that is, supply-siders work for the vast right-wing conspiracy. What gives supply-side economics influence is its connection with a powerful network of institutions that want to shrink the government and see tax cuts as a way to achieve that goal. Supply-side economics is a feel-good cover story for a political movement with a much harder-nosed agenda.

This isn't just speculation. Irving Kristol, in his role as co-editor of *The Public Interest*, was arguably the single most important proponent of supply-side economics. But years later, he suggested that he himself wasn't all that persuaded by the doctrine: "I was not certain of its economic merits but quickly saw its political possibilities." Writing in 1995, he explained that his real aim was to shrink the government and that tax cuts were a means to that end: "The task, as I saw it, was to create a new majority, which evidently would mean a conservative majority, which came to mean, in turn, a Republican majority—so political effectiveness was the priority, not the accounting deficiencies of government."

In effect, what Kristol said in 1995 was that he and his associates set out to deceive the American public. They sold tax cuts on the pretense that they would be painless, when they themselves believed that it would be necessary to slash public spending in order to make room for those cuts.

But one supposes that the response would be that the end justified the means—that the tax cuts did benefit all Americans because they led to faster economic growth. Did they?

4. From Reaganomics to Clintonomics

Ronald Reagan put supply-side theory into practice with his 1981 tax cut. The tax cuts were modest for middle-class families but very large for the well-off. Between 1979 and 1983, according to Congressional Budget Office estimates, the average federal tax rate on the top 1 percent of families fell from 37 to 27.7 percent.

So did the tax cuts promote economic growth? You might think that all we have to do is look at how the economy performed. But it's not that simple, because different observers read different things from Reagan's economic record.

Here's how tax-cut advocates look at it: after a deep slump between 1979 and 1982, the U.S. economy began growing rapidly. Between 1982 and 1989 (the first year of the first George Bush's presidency), the economy grew at an average annual rate of 4.2 percent. That's a lot better than the growth rate of the economy in the late 1970s, and supply-siders claim that these "Seven Fat Years" (the title of a book by Robert L. Bartley, the longtime editor of *The Wall Street Journal*'s editorial page) prove the success of Reagan's 1981 tax cut.

But skeptics say that rapid growth after 1982 proves nothing: a severe recession is usually followed by a period of fast growth, as unemployed workers and factories are brought back on line. The test of tax cuts as a spur to economic growth is whether they produced more than an ordinary business cycle recovery. Once the economy was back to full employment, was it bigger than you would otherwise have expected? And there Reagan fails the test: between 1979, when the big slump began, and 1989, when the economy finally achieved more or less full employment again, the growth rate was 3 percent, the same as the growth rate between the two previous business cycle peaks in 1973 and 1979. Or to put it another way, by the late 1980s the U.S. economy was about where you would have expected it to be, given the trend in the 1970s. Nothing in the data suggests a supply-side revolution.

Does this mean that the Reagan tax cuts had no effect? Of course not. Those tax cuts, combined with increased military spending, provided a good old-fashioned Keynesian boost to demand. And this boost was one factor in the rapid recovery from recession that developed at the end of 1982, though probably not as important as the rapid expansion of the money supply that began in the summer of that year. But the supposed supply-side effects are invisible in the data.

While the Reagan tax cuts didn't produce any visible supply-side gains, they did lead to large budget deficits. From the point of view of most economists, this was a bad thing. But for starve-the-beast tax-cutters, deficits are potentially a good thing, because they force the government to shrink. So did Reagan's deficits shrink the beast?

A casual glance at the data might suggest not: federal spending as a share of gross domestic product was actually slightly higher at the end of the 1980s than it was at the end of the 1970s. But that number includes both defense spending and "entitlements," mainly Social Security and Medicare, whose growth is automatic unless Congress votes to cut benefits. What's left is a grab bag known as domestic discretionary spending, including everything from courts and national parks to environmental cleanups and education. And domestic discretionary spending fell from 4.5 percent of GDP in 1981 to 3.2 percent in 1988.

But that's probably about as far as any president can shrink domestic discretionary spending. And because Reagan couldn't shrink the belly of the beast, entitlements, he couldn't find enough domestic spending cuts to offset his military spending increases and tax cuts. The federal budget went into persistent, alarming, deficit. In response to these deficits, George Bush the elder went back on his "read my lips" pledge and raised taxes. Bill Clinton raised them further. And thereby hangs a tale.

For Clinton did exactly the opposite of what supply-side economics said you should do: he raised the marginal rate on high-income taxpayers. In 1989, the top 1 percent of families paid, on average, only 28.9 percent of their income in federal taxes; by 1995, that share was up to 36.1 percent.

Conservatives confidently awaited a disaster—but it failed to materialize. In fact, the economy grew at a reasonable pace through Clinton's first term, while the deficit and the unemployment rate went steadily down. And then the news got even better: unemployment fell to its lowest level in decades without causing inflation, while productivity growth accelerated to rates not seen since the 1960s. And the budget deficit turned into an impressive surplus.

Tax-cut advocates had claimed the Reagan years as proof of their doctrine's correctness; as we have seen, those claims wilt under close examination. But the Clinton years posed a much greater challenge: here was a president who sharply raised the marginal tax rate on high-income taxpayers, the very rate that the tax-cut movement cares most about. And instead of presiding over an economic disaster, he presided over an economic miracle.

Let's be clear: very few economists think that Clinton's policies were primarily responsible for that miracle. For the most part, the Clinton-era surge probably reflected the maturing of information technology: businesses finally figured out how to make effective use of computers, and the resulting surge in productivity drove the economy forward. But the fact that America's best growth in a generation took place after the government did exactly the opposite of what tax-cutters advocate was a body blow to their doctrine.

They tried to make the best of the situation. The good economy of the late 1990s, ardent tax-cutters insisted, was caused by the 1981 tax cut. Early in 2000, Lawrence Kudlow and Stephen Moore, prominent supply-siders, published an article titled "It's the Reagan Economy, Stupid."

But anyone who thought about the lags involved found this implausible—indeed, hilarious. If the tax-cut movement attributed the booming economy of 1999 to a tax cut Reagan pushed through 18 years earlier, why didn't they attribute the economic boom of 1983 and 1984—Reagan's "Morning in America"—to whatever Lyndon Johnson was doing in 1965 and 1966?

By the end of the 1990s, in other words, supply-side economics had become something of a laughingstock, and the whole case for tax cuts as a route to economic growth was looking pretty shaky. But the tax-cut crusade was nonetheless, it turned out, poised for its biggest political victories yet. How did that happen?

5. Second Wind: The Bush Tax Cuts

As the economic success of the United States under Bill Clinton became impossible to deny, there was a gradual shift in the sales strategy for tax cuts. The supposed economic benefits of tax cuts received less emphasis; the populist rationale—you, personally, pay too much in taxes—was played up.

I began this article with an example of this campaign's success: the creator of Mallard Fillmore apparently believes that typical families pay twice as much in taxes as they in fact do. But the most striking example of what skillful marketing can accomplish is the campaign for repeal of the estate tax.

As demonstrated, the estate tax is a tax on the very, very well off. Yet advocates of repeal began portraying it as a terrible burden on the little guy. They renamed it the "death tax" and put out reports decrying its impact on struggling farmers and businessmen—reports that never provided real-world examples because actual cases of family farms or small businesses broken up to pay estate taxes are almost impossible to find. This campaign succeeded in creating a public perception that the estate tax falls broadly on the population. Earlier this year, a poll found that 49 percent of Americans believed that most families had to pay the estate tax, while only 33 percent gave the right answer that only a few families had to pay.

Still, while an insistent marketing campaign has convinced many Americans that they are overtaxed, it hasn't succeeded in making the issue a top priority with the public. Polls consistently show that voters regard safeguarding Social Security and Medicare as much more important than tax cuts.

Nonetheless, George W. Bush has pushed through tax cuts in each year of his presidency. Why did he push for these tax cuts, and how did he get them through?

You might think that you could turn to the administration's own pronouncements to learn why it has been so determined to cut taxes. But even if you try to take the administration at its word, there's a problem: the public rationale for tax cuts has shifted repeatedly over the past three years.

During the 2000 campaign and the initial selling of the 2001 tax cut, the Bush team insisted that the federal government was running an excessive budget surplus, which should be returned to taxpayers. By the summer of 2001, as it became clear that the projected budget surpluses would not materialize, the administration shifted to touting the tax cuts as a form of demand-side economic stimulus: by putting more money in consumers' pockets, the tax cuts would stimulate spending and help pull the economy out of recession. By 2003, the rationale had changed again: the administration argued that reducing taxes on dividend income, the core of its plan, would improve incentives and hence long-run growth—that is, it had turned to a supply-side argument.

These shifting rationales had one thing in common: none of them were credible. It was obvious to independent observers even in 2001 that the budget projections used to justify that year's tax cut exaggerated future revenues and understated future costs. It was similarly obvious that the 2001 tax cut was poorly designed as a demand stimulus. And we have already seen that the supply-side rationale for the 2003 tax cut was tested and found wanting by the Congressional Budget Office.

So what were the Bush tax cuts really about? The best answer seems to be that they were about securing a key part of the Republican base. Wealthy campaign contributors have a lot to gain from lower taxes, and since they aren't very likely to depend on Medicare, Social Security or Medicaid, they won't suffer if the beast gets starved. Equally important was the support of the party's intelligentsia, nurtured by policy centers like Heritage and professionally committed to the tax-cut crusade. The original Bush tax-cut proposal was devised in late 1999 not to win votes in the national election but to fend off a primary challenge from the supply-sider Steve Forbes, the presumptive favorite of that part of the base.

This brings us to the next question: How have these cuts been sold?

At this point, one must be blunt: the selling of the tax cuts has depended heavily on chicanery. The administration has used accounting trickery to hide the true budget impact of its proposals, and it has used misleading presentations to conceal the extent to which its tax cuts are tilted toward families with very high income.

The most important tool of accounting trickery, though not the only one, is the use of "sunset clauses" to understate the long-term budget impact of tax cuts. To keep the official 10-year cost of the 2001 tax cut down, the administration's Congressional allies wrote the law so that tax rates revert to their 2000 levels in 2011. But, of course, nobody expects the sunset to occur: when 2011 rolls around, Congress will be under immense pressure to extend the tax cuts.

The same strategy was used to hide the cost of the 2003 tax cut. Thanks to sunset clauses, its headline cost over the next decade was only $350 billion, but if the sunsets are canceled—as the president proposed in a speech early this month—the cost will be at least $800 billion.

Meanwhile, the administration has carried out a very successful campaign to portray these tax cuts as mainly aimed at middle-class families. This campaign is similar in spirit to the selling of estate-tax repeal as a populist measure, but considerably more sophisticated.

The reality is that the core measures of both the 2001 and 2003 tax cuts mainly benefit the very affluent. The centerpieces of the 2001 act were a reduction in the top income-tax rate and elimination of the estate tax—the first, by definition, benefiting only people with high incomes; the second benefiting only heirs to large estates. The core of the 2003 tax cut was a reduction in the tax rate on dividend income. This benefit, too, is concentrated on very high-income families.

According to estimates by the Tax Policy Center—a liberal-oriented institution, but one with a reputation for scrupulous accuracy—the 2001 tax cut, once fully phased in, will deliver 42 percent of its benefits to the top 1 percent of the income distribution. (Roughly speaking, that means families earning more than $330,000 per year.) The 2003 tax cut delivers a somewhat smaller share to the top 1 percent, 29.1 percent, but within that concentrates its benefits on the really, really rich. Families with incomes over $1 million a year—a mere 0.13 percent of the population—will receive 17.3 percent of this year's tax cut, more than the total received by the bottom 70 percent of American families. Indeed, the 2003 tax cut has already proved a major boon to some of America's wealthiest people: corporations in which executives or a single family hold a large fraction of stocks are suddenly paying much bigger dividends, which are now taxed at only 15 percent no matter how high the income of their recipient.

It might seem impossible to put a populist gloss on tax cuts this skewed toward the rich, but the administration has been remarkably successful in doing just that.

One technique involves exploiting the public's lack of statistical sophistication. In the selling of the 2003 tax cut, the catch phrase used by administration spokesmen was "92 million Americans will receive an average tax cut of $1,083." That sounded, and was intended to sound, as if every American family would get $1,083. Needless to say, that wasn't true.

Yet the catch phrase wasn't technically a lie: the Tax Policy Center estimates that 89 million people will receive tax cuts this year and that the total tax cut will be $99 billion, or about $1,100 for each of those 89 million people. But this calculation carefully leaves out the 50 million taxpayers who received no tax cut at all. And even among those who did get a tax cut, most got a lot less than $1,000, a number inflated by the very big tax cuts received by a few wealthy people. About half of American families received a tax cut of less than $100; the great majority, a tax cut of less than $500.

But the most original, you might say brilliant, aspect of the Bush administration's approach to tax cuts has involved the way the tax cuts themselves are structured.

David Stockman famously admitted that Reagan's middle-class tax cuts were a "Trojan horse" that allowed him to smuggle in what he really wanted, a cut in the top marginal rate. The Bush administration similarly follows a Trojan horse strategy, but an even cleverer one. The core measures in Bush's tax cuts benefit only the wealthy, but there are additional features that provide significant benefits to some—but only some—middle-class families. For example, the 2001 tax cut included a $400 child credit and also created a new 10 percent tax bracket, the so-called cutout. These measures had the effect of creating a "sweet spot" that could be exploited for political purposes. If a couple had multiple children, if the children were all still under 18 and if the couple's income was just high enough to allow it to take full advantage of the child credit, it could get a tax cut of as much as 4 percent of pretax income. Hence the couple with two children and an income of $40,000, receiving a tax cut of $1,600, who played such a large role in the administration's rhetoric. But while most couples have children, at any given time only a small minority of families contains two or more children under 18—and many of these families have income too low to take full advantage of the child tax credit. So that "typical" family wasn't typical at all. Last year, the actual tax break for families in the middle of the income distribution averaged $469, not $1,600.

So that's the story of the tax-cut offensive under the Bush administration: through a combination of hardball politics, deceptive budget arithmetic, and systematic misrepresentation of who benefits, Bush's team has achieved a major reduction of taxes, especially for people with very high incomes.

But where does that leave the country?

6. A Planned Crisis

Right now, much of the public discussion of the Bush tax cuts focuses on their short-run impact. Critics say that the 2.7 million jobs lost since March 2001 prove that the administration's policies have failed, while the administration says that things would have been even worse without the tax cuts and that a solid recovery is just around the corner.

But this is the wrong debate. Even in the short run, the right question to ask isn't whether the tax cuts were better than nothing; they probably were. The right question is whether some other economic-stimulus plan could have achieved better results at a lower budget cost. And it is hard to deny that, on a jobs-per-dollar basis, the Bush tax cuts have been extremely ineffective. According to the Congressional Budget Office, half of this year's $400 billion budget deficit is due to Bush tax cuts. Now $200 billion is a lot of money; it is equivalent to the salaries of four million average workers. Even the administration doesn't claim its policies have created four million jobs. Surely some other policy—aid to state and local governments, tax breaks for the poor and middle class rather than the rich, maybe even W.P.A.-style public works— would have been more successful at getting the country back to work.

Meanwhile, the tax cuts are designed to remain in place even after the economy has recovered. Where will they leave us?

Here's the basic fact: partly, though not entirely, as a result of the tax cuts of the last three years, the government of the United States faces a fundamental fiscal shortfall. That is, the revenue it collects falls well short of the sums it needs to pay for existing programs. Even the U.S. government must, eventually, pay its bills, so something will have to give.

The numbers tell the tale. This year and next, the federal government will run budget deficits of more than $400 billion. Deficits may fall a bit, at least as a share of gross domestic product, when the economy recovers. But the relief will be modest and temporary. As Peter Fisher, under secretary of the treasury for domestic finance, puts it, the federal government is "a gigantic insurance company with a sideline business in defense and homeland security." And about a decade from now, this insurance company's policyholders will begin making a lot of claims. As the baby boomers retire, spending on Social Security benefits and Medicare will steadily rise, as will spending on Medicaid (because of rising medical costs). Eventually, unless there are sharp cuts in benefits, these three programs alone will consume a larger share of GDP than the federal government currently collects in taxes.

Alan Auerbach, William Gale, and Peter Orszag, fiscal experts at the Brookings Institution, have estimated the size of the "fiscal gap"—the increase in revenues or reduction in spending that would be needed to make the nation's finances sustainable in the long run. If you define the long run as 75 years, this gap turns out to be 4.5 percent of GDP Or to put it another way, the gap is equal to 30 percent of what the federal government spends on all domestic programs. Of that gap, about 60 percent is the result of the Bush tax cuts. We would have faced a serious fiscal problem even if those tax cuts had never happened. But we face a much nastier problem now that they are in place. And more broadly, the tax-cut crusade will make it very hard for any future politicians to raise taxes.

So how will this gap be closed? The crucial point is that it cannot be closed without either fundamentally redefining the role of government or sharply raising taxes.

Politicians will, of course, promise to eliminate wasteful spending. But take out Social Security, Medicare, defense, Medicaid, government pensions, homeland security, interest on the public debt, and veterans' benefits—none of them what people who complain about waste usually have in mind—and you are left with spending equal to about 3 percent of gross domestic product. And most of that goes for courts, highways, education, and other useful things. Any savings from elimination of waste and fraud will amount to little more than a rounding-off error.

So let's put a few things back on the table. Let's assume that interest on the public debt will be paid, that spending on defense and homeland security will not be compromised, and that the regular operations of government will continue to be financed. What we are left with, then, are the New Deal and Great Society programs: Social Security, Medicare, Medicaid, and unemployment insurance. And to close the fiscal gap, spending on these programs would have to be cut by around 40 percent.

It's impossible to know how such spending cuts might unfold, but cuts of that magnitude would require drastic changes in the system. It goes almost without saying that the age at which Americans become eligible for retirement benefits would rise, that Social Security payments would fall sharply compared with average incomes, that Medicare patients would be forced to pay much more of their expenses out of pocket—or do without. And that would be only a start.

All this sounds politically impossible. In fact, politicians of both parties have been scrambling to expand, not reduce, Medicare benefits by adding prescription drug coverage. It's hard to imagine a situation under which the entitlement programs would be rolled back sufficiently to close the fiscal gap.

Yet closing the fiscal gap by raising taxes would mean rolling back all of the Bush tax cuts, and then some. And that also sounds politically impossible.

For the time being, there is a third alternative: borrow the difference between what we insist on spending and what we're willing to collect in taxes. That works as long as lenders believe that someday, somehow, we're going to get our fiscal act together. But this can't go on indefinitely. Eventually—I think within a decade, though not everyone agrees—the bond market will tell us that we have to make a choice.

In short, everything is going according to plan.

For the looming fiscal crisis doesn't represent a defeat for the leaders of the tax-cut crusade or a miscalculation on their part. Some supporters of President Bush may have really believed that his tax cuts were consistent with his promises to protect Social Security and expand Medicare; some people may still believe that the wondrous supply-side effects of tax cuts will make the budget deficit disappear. But for starve-the-beast tax-cutters, the coming crunch is exactly what they had in mind.

7. What Kind of Country?

The astonishing political success of the antitax crusade has, more or less deliberately, set the United States up for a fiscal crisis. How we respond to that crisis will determine what kind of country we become.

If Grover Norquist is right—and he has been right about a lot—the coming crisis will allow conservatives to move the nation a long way back toward the kind of limited government we had before Franklin Roosevelt. Lack of revenue, he says, will make it possible for conservative politicians—in the name of fiscal necessity—to dismantle immensely popular government programs that would otherwise have been untouchable.

In Norquist's vision, America a couple of decades from now will be a place in which elderly people make up a disproportionate share of the poor, as they did before Social Security. It will also be a country in which even middle-class elderly Americans are, in many cases, unable to afford expensive medical procedures or prescription drugs and in which poor Americans generally go without even basic health care. And it may well be a place in which only those who can afford expensive private schools can give their children a decent education.

But as Governor Riley of Alabama reminds us, that's a choice, not a necessity. The tax-cut crusade has created a situation in which something must give. But what gives—whether we decide that the New Deal and the Great Society must go or that taxes aren't such a bad thing after all—is up to us. The American people must decide what kind of a country we want to be.

Playing Defense
Michael Crowley

The New Republic | March 15, 2004

Is the U.S. better equipped to prevent or respond to terrorist attacks than we were three years ago? A number of recent reports suggest that America's homeland security efforts have been seriously mismanaged. A March 19, 2004, Time *magazine article, for instance, reported that the "vast majority" of the $13 billion appropriated for homeland security since 9/11 "was distributed with no regard for the threats, vulnerabilities, and potential consequences faced by each region." Meanwhile, an April 28, 2004* New York Times *article said that, according to congressional officials, "[m]ore than $5 billion in federal money to help communities brace for terrorist attacks has not yet reached the local authorities and remains stuck in the administrative pipeline."*

The Times *report credited the newly formed Department of Homeland Security (DHS) for getting better at moving the grants along, but the DHS has come in for plenty of criticism as well. A September 7, 2003,* Washington Post *article noted that, while flying had become safer thanks to the hiring of 50,000 new airline screeners and expansion of the air marshal program, "[e]fforts to organize the government's ten or so disparate lists of potential terrorism suspects, secure airline cargo against terrorist plots, and advise local police and firefighters on training and equipment have all foundered."*

In the following New Republic *article, Michael Crowley also finds big problems in the alphabet-soup world of counterterrorist agencies. One note of interest: The Terrorist Threat Integration Center (TTIC) mentioned below was back in the headlines as we went to press for having provided flawed figures for a government report on 2003 terrorist activity that understated the year's incidents and casualites—a mistake that was discovered only after two professors checked the TTIC's figures. Among other things, the revised statistics showed that worldwide injuries from terrorist attacks went up sharply from 2002 to 2003, rather than declining as originally reported. . . .*

Last December, I called the Department of Homeland Security's (DHS) main line. "Thank you for your interest in the Department of Homeland Security," a recorded voice responded. "Due to the high level of interest in the department all lines are currently busy. . . . We encourage you to call back soon." A beep was followed by a click. It was a good thing I wasn't calling to report an anthrax attack, because I'd been disconnected. As advised, I tried calling back "soon"—and got the same recording. Just a bad week, perhaps? Apparently not. A few weeks later, a *Roll Call* reporter had the same experience.

Unanswered phones are a small but telling example of how DHS is faring one year after the department opened its doors last March. Far from being greater than the sum of its parts, DHS is a bureaucratic Frankenstein, with clumsily stitched-together limbs and an inadequate, misfiring brain. No one says merging 170,000 employees from 22 different agencies should have been easy. But, even allowing for inevitable transition problems, DHS has been a disaster: underfunded, undermanned, disorganized, and unforgivably slow-moving.

And, yet, George W. Bush can't stop praising it. His January State of the Union address hailed "the men and women of our new Homeland Security Department [who] are patrolling our coasts and borders," whose "vigilance is protecting America." In a September 11 anniversary address at Quantico, Virginia, Bush mentioned DHS no less than twelve times, saying, "Secretary [Tom] Ridge and his team have done a fine job in getting the difficult work of organizing the department [sic]." And, at an event celebrating the department's one-year anniversary this week, Bush declared that the department had "accomplished an historic task," and that Ridge has done a "fantastic job" of making the United States safer.

That's nonsense. DHS has failed to address some of our most serious vulnerabilities, from centralizing intelligence to protecting critical infrastructure to organizing against bioterror. Many a policy wonk who has evaluated the department has come away despondent. Zoe Lofgren, a senior Democrat on two House committees that oversee DHS, puts it this way: "We are arguably in worse shape than we were before [the creation of the department]. . . . If the American people knew how little has been done, they would be outraged."

If the September 11 attacks provided one essential lesson about the federal bureaucracy, it is that rival agencies need to better share intelligence so they can "connect the dots" and more quickly track down suspected terrorists. Improving intelligence coordination was a fundamental rationale for creating DHS, and so the bill establishing the department also gave birth to a brand new government office, the directorate of Information Analysis and Infrastructure Protection (IAIP). IAIP was designed to receive vast amounts of both raw and analyzed data from intelligence agencies like the CIA and FBI, allowing DHS analysts to search for patterns that individual agencies might have missed. Bush called this one of DHS's "primary tasks": "to review intelligence and law enforcement information from all agencies of government and produce a single daily picture of threats against our homeland."

But, even before DHS opened its doors, Bush dramatically undermined the IAIP—and, by extension, the entire department. Without consulting Congress—or telling the IAIP's planning staff—he announced the creation of the Terrorist Threat Integration Center (TTIC), a quasi-independent agency that would assume most of the intelligence powers originally intended for the new department. Now TTIC, and not DHS, would become the clearinghouse of anti-terror intelligence. The decision not only eliminated the chief rationale for IAIP's existence; it exacerbated a problem the new agency had been created to improve. That is, rather than cutting through bureaucratic turf battles, TTIC may have complicated them further. Staffed by officials from a variety of existing intelligence agencies, TTIC is housed in the CIA's offices in Langley, Virginia, and its director reports to CIA Director George Tenet. Explained a former administration anti-terror official, "Tenet said the CIA is not going to give up its responsibility on threat reporting and threat analysis.

He put a mark in the sand and said, 'No way am I going to give this up to a new organization [DHS] that doesn't know its ass from its elbow.' "

But TTIC has only further confused the interagency intelligence picture, according to a recent report on homeland security information-sharing by the Markle Foundation. "TTIC's creation has caused confusion among state and local entities, and within the federal government itself, about the respective roles of the TTIC and DHS," explained the report, which was overseen by former Aetna executive Zoe Baird and former Netscape CEO James Barksdale. "This confusion needs to be resolved." Even the agency's deputy director, Russell Travers, conceded as much in testimony to the 9/11 Commission in January: "There is a degree of ambiguity between our mission and some other analytic organizations within the government." Internally, TTIC analysts—who tend to be junior and inexperienced—still need permission from intelligence agencies before sharing their data with other parts of the government. The Markle report says that approach "further locks the government into a system that has proven unsuccessful for the sharing of information in the past." Perhaps worst of all, there's no requirement that other intelligence agencies share with TTIC at all. "The original idea [behind DHS] was that a fusion center doesn't allow anyone to make decisions about what flows into it. The analysts are there to look and decide," says a Senate Democratic aide. So much for that idea.

Then again, it's not clear why anyone would trust DHS with something as important as raw intelligence. Consider the story of Paul Redmond, IAIP's first director. Although most of IAIP's intelligence-analysis duties have been given to TTIC, it is still responsible for finding and fixing vulnerabilities in the nation's infrastructure. However, when Redmond appeared before a House subcommittee last June, it was clear that IAIP couldn't handle even this task. Redmond reported that, three months after DHS had begun operations, IAIP had filled just one-quarter of its analyst slots, "because we do not have the [office] space for them." Committee members of both parties were appalled. "Why should I feel comfortable today, Mister Redmond?" asked Republican Representative Chris Shays. "Why should I feel that we made a good decision [about creating IAIP]? . . . Do you feel that, given the incredible importance of your office, that that's a pretty surprising statement to make before this committee?" Apparently, Redmond's performance didn't go over well with the Bush administration, either. Soon after, he quietly announced his resignation for "health reasons."

Redmond was only running IAIP to begin with because the best man for the job had been passed over. That man was John Gannon, formerly a top official at the CIA. Gannon had run IAIP's transition team and was expected to become its director. "If there was anyone in government qualified to do that job, he was the guy," says a person familiar with the IAIP. But the administration didn't turn to Gannon—some suspect because he was a Clinton appointee. Unfortunately, the Pentagon official who was the administration's first choice to fill the position said no. So did the next candidate. And the next. In all, more than 15 people turned down entreaties that they apply for the job, according to the *Washington Post*. "When [the administration] finally realized there was nobody but Gannon to offer the job [to, Gannon] was so pissed off he went elsewhere," says Rand Beers, a former administration counterterrorism official now advising John Kerry. (Gannon is now staff director of the House Homeland Security Committee.)

The story illustrates the trouble the administration has had bringing topflight talent to DHS. "They definitely were not attracting the superstars," says a former administration national security official. "I often felt like I was dealing with the B team or even the C team. You can chalk that up to growing pains, . . . [but] it doesn't leave you that comforted." For instance, although several agents from an existing FBI critical infrastructure protection office were expected to make the leap to DHS, virtually none were willing to do so. "A lot of agents said, 'Why would I go *there*?' " reports one former administration official. "[I]ntelligence professionals have been much more willing to go to the CIA or Departments of Justice, Defense, or State," reported the Gilmore Commission, a group of homeland security experts assembled by Congress and charged with periodically reviewing U.S. defenses against terrorism. It's not just skilled bureaucrats who shun DHS but technical experts, too. For instance, the department has few top bioterrorism scientists in its ranks, according to Tara O'Toole, director of the Center for Biosecurity at the University of Pittsburgh Medical Center and one of the nation's leading bioterror authorities. DHS has "a very minimal team in terms of senior people with appropriate technical backgrounds. That's got to change," O'Toole says.

Meanwhile, DHS's leadership has already suffered a slew of defections. Within six months, several key officials who helped launch the new department were gone—including Ridge's chief of staff, Bruce Lawlor, and deputy secretary, Gordon England, both of whom left on rocky terms. The department's chief financial officer, Bruce Carnes, also departed in December. Such defections have further stalled the department's progress. "A lot of time has been lost because the department's management hasn't been tip-top," says a Senate Democratic aide.

And, in case you were wondering, the search for someone to run IAIP settled on a former Marine Corps general named Frank Libutti. But Libutti, while an experienced soldier, lacks any intelligence background. And his pile-driving, military style isn't winning many converts. At a meeting of state homeland security directors at a Virginia Marriott hotel last October, Libutti took the stage as the theme from *Rocky* blared through a loudspeaker and a laser light show bounced off the walls. He then proceeded to drop and perform one-armed push-ups for the bewildered crowd. Over the course of the conference, multiple sources say, Libutti further alienated the state officials with a crude machismo that caused at least one woman to walk out in disgust.

It's not just the department's weak leadership that's causing problems. DHS has also been hamstrung by the forced assimilation of rival agencies. "[M]any of the agencies and employees subsumed by the integration continue to have no identity with or 'buy-in' to their parent organization," the Gilmore Commission warns. Nowhere is this more true than in DHS's new Border and Transportation Security (BTS) directorate, which combined the Immigration and Naturalization Service (INS) with the old Customs Service. The basic idea made sense: INS and Customs had lots of overlapping duties. And, for years, INS had been a reform-resistant organizational disaster. But combining the two has pleased neither agency. Customs officials complain they were forced to incorporate many of the INS's worst management elements into their relatively efficient culture, especially at the Immigrations and Customs Enforcement agency (ICE), which is BTS's investigative arm. "The INS has not been abolished," says a mid-level ICE worker in a Northeastern city. "It's alive and well, and running ICE." Customs had a good computer system but was forced to inherit INS's notoriously "horrible" one, this worker complains. He adds that the INS-based system in his office is so baffling that he needs a new staffer "basically full-time to operate [it]." Some Customs officials have even had to revert to pen and paper for record-keeping.

Of course, former INS workers see it differently. "Basically, [Customs officials] are saying, . . . '[N]ow you live in our house and you're going to play by our rules,' " says Michael Knowles, a union representative for former INS workers at the American Federation of Government Employees. The two sides have clashed about details as small as what sort of gun ICE agents should carry—the 9-mm pistol that was standard-issue at Customs or the INS's 40-caliber handgun. ("The 40-cal is a superior round. It ends the situation in a more efficient manner," Knowles insists.) There's even been squabbling about what name to give ICE, which has already been renamed once (from "BICE") and may be rechristened yet again.

The squabbling has fostered resentment toward the Bush administration. "Some of the people up there writing the law didn't have any clue what was happening on the ground," the ICE worker fumes. "They pushed these agencies together so fast that there was very little opportunity for these guys to figure out how to make things work." And it may be affecting job performance. In a November letter to the Senate Judiciary Committee, Allen Martin, an ICE official who is head of the Customs Investigators Association, warned that "[m]orale in the field is at an all-time low. There is a real lack of identity, mission focus, and direction."

In some cases, however, dueling government agencies were never merged in the first place—even though Bush had explained that "ending duplication and overlap" would save money and coordinate anti-terror efforts. Take the array of offices within DHS that manage grants and training for local first responders. The White House had initially intended to combine programs run by the Federal Emergency Management Agency and the Department of Justice's Office of Domestic Preparedness (ODP). But, after protests from both agencies—and members of Congress who have come to love ODP as a useful pork-delivery mechanism—they were kept separate. (Instead of being merged into DHS's Emergency Response and Preparedness directorate, ODP was nonsensically stashed in the department's border-security division.) "The current structure suffers from a duplication of preparedness efforts and a lack of coordination among relevant entities," the Gilmore Commission found—another way of saying, "What a mess." "They have created a completely illogical system," says Seth Jones of the RAND Corporation, who helped to write the Gilmore report. "The point is that not all the decisions about how to build the department were done logically. There are some pretty clear structural issues."

Poor planning has led to confusion throughout DHS. "There are some people over there who still don't know what's going on," says a state homeland security policy expert. "It's not that they're not smart. They literally don't know where they fit in." One official I spoke to recently wasn't sure of the current name of her office. Bio-expert Tara O'Toole says such disorder has very real consequences. "I don't know who's in charge of biodefense for the United States. And, given that I do this all the time," she says, "that's very alarming to me."

B-grade talent and organizational confusion would be less of a problem if the department were showing better results. But, so far, there's been little progress. In many areas it seems that, in the race against the terrorists, DHS is wearing boots of lead.

Take the department's failure to create a consolidated terrorist "watch list." When it was discovered that the CIA had been watching two of the eventual September 11 hijackers as early as 2000 but never notified other agencies that might have stopped their entry into the United States, no task became more urgent than combining the government's twelve separate rosters of suspected terrorists. Outside experts, including the Markle task force, said that merging the watch lists could take as little as six to twelve months. The task initially fell to DHS, which claimed last year to be making progress. "I think we're fairly close to finalizing the consolidation itself," Ridge told a Senate committee last April. Five months later, a DHS press release assured that all federal agents would soon be working "off the same unified, comprehensive set of anti-terrorist information." Six months later, the lists are still not merged—and responsibility for the job has been transferred from Ridge's hapless department to the FBI.

Indeed, information-sharing among government agencies remains hamstrung. Unifying computers and sharing data is inherently complex, and the Bush administration has given DHS few resources for such a massive task. Insufficient funding for new employees at DHS—whose leadership the White House has kept skeletal for fear of growing the bureaucracy—has left the department's information-technology (I.T.) offices badly undermanned, slowing the process of interfacing government computers. For instance, in the office of Chief Information Officer Steve Cooper, "[I]f two people go out to lunch, there's no one to answer the phones," says James Carafano, a homeland security specialist at the Heritage Foundation. Nor does Cooper seem to have the kind of decisive authority his job requires. Last year, for instance, the department issued a $500 million I.T. purchase agreement that he tried, unsuccessfully, to block. "What's the point of having a CIO if he is not given budget control over the department's I.T.?" asked one private-sector tech CEO at a House hearing last fall. Adding to the indignity, when a House sub-committee recently ranked the cybersecurity of various federal departments and agencies, DHS finished with the lowest score and a failing grade.

More serious is the flow of information between DHS and state and local governments. In an address last week commemorating the department's one-year anniversary, Ridge bragged that DHS has "created a powerful and con-stant two-way flow of information." But the Markle Foundation saw things differently. "The sharing of terrorist-related information between relevant agencies at different levels of government has only been marginally improved in the last year" and is "ad hoc and sporadic at best," the report found. Last week, Ridge unveiled a new high-tech system that will connect DHS with state and local agencies and ameliorate the communication problem. But, from Ridge's description, it sounds mainly like he has discovered WiFi. "We'll be able to send photos and maps, even streaming video," Ridge bragged. "We'll even be able to access data at the scene of a crime . . . through wireless lap-tops." Alas, it's not clear that the system Ridge so breathlessly described is a solution. The real problems with info-sharing involve a lack of guidelines for classifying data, deciding who gets to see it, and teaching local officials proper analytical skills. The new system is "a step in the right direction," Carafano allows. "But there's a long way to go."

DHS is also having trouble holding its own against other government agen-cies, falling prey to the very sort of bureaucratic sumo wrestling it was sup-posed to supercede. For instance, last May Ridge signed an agreement with Attorney General John Ashcroft ceding most control over terrorism-financing investigations to the Department of Justice, even though former Customs offi-cials, now at ICE, had traditionally had that job and wanted to keep it. ICE workers were dismayed at Ridge's decision, and, according to one depart-ment official, felt his inexperienced staff had been outmaneuvered by wilier FBI and Justice Department officials.

The Department of Defense (DOD) has also toyed with DHS. The Pentagon has reportedly been territorial about encroachments onto its own homeland defense functions, willing to share only unglamorous duties it never wanted in the first place—such as anti-drug-trafficking responsibilities. The Pentagon is "punting stuff they don't really want" to the new department, says a DHS official. Otherwise, says a congressional aide, "DOD just ignores them." A lack of respect for DHS's authority may help explain the delay in efforts like uni-fying terrorist watch lists. "Ridge can't bang heads outside the department," says Rob Atkinson, vice president of the Progressive Policy Institute.

But that wouldn't explain the department's failure to begin securing the nation's infrastructure. Assessing the nation's thousands of vulnerable industrial sites, railways, electric grids, and so on is supposed to be central to the DHS mission. But thirty months after September 11, almost nothing has been done. Last year, an impatient Congress asked DHS to produce a plan for its nationwide risk assessment—not the actual assessment, just a plan for devising it—by December 15, 2003. The deadline came and went. Two days later, the White House quietly issued a directive giving DHS an entire year to develop a "plan" explaining its "strategy" for how to examine infrastructure. An actual infrastructure analysis, one DHS official told Congress last fall, could take five years. No one says it is easy to inventory the vulnerabilities of all fifty states. But DHS looks curiously slow when you consider that, by last summer, a George Mason University graduate student had used publicly available data to map every commercial and industrial sector in the country, complete with their fiber-optic network connections. And, as DHS struggles with devising an infrastructure-assessment plan, it is doing nothing to oversee critical facilities, like the hundreds of chemical plants nationwide—most of which still have little or no security.

It's tempting to blame Tom Ridge for his department's shortfalls. Certainly, he has been a flawed spokesman. At a town-hall meeting in a Washington, D.C., suburb this week, Ridge admitted that most Americans still don't know what to do in the event of an attack. "A massive public education campaign needs to take place before an incident occurs," Ridge said—a strange assertion from someone who has had two years to conduct one (remember, Ridge was director of the White House Office of Homeland Security before he became DHS secretary last January). Then again, Ridge's prior communication efforts have left something to be desired. Everyone seems to hate his department's color-coded alert system, which Congress is determined to revamp. When the department's public-information website, Ready.gov, was unveiled a year ago, it was filled with useless and even misleading information (among other things, it vastly overstated the destructive power of a dirty bomb). And then, of course, there was Ridge's advice about buying duct tape last February, which touched off a semi-panicked rush to hardware stores and made Ridge a laughingstock on late-night television. (DHS's press office did not respond to my request to interview Ridge and other officials.)

Of course, Tom Ridge can only be as effective as the White House makes him. And, so far, Bush hasn't given Ridge the money or authority to match his "urgent and overriding mission." One indicator is the department's frugal budget. Last month, the White House unveiled a $40 billion budget for DHS, which it touted as a 10 percent spending increase from the previous year. But that figure is hardly as generous as it seems. More than half the new spending will go to tax incentives for pharmaceutical companies to develop new vaccines. In other words, there's very little new money for beefing up the department's shoddy management. Indeed, Bush's budget *cuts* several vital DHS projects, such as funding for local first responders, border patrol, and federal air marshals.

Homeland security experts say this parsimony reflects a lack of White House commitment to the new department. "The reality of Washington is that, if you have a new organization and there's not leadership from the top saying, 'You need to take on this role, and you have my authority behind you,' it's just not going to happen," says one person who helped produce the Markle report. "I think what is lacking now, for whatever reason, is White House muscle and leadership. There's just been no sustained attention." Adds a person who worked on the Gilmore Commission report: "Unless the president says, 'OK, Mister Secretary of Defense, Mister CIA Director, Mister Attorney General: You all get your little shits together, or you're gonna be on the street,' [DHS] is going to be marginalized."

Ultimately, perhaps we shouldn't be surprised. The president, after all, never wanted this department in the first place. The original idea came from Joe Lieberman—and Bush only embraced it when it looked like Lieberman's plan might pass without his support. But Bush certainly does like using DHS as a rhetorical weapon. His 2002 battle with Senate Democrats over union provisions in the DHS bill—during which he said the bill's opponents were "more interested in special interests in Washington and not interested in the security of the American people"—helped Republicans win back the Senate that November. No doubt Bush will be telling voters this fall that it was he who championed the department, implying that a Democrat couldn't be trusted to run it.

Bush may have inadvertently revealed his real motives a day after calling for the new department in June of 2002. Sitting in the Cabinet Room of the White House, flanked by his GOP allies, Bush declared that the new department would "enable all of us to tell the American people that we're doing everything in our power to protect the homeland." In the case of the Department of Homeland Security, Bush seems to prefer the telling to the doing.

Crimes Against Nature

Robert Kennedy Jr.

Rolling Stone | December 11, 2003

The war in Iraq and the slowly resurging economy garnered most of the headlines this past year, but environmental advocates have continued to raise the alarm over what they perceive to be the Bush administration's disastrous environmental policies. The administration has never hidden its belief that existing environmental regulations were too stringent and were hurting American businesses, nor have officials been shy about hiring ex-lobbyists to regulate the companies they used to represent. The administration has also made an art form out of naming their programs: "Clear Skies," for a plan to ease emissions restrictions, and "Healthy Forests," for a plan that opens up wilderness areas to logging.

Administration backers say that this new approach strikes a better balance between economic and environmental interests. Opponents accuse Bush of distorting science and undermining existing laws. In July, 2003, for example, the New York Times *reported that "[Environmental Protection] Agency employees say they have been told either not to analyze or not to release information about mercury, carbon dioxide, and other air pollutants." A month before that, text supporting the concept of global warming was quietly deleted from an EPA report.*

More recently, the White House enraged environmentalists by backing an EPA plan that would let coal-burning power plants trade mercury pollution rights (rather than require each plant to meet strict reduction targets by 2007, as called for by the Clean Air Act), and by proposing to lump farm-raised and wild salmon together as a means of shifting salmon off the endangered species list (a move that would give industry greater latitude to deplete the wild salmon supply in rivers).

Here, Robert Kennedy Jr., senior attorney for the Natural Resources Defense Council, lays out the enviromental lobby's case against the Bush administration. . . .

George W. Bush will go down in history as America's worst environmental president.

In a ferocious three-year attack, the Bush administration has initiated more than 200 major rollbacks of America's environmental laws, weakening the protection of our country's air, water, public lands and wildlife. Cloaked in meticulously crafted language designed to deceive the public, the administration intends to eliminate the nation's most important environmental laws by the end of the year.

Under the guidance of Republican pollster Frank Luntz, the Bush White House has actively hidden its anti-environmental program behind deceptive rhetoric, telegenic spokespeople, secrecy, and the intimidation of scientists and bureaucrats.

The Bush attack was not entirely unexpected. George W. Bush had the grimmest environmental record of any governor during his tenure in Texas. Texas became number one in air and water pollution and in the release of toxic chemicals. In his six years in Austin, he championed a short-term pollution-based prosperity, which enriched his political contributors and corporate cronies by lowering the quality of life for everyone else. Now President Bush is set to do the same to America. After three years, his policies are already bearing fruit, diminishing standards of living for millions of Americans.

I am angry both as a citizen and a father. Three of my sons have asthma, and I watch them struggle to breathe on bad-air days. And they're comparatively lucky: One in four African-American children in New York shares this affliction; their suffering is often unrelieved because they lack the insurance and high-quality health care that keep my sons alive. My kids are among the millions of Americans who cannot enjoy the seminal American experience of fishing locally with their dad and eating their catch. Most freshwater fish in New York and all in Connecticut are now under consumption advisories. A main source of mercury pollution in America, as well as asthma-provoking ozone and particulates, is the coal-burning power plants that President Bush recently excused from complying with the Clean Air Act.

Furthermore, the deadly addiction to fossil fuels that White House policies encourage has squandered our treasury, entangled us in foreign wars, diminished our international prestige, made us a target for terrorist attacks, and increased our reliance on petty Middle Eastern dictators who despise democracy and are hated by their own people.

When the Republican right managed to install George W. Bush as president in 2000, movement leaders once again set about doing what they had attempted to do since the Reagan years: eviscerate the infrastructure of laws and regulations that protect the environment. For twenty-five years it has been like the zombie that keeps coming back from the grave.

The attacks began on inauguration day, when President Bush's chief of staff and former General Motors lobbyist Andrew Card quietly initiated a moratorium on all recently adopted regulations. Since then, the White House has enlisted every federal agency that oversees environmental programs in a coordinated effort to relax rules aimed at the oil, coal, logging, mining, and chemical industries as well as automakers, real estate developers, corporate agribusiness, and other industries.

Bush's Environmental Protection Agency has halted work on sixty-two environmental standards, the federal Department of Agriculture has stopped work on fifty-seven standards, and the Occupational Safety and Health Administration has halted twenty-one new standards. The EPA completed just two major rules—both under court order and both watered down at industry request—compared to twenty-three completed by the Clinton administration and fourteen by the Bush Sr. administration in their first two years.

This onslaught is being coordinated through the White House Office of Management and Budget—or, more precisely, OMB's Office of Information and Regulatory Affairs, under the direction of John Graham, the engine-room mechanic of the Bush stealth strategy. Graham's specialty is promoting changes in scientific and economic assumptions that underlie government regulations—such as recalculating cost-benefit analyses to favor polluters. Before coming to the White House, Graham was the founding director of the Harvard Center for Risk Analysis, where he received funding from America's champion corporate polluters: Dow Chemical, DuPont, Monsanto, Alcoa, Exxon, General Electric, and General Motors.

Under the White House's guidance, the very agencies entrusted to protect Americans from polluters are laboring to destroy environmental laws. Or they've simply stopped enforcing them. Penalties imposed for environmental violations have plummeted under Bush. The EPA has proposed eliminating 270 enforcement staffers, which would drop staff levels to the lowest level ever. Inspections of polluting businesses have dipped fifteen percent. Criminal cases referred for federal prosecution have dropped 40 percent. The EPA measures its success by the amount of pollution reduced or prevented as a result of its own actions. Last year, the EPA's two most senior career enforcement officials resigned after decades of service. They cited the administration's refusal to carry out environmental laws.

The White House has masked its attacks with euphemisms that would have embarrassed George Orwell. George W. Bush's "Healthy Forests" initiative promotes destructive logging of old-growth forests. His "Clear Skies" program, which repealed key provisions of the Clean Air Act, allows more emissions.

The administration uses misleading code words such as streamlining or reforming instead of weakening, and thinning instead of logging.

In a March 2003 memo to Republican leadership, pollster Frank Luntz frankly outlined the White House strategy on energy and the environment: "The environment is probably the single issue on which Republicans in general and President Bush in particular are most vulnerable," he wrote, cautioning that the public views Republicans as being "in the pockets of corporate fat cats who rub their hands together and chuckle maniacally as they plot to pollute America for fun and profit." Luntz warned, "Not only do we risk losing the swing vote, but our suburban female base could abandon us as well." He recommended that Republicans don the sheep's clothing of environmental rhetoric while dismantling environmental laws.

I prosecute polluters on behalf of the Natural Resources Defense Council, Riverkeeper, and Waterkeeper Alliance. As George W. Bush began his presidency, I was involved in litigation against the factory-pork industry, which is a large source of air and water pollution in America. Corporate pork factories cannot produce more efficiently than traditional family farmers without violating several federal environmental statutes. Industrial farms illegally dump millions of tons of untreated fecal and toxic waste onto land and into the air and water. Factory farms have contaminated hundreds of miles of waterways, put tens of thousands of family farmers and fishermen out of work, killed billions of fish, sickened consumers, and subjected millions of farm animals to unspeakable cruelty.

On behalf of several farm groups and fishermen, we sued Smithfield Foods and won a decision that suggested that almost all of American factory farms were violating the Clean Water Act. The Clinton EPA had also brought its own parallel suits addressing chronic air and water violations by hog factories. But almost immediately after taking office, the Bush administration ordered the EPA to halt its Clean Air Act investigations of animal factories and weaken the water rules to allow them to continue polluting indefinitely.

Several of my other national cases were similarly derailed. Eleven years ago, I sued the EPA to stop massive fish kills at power plants. Using antiquated technology, power plants often suck up the entire fresh water volume of large rivers, killing obscene numbers of fish. Just one facility, the Salem nuclear plant in New Jersey, kills more than 3 billion Delaware River fish each year, according to Martin Marietta, the plant's own consultant. These fish kills are illegal, and in 2001 we finally won our case. A federal judge ordered the EPA to issue regulations restricting power-plant fish kills. But soon after President

Bush's inauguration, the administration replaced the proposed new rule with clever regulations designed to allow the slaughter to continue unabated. The new administration also trumped court decisions that would have enforced greater degrees of wetlands protection and forbidden coal moguls from blasting off whole mountain-tops to get at the coal beneath.

The fishermen I represent are traditionally Republican. But, without exception, they see this administration as the largest threat not just to their livelihoods but to their values and their idea of what it means to be American. "Why," they'll ask, "is the president allowing coal, oil, power, and automotive interests to fix the game?"

Back to the Dark Ages

George W. Bush seems to be trying to take us all the way back to the Dark Ages by undermining the very principles of our environmental rights, which civilized nations have always recognized. Ancient Rome's Code of Justinian guaranteed the use to all citizens of the "public trust" or commons—those shared resources that cannot be reduced to private property—the air, flowing water, public lands, wandering animals, fisheries, wetlands and aquifers.

When Roman law broke down in Europe during the Dark Ages, feudal kings began to privatize the commons. In the early thirteenth century, when King John also attempted to sell off England's fisheries and erect navigational tolls on the Thames, his subjects rose up and confronted him at Runnymede, forcing him to sign the Magna Carta, which includes provisions guaranteeing the rights of free access to fisheries and waters.

Clean-air laws in England, passed in the fourteenth century, made it a capital offense to burn coal in London, and violators were executed for the crime. These "public trust" rights to unspoiled air, water, and wildlife descended to the people of the United States following the American Revolution. Until 1870, a factory releasing even small amounts of smoke onto public or private property was operating illegally.

But during the Gilded Age, when the corporate robber barons captured the political and judicial systems, those rights were stolen from the American people. As the Industrial Revolution morphed into the postwar industrial boom, Americans found themselves paying a high price for the resulting pollution. The wake-up call came in the late '60s, when Lake Erie was declared dead and Cleveland's Cuyahoga River exploded in colossal infernos.

In 1970, more than 20 million Americans took to the streets protesting the state of the environment on the first Earth Day. Whether they knew it or not, they were demanding a return of ancient rights.

During the next few years, Congress passed twenty-eight major environmental statutes, including the Clean Air Act, the Clean Water Act, and the Endangered Species Act, and it created the Environmental Protection Agency to apply and enforce these new laws. Polluters would be held accountable; those planning to use the commons would have to compile environmental-impact statements and hold public hearings; citizens were given the power to prosecute environmental crimes. Right-to-know and toxic-inventory laws made government and industry more transparent on the local level and our nation more democratic. Even the most vulnerable Americans could now participate in the dialogue that determines the destinies of their communities.

Earth Day caught polluters off guard. But in the next thirty years, they mounted an increasingly sophisticated and aggressive counterattack to undermine these laws. The Bush administration is a culmination of their three-decade campaign.

Strangling the Environment

In 1980, candidate Ronald Reagan declared, "I am a Sagebrush Rebel," marking a major turning point of the modern anti-environmental movement. In the early 1980s, the Western extractive industries, led by one of Colorado's worst polluters, brewer Joseph Coors, organized the Sagebrush Rebellion, a coalition of industry money and right-wing ideologues that helped elect Reagan president.

The big polluters who started the Sagebrush Rebellion were successful because they managed to broaden their constituency with anti-regulatory, anti-labor, and anti-environmental rhetoric that had great appeal both among Christian fundamentalist leaders such as Jerry Falwell and Pat Robertson, and in certain Western communities where hostility to government is deeply rooted. Big polluters found that they could organize this discontent into a potent political force that possessed the two ingredients of power in American democracy: money and intensity. Meanwhile, innovations in direct-mail and computer technologies gave this alliance of dark populists and polluters a deafening voice in American government.

Coors founded the Mountain States Legal Foundation in 1976 to bring lawsuits designed to enrich giant corporations, limit civil rights, and attack unions, homosexuals, and minorities. He also founded the right-wing Heritage Foundation, to provide a philosophical underpinning for the anti-environmental movement. While the foundation and its imitators—the Competitive Enterprise Institute, the American Enterprise Institute, the Reason Foundation, the Federalist Society, the Marshall Institute and others—claim to advocate free markets and property rights, their agenda is more pro-pollution than anything else.

From its conception, the Heritage Foundation and its neoconservative cronies urged followers to "strangle the environmental movement," which Heritage named "the greatest single threat to the American economy." Ronald Reagan's victory gave Heritage Foundation and the Mountain States Legal Foundation immeasurable clout. Heritage became known as Reagan's "shadow government," and its 2,000-page manifesto, "Mandate for Change," became a blueprint for his administration. Coors handpicked his Colorado associates: Anne Gorsuch became the EPA administrator; her husband, Robert Burford, a cattle baron who had vowed to destroy the Bureau of Land Management, was selected to head that very agency. Most notorious, Coors chose James Watt, president of the Mountain States Legal Foundation, as the secretary of the interior. Watt was a proponent of "dominion theology," an authoritarian Christian heresy that advocates man's duty to "subdue" nature. His deep faith in laissez-faire capitalism and apocalyptic Christianity led Secretary Watt to set about dismantling his department and distributing its assets rather than managing them for future generations. During a Senate hearing, he cited the approaching Apocalypse to explain why he was giving away America's sacred places at fire-sale prices: "I do not know how many future generations we can count on before the Lord returns."

Meanwhile, Anne Gorsuch enthusiastically gutted EPA's budget by sixty percent, crippling its ability to write regulations or enforce the law. She appointed lobbyists fresh from their hitches with the paper, asbestos, chemical, and oil companies to run each of the principal agency departments. Her chief counsel was an Exxon lawyer; her head of enforcement was from General Motors.

These attacks on the environment precipitated a public revolt. By 1983, more than a million Americans and all 125 American-Indian tribes had signed a petition demanding Watt's removal. After being forced out of office, Watt was indicted on twenty-five felony counts of influence-pedaling. Gorsuch and twenty-three of her cronies were forced to resign following a congressional investigation of sweetheart deals with polluters, including Coors. Her first deputy, Rita Lavelle, was jailed for perjury.

The indictments and resignations put a temporary damper on the Sagebrush

Rebels, but they quickly regrouped as the "Wise Use" movement. Wise Use founder, the timber-industry flack Ron Arnold, said, "Our goal is to destroy, to eradicate the environmental movement. We want to be able to exploit the environment for private gain, absolutely."

By 1994, Wise Use helped propel Newt Gingrich to the Speaker's chair of the U.S. House of Representatives and turn his anti-environmental manifesto, "The Contract With America," into law. Gingrich's chief of environmental policy was Representative Tom DeLay, the one-time Houston exterminator who was determined to rid the world of pesky pesticide regulations and to promote a biblical worldview. He targeted the Endangered Species Act as the second-greatest threat to Texas after illegal aliens. He also wanted to legalize the deadly pesticide DDT, and he routinely referred to the EPA as "the Gestapo of government." In January 1995, DeLay invited a group of 350 lobbyists representing some of America's biggest polluters to collaborate in drafting legislation to dismantle federal health, safety, and environmental laws.

Gingrich and DeLay had learned from the James Watt debacle that they had to conceal their radical agenda. Carefully eschewing public debates on their initiatives, they mounted a stealth attack on America's environmental laws. Rather than pursue a frontal assault against popular statutes such as the Endangered Species, Clean Water, and Clean Air acts, they tried to undermine these laws by attaching silent riders to must-pass budget bills.

But the public got wise. Moderate Republicans teamed up with the Clinton administration to block the worst of it. My group, the NRDC, as well as the Sierra Club and the U.S. Public Interest Research Group, generated more than 1 million letters to Congress. When President Clinton shut down the government in December 1995 rather than pass a budget bill spangled with anti-environmental riders, the tide turned against Gingrich and DeLay. By the end of that month, even conservatives disavowed the attack. "We lost the battle on the environment," DeLay conceded.

Undermining the Scientists

Today, with the presidency and both houses of Congress under the anti-environmentalists' control, they are set to eviscerate the despised laws. White House strategy is to promote its unpopular policies by lying about its agenda, cheating on the science and stealing the language and rhetoric of the environmental movement.

Even as Republican pollster Luntz acknowledged that the scientific evidence is against the Republicans on issues like global warming, he advised them to find scientists willing to hoodwink the public. "You need to continue to make the lack of scientific certainty a primary issue," he told Republicans, "by becoming even more active in recruiting experts sympathetic to your view."

In the meantime, he urged them to change their rhetoric. " 'Climate change,' " he said, "is less threatening than 'global warming.' While global-warming has catastrophic connotations attached to it, climate change suggests a more controllable and less emotional challenge."

The EPA's inspector general received broad attention for his August 21, 2003, finding that the White House pressured the agency to conceal the public-health risks from poisoned air following the September 11th World Trade Center attacks. But this 2001 deception is only one example of the administration's pattern of strategic distortion. Earlier this year, it suppressed an EPA report warning that millions of Americans, especially children, are being poisoned by mercury from industrial sources.

This behavior is consistent throughout the Bush government. Consider the story of James Zahn, a scientist at the Department of Agriculture who resigned after the Bush administration suppressed his taxpayer-funded study proving that billions of antibiotic-resistant bacteria can be carried daily across property lines from meat factories into neighboring homes and farms. In March 2002, Zahn accepted my invitation to present his findings to a convention of family-farm advocates in Iowa. Several weeks before the April conference, pork-industry lobbyists learned of his appearance and persuaded the Department of Agriculture to forbid him from appearing. Zahn told me he had been ordered to cancel a dozen appearances at county health departments and similar venues.

In May, the White House blocked the EPA staff from publicly discussing contamination by the chemical perchlorate—the main ingredient in solid rocket fuel. The administration froze federal regulations on perchlorate, even as new research reveals alarmingly high levels of the chemical in the nation's drinking water and food supply, including many grocery-store lettuces. Perchlorate pollution has been linked to neurological problems, cancer, and other life-threatening illnesses in some twenty states. The Pentagon and several defense contractors face billions of dollars in potential cleanup liability.

The administration's leading expert in manipulating scientific data is Interior Secretary Gale Norton. During her nomination hearings, Norton promised not to ideologically slant agency science. But as her friend Thomas Sansonetti, a coal-industry lobbyist who is now assistant attorney general, predicted, "There won't be any biologists or botanists to come in and pull the wool over her eyes."

In autumn 2001, Secretary Norton provided the Senate Committee on Energy and Natural Resources with her agency's scientific assessment that Arctic oil drilling would not harm hundreds of thousands of caribou. Not long afterward, Fish and Wildlife Service biologists contacted the Public Employees for Environmental Responsibility, which defends scientists and other professionals working in state and federal environmental agencies. "The scientists provided us the science that they had submitted to Norton and the altered version that she had given to Congress a week later," said the group's executive director, Jeff Ruch. There were seventeen major substantive changes, all of them minimizing the reported impacts. When Norton was asked about the alterations in October 2001, she dismissed them as typographical errors.

Later, she and White House political adviser Karl Rove forced National Marine Fisheries scientists to alter findings on the amount of water required for the survival of salmon in Oregon's Klamath River, to ensure that large corporate farms got a bigger share of the river water. As a result, more than 33,000 chinook and coho salmon died—the largest fish kill in the history of America. Mike Kelly, the biologist who drafted the original opinion (and who has since been awarded federal whistle-blower status), told me that the coho salmon is probably headed for extinction. "Morale is low among scientists here," Kelly says. "We are under pressure to get the right results. This administration is putting the species at risk for political gain—and not just in the Klamath."

Norton has also ordered the rewriting of an exhaustive twelve-year study by federal biologists detailing the effects that Arctic drilling would have on populations of musk oxen and snow geese. She reissued the biologists' report two weeks later as a two-page paper showing no negative impact to wildlife. She also ordered suppression of two studies by the Fish and Wildlife Service concluding that the drilling would threaten polar-bear populations and violate the international treaty protecting bears. She then instructed the Fish and Wildlife Service to redo the report to "reflect the Interior Department's position." She suppressed findings that mountaintop mining would cause "tremendous destruction of aquatic and terrestrial habitat" and a Park Service report that found that snowmobiles were hurting Yellowstone's air quality, wildlife, and the health of its visitors and employees.

Norton's Fish and Wildlife Service is the first ever not to voluntarily list a single species as endangered or threatened. Her officials have blackballed scientists and savaged studies to avoid listing the trumpeter swan, revoke the listing of the grizzly bear, and shrink the remnant habitat for the Florida panther. She disbanded the service's oldest scientific advisory committee in order to halt protection of desert fish in Arizona, New Mexico, and Texas that are headed for extinction. Interior career staffers and scientists say they are monitored by Norton's industry appointees to ensure that future studies do not conflict with industry profit-making.

Cooking the Books on Global Warming

There is no scientific debate in which the White House has cooked the books more than that of global warming. In the past two years the Bush administration has altered, suppressed, or attempted to discredit close to a dozen major reports on the subject. These include a ten-year peer-reviewed study by the International Panel on Climate Change, commissioned by the president's father in 1993 in his own efforts to dodge what was already a virtual scientific consensus blaming industrial emissions for global warming.

After disavowing the Kyoto Protocol, the Bush administration commissioned the federal government's National Academy of Sciences to find holes in the IPCC analysis. But this ploy backfired. The NAS not only confirmed the existence of global warming and its connection to industrial greenhouse gases, it also predicted that the effects of climate change would be worse than previously believed, estimating that global temperatures will rise between 2.5 and 10.4 degrees by 2100.

A May 2002 report by scientists from the EPA, NASA, and the National Oceanic and Atmospheric Administration, approved by Bush appointees at the Council on Environmental Quality and submitted to the United Nations by the U.S., predicted similarly catastrophic impacts. When confronted with the findings, Bush dismissed it with his smirking condemnation: "I've read the report put out by the bureaucracy. . . . "

Afterward, the White House acknowledged that, in fact, he hadn't. Having failed to discredit the report with this untruth, George W. did what his father had done: He promised to study the problem some more. Last fall, the White House announced the creation of the Climate Research Initiative to study global warming. The earliest results are due next fall. But the White House's draft plan for CRI was derided by the NAS in February as a rehash of old studies and established science lacking "most elements of a strategic plan."

In September 2002, administration censors released the annual EPA report on air pollution without the agency's usual update on global warming, that section having been deleted by Bush appointees at the White House. On June

19, 2003, a "State of the Environment" report commissioned by the EPA in 2001 was released after language about global warming was excised by flat-earthers in the White House. The redacted studies had included a 2001 report by the National Research Council, commissioned by the White House. In their place was a piece of propaganda financed by the American Petroleum Institute challenging these conclusions.

This past July, EPA scientists leaked a study, which the agency had ordered suppressed in May, showing that a Senate plan—co-sponsored by Republican Senator John McCain—to reduce the pollution that causes global warming could achieve its goal at very small cost. Bush reacted by launching a $100 million ten-year effort to prove that global temperature changes have, in fact, occurred naturally, another delay tactic for the fossil-fuel barons at taxpayer expense.

Princeton geo-scientist Michael Oppenheimer told me, "This administration likes to emphasize what we don't know while ignoring or minimizing what we do know, which is a prescription for paralysis on policy. It's hard to imagine what kind of scientific evidence would suffice to convince the White House to take firm action on global warming."

Across the board, the administration yields to Big Energy. At the request of ExxonMobil, and with the help of a lobbying group working for coal-burning utility Southern Co., the Bush administration orchestrated the removal of U.S. scientist Robert Watson, the world-renowned former NASA atmospheric chemist who headed the United Nations' IPCC. He was replaced by a little-known scientist from New Delhi, India, who would be generally unavailable for congressional hearings.

The Bush administration now plans to contract out thousands of environmental-science jobs to compliant industry consultants already in the habit of massaging data to support corporate profit-taking, effectively making federal science an arm of Karl Rove's political machine. The very ideologues who derided Bill Clinton as a liar have institutionalized dishonesty and made it the reigning culture of America's federal agencies. "At its worst," Oppenheimer says, "this approach represents a serious erosion in the way a democracy deals with science."

Inside the Cheney Task Force

There is no better example of the corporate cronyism now hijacking American democracy than the White House's cozy relationship with the energy industry. It's hard to find anyone on Bush's staff who does not have extensive corporate connections, but fossil-fuel executives rule the roost. The energy industry contributed more than $48.3 million to Republicans in the 2000 election cycle, with $3 million to Bush. Now the investment has matured. Both Bush and Cheney came out of the oil patch. Thirty-one of the Bush transition team's forty-eight members had energy-industry ties. Bush's cabinet and White House staff is an energy-industry dream team—four cabinet secretaries, the six most powerful White House officials, and more than twenty high-level appointees are alumni of the industry and its allies.

The potential for corruption is staggering. Take the case of J. Steven Griles, deputy secretary of the Interior Department. During the first Reagan administration, Griles worked directly under James Watt at Interior, where he helped the coal industry evade prohibitions against mountaintop-removal strip mining. In 1989, Griles left government to work as a mining executive and then as a lobbyist with National Environmental Strategies, a Washington, D.C., firm that represented the National Mining Association and Dominion Resources, one of the nation's largest power producers. When Griles got his new job at Interior, the National Mining Association hailed him as "an ally of the industry."

It's bad enough that a former mining lobbyist was put in charge of regulating mining on public land. But it turns out that Griles is still on the industry's payroll. In 2001, he sold his client base to his partner Marc Himmelstein for four annual payments of $284,000, making Griles, in effect, a continuing partner in the firm.

Because Griles was an oil and mining lobbyist, the Senate made him agree in writing that he would avoid contact with his former clients as a condition of his confirmation. Griles has nevertheless repeatedly met with former coal clients to discuss new rules allowing mountaintop mining in Appalachia and destructive coal-bed methane drilling in Wyoming. He also met with his former oil clients about offshore leases. These meetings prompted Senator Joseph Lieberman to ask the Interior Department to investigate Griles. With Republicans in control of congressional committees, no subpoenas have interrupted the Griles scandals.

With its operatives in place, the Bush energy plan became an orgy of industry plunder. Days after his inauguration, Bush launched the National Energy Policy Development Group, chaired by Cheney. For three months, the task force held closed-door meetings with energy-industry representatives—then refused to disclose the names of the participants.

For the first time in history, the nonpartisan General Accounting Office sued the executive branch, for access to these records. NRDC put in a Freedom of Information Act request, and when Cheney did not respond, we also sued. On February 21, 2002, U.S. District Judge Gladys Kessler ordered Energy Secretary Spencer Abraham and other agency officials to turn over the records relating to their participation in the work of the energy task force. Under this court order, NRDC has obtained some 20,000 documents. Although none of the logs on the vice president's meetings have been released yet and the pages were heavily redacted to prevent disclosure of useful information, the documents still allow glimpses of the process.

The task force comprised Cabinet secretaries and other high-level administration officials with energy-industry pedigrees. The undisputed leader was Cheney, who hails from Wyoming, the nation's largest coal producer, and who, for six previous years, was CEO of Halliburton, the oil-service company. Treasury Secretary Paul O'Neill was chairman of the Aluminum Company of America for thirteen years. Aluminum-industry profits are directly related to energy prices. O'Neill promised to immediately sell his extensive stock holdings in his former company (worth more than $100 million) to avoid conflicts of interest, but he delayed the sale until after the energy plan was released. By then, thanks partly to the administration's energy policies, Alcoa's stock had risen thirty percent. Energy Secretary Abraham, a former one-term senator from Michigan, received $700,000 from the auto industry in his losing 2000 campaign, more than any other Senate candidate. At Energy, Abraham led the administration effort to scuttle fuel-economy standards, allow SUVs to escape fuel-efficiency minimums, and create obscene tax incentives for Americans to buy the largest gas guzzlers.

Joe Allbaugh, director of the Federal Energy Regulatory Commission, sat next to Abraham on the task force. Allbaugh's wife, Diane, is an energy-industry lobbyist and represents three firms—Reliant Energy, Entergy, and TXU, each of which paid her $20,000 in the three months of the task force's deliberation. Joe Allbaugh participated in task-force meetings on issues directly affecting those companies, including debates about environmental rules for power plants and—his wife's specialty—electricity deregulation.

Commerce Secretary Don Evans, an old friend of the president from their early days in the oil business, was CEO of Tom Brown Inc., a Denver oil-and-gas company, and a trustee of another drilling firm. Interior Secretary Gale Norton, a mining-industry lawyer, accepted nearly $800,000 from the energy industry during her 1996 run in Colorado for the U.S. Senate.

In the winter and spring of 2001, executives and lobbyists from the oil, coal, electric-utility, and nuclear industries tramped in and out of the Cabinet room and Cheney's office. Many of the lobbyists had just left posts inside Bush's presidential campaign to work for companies that had donated lavishly to that effort. Companies that made large contributions were given special access. Executives from Enron Corp., which contributed $2.5 million to the GOP from 1999 to 2002, had contact with the task force at least ten times, including six face-to-face meetings between top officials and Cheney.

After one meeting with Enron CEO Kenneth Lay, Cheney dismissed California Governor Gray Davis's request to cap the state's energy prices. That denial would enrich Enron and nearly bankrupt California. It has since emerged that the state's energy crisis was largely engineered by Enron. According to the *New York Times*, the task-force staff circulated a memo that suggested "utilizing" the crisis to justify expanded oil and gas drilling. President Bush and others would cite the California crisis to call for drilling in the Arctic National Wildlife Refuge.

Energy companies that had not ponied up remained under pressure to give to Republicans. When Westar Energy's chief executive was indicted for fraud, investigators found an e-mail written by Westar executives describing solicitations by Republican politicians for a political action committee controlled by Tom DeLay as the price for a "seat at the table" with the task force.

Task-force members began each meeting with industry lobbyists by announcing that the session was off the record and that participants were to share no documents. A National Mining Association official told reporters that the industry managed to control the energy plan by keeping the process secret. "We've probably had as much input as anybody else in town," he said. "I have to take my hat off to them—they've been able to keep a lid on it."

When it was suggested that access to the administration was for sale, Cheney hardly apologized. "Just because somebody makes a campaign contribution doesn't mean that they should be denied the opportunity to express their view to government officials," he said. Although they met with hundreds of industry officials, Cheney and Abraham refused to meet with any environmental groups. Cheney made one exception to the secrecy policy: On May 15, 2001, the day before the task force sent its plan to the president, CEOs from wind-, solar-,and geothermal-energy companies were granted a short meeting with Cheney. Afterward, they were led into the Rose Garden for a press conference and a photo op.

While peddling influence to energy tycoons, the White House quietly dropped criminal and civil charges against Koch Industries, America's largest privately held oil company. Koch faced a ninety-seven-count federal felony indictment and $357 million in fines for knowingly releasing ninety metric tons of carcinogenic benzene and concealing the releases from federal regulators. Koch executives contributed $800,000 to Bush's presidential campaign and to other top Republicans.

Last March, the Federal Trade Commission dropped a Clinton-era investigation of price gouging by the oil and gas industries, even as Duke Energy, a principal target of the probe, admitted to selling electricity in California for more than double the highest previously reported price. The Bush administration said that the industry deserved a "gentler approach." Administration officials also winked at a scam involving a half-dozen oil companies cheating the government out of $100 million per year in royalty payments.

Southern Co. was among the most adept advocates for its own self-interest. The company, which contributed $1.6 million to Republicans from 1999 to 2002, met with Cheney's task force seven times. Faced with a series of EPA prosecutions at power plants violating air-quality standards, the company retained Haley Barbour, former Republican National Committee chairman and now governor-elect of Mississippi, to lobby the administration to ignore Southern's violations.

The White House then forced the Justice Department to drop the prosecution. Justice lawyers were "astounded" that the administration would interfere in a law-enforcement matter that was "supposed to be out of bounds from politics." The EPA's chief enforcement officer, Eric Schaeffer, resigned. "With the Bush administration, whether or not environmental laws are enforced depends on who you know," Schaeffer told me. "If you've got a good lobbyist, you can just buy your way out of trouble."

Along with Barbour, Southern retained current Republican National Committee chairman and former Montana governor Marc Racicot. Barbour and Racicot repeatedly conferred with Abraham and Cheney, urging them to ease limits on carbon-dioxide pollution from power plants and to gut the Clean Air Act. On May 17, 2001, the White House released its energy plan. Among the recommendations were exempting old power plants from Clean Air Act compliance and adopting Barbour's arguments about carbon-dioxide restrictions. Barbour repaid the favor that week by raising $250,000 at a May 21 GOP gala honoring Bush. Southern donated $150,000 to the effort.

Cheney's task force had at least nineteen contacts with officials from the nuclear-energy industry—whose trade association, the Nuclear Energy Institute, donated $100,000 to the Bush inauguration gala and $437,000 to Republicans from 1999 to 2002. The report recommended loosening environmental controls on the industry, reducing public participation in the siting of nuclear plants, and adding billions of dollars in subsidies for the nuclear industry.

Cheney wasn't embarrassed to reward his old cronies at Halliburton, either. The final draft of the task-force report praises a gas-recovery technique controlled by Halliburton—even though an earlier draft had criticized the technology. The technique, which has been linked to the contamination of aquifers, is currently being investigated by the EPA. Somehow, that got edited out of the report.

Big Coal and the Destruction of Appalachia

Coal companies enjoyed perhaps the biggest payoff. At the West Virginia Coal Association's annual conference in May 2002, president William D. Raney assured 150 industry moguls, "You did everything you could to elect a Republican president." Now, he said, "you are already seeing in his actions the payback."

Peabody Energy, the world's largest coal company and a major contributor to the Bush campaign, was one of the first to cash in. Immediately after his inauguration, Bush appointed two executives from Peabody and one from its Black Beauty subsidiary to his energy advisory team.

When the task force released its final report, it recommended accelerating coal production and spending $2 billion in federal subsidies for research to make coal-fired electricity cleaner. Five days later, Peabody issued a public-stock offering, raising $60 million more than analysts had predicted. Company vice president Fred Palmer credited the Bush administration. "I am sure it affected the valuation of the stock," he told the *Los Angeles Times*.

Peabody also wanted to build the largest coal-fired power plant in thirty years upwind of Mammoth Cave National Park in Kentucky, a designated UNESCO World Heritage site and International Biosphere Reserve. With arm-twisting from Deputy Interior Secretary Steven Griles and another $450,000 in GOP contributions, Peabody got what it wanted. A study on the air impacts was suppressed, and park scientists who feared that several endangered species might go extinct due to mercury and acid-rain deposits were silenced.

At the Senate's request, Griles had signed a "statement of disqualification" on August 1, 2001, committing himself to avoiding issues affecting his former clients. Three days later, he nevertheless appeared before the West Virginia Coal Association and promised executives that "we will fix the federal rules very soon on water and soil placement." That was fancy language for pushing whole mountaintops into valleys, a practice worth billions to the industry.

As a Reagan official, Griles helped devise the practice, which a federal court declared illegal in 2002, after 1,200 miles of streambeds had been filled and 380,000 acres of Appalachian forestlands had been rendered barren moonscapes.

Now Griles was promising his former coal clients he would fix these rules. In May 2002, the EPA and the Army Corps of Engineers adopted the language recommended by his former client, the National Mining Association. Had Griles not intervened, the practice of mountaintop-removal mining would have been severely restricted. Griles also pushed EPA deputy administrator Linda Fisher to overrule career personnel in the agency's Denver office who had given a devastating assessment to a proposal to produce coal-bed methane gas in the Powder River basin in Wyoming. Although Griles had recused himself from any discussion of this subject because it would directly enrich his former clients, he worked aggressively behind the scenes on behalf of a proposal to build 51,000 wells. The project will require 26,000 miles of new roads and 48,000 miles of pipeline, and will foul pristine landscapes with trillions of gallons of toxic wastewater.

Blueprint for Plunder

The energy-task-force plan is a $20 billion subsidy to the oil, coal, and nuclear industries, which are already swimming in record revenues. In May 2003, as the House passed the plan and as the rest of the nation stagnated in a recession abetted by high oil prices, Exxon announced that its profits had tripled from the previous quarter's record earnings. The energy plan recommends opening protected lands and waters to oil and gas drilling and building up to 1,900 electric-power plants. National treasures such as the California and Florida coasts, the Arctic National Wildlife Refuge and the areas around Yellowstone Park will be opened for plunder for the trivial amounts of fossil fuels that they contain. While increasing reliance on oil, coal, and nuclear power, the plan cuts the budget for research into energy efficiency and alternative power sources by nearly a third. "Conservation may be a sign of personal virtue," Cheney explained, but it should not be the basis of "comprehensive energy policy."

As if to prove that point, Republicans simultaneously eliminated the tax credit that had encouraged Americans to buy gas-saving hybrid cars, and weakened efficiency standards for everything from air conditioners to automobiles. They also created an obscene $100,000 tax break for Hummers and the thirty-eight biggest gas guzzlers. Then, adding insult to injury, the Energy

Department robbed $135,615 from the anemic solar, renewables, and energy-conservation budget to produce 10,000 copies of the White House's energy plan.

To lobby for the plan, more than 400 industry groups enlisted in the Alliance for Energy and Economic Growth, a coalition created by oil, mining, and nuclear interests and guided by the White House. It cost $5,000 to join, "a very low price," according to Republican lobbyist Wayne Valis. The prerequisite for joining, he wrote in a memo, was that members "must agree to support the Bush energy proposal in its entirety and not lobby for changes." Within two months, members had contributed more than $1 million. The price for disloyalty was expulsion from the coalition and possible reprisal by the administration. "I have been advised," wrote Valis, "that this White House 'will have a long memory.' "

The plan represents a massive transfer of wealth from the public to the energy sector. Indeed, Bush views his massive tax cuts as a way of helping Americans pay for inflated energy bills. "If I had my way," he declared, "I'd have [the tax cuts] in place tomorrow so that people would have money in their pockets to deal with high energy prices."

Looting the Commons

Although Congress will have its final vote on the plan in November, the White House has already devised ways to implement most of its worst provisions without congressional interference. In October 2001, the administration removed the Interior Department's power to veto mining permits, even if the mining would cause "substantial and irreparable harm" to the environment. That December, Bush and congressional Republicans passed an "economic-stimulus package" that proposed $2.4 billion worth of tax breaks, credits, and loopholes for Chevron, Texaco, Enron, and General Electric. The following February, the White House announced it would abandon regulations for three major pollutants—mercury, sulfur dioxide, and nitrogen oxide.

Early in the Bush administration, Vice President Cheney had solicited an industry wish list from the United States Energy Association, the lobbying arm for trade associations including the American Petroleum Institute, the National Mining Association, the Nuclear Energy Institute, and the Edison Institute. The USEA responded by providing 105 specific recommendations from its members for plundering our natural resources and polluting America's air and water. In a speech to the group in June 2002, Energy Secretary Abraham reported that the administration had already implemented three-quarters of the industry's recommendations and predicted the rest would pass through Congress shortly.

On August 27, 2002—while most of America was heading off for a Labor Day weekend—the administration announced that it would redefine carbon dioxide, the primary cause of global warming, so that it would no longer be considered a pollutant and would therefore not be subject to regulation under the Clean Air Act. The next day, the White House repealed the act's "new source review" provision, which requires companies to modernise pollution control when they modify their plants.

According to the National Academy of Sciences, the White House rollback will cause 30,000 Americans to die prematurely each year. Although the regulation will probably be reversed in the courts, the damage will have been done, and power utilities such as Southern Co. will escape criminal prosecution. As soon as the new regulations were announced, John Pemberton, chief of staff to the EPA's assistant administrator for air, left the agency to work for Southern. The EPA's congressional office chief also left, to join Southern's lobbying shop, Bracewell, Patterson.

By summer 2003, the White House had become a virtual pinata for energy moguls. In August, the administration proposed limiting the authority of states to object to offshore-drilling decisions, and it ordered federal land managers across the West to ease environmental restrictions for oil and gas drilling in national forests. The White House also proposed removing federal protections for most American wetlands and streams. As an astounded Republican, Representative Christopher Shays, told me, "It's almost like they want to alienate people who care about the environment, as if they believe that this will help them with their core."

EPA: From Bad to Worse

On August 30, 2003, President Bush nominated Utah's three-term Republican governor Mike Leavitt to replace his beleaguered EPA head, Christine Todd Whitman, who was driven from office, humiliated in even her paltry efforts to moderate the pillage. In October, Leavitt was confirmed by the Senate.

Like Gale Norton, Leavitt has a winning personality and a disastrous environmental record. Under his leadership, Utah tied for last as the state with the worst environmental enforcement record and ranked second-worst (behind Texas) for both air quality and toxic releases. As governor, Leavitt displayed the same contempt for science that has characterized the Bush administration.

He fired more than seventy scientists employed by state agencies for producing studies that challenged his political agenda. He fired a state enforcement officer who penalized one of Leavitt's family fish farms for introducing whirling disease into Utah, devastating the state's wild-trout populations.

Leavitt has a penchant for backdoor deals to please corporate polluters. Last year he resurrected a frivolous and moribund Utah lawsuit against the Interior Department and then settled the suit behind closed doors without public involvement, stripping 6 million acres of wilderness protections. This track record does not reflect the independence, sense of stewardship, and respect for science and law that most Americans have the right to expect in our nation's chief environmental guardian.

The Threat to Democracy

Generations of Americans will pay the Republican campaign debt to the energy industry with global instability, depleted national coffers, and increased vulnerability to price shocks in the oil market.

They will also pay with reduced prosperity and quality of life at home. Pollution from power plants and traffic smog will continue to skyrocket. Carbon-dioxide emissions will aggravate global warming. Acid rain from Midwestern coal plants has already sterilized half the lakes in the Adirondacks and destroyed the forest cover in the high peaks of the Appalachian range up into Canada. The administration's attacks on science and the law have put something even greater at risk. Americans need to recognize that we are facing not just a threat to our environment but to our values, and to our democracy.

Growing up, I was taught that communism leads to dictatorship and capitalism to democracy. But as we've seen from the the Bush administration, the latter proposition does not always hold. While free markets tend to democratize a society, unfettered capitalism leads invariably to corporate control of government.

America's most visionary leaders have long warned against allowing corporate power to dominate the political landscape. In 1863, in the depths of the Civil War, Abraham Lincoln lamented, "I have the Confederacy before me and the bankers behind me, and I fear the bankers most." Franklin Roosevelt echoed that sentiment when he warned that "the liberty of a democracy is not safe if the people tolerate the growth of private power to a point where it becomes stronger than their democratic state itself. That, in its essence, is fascism—ownership of government by an individual, by a group or by any controlling power."

Today, more than ever, it is critical for American citizens to understand the difference between the free-market capitalism that made our country great and the corporate cronyism that is now corrupting our political process, strangling democracy, and devouring our national treasures.

Corporate capitalists do not want free markets, they want dependable profits, and their surest route is to crush competition by controlling government. The rise of fascism across Europe in the 1930s offers many informative lessons on how corporate power can undermine a democracy. In Spain, Germany, and Italy, industrialists allied themselves with right-wing leaders who used the provocation of terrorist attacks, continual wars, and invocations of patriotism and homeland security to tame the press, muzzle criticism by opponents, and turn government over to corporate control. Those governments tapped industrial executives to run ministries and poured government money into corporate coffers with lucrative contracts to prosecute wars and build infrastructure. They encouraged friendly corporations to swallow media outlets, and they enriched the wealthiest classes, privatized the commons, and pared down constitutional rights, creating short-term prosperity through pollution-based profits and constant wars. Benito Mussolini's inside view of this process led him to complain that "fascism should really be called 'corporatism.'"

While the European democracies unraveled into fascism, America confronted the same devastating Depression by reaffirming its democracy. It enacted minimum-wage and Social Security laws to foster a middle class, passed income taxes and anti-trust legislation to limit the power of corporations and the wealthy, and commissioned parks, public lands, and museums to create employment and safeguard the commons.

The best way to judge the effectiveness of a democracy is to measure how it allocates the goods of the land: Does the government protect the commonwealth on behalf of all the community members, or does it allow wealth and political clout to steal the commons from the people?

Today, George W. Bush and his court are treating our country as a grab bag for the robber barons, doling out the commons to large polluters. Last year, as the calamitous rollbacks multiplied, the corporate-owned TV networks devoted less than 4 percent of their news minutes to environmental stories. If they knew the truth, most Americans would share my fury that this president is allowing his corporate cronies to steal America from our children.

National Conversation: Gay Marriage

"We're already married"

Ruth Rosen

San Francisco Chronicle | February 18, 2004

After simmering for years, the issue of same-sex marriage burst onto the national scene late in 2003. The precipitating event was a 4-3 ruling by the Massachusetts State Supreme Court in November, upholding the right of same-sex couples to be married under the Massachusetts state constitution beginning in May 2004. Republican governor Mitt Romney immediately called for a state constitutional amendment banning same-sex marriages. A deadlocked Massachusetts legislature failed to pass such an amendment, however, calling it quits after a raucous two-day constitutional convention in mid-February—the same week that newly elected San Francisco mayor Gavin Newsom surprised the nation by declaring that the county of San Francisco would start issuing marriage licenses to same-sex couples, in direct defiance of California's Defense of Marriage Act.

Overnight, San Francisco became a magnet for thousands of couples eager to take advantage of his offer. In this column, the San Francisco Chronicle's *Ruth Rosen reports from the steps of City Hall on the history-making event. . . .*

Who are all the gay and lesbian couples streaming into San Francisco's City Hall to get married? What hopes and dreams did they bring to these sudden and unexpected marriage ceremonies?

Last Friday, I talked with some of the these couples who, in defiance of state law, married in San Francisco. Even though their marriage licenses may be judged invalid by the courts, they came because they wanted to participate in this historic event and to have, even temporarily, the same rights enjoyed by heterosexual couples.

Some of the women, dressed in stunning white gowns, juggled babies and bouquets. Some of the men, dressed in elegant tuxedos, sported a carnation in their lapels and cradled babies, while friends held their paperwork. One man pushed his partner in a wheelchair, a broad smile spreading across his face.

Beaming faces spread an intoxicating sense of joy throughout the building. As couples looked into each other's eyes, arms wrapped around each other, their friends took snapshots and the national media documented the occasion for the evening news. I chatted with one veteran cameraman who was overwhelmed by the scene and, much to his surprise, found himself blinking back tears.

Jennifer Shifflet, 31, and Kati Keyser, 29, both graduate students, live in Berkeley and have been together for eight years. The day before, Jennifer had telephoned Kati at work and said, "Let's do it tomorrow; it's such a historic event." Neither one had a chance to tell their parents of their plan.

But their parents wouldn't be surprised. With pride, they showed me pictures of the family members and friends who gathered around them at their commitment ceremony. During that event, they had expressed their gratitude to all the earlier activists who had struggled for gay rights. Kati said they had come "to support this historic event."

What do they imagine might change, now that they are married? "I won't have to call her my partner or girlfriend at a doctor's office or a hospital," said Jennifer. "She's now my spouse."

"We want to have children," said Kati. "Someday I can call a child-care center or a school and say that my spouse will be picking up our child. We'll be viewed as a valid family."

"It's an honor to be part of this. I'm thrilled," said Jennifer. "But the truth is, we had already made this commitment and felt married."

Randa Johnson and Adreanna Riles, both social workers in their late 30s, jointly own a house in Felton. They also felt that they had already married. Still, the day before they traveled to the steps of San Francisco's City Hall, they had asked each other: "Should we wait? No! We've got to be a part of it."

They too, have been together for eight years, but, as Adreanna put it, "I never imagined that we'd be able to marry in my lifetime." Draped in the white dresses they had worn at their commitment ceremony four years ago, they both felt they were "renewing" vows.

Why, then did they want to wed? Aside from the possibility of getting health and retirement benefits reserved for spouses, they said that their religious friends would regard their relationship as more legitimate now that they are married. They also want to have children and feel that they and their children will be viewed as a more legitimate family by teachers and others in their community.

Glowing with happiness, the two women looked like—and spoke like—any other married couple who deeply love and respect each other.

There may have been couples who had just met, were swept up in the heady passion of a new romance, and decided to rush down to City Hall to get married.

But that's not what I saw. I met couples who already had made a spiritual commitment to each other and whose love had been tested by time and travail.

For them, a marriage license meant greater social legitimacy and fewer logical and legal hassles.

That's how Andy Anderson, 42, and Marcus Wonacott, 49, viewed it. Long-time residents of San Francisco, the men had already shared sixteen years of their lives. They, too, already felt they had wed.

As they approached the steps to City Hall, a friend greeted them and pinned roses on their suit jackets. Their faces beamed as they held hands. "We're really very grateful to Mayor Gavin Newsom," said Andy. "This really makes a statement. He deserves so much credit for being so bold and daring."

"It a historic milestone," said Marcus. "We're part of history and we know it."

Then, with joyful smiles, they eagerly entered City Hall to renew vows they had made eight years ago, at their commitment ceremony.

A Political Recalculation on Gay Marriage
Terry Neal

WashingtonPost.com | February 26, 2004

One of the earliest gay-marriage showdowns occurred in Hawaii, when the state supreme court ruled in 1993 that Hawaii's ban on same-sex marriages was unconstitutional. Suddenly, it appeared that same-sex marriage was on the verge of becoming legal in our fiftieth state. It never happened—Hawaiians eventually passed a state amendment banning gay marriage, which was upheld by the state supreme court—but at the time, thirty states, worried that they might have to recognize Hawaii's same-sex marriages, quickly enacted laws outlawing such marriages. In 1996 the U.S. Congress also joined the fray by passing the Defense of Marriage Act, which denied federal recognition to same-sex marriages and gave states the right not to recognize such marriages licensed by other states.

When the issue heated up again in 2003, social conservatives—for whom a ban on gay marriage had become a top priority—began to lobby for something stronger: A U.S. Constitutional amendment limiting marriage to heterosexual couples. President Bush had said repeatedly that he opposed gay marriage but was in favor of same-sex civil unions (a position most of the Democratic presidential candidates took as well) but amendment proponents wanted him to announce his outright support. On

February 25, 2004, he finally complied—"acting," the New York Times *reported, "under enormous pressure from conservative supporters, who insisted that he speak out in an election year on a matter of critical importance to many of his Christian backers." In this edition of his regular online column, Terry Neal looks at the politics behind the president's endorsement. . . .*

President Bush and his supporters have often claimed he makes his policy decisions without political calculation or attention to polls. But his decision this week to advocate a constitutional amendment banning same-sex marriage raises fresh questions about that claim.

From a political standpoint, calling for a constitutional amendment banning same-sex marriage was probably a "win-win" for the White House. Polls show most Americans support banning same-sex marriage, even while many of them support allowing some form of civil unions.

The White House's calculation is that—given support in the polls for banning same-sex marriage—the president won't face a backlash from moderate voters. And those who are most likely to be angered aren't going to vote for him anyway.

On the other hand, the president appeases a base that has grown frustrated with his reluctance to insert himself into the culture wars that dominated the early 1980s.

Bush campaign spokesman Terry Holt said necessity, not politics, dictated the president's announcement. He said Bush felt that his hand was forced by "activist judges" in Massachusetts and San Francisco Mayor Gavin Newsom's decision to allow same sex couples to marry in the city.

Opponents of same-sex marriage were putting pressure on the president to do something now. In an interview last week—a week before the president made his announcement—conservative activist Gary Bauer offered a less than enthusiastic endorsement of Bush, whom he ran against for the Republican presidential nomination in 2000. Of course, the people Bauer represents won't vote for a Democrat in November, but they could decide to stay home on election day.

This isn't the first time Bauer and conservatives have pressured Bush on the issue. Bauer ran against Bush for the GOP nomination in 2000 and helped keep the spotlight on issues important to social conservatives.

During the 2000 primary battle, Bush refused to meet with leaders of the Log Cabin Republicans, a gay political group, in Austin. After effectively wrapping up the nomination, however, Bush's refusal to meet with gay leaders threatened to undermine his campaign theme of being a "uniter not a divider" and a "compassionate conservative."

By April 2000, the Bush campaign was shifting gears and knew there was more to gain than lose by meeting with gay leaders. After all, what were the social conservatives going to do, vote for Al Gore? As the *Washington Post*'s beat reporter covering the Bush campaign, I attended the news conference at the statehouse in Austin after Bush met with the Log Cabin Republicans.

"The meeting was a wide-ranging discussion on issues," Bush declared to the press corps. "I'm a better person for the meeting. I enjoyed it."

Pragmatism—the desire to take back the White House at all cost—muted the discontent among the party faithful. The Bush campaign touted the meeting as a sign that he was a "new kind of Republican," even though he never wavered from positions such as opposition to same-sex marriage.

The meeting was summed up succinctly by Human Rights Campaign spokesman David Smith, whom I quoted afterward saying: "Politically, obviously, it's a win-win for him. He gets to look tolerant and moderate, and, at the same time, he can say to his ultraconservative followers that he has not changed any of his policy positions."

At this point in the 2004 cycle, Bush appears to be more concerned about shoring up his conservative base than winning swing voters. In some ways this was a preemptive strike; there is no reason they had to do this now, according to past positions taken by both Bush and Vice President Cheney. Both have said they supported leaving the issue to the states. And the federal Defense of Marriage Act of 1996 ensured that no state had to recognize same-sex marriages performed in another state—such as those performed recently in New Mexico and California. Many Republicans in Congress preferred to let the issue play out in the courts first.

But Keith Appell, a well-known Republican media adviser in Washington, said same-sex marriage is issue number one now for social conservatives. He has close ties to people like Focus on the Family founder James Dobson and Concerned Women for America president Sandy Rios—the sort of people who can pick up the phone and get Karl Rove at the White House. In fact, Dobson and Rios have done just that, lobbying the White House intensely on this issue, Appell said.

Appell and others point specifically to polls that Americans overwhelmingly oppose same-sex marriage. He said the fight over same-sex marriage would hinge on whether his side could get Americans to reject the idea that popular opposition to same-sex marriage isn't comparable to popular support in the past for issues that eventually became wildly unpopular—slavery, for example.

"Religious conservatives see this issue very clearly," he said. "They don't see heterosexuals and homosexuals being equal. Homosexuality, unlike race, is not an immutable characteristic. We've met plenty of people who are no longer gay. We don't know anyone who was formerly black or Hispanic."

Appell referred to Stephen Bennett, a Connecticut-based conservative activist who said he had sex with men until he was 29. Now married with two children, Bennett said his homosexuality was based on environmental factors—primarily a long, painful estrangement from his father. He said he left the lifestyle and became a heterosexual after reconciling with his father and finding religion.

"We start from the premise that homosexuality is wrong and that it develops out of dysfunction," said Bennett, who regularly speaks at Concerned Women for America events. "We want to help people come out of it. I don't think [banning gay marriage] is depriving anyone of rights. I know many gays and lesbians, and they have as many rights as anyone else. But the Bible says marriage is between a man and a woman."

But there are risks for the president, and the White House knows it. Bush has never been particularly enthusiastic about wading into the culture wars. During his last campaign he observed how some of the party's harsh rhetoric about "welfare queens" and gays and the focus on Bill Clinton's sex life turned off many moderate voters in the mid-1990s, after the Republican revolution of 1994. Even if a majority of Americans opposes same-sex marriage, the rhetoric from the right could prove damaging if the debate gets out of control this year.

Gay rights advocates see this issue as the front of a new civil rights movement. "The issue isn't whether you agree with the lifestyle we live," said Amy Errett, a board member of the Human Rights Campaign. "The issue is that we're American, and we deserve this civil right. We fight in the military. We're police officers. We're CEOs. We're your next door neighbors."

Errett is the CEO of Olivia Cruises and Resorts, a lifestyle and travel company for lesbian couples. She and her partner are among the scores of gay and lesbian couples who have wed in San Francisco in recent weeks. "I'm outraged," she said. "I really feel that the whole issue of a constitutional amendment to define what committed relationships are is outrageous. I don't see divorce being made illegal or adultery being made illegal."

Errett said Appell and Bennett's argument was specious. Certainly some people were gay by choice, but many others feel strongly that they were born that way. That argument is irrelevant anyway, she said, because the same can be said of straight people: They have chosen their sexual preference. Why then should one group who chooses one adult behavior between consulting adults be given preferential treatment over another that simply makes a different choice?

Errett argued that Republicans were promoting a double standard, promoting states' rights only when it was convenient to them. "The whole concept is quite hypocritical and contrary to what this administration had made crystal clear, which is that there should be less government and that the states should make their own decisions.

"This constitutional amendment clearly does the opposite of that. This amendment sounds very much like a double standard. It has been very much drawn from a religious perspective and not being looked at for what it is, a civil rights issue, not a religious issue."

Revolution, Televised
Andrew Sullivan

The New Republic | March 1, 2004

In early March 2004, the California Supreme Court ordered a temporary halt to San Francisco's same-sex weddings. By then, however, other states were joining the battle. On Feburary 27, Jason West, the mayor of New Paltz, New York, presided over twenty-five same-sex ceremonies before the local district attorney put a stop to the proceedings by threatening to throw West in jail. In Portland, Oregon, officials began giving out same-sex marriage licenses after the county attorney took the opposite stance, ruling that the county was required to do so. The city of Asbury Park, New Jersey, also started accepting same-sex marriage applications until the state attorney general issued a warning; the city council then voted to sue the state over the issue.

Opponents were busy as well: As of the first week in March, the Wisconsin Assembly and Kansas House of Representatives had voted for state amendments banning same-sex marriages, while similar amendments had been defeated in the Idaho Senate and were due to be voted on in Michigan. There was a growing sense, however, that the anti-gay marriage forces were on the losing side of history. In this essay, New Republic *senior editor Andrew Sullivan—a self-described conservative gay man—analyzes what he feels is a watershed moment for America's gay community. . . .*

It turned out to be a different kind of Valentine's Day. On television, you could watch hundreds of gay couples lining up in the rain and waiting through the night to receive (largely symbolic) marriage licenses from the mayor of San Francisco. Back here in Washington, two friends of mine who have been together for about seven years also embarked on something new. Doug took his boyfriend, Chip, to the steps of the Supreme Court, got down on his knees, and proposed. It was after dusk, and a nervous cop shined his flashlight on them to make sure they weren't doing anything improper. More symbolism: For decades, cops had shone lights on gay men in public places to see if they were having illicit sex. Now the light was on a gay couple for seeking the right to marry. The cop saw what was going on, turned off his flashlight, and moved on.

Something is happening in gay America. From an abstract argument pioneered by a few, the reality of marriage has now clearly been embraced by the vast majority. The silent types in gay culture are now in the vanguard— the ones whose relationships are conducted away from the streets and the parades and the bars, in suburbs or small towns or residential neighborhoods in big cities. Many have clearly decided that they do not need to wait any more for others to approve their relationships. They are already married in fact if not in law, in the eyes of their family and friends, and sometimes even in the eyes of their church. But they still lack the legal protections that make marriage a civil reality. Today, they no longer ask for these. They demand them.

This is the changed consciousness that every civil rights movement aims for. And, in that sense, we have already won. I've long believed that one thing holding gay America back from full equality is a residual lack of self-esteem and self-belief. That's changing. Marriage—the very institution long used to stigmatize, marginalize, and disenfranchise gays—might now be opening to them. It already exists in Canada and is emerging in Hawaii and Alaska and Vermont and now Massachusetts. Every debate we have entrenches it further in the public mind—gay and straight alike. And, once you have internalized the notion that you really are as good as any heterosexual, it is hard to snuff out the empowerment that accompanies it. In this sense, San Francisco is merely a start, a gesture. When legal marriages emerge in Massachusetts in May, the gesture will become real.

And that, I think, will shift the whole dynamic of the debate. The question will no longer be whether we should agree to some new idea of marriage, but whether we intend to strip existing marriages of their legal protections; whether children of lawful parents will be made suddenly illegitimate; whether shared property must be unraveled; whether joint commitments can be legally undone by outsiders. Suddenly, it will be the religious right attacking marriage and the Catholic Church proposing divorce.

Some say gay marriage should not be imposed by the courts. But almost all civil rights breakthroughs in U.S. history have come through the courts. And Massachusetts is already contemplating legislative responses, including a state constitutional amendment. The voters will have their say. Others argue that marriage is a religious matter that gays shouldn't touch. But civil marriage is not a religious matter; it's a civil matter. When President Bush calls marriage a "sacred institution," he is stepping beyond the bounds of his secular office. If civil marriage is "sacred," why, after all, should atheists be allowed to marry?

For gay conservatives, and especially gay Republicans, this is a particularly fraught time. They are discovering that the fundamentalist core of the Republican Party is opposed not just to gay sex but also to gay love. Gays will be condemned for promiscuity, and they will be condemned for monogamy. The point is the condemnation. The president, for his part, wants to bar marriage and any civil protections to gay couples but without explicitly condemning them. He is two decades too late. Gay people are no longer so beaten down that they can be corralled to support their own disenfranchisement. Nor will gay conservatives sign on to a constitutional amendment that is the antithesis of traditional conservatism. The proposed amendment, drafted by some of the most radical "natural law" jurists in the country, would not simply rob states of any autonomy with regard to marriage rights, ending centuries of U.S. constitutional practice. It would forbid state judges from interpreting their own state constitutions and void any civil unions for gay couples that included the "legal incidents" of marriage. It would also be the first amendment designed specifically to target a minority and curtail their civil rights. Gay Republicans know this. They are terrified of what might happen and horrified by what their party has become. But they are ready to fight as well.

Can we avoid the war? I wish we could. Some kind of state-by-state solution is obviously the best recourse. But the religious right feels that allowing for marriage rights in even one state would represent the end of civilization.

A federal civil-unions bill could undermine the calls for marriage rights—but, again, the religious right would not countenance it. Or there could be civil unions on the state level—but, if ratified, the amendment would gut them of any legal force as well. So the stakes mount. No one knows what lies ahead. We have never lived in a time of greater promise for gay Americans, nor a time of greater foreboding. After years on the margins, we are grappling toward a new dignity. But that dignity will be fiercely contested, debated, attacked.

In the face of this, perhaps the best psychological insulation is remembering what this is really about: cementing our loves and relationships regardless of what the world does or doesn't do. We can propose on the steps of the Supreme Court or in the pouring rain outside San Francisco City Hall. We can marry in our hearts and in our homes before we marry under the law. We can love each other as human beings before we can love each other as equal citizens. And that they can never take away.

Without the Consent of the Governed
Hugh Hewitt

Weekly Standard Online | March 25, 2004

In this piece, Weekly Standard *columnist Hugh Hewitt accuses gay-marriage supporters (including, specifically, Andrew Sullivan, the author of the preceding column in this collection) of working through the courts to impose their will on a reluctant majority of U.S. citizens. "Across the country, even in the liberal precincts of California," he notes, "supermajorities continue to believe that marriage is the union of a man and a woman, and presented with the question on ballots, have continually affirmed the millennia-old standard." Hewitt goes on to praise the proposed Federal Marriage Amendment—which Sullivan has called "the biggest assault on gay rights in U.S. history"—as "a necessary, indeed urgently required antidote to such a radical assault on the bedrock of the American experience." . . .*

The *Washington Post* opened its Wednesday coverage of Tuesday's Senate Judiciary Committee hearing on an amendment to the United States Constitution concerning marriage with the hardly neutral declaration that "[d]espite indications that a bill to amend the Constitution to ban gay marriages has little hope of passage, GOP congressional leaders continued to push the amendment yesterday, prompting Democrats to charge that Republicans are orchestrating an emotionally divisive issue for the fall elections."

Such transparently hostile coverage from elite media will mark the amendment's progress through this year and the years ahead, but proponents of the amendment have grown increasingly confident that a sustained battle to defend the thousands of years–old definition of marriage will succeed. They have coalesced around language that would leave civil-union laws untouched and they have been cheered by public opinion polls showing surging support in the aftermath of the antics in San Francisco and elsewhere. Intellectual leaders of the battle are emerging, with folks like Maggie Gallagher and Stanley Kurtz producing the numerous pieces necessary to sustain the argument in today's opinions-by-the-pound environment.

There is one aspect of the debate that has not yet been fully joined, perhaps because it is so simple to state and so impossible for proponents of gay marriage to rebut: It concerns the consent of the governed.

The consent of the governed is arguably the bedrock principle of the American republic, animating the Declaration of Independence, the Constitution, Lincoln's restatement of the Declaration at Gettysburg, and the 14th Amendment. The great civil rights laws of the 1960s were also built upon the notion that any lasting public ethic had to proceed from an act of legislative will, thus anchoring that ethic to the consent of the governed.

Never in the 228 years since the Declaration has any legislative body at the federal or state level passed any law with the intent of establishing the proposition that two people of the same sex could marry. Not once. The principle of equality between religions was consented to in the First Amendment; between races, in the 14th Amendment; between genders, in the 19th Amendment. Each of these principles had long and difficult passages to majoritarian and statutory status. Courts could not and did not impose them because courts cannot will majorities into being—they can only articulate the implications of previously established legislative actions.

Had the proponents of gay marriage taken their cause to state legislatures, they would have been rebuffed, at least today and in the foreseeable future. Across the country, even in the liberal precincts of California, supermajorities continue to believe that marriage is the union of a man and a woman, and presented with the question on ballots, have continually affirmed the millennia-old standard. And off course the Congress has already passed, by supermajorities in both houses, the Defense of Marriage Act.

Faced with this wall of resistance, proponents of a radical new view of marriage wish to bypass the consent of the governed and impose their vision. Andrew Sullivan has taken to branding opponents of gay marriage as "theocrats," but of course those seeking to impose their own vision of society—without even a single instance of elected officials acting in legislative bodies to endorse their view—are acting in the tradition currently on display in Iran, where the reigning mullahs do everything in their power to prevent majorities from electing legislatures to represent their own desires and views. The theocrats of the gay marriage movement have set their goals above the consent of the governed.

The marriage amendment is a necessary, indeed urgently required antidote to such a radical assault on the bedrock of the American experience. If imposition of new norms can be accomplished without even one law anywhere ever having being passed, then it can happen again and again whenever willful minorities can persuade robed elites to act without conscience against the idea that all law proceeds from the people.

It has become quaint to quote the Framers or to summon up Lincoln. In an age of *Queer Eye for the Straight Guy*, *Sex and the City*, and Howard Stern, there isn't a lot of mileage in arguments about the essence of civil society requiring legislative action. But Lincoln was standing over a cemetery that was the final home to thousands who had died to preserve a union when he described the essence of America as "government of the people, by the people, for the people." There is no law that can be legitimate without the consent of the people.

The Marriage Amendment is to me and hopefully millions more primarily about preserving the essential structure of representative government against those who are frustrated by that structure's processes and values, and who would rather do great and lasting injury to that structure to achieve their ends than work within it to achieve legitimate laws.

Who Knows Hearts, Minds of Voters?
Scot Lehigh

The Boston Globe | April 2, 2004

In mid-March, after handing out some 4,000 marriage licenses, San Francisco was ordered by the California Supreme Court to halt the practice—shifting the debate to the California judicial system. Massachusetts was a different story, however. At 12:01 on the morning of May 17, 2004, after the failure of several last-ditch legal attempts by opponents, the Bay State became the first state to legalize same-sex marriages (Vermont has endorsed same-sex "civil unions" since 2000).

In the first week of legalization, 2,500 couples applied for marriage licenses. Still, the fight promised to continue on various fronts: Governor Mitt Romney threatened to overturn any marriages of non-Massachusetts residents—citing a 1913 law that was originally passed to prevent interracial couples from wedding—while officials in Provincetown, Worcester, and Somerville vowed they would accept applications from out-of-staters anyway. Meanwhile, the Massachusetts state legislature was in the process of voting on a state amendment that would allow same-sex civil unions, but not marriages. Here, Scot Lehigh parses the proposed amendment. . . .

Who are you? It's a question worth asking in a week that saw the Legislature give the first of two required approvals to a "compromise" constitutional amendment that would establish civil unions for gays but ban them from marrying.

No one, it's said, is passionate in defense of a compromise, and that's doubly true of this one. Conservatives still prefer a ban on gay marriage with no strong provision for civil unions. Liberals still want outright gay marriage. Thus it's impossible to know whether the compromise will ever reach the ballot.

But as the debate rolls on, here's an illuminating question: What do the various sides think or hope of you, the voters? So, to generalize a little:

Conservatives, who maneuvered to put a stricter amendment on the ballot, believe you're so put off by the idea of homosexual pairs sharing the same civil status as heterosexual couples that you'll vote to ban gay marriage even with no guarantees that serious provisions will be made for homosexual couples and their families.

In the broad middle, one finds people of cautious good will, legislators willing to ensure gays and lesbians every state right that comes with marriage but not marriage itself. They think you are basically decent, tolerant people—but that you just can't stretch far enough to accept equality for gays and lesbians.

Here's how the Senate minority leader, Brian Lees, a key player in winning approval for the compromise amendment, sees it: "I don't want to take away any rights that are already there or that people get as of May 17," the date gay marriage takes effect.

However, if the civil unions compromise did become part of the Constitution, it would also ban gay marriage. Which means that if gay marriage should ever win national recognition, Massachusetts same-sex couples would be denied hundreds of federal benefits that come with marital status.

Asked about that, Lees replies: "You can't look at things in the future." Not and continue to think that writing a gay marriage ban into the state Constitution is wise public policy, at any rate. If the state does adopt such a ban, what would happen if federal recognition of gay marriage someday takes place? "If it ever got recognized nationally, we would move to change that back, probably," says Lees.

OK, but wouldn't it be better not to have enacted the constitutional ban in the first place?

It's the gay community that ultimately has the highest hopes about how you'll react. Yes, gay and lesbian activists and their allies are fighting hard to keep anything from coming to the ballot. But they also recognize that the strategy they have pursued has very real risks. If the compromise is derailed, support could well grow for a strict gay marriage ban aimed at a later ballot. If done as a petition drive, such a measure would need the votes not of a majority of two constitutional conventions but the approval of only 25 percent of lawmakers in those joint sessions. And in the aftermath of the Supreme Judicial Court's Goodridge ruling, using parliamentary ploys to kill such an amendment would be exceedingly unlikely.

Still, rather than compromise away the possibility of full marriage rights by supporting the civil unions amendment, the gay community is hoping that if something does come to the ballot, their fellow citizens will cast a vote for fairness and against discrimination.

"Our hope is that come May 17, people will see gay couples get married around the state and they'll notice the very next day that nothing in their lives has changed, that the only people whose lives have changed are those gay couples who got married and that for the rest of the world it will be one big yawn," says Arline Isaacson, cochair of the Massachusetts Gay and Lesbian Political Caucus.

There, then, are the competing ideas about you, the voters:

- That you would vote to ban gay marriage without any real consideration for gays and lesbians or their children.
- That you're willing to be accepting as long as gays and lesbians don't
  try to assert that their relationships are the equal of your marriage.
- Or that over the next few years, you'll give serious thought to the claims
  of equity and equality—and ultimately decide that those values are
  important enough to overcome any qualms you may have about gay
  marriage.

It's time to start thinking about who you really are.

Abolish Marriage
Michael Kinsley

Slate.com | July 2, 2003

*For the final column of this section we go back in time to mid-2003, just after the
U.S. Supreme Court's historic ruling striking down anti-sodomy laws in Texas. The decision, which included strong language protecting citizens from discrimination based
on their sexual preference, laid the groundwork for the subsequent gay marriage showdown in various state courthouses around the nation.*

*In this commentary on the decision and its implications, Michael Kinsley asks why
the government should be involved in ratifying marriage at all. Don't count on the
U.S. Congress to buy this argument anytime soon, however: As we went to press, Senate
Majority Leader Bill Frist announced that he planned to bring the federal Marriage
Amendment—which would amend the consitution to ban same-sex marriages—up
for a vote before the full Senate (Late note: it was defeated). . . .*

Critics and enthusiasts of *Lawrence v. Texas*, last week's Supreme Court decision invalidating state anti-sodomy laws, agree on one thing: The next argument is going to be about gay marriage. As Justice Scalia noted in his tart
dissent, it follows from the logic of *Lawrence*. Mutually consenting sex with

the person of your choice in the privacy of your own home is now a basic right of American citizenship under the Constitution. This does not mean that the government must supply it or guarantee it. But the government cannot forbid it, and the government also should not discriminate against you for choosing to exercise a basic right of citizenship. Offering an institution as important as marriage to male-female couples only is exactly this kind of discrimination. Or so the gay rights movement will now argue. Persuasively, I think.

Opponents of gay rights will resist mightily, although they have been in retreat for a couple of decades. General anti-gay sentiments are now considered a serious breach of civic etiquette, even in anti-gay circles. The current line of defense, which probably won't hold either, is between social toleration of homosexuals and social approval of homosexuality. Or between accepting the reality that people are gay, even accepting that gays are people, and endorsing something called "the gay agenda." Gay marriage, the opponents will argue, would cross this line. It would make homosexuality respectable and, worse, normal. Gays are welcome to exist all they want, and to do their inexplicable thing if they must, but they shouldn't expect a government stamp of approval.

It's going to get ugly. And then it's going to get boring. So, we have two options here. We can add gay marriage to the short list of controversies—abortion, affirmative action, the death penalty—that are so frozen and ritualistic that debates about them are more like Kabuki performances than intellectual exercises. Or we can think outside the box. There is a solution that ought to satisfy both camps and may not be a bad idea even apart from the gay-marriage controversy.

That solution is to end the institution of marriage. Or rather (he hastens to clarify, Dear) the solution is to end the institution of government-sanctioned marriage. Or, framed to appeal to conservatives: End the government monopoly on marriage. Wait, I've got it: Privatize marriage. These slogans all mean the same thing. Let churches and other religious institutions continue to offer marriage ceremonies. Let department stores and casinos get into the act if they want. Let each organization decide for itself what kinds of couples it wants to offer marriage to. Let couples celebrate their union in any way they choose and consider themselves married whenever they want. Let others be free to consider them not married, under rules these others may prefer. And, yes, if three people want to get married, or one person wants to marry herself, and someone else wants to conduct a ceremony and declare them married, let 'em. If you and your government aren't implicated, what do you care?

In fact, there is nothing to stop any of this from happening now. And a lot of it does happen. But only certain marriages get certified by the government. So, in the United States we are about to find ourselves in a strange situation where the principal demand of a liberation movement is to be included in the red tape of a government bureaucracy. Having just gotten state governments out of their bedrooms, gays now want these governments back in. Meanwhile, social-conservative anti-gays, many of them southerners, are calling on the government in Washington to trample states' rights and nationalize the rules of marriage, if necessary, to prevent gays from getting what they want. The Senate Majority Leader, Bill Frist of Tennessee, responded to the Supreme Court's *Lawrence* decision by endorsing a constitutional amendment, no less, against gay marriage.

If marriage were an entirely private affair, all the disputes over gay marriage would become irrelevant. Gay marriage would not have the official sanction of government, but neither would straight marriage. There would be official equality between the two, which is the essence of what gays want and are entitled to. And if the other side is sincere in saying that its concern is not what people do in private, but government endorsement of a gay "lifestyle" or "agenda," that problem goes away, too.

Yes, yes, marriage is about more than sleeping arrangements. There are children, there are finances, there are spousal job benefits like health insurance and pensions. In all these areas, marriage is used as a substitute for other factors that are harder to measure, such as financial dependence or devotion to offspring. It would be possible to write rules that measure the real factors at stake and leave marriage out of the matter. Regarding children and finances, people can set their own rules, as many already do. None of this would be easy. Marriage functions as what lawyers call a "bright line," which saves the trouble of trying to measure a lot of amorphous factors. You're either married or you're not. Once marriage itself becomes amorphous, who-gets-the-kids and who-gets-health-care become trickier questions.

So, sure, there are some legitimate objections to the idea of privatizing marriage. But they don't add up to a fatal objection. Especially when you consider that the alternative is arguing about gay marriage until death do us part.

Part Four:
(Not) Politics as Usual

Lie Down for America

Thomas Frank

from *Harper's Magazine* | April 2004

An abiding frustration among left-wing policy makers and politicians is the fact that so many people who, in theory, would benefit more from liberal government policies still insist on voting for conservative candidates who support policies that tilt toward the wealthy. In this passage—actually the opening section of a much longer essay that appeared in Harper's Magazine—*Thomas Frank offers an eloquent rumination on this great American paradox. . . .*

The poorest county in America isn't in Appalachia or the Deep South. It is on the Great Plains, a region of struggling ranchers and dying farm towns, and in the election of 2000 the Republican candidate for president, George W. Bush, carried it by a majority of greater than 75 percent.*

This puzzled me when I first read about it, as it puzzles many of the people I know. For us it is the Democrats that are the party of workers, of the poor, of the weak and the victimized. Figuring this out, we think, is basic; it is part of the ABCs of adulthood. When I told a friend of mine about that impoverished High Plains county so enamored of President Bush, she was perplexed. "How can anyone who has ever worked for someone else vote Republican?" she asked. How could so many people get it so wrong?

Her question is apt; it is, in many ways, the preeminent question of our times. People getting their fundamental interests wrong is what American political life is all about. This species of derangement is the bedrock of our civic order; it is the foundation on which all else rests. This derangement has put the Republicans in charge of all three branches of government; it has elected presidents, senators, governors; it shifts the Democrats to the right and then impeaches Bill Clinton just for fun.

*I am referring to Loup County, Nebraska. According to the Bureau of Economic Analysis, the county's per capita personal income was only $6,235 in 2002. In 2000, the poorest county was McPherson, also in Nebraska, which went for George W. Bush by more than 80 percent. On the sad phenomenon of High Plains poverty, see the study by Patricia Funk and Jon Bailey, "Trampled Dreams: The Neglected Economy of the Rural Great Plains" (Walthill, Nebr.: Center for Rural Affairs, 2000).

If you earn more than $300,000 a year, you owe a great deal to this derangement. Raise a glass sometime to those indigent High Plains Republicans as you contemplate your good fortune: It is thanks to their self-denying votes that you are no longer burdened by the estate tax, or troublesome labor unions, or meddlesome banking regulators. Thanks to the allegiance of these sons and daughters of toil you have escaped what your affluent forebears used to call "confiscatory" income-tax levels. It is thanks to them that you were able to buy two Rolexes this year instead of one and take delivery on that limited-edition Segway with the gold trim.

Or perhaps you are one of those many, many millions of average-income Americans who see nothing deranged about this at all. For you this picture of hard-times conservatism makes perfect sense, and it is the opposite phenomenon—working-class people who insist on voting for liberals—that strikes you as an indecipherable puzzlement. Maybe you see it the way the bumper sticker I spotted at a Kansas City gun show puts it: A WORKING PERSON THAT SUPPORTS DEMOCRATS IS LIKE A CHICKEN THAT SUPPORTS COL. SANDERS!

Maybe you've seen it that way for so long that it's hard for you to remember why blue-collar people were ever Democrats in the first place. Maybe you stood up for America way back in 1968, sick and tired of those rich kids in beads bad-mouthing the country. Or maybe Ronald Reagan brought you over, the way he talked about that sunshiny, Glenn Miller America that you remembered from the time before the world went to hell. Or maybe Bill Clinton made a Republican out of you, with his obvious contempt for non-Ivy Americans, the ones he had the nerve to order into combat even though he himself took the coward's way out when his turn came.

Nearly everyone has a conversion story of this kind that they can tell: how their dad had been a union steelworker and a stalwart Democrat, but how all their brothers and sisters started voting Republican; or how their cousin gave up on Methodism and started going to the Pentecostal church out on the edge of town; or how they themselves just got so sick of being scolded for eating meat or for wearing clothes emblazoned with the State U's Indian mascot that one day Fox News started to seem "fair and balanced" to them after all.

Welcome to the Great Backlash, a style of conservatism that is anything but complacent. Whereas earlier forms of conservatism emphasized fiscal sobriety, the backlash mobilizes voters with explosive social issues—summoning public outrage over everything from busing to un-Christian art—which it then marries to probusiness economic policies. Cultural anger is marshaled to achieve economic ends. And it is these economic achievements—not the forgettable skirmishes of the never-ending culture wars—that are the movement's greatest monuments. The backlash is what has made possible the international free-market consensus of recent years, with all the privatization, deregulation, and deunionization that are its components. Backlash ensures that Republicans will continue to be returned to office even when their free-market miracles fail and their libertarian schemes don't deliver and their "New Economy" collapses. It makes possible the policy pushers' fantasies of "globalization" and a free-trade empire that are foisted upon the rest of the world with such self-assurance. Because some artist decides to shock the hicks by dunking Jesus in urine, the entire planet must remake itself along the lines preferred by the Republican Party, U.S.A.

The Great Backlash has made the laissez-faire revival possible, but this does not mean that it speaks to us in the manner of the capitalists of old, invoking the divine right of money or demanding that the lowly learn their place in the great chain of being. On the contrary: The backlash imagines itself as a foe of the elite, as the voice of the unfairly persecuted, as a righteous protest of the people on history's receiving end. That its champions today control all three branches of government matters not a whit. That its greatest beneficiaries are the wealthiest people on the planet does not give it pause.

In fact, backlash leaders systematically downplay the politics of economics. The movement's basic premise is that culture outweighs economics as a matter of public concern—that *Values Matter Most*, as one backlash book title has it. On those grounds it rallies citizens who would once have been reliable partisans of the New Deal to the standard of conservatism. Old-fashioned values may count when conservatives appear on the stump, but once conservatives are in office the only old-fashioned situation they care to revive is the regimen of low wages and lax regulations. Over the last three decades they have smashed the welfare state, reduced the tax burden on corporations and the wealthy, and generally facilitated the country's return to a nineteenth-century pattern of wealth distribution. Thus the primary contradiction of the backlash: It is a working-class movement that has done incalculable, historic harm to working-class people.

The leaders of the backlash may talk Christ, but they walk corporate. Values may "matter most" to voters, but they always take a back seat to the needs of money once the elections are won. This is a basic earmark of the phenomenon, absolutely consistent across its decades-long history. Abortion is never halted. Affirmative action is never abolished. The culture industry is never forced to clean up its act. Even the greatest culture-warrior of them all, Ronald Reagan, was a notorious cop-out once it came time to deliver.

One might expect this reality to vex the movement's true believers. Their grandstanding leaders never produce, their fury mounts and mounts, and nevertheless they turn out every two years to return their right-wing heroes to office for a second, a third, a twentieth try. The trick never ages, the illusion never wears off. *Vote* to stop abortion; *receive* a rollback in capital-gains taxes. *Vote* to make our country strong again; *receive* deindustrialization. *Vote* to screw those politically correct college professors; *receive* electricity deregulation. *Vote* to get government off our backs; *receive* conglomeration and monopoly everywhere from media to meatpacking. *Vote* to stand tall against terrorists; *receive* Social Security privatization efforts. *Vote* to strike a blow against elitism; *receive* a social order in which wealth is more concentrated than ever before in our lifetimes, in which workers have been stripped of power and CEOs are rewarded in a manner beyond imagining.

Backlash theorists imagine countless conspiracies in which the wealthy, powerful, and well-connected—the liberal media, the atheistic scientists, the obnoxious eastern elite—pull the strings and make the puppets dance. And yet the backlash itself has been a political trap so devastating to the interests of Middle America that even the most diabolical of string-pullers would have had trouble dreaming it up. Here, after all, is a rebellion against "the establishment" that has wound up abolishing the tax on inherited estates. Here is a movement whose response to the power structure is to make the rich even richer; whose answer to the undeniable degradation of working-class life is to lash out angrily at labor unions and liberal workplace-safety programs; whose solution to the rise of ignorance in America is to pull the rug out from under public education.

Like a French Revolution in reverse—one in which the *sans-culottes* pour down the streets demanding more power to the aristocracy—the backlash pushes the spectrum of the acceptable to the right, to the right, further to the right. It may never bring prayer back to the schools, but it has rescued all manner of right-wing economic nostrums from history's dustbin. Having rolled back the landmark economic reforms of the sixties (the war on poverty) and those of the thirties (labor law, agricultural price supports, banking regulation), its leaders now turn their guns on the accomplishments of the earliest years of progressivism (Wilson's estate tax, Theodore Roosevelt's antitrust measures). With a little more effort, the backlash may well repeal the entire twentieth century.

Mad About You
Jonathan Chait

The New Republic | September 29, 2003

After witnessing eight years of nonstop Clinton-bashing by conservatives, the liberal camp found themselves chuckling in amazement when right-wing pundits began complaining about how a new phenomenon known as "Bush hatred" was poisoning the well of political discourse. In this essay, Jonathan Chait analyzes the left's widely-shared animus for our forty-third president. . . .

I hate President George W. Bush. There, I said it. I think his policies rank him among the worst presidents in U.S. history. And, while I'm tempted to leave it at that, the truth is that I hate him for less substantive reasons, too. I hate the inequitable way he has come to his economic and political achievements and his utter lack of humility (disguised behind transparently false modesty) at having done so. His favorite answer to the question of nepotism— "I inherited half my father's friends and all his enemies"—conveys the laughable implication that his birth bestowed more disadvantage than advantage. He reminds me of a certain type I knew in high school—the kid who was given a fancy sports car for his sixteenth birthday and believed that he had somehow earned it. I hate the way he walks—shoulders flexed, elbows splayed out from his sides like a teenage boy feigning machismo. I hate the way he talks— blustery self-assurance masked by a pseudo-populist twang. I even hate the things that everybody seems to like about him. I hate his lame nickname-bestowing—a way to establish one's social superiority beneath a veneer of chumminess (does anybody give their boss a nickname without his consent?). And, while most people who meet Bush claim to like him, I suspect that, if I got to know him personally, I would hate him even more.

There seem to be quite a few of us Bush haters. I have friends who have a viscerally hostile reaction to the sound of his voice or describe his existence as a constant oppressive force in their daily psyche. Nor is this phenomenon limited to my personal experience: Pollster Geoff Garin, speaking to the *New York Times*, called Bush hatred "as strong as anything I've experienced in 25 years now of polling." Columnist Robert Novak described it as a "hatred . . . that I have never seen in 44 years of campaign watching."

Yet, for all its pervasiveness, Bush hatred is described almost exclusively as a sort of incomprehensible mental affliction. James Traub, writing last June in the *New York Times Magazine*, dismissed the "hysteria" of Bush haters. Conservatives have taken a special interest in the subject. "Democrats are seized with a loathing for President Bush—a contempt and disdain giving way to a hatred that is near pathological—unlike any since they had Richard Nixon to kick around," writes Charles Krauthammer in *Time* magazine. "The puzzle is where this depth of feeling comes from." Even writers like David Brooks and Christopher Caldwell of *The Weekly Standard*—the sorts of conservatives who have plenty of liberal friends—seem to regard it from the standpoint of total incomprehension. "Democrats have been driven into a frenzy of illogic by their dislike of George W. Bush," explains Caldwell. "It's mystifying," writes Brooks, noting that Democrats have grown "so caught up in their own victimization that they behave in ways that are patently not in their self-interest, and that are almost guaranteed to perpetuate their suffering."

Have Bush haters lost their minds? Certainly some have. Antipathy to Bush has, for example, led many liberals not only to believe the costs of the Iraq war outweigh the benefits but to refuse to acknowledge any benefits at all, even freeing the Iraqis from Saddam Hussein's reign of terror. And it has caused them to look for the presidential nominee who can best stoke their own anger, not the one who can win over a majority of voters—who, they forget, still like Bush. But, although Bush hatred can result in irrationality, it's not the product of irrationality. Indeed, for those not ideologically or personally committed to Bush's success, hatred for Bush is a logical response to the events of the last few years. It is not the slightest bit mystifying that liberals despise Bush. It would be mystifying if we did not.

One reason Bush hatred is seen as inherently irrational is that its immediate precursor, hatred of Bill Clinton, really did have a paranoid tinge. Conservatives, in retrospect, now concede that some of the Clinton haters were a little bit nutty. But they usually do so only in the context of declaring that Bush hatred is as bad or worse. "Back then, [there were] disapproving articles—not to mention armchair psychoanalysis—about Clinton-hating," complains Byron York in a *National Review* story this month. "Today, there appears to be less concern." Adds Brooks, "Now it is true that you can find conservatives and Republicans who went berserk during the Clinton years, accusing the Clintons of multiple murders and obsessing how Vince Foster's body may or may not have been moved. . . . But the Democratic mood is more pervasive, and potentially more self-destructive."

It's certainly true that there is a left-wing fringe of Bush haters whose lurid conspiracy-mongering neatly parallels that of the Clinton haters. York cites various left-wing websites that compare Bush to Hitler and accuse him of murder. The trouble with this parallel is, first, that this sort of Bush-hating is entirely confined to the political fringe. The most mainstream anti-Bush conspiracy theorist cited in York's piece is Alexander Cockburn, the ultra-left, rabidly anti-Clinton newsletter editor. Mainstream Democrats have avoided delving into Bush's economic ties with the bin Laden family or suggesting that Bush invaded Iraq primarily to benefit Halliburton. The Clinton haters, on the other hand, drew from the highest ranks of the Republican Party and the conservative intelligentsia. Bush's solicitor general, Theodore Olson, was involved with *The American Spectator*'s "Arkansas Project," which used every conceivable method—including paying sources—to dig up dirt from Clinton's past. Mainstream conservative pundits, such as William Safire and Rush Limbaugh, asserted that Vince Foster had been murdered, and GOP Government Reform Committee Chairman Dan Burton attempted to demonstrate this theory forensically by firing a shot into a dummy head in his backyard.

A second, more crucial difference is that Bush is a far more radical president than Clinton was. From a purely ideological standpoint, then, liberal hatred of Bush makes more sense than conservatives' Clinton fixation. Clinton offended liberals time and again, embracing welfare reform, tax cuts, and free trade, and nominating judicial moderates. When budget surpluses first appeared, he stunned the left by reducing the national debt rather than pushing for more spending. Bush, on the other hand, has developed into a truly radical president. Like Ronald Reagan, Bush crusaded for an enormous supply-side tax cut that was anathema to liberals. But, where Reagan followed his cuts with subsequent measures to reduce revenue loss and restore some progressivity to the tax code, Bush proceeded to execute two additional regressive tax cuts. Combined with his stated desire to eliminate virtually all taxes on capital income and to privatize Medicare and Social Security, it's not much of an exaggeration to say that Bush would like to roll back the federal government to something resembling its pre–New Deal state.

And, while there has been no shortage of liberal hysteria over Bush's foreign policy, it's not hard to see why it scares so many people. I was (and remain) a supporter of the war in Iraq. But the way Bush sold it—by playing upon the public's erroneous belief that Saddam had some role in the September 11 attacks—harkened back to the deceit that preceded the Spanish-American War. Bush's doctrine of preemption, which reserved the right to invade just about any nation we desired, was far broader than anything he needed to validate invading a country that had flouted its truce agreements for more than a decade. While liberals may be overreacting to Bush's foreign policy decisions—remember their fear of an imminent invasion of Syria?—the president's shifting and dishonest rationales and tendency to paint anyone who disagrees with him as unpatriotic offer plenty of grounds for suspicion.

It was not always this way. During the 2000 election, liberals evinced far less disdain for Bush than conservatives did for Al Gore. As the *New York Times* reported on the eve of the election, "The gap in intensity between Democrats and Republicans has been apparent all year." This "passion gap" manifested itself in the willingness of many liberals and leftists to vote for Ralph Nader, even in swing states. It became even more obvious during the Florida recount, when a December 2000 ABC News/*Washington Post* poll showed Gore voters more willing to accept a Bush victory than vice-versa, by a 47 to 28 percent margin. "There is no great ideological chasm dividing the candidates," retiring Democratic Senator Pat Moynihan told the *Times*. "Each one has his prescription-drugs plan, each one has his tax-cut program, and the country obviously thinks one would do about as well as the other."

Most Democrats took Bush's victory with a measure of equanimity because he had spent his campaign presenting himself as a "compassionate conservative"—a phrase intended to contrast him with the GOP ideologues in Congress—who would reduce partisan strife in Washington. His loss of the popular vote, and the disputed Florida recount, followed by his soothing promises to be "president of all Americans," all fed the widespread assumption that Bush would hew a centrist course. "Given the circumstances, there is only one possible governing strategy: a quiet, patient, and persistent bipartisanship," intoned a *New Yorker* editorial written by Joe Klein.

Instead, Bush has governed as the most partisan president in modern U.S. history. The pillars of his compassionate-conservative agenda—the faith-based initiative, charitable tax credits, additional spending on education—have been abandoned or absurdly underfunded. Instead, Bush's legislative strategy has revolved around wringing out narrow, party-line votes for conservative priorities by applying relentless pressure to GOP moderates—in one case, to the point of driving Vermont's James Jeffords out of the party. Indeed, when bipartisanship shows even the slightest sign of life, Bush usually responds by ruthlessly tamping it down. In 2001, he convinced GOP Representative Charlie Norwood to abandon his long-cherished patients' bill of rights, which enjoyed widespread Democratic support. According to a *Washington Post* account, Bush and other White House officials "met with Norwood for hours and issued endless appeals to party loyalty." Such behavior is now so routine that it barely rates notice. Earlier this year, a column by Novak noted almost in passing that "senior lawmakers are admonished by junior White House aides to refrain from being too chummy with Democrats."

When the September 11 attacks gave Bush an opportunity to unite the country, he simply took it as another chance for partisan gain. He opposed a plan to bolster airport security for fear that it would lead to a few more union jobs. When Democrats proposed creating a Department of Homeland Security, he resisted it as well. But later, facing controversy over disclosures of pre–September 11 intelligence failures, he adopted the idea as his own and immediately began using it as a cudgel with which to bludgeon Democrats. The episode was telling: Having spent the better part of a year denying the need for any Homeland Security Department at all, Bush aides secretly wrote up a plan with civil service provisions they knew Democrats would oppose and then used it to impugn the patriotism of any Democrats who did—most notably Georgia senator Max Cleland, a triple-amputee veteran running for reelection who, despite his support for the war with Iraq and general hawkishness, lost his Senate race thanks to an ugly GOP ad linking him to Osama bin Laden.

All this helps answer the oft-posed question of why liberals detest Bush more than Reagan. It's not just that Bush has been more ideologically radical; it's that Bush's success represents a breakdown of the political process. Reagan didn't pretend to be anything other than what he was; his election came at the crest of a twelve-year-long popular rebellion against liberalism. Bush, on the other hand, assumed office at a time when most Americans approved of Clinton's policies. He triumphed largely because a number of democratic safeguards failed. The media overwhelmingly bought into Bush's compassionate-conservative facade and downplayed his radical economic conservatism. On top of that, it took the monomania of a third-party spoiler candidate, plus an electoral college that gives disproportionate weight to GOP voters—the voting population of Gore's blue-state voters exceeded that of Bush's red-state voters—even to bring Bush close enough that faulty ballots in Florida could put him in office.

But Bush is never called to task for the radical disconnect between how he got into office and what he has done since arriving. Reporters don't ask if he has succeeded in "changing the tone." Even the fact that Bush lost the popular vote is hardly ever mentioned. Liberals hate Bush not because he has succeeded but because his success is deeply unfair and could even be described as cheating.

It doesn't help that this also happens to be a pretty compelling explanation of how Bush achieved his station in life. He got into college as a legacy; his parents' friends and political cronies propped him up through a series of failed business ventures (the founder of Harken Energy summed up his economic appeal thusly: "His name was George Bush"); he obtained the primary source of his wealth by selling all his Harken stock before it plunged on bad news, triggering an inconclusive Securities Exchange Commission insider-trading investigation; the GOP establishment cleared a path for him through the primaries by showering him with a political war chest of previously unthinkable size; and conservative justices (one appointed by his father) flouted their own legal principles—adopting an absurdly expansive federal role to enforce voting rights they had never even conceived of before—to halt a recount that threatened to put his more popular opponent in the White House.

Conservatives believe liberals resent Bush in part because he is a rough-hewn Texan. In fact, they hate him because they believe he is not a rough-hewn Texan but rather a pampered frat boy masquerading as one, with his pickup truck and blue jeans serving as the perfect props to disguise his plutocratic nature. The liberal view of Bush was captured by *Washington Post* (and former *New Republic*) cartoonist Tom Toles, who once depicted Bush being informed by an adviser that he "didn't hit a triple. You were born on third base." A puzzled Bush replies, "I thought I was born at my beloved hard-scrabble Crawford ranch," at which point his subordinate reminds him, "You bought that place a couple years ago for your presidential campaign."

During the 1990s, it was occasionally noted that conservatives despised Clinton because he flouted their basic values. From the beginning, they saw him as a product of the 1960s, a moral relativist who gave his wife too much power. But what really set them off was that he cheated on his wife, lied, and got away with it. "We must teach our children that crime does not pay," insisted former California representative and über–Clinton hater Bob Dornan. "What kind of example does this set to teach kids that lying like this is OK?" complained Andrea Sheldon Lafferty, executive director of the Traditional Values Coalition.

In a way, Bush's personal life is just as deep an affront to the values of the liberal meritocracy. How can they teach their children that they must get straight *As* if the president slid through with *Cs*—and brags about it!—and then, rather than truly earning his living, amasses a fortune through crony capitalism? The beliefs of the striving, educated elite were expressed, fittingly enough, by Clinton at a meeting of the Aspen Institute last month. Clinton, according to *New York* magazine reporter Michael Wolff, said of the Harken deal that Bush had "sold the stock to buy the baseball team which got him the governorship which got him the presidency." Every aspect of Bush's personal history points to the ways in which American life continues to fall short of the meritocratic ideal.

But perhaps most infuriating of all is the fact that liberals do not see their view of Bush given public expression. It's not that Bush has been spared from any criticism—far from it. It's that certain kinds of criticism have been largely banished from mainstream discourse. After Bush assumed office, the political media pretty much decided that the health of U.S. democracy, having edged uncomfortably close to chaos in December 2000, required a cooling of overheated passions. Criticism of Bush's policies—after a requisite honeymoon—was fine. But the media defined any attempt to question Bush's legitimacy as out-of-bounds. When, in early February, Democratic National Committee Chairman Terry McAuliffe invoked the Florida debacle, *The Washington Post* reported it thusly: "Although some Democratic leaders have concluded that the public wants to move past the ill will over the post-election maneuvering that settled the close Florida contest, McAuliffe plainly believes that with some audiences—namely, the Democratic base of activists he was addressing yesterday—a backward-looking appeal to resentment is for now the best way to motivate and unite an often-fractious party." (This was in a news story!) "It sounds like you're still fighting the election," growled NBC's Tim Russert on *Meet the Press*. "So much for bipartisanship!" huffed ABC's Sam Donaldson on *This Week*.

Just as mainstream Democrats and liberals ceased to question Bush's right to hold office, so too did they cease to question his intelligence. If you search a journalistic database for articles discussing Bush's brainpower, you will find something curious. The idea of Bush as a dullard comes up frequently—but nearly always in the context of knocking it down. While it's described as a widely held view, one can find very few people who will admit to holding it. Conservatives use the theme as a taunt—if Bush is so dumb, how come he keeps winning? Liberals, spooked, have concluded that calling Bush dumb is a strategic mistake. "You're not going to get votes by assuming that, as a party, you're a lot smarter than the voters," argued Democratic Leadership Council President Bruce Reed last November. "Casting Bush as a dummy also plays into his strategy of casting himself as a Texas common man," wrote *Washington Post* columnist E.J. Dionne in March 2001.

Maybe Bush's limited brainpower hasn't hampered his political success. And maybe pointing out that he's not the brightest bulb is politically counterproductive. Nonetheless, however immaterial or inconvenient the fact may be, it remains true that Bush is just not a terribly bright man. (Or, more precisely, his intellectual incuriosity is such that the effect is the same.) On the rare occasions Bush takes an extemporaneous question for which he hasn't prepared, he usually stumbles embarrassingly. When asked in July whether, given that Israel was releasing Palestinian prisoners, he would consider releasing famed Israeli spy Jonathan Pollard, Bush's answer showed he didn't even know who Pollard is. "Well, I said very clearly at the press conference with Prime Minister [Mahmoud] Abbas, I don't expect anybody to release somebody from prison who'll go kill somebody," he rambled. Bush's unscripted replies have caused him to accidentally change U.S. policy on Taiwan. And, while Bush's inner circle remains committed to the pretense of a president in total command of his staff, his advisers occasionally blurt out the truth. In the July issue of *Vanity Fair*, Richard Perle admitted that, when he first met Bush, "he didn't know very much."

While liberals have pretty much quit questioning Bush's competence, conservatives have given free rein to their most sycophantic impulses. Some of this is Bush's own doing—most notably, his staged aircraft-carrier landing, a naked attempt to transfer the public's admiration for the military onto himself (a man, it must be noted, who took a coveted slot in the National Guard during Vietnam and who then apparently declined to show up for a year of duty). Bush's supporters have spawned an entire industry of hagiographic kitsch. You can buy a twelve-inch doll of Bush clad in his "Mission Accomplished" flight suit or, if you have a couple thousand dollars to spend, a bronze bust depicting a steely-eyed "Commander-in-Chief" Bush. *National Review* is enticing its readers to fork over $24.95 for a book-length collection of Bush's post-September 11, 2001, speeches—any and all of which could be downloaded from the White House website for free. The collection recasts Bush as Winston Churchill, with even his most mundane pronouncements ("Excerpted Remarks by the President from Speech at the Lighting of the National Christmas Tree," "Excerpted Remarks by the President from Speech to the Missouri Farmers Association") deemed worthy of cherishing in bound form. Meanwhile, the recent Showtime pseudo-documentary *DC 9/11* renders the president as a Clint Eastwood figure, lording over a cringing Dick Cheney and barking out such implausible lines as "If some tinhorn terrorist wants me, tell him to come on over and get me. I'll be here!"

Certainly Clinton had his defenders and admirers, but no similar cult of personality. Liberal Hollywood fantasies—*The West Wing*, *The American President*—all depict imaginary presidents who pointedly lack Clinton's personal flaws or penchant for compromise. The political point was more to highlight Clinton's deficiencies than to defend them.

The persistence of an absurdly heroic view of Bush is what makes his dullness so maddening. To be a liberal today is to feel as though you've been transported into some alternative universe in which a transparently mediocre man is revered as a moral and strategic giant. You ask yourself why Bush is considered a great, or even a likeable, man. You wonder what it is you have been missing. Being a liberal, you probably subject yourself to frequent periods of self-doubt. But then you conclude that you're actually not missing anything at all. You decide Bush is a dullard lacking any moral constraints in his pursuit of partisan gain, loyal to no principle save the comfort of the very rich, unburdened by any thoughtful consideration of the national interest, and a man who, on those occasions when he actually does make a correct decision, does so almost by accident.

There. That feels better.

Californication
Lisa DePaulo

GQ | October 2003

As it turns out, Arnold Schwarzenegger has done a remarkably effective job so far as governor of California. The former movie star's approval ratings were floating above 60 percent when this book went to press, after having cajoled the state's voters into backing a $15-billion dollar bond issue that was essential to California's immediate fiscal future, trimming the state budget by pushing a bill through the legislature reforming workers' compensation rules, striking a slot-machine deal with five Native American tribes that brought the state a quick $1 billion in cash, and generally encouraging Democrats and Republicans to work together in a way that would have seemed impossible eight months earlier.

Who knew? Still, we can't help but look back with nostalgia on those zany days of the California recall, when 135 candidates strode the stage, and a Schwarzenegger governorship was still a gleam in Jay Leno's eye. In this article, Lisa DePaulo offers an up-close-and-personal report on those frothy days of last autumn, including a poignant portrait of Gray Davis, the soon-to-be-ex governor, as he limps through his final weeks in office. . . .

On a Tuesday night in mid-August, after the worst week of any living politician's life—with the exception of Bill, but at least he got sex out of it—Gray Davis agrees to a meeting. He's holed up in his L.A. bunker, a cluttered rented spread on Pico Boulevard that serves as headquarters for "Californians Against the *Costly* Recall," as his staff is now forced to answer the phones, where every piece of furniture is temporary—including, perhaps, the governor—and where the air-conditioning snaps off at 5 PM but the governor does not. No, sirree, he will *stay here and sweat*, late into the night, won't even loosen that noose of a necktie—clearly, the man has not been tortured enough—all in the service of the good people of California, who, in the next poll, will claim they hate him every bit as much as Richard Nixon.

"We are *so* sorry," a succession of aides bearing water repeat for the next hour or so, but the gov is in a Very Important Meeting with a Very Important Visitor and is running late. At one point, Davis himself comes out to apologize, and his eyes dart to the TV, which is blasting Fox News and the latest on Arnold. "Can we get someone to switch to CNN so we don't have to watch the enemy?" he asks. (He is referring to Fox News.)

It's been six days since Arnold's "surprise" announcement on *The Tonight Show with Jay Leno* and three days since the Saturday from hell, when Davis first learned precisely which other fine people would by vying to replace him. The diminutive Gary Coleman, the Greek millionairess Arianna Huffington, the fuck-flick queen Mary Carey, the billboard freak with the pink Maltese, his own lieutenant governor . . . and then, just this afternoon, a small mercy: Father Guido Sarducci has failed to obtain the necessary signatures.

How? *How?* How has a man as famously dull as Gray Davis managed to catalyze such chaos?

A little after eight, the governor emerges with his Very Important Visitor in tow.

"So," he says, springing his robotic arms in the air and doing a little hop thing that would translate as awkward even it weren't Gray Davis doing it, "who's better dressed?"

Warren Beatty arches an eyebrow as only Warren Beatty can. (Quick: Who has the scarier face-lift, Warren or Arnold?) Forget the obvious question, about how pissed Arianna's going to be that her good buddy Warren has just spent over an hour offering "lots of thoughtful ideas," as Davis later puts it, to the governor she vants to replace. *What's up with the belt?*

Warren, whose right eyebrow is still in a fixed arch (is it stuck?), has noticed it, too. How could he not? That is one gaudy—and we mean worse-than-any-of-Arnold's-rings gaudy—star-spangled belt buckle that Davis, who is otherwise dressed as usual, like an undertaker, is sporting this evening.

"You like it?" Davis asks. Warren Beatty says nothing. It's hard to insult a guy who's being pummeled out of office.

"We just bought it this weekend," adds Davis's wife, Sharon. "It's *inlay*, not rhinestones." Whew. "You think it counterbalances the image that he's boring and stiff?"

So this is what it's come to.

Gray Davis has busted his ass for twenty-eight years as a public servant. Even if you hate the guy, twenty-eight years is a long time to devote to waste bills and leash laws. Ploddingly, tediously, he rose up the political ladder, step by dreary step—from his first job in the '70s, carrying Jerry Brown's lava lamp as the governor's chief of staff, to obscure assemblyman to obscure controller to obscure lieutenant governor to governor. This is not a guy who is going to go quietly, even if nobody notices.

Except for his wife, he has nothing but the job. He lives in a condo the size of a nice hotel room, has the social life of a monk, doesn't own a car (he sold the Taurus a while ago), attends mass at the Good Shepherd every Saturday night, eats take-out chicken every night, and frets about the toxic chemicals in the drinking water, the poor suffering trees, SAT scores, and little missing girls even before Larry King starts booking them.

He is the most boring white man in America, but that didn't stop Californians from voting him into office seven times, five times statewide.

Then, *wham*. Suddenly, the guy whose blandness was a virtue is the eye of the biggest political hurricane since President Clinton accepted the wrong pizza delivery. Mr. Personality has somehow managed to incite a most public and pathetic display of everything people loathe about flaky, freaky, phony, fake-titted California. Which is everything he's not. Gray Davis *liked* being bland. He took pride in it—at not emoting, at not making a spectacle of himself, at quietly getting the job done. Now the spectacle has come to him.

Davis had just been reelected to his second term as governor when the effort to throw him out of office began. "They were circulating the petition thirty-one days after I was inaugurated," he says. "I barely had time for a cup of coffee." His enemies—which is to say the Republicans—would have you believe that Californians despised him so much (even though they'd just gone to the polls to reelect him) that suddenly they came out with their torches and pitchforks in mass revolt. They will tell you that the *real* impetus for the recall was the lingering anger Californians felt about the energy crisis of 2001, combined with how pissed they were to discover that the state's deficit was $38 billion rather than the $12 billion Davis had announced at the beginning of the campaign. And so, they say, there was a groundswell of passion and outrage! Democracy in Action! Davis's allies—at least those who are left—say that this was nothing but a right-wing power play, another "attempt by Republicans to steal elections they cannot win," as Davis recently put it. Driven not by the passions of the people but by a nut job with a couple million to blow.

That nut job would be Darrell Issa, an alleged car thief turned Republican congressman who'd amassed a huge personal fortune selling . . . car alarms. (That annoying voice you hear, *"Please step away from the car"*? That's Darrell Issa.) The congressman, who claims he was motivated purely by his love and concern for California, pumped nearly $2 million of his own loot into jump-starting the recall effort—money that paid for flyers and for sending people around to places like Home Depot to collect the necessary signatures, which came out to about a buck a pop. Oh, and he also declared his own candidacy.

That was when it really got fun. In no time, juicy revelations about his criminal record—which includes not only those pesky car-theft arrests but also charges of arson and carrying a concealed weapon—got dug up by the *L.A. Times* and the *San Francisco Chronicle*. Still, he soldiered on.

"Issa is a rich egomaniac who didn't have the *balls* to run when we had a regularly scheduled election last fall because he would have had to give up his safe seat in northern San Diego County," says Garry South, Davis's longtime strategist. "This was an incredible act of arrogance and hubris." Also, he adds with a grin, "stealing cars is not a great thing to have on your résumé when running for governor of California."

In the end, Issa's own flames would consume him. Despite his largesse, the GOP, of course, had no intention of actually supporting this dude for governor. Within twenty-four hours of Arnold's grand announcement, Issa quit the race, in a press conference during which he broke down in sobs. The media might have as well.

Monday, August 4, 1:00 P.M.
They Can All Go Screw Themselves!

Democracy in Action begins when fifty members of the press show up in the offices of *Hustler* magazine to hear Larry Flynt declare his candidacy. His publicist, Kim-from-L.A.—that's her name, and that's what you are to call her—bounces around Flynt's gilded lair in a black micromini suit, assuring the throng that he will roll in any minute and searching to make sure "the *New York Times* guy" has shown up. "The *Today* show is setting up in the apartment," beams Kim-from-L.A.

For a while, reporters have to make do with Corky, Flynt's dog.

"That's Corky Flynt," says Kim-from-L.A.

"Corky! Corky! Over here, Corky!" shout the cameramen, as the caffeinated little terrier darts around the nude statues in the room.

A photographer from one of the papers snaps away, then in a most serious tone asks Kim-from-L.A., "How is Corky's name spelled, please? . . . Thank you."

Flynt arrives, and his sunglassed security goon positions the gold-plated wheelchair at his desk, which is adorned with a framed picture of Flynt and his wife and a display of some of his prize works, such as *Honeybuns* and *Girl+Girl*.

"Jesse Ventura was an *asshole!*" says Flynt, when reporters who are peppering him with questions ask if he sees similarities in their campaigns. Flynt promises to balance the California budget by bringing slot machines to the state and basically delivers some of Arnold's best lines before Arnold delivers them on *Leno* two days hence. "There's one thing for sure: I can't be bought," he says. "I don't have one penny of special-interest support. They can all go screw themselves!" When asked about Arnold, Flynt smiles menacingly. "I've heard a few stories," he says.

"Mr. Flynt!" shouts another reporter. "How is your health?"

"My health couldn't be better," he says, "except for the fact that I can't walk." Grin. "I may be paralyzed from the waist down, but unlike Gray Davis I'm not paralyzed from the neck up."

Back on Pico Boulevard, Warren has left the building. Gray Davis retreats to his inner sanctum—a sterile Staples-furnished conference room that is as neat as a military barracks. At the end of the long table where he sits—oddly, in the only chair where it's impossible to take in the view of West Hollywood— a pile of memos is neatly arranged. A spiral notebook filled with his impeccable Catholic-school handwriting (this is not a guy who colors outside the lines) is opened to a page where he has written, among other things, *Energy* and *Arnold Schwarzenegger*.

He narrates a tour of newspaper cartoons and caricatures, from his campaigns over the years, that he has framed and displayed on the conference-room wall. "This is when they called me 'Roadkill' in '98," he says. "See there—I'm the little tortoise."

What I really wanted to know is what it's like to be so despised, how it feels to—

"Sweetheart, I've got to run some errands," says his pretty blond wife, Sharon, who has breezed in to say good-bye. She plants a big warm smack on his lips. "Your dinner's here," she adds.

"Okay, sweetheart. I'll see you at home."

So what's for dinner? I ask.

"The same thing," Davis says.

The same thing?

He likes to eat the exact same dinner every night, he explains. Not sort of the same. Exactly the same. Skinless chicken from Koo Koo Roo. "With steamed broccoli. And they have these nice tomatoes. . . . " He describes in detail the process by which he uses the microwave to heat up the chicken, if he's at home. And how he'll "put a little garlic in the tomato salad." Sometimes the Davises eat their dinner, Sharon has already divulged, on TV tables in bed, watching movies. "Well, I put on *SportsCenter*, but she switches it," he says. Lunch, apparently, is a similar drill. Turkey sandwich from Koo Koo Roo, hold the mayo, or that same old chicken. Every fucking day.

And this Koo Koo Roo thing is what? Fast food?

Davis gets animated. "So you don't think it's *junk* food," he says defensively, "the UCLA School of Public Health ranked it number one of fast-food restaurants. It's pretty healthy. *Trust* me."

Why do we get the feeling that Mary Carey isn't having this conversation right now?

While the little people and strippers vie for prime-time coverage, Davis gets to hear, every day, what a drag he is. How predictable. How uninspiring. For months now, almost every newspaper in the country has described him as "unpopular" and "unlikable." His buddy Willie Brown—at least he *thought* Brown was his buddy—made the point of announcing to the press that Davis had "zero personal relationships" (the same day, Davis's wife says, Brown visited them to talk about "what he was doing to help out"). Davis's wife has been referred to as "the only person who actually likes Gray Davis." Several political people who came billed as his "close friends" backpedaled when asked if that was true. "Well, I wouldn't call us *friends*," they each said. Sharon Davis says her husband is always surprised when he hears these things. "He probably feels closer to people than they feel to him," says Sharon. Even some of his paid staff, when asked if they like the guy, hesitate. "He's not the kind of guy you want to go have drinks with," as one puts it.

Actually, he's not so bad in person.

"Thanks. Then it's working," he says with what seems to be a genuine laugh. "I prefer to be underestimated. That's my greatest strength, when people think I cannot do something. First of all, it motivates me. And second, they've lowered the bar for me to impress them. If you expected me to be, you know, like Warren Beatty, you'd say, 'Hey, that guy's kind of a dud.' But if you expect to fall asleep listening to me and I hold your attention, you say, 'Hey, well, he wasn't that bad.' "

In fact, that's the entire campaign strategy: The more insanely exciting this gets, the better boring ol' Gray will start to look. He's run on the I'm-not-that-bad platform before. "People kept telling me in '98 that I couldn't get elected 'cause I was too boring and dull," Davis says. That election, when he first became governor in what seemed an unwinnable race—for starters, he was outspent by almost $50 million in the primary—was worse than this. "Because almost none of my longtime friends"—at least he *thought* they were his friends—"believed that I could win. Many of them endorsed other candidates. They said, 'We like you, Gray, but you don't have the money, you don't have the charisma, you're just not gonna make it.' That was the low point of my life." He won, but he never did get over the friend thing.

So what condition is his ego in right now?

"I don't know how to answer that."

To hear every day that no one likes you, that you're a loser . . .

"I don't let it become personal," he says.

But really, it's got to hurt.

"Yeah." Pause. "But see, I just—I'm not gonna go there. Because I don't think people give a, a . . . two cents about how I feel."

That's debatable. The man who's gotten through a lifetime of politics without ever emoting, without ever even betraying a scintilla of charisma, is in a whole new ball game this time.

Monday, August 4, 7:00 P.M.
The Ego Has Landed

Two nights before the Leno shocker, Arnold's Cigar Night is in full swing at Schatzi's on Main in Santa Monica. Arnold owns the property. Arnold's pictures are all over the walls. And some of the crowd even looks like Arnold—which shouldn't be all that surprising, considering they're his body doubles and his stuntmen. Once a month, he hosts a party for fifty or so of his closest pals. Any tables left over are doled out to his fans—who, for a mere $100, are allowed to bask in his aura.

Tonight is a part of the big fake out. Even Arnold's political strategist, George Gorton, is here, trying to divine what Arnold's final decision will really be. "Sometimes he gets up and walks around to every table and says hello," Gorton says. "It depends how he feels." The strategist believes that if Arnold greets the peons tonight, then maybe it's a sign he's running! Hmmmm. No one believes he is actually going to run, but Gorton, whose career goes back to Nixon, would give his left nut to do a Schwarzenegger race. He and his wife, Kiki, even moved from San Diego to be closer to Arnold and his "political needs."

By eight the joint is mobbed, and everybody is waiting for Arnold. Among the stuntmen, body doubles and freshly carved blonds who do gain entry are a lot of men with Austrian accents, the runner-up to Mr. Universe, the guy who designed Arnold's Mr. Freeze costume for *Batman & Robin*, the man who's handled Arnold's security for seventeen years and a man who Schatzi proprietor Charly Temmel says "has been in 3,200 porns."

Constituents all.

"You can see this isn't a big *political* crowd," Gorton says. "I think it would be if he were running."

When Arnold finally arrives, you can almost see the breasts perk up in the crowd—particularly Gorton's. But Arnold blows everybody off as his bodyguards escort him straight to his office upstairs. What does that mean? the people wonder. But then a half hour later, smiling, beaming, pumping hands, he comes downstairs and delivers himself to his subjects, soon to be the voters. "He made eye contact with me!" squeals a young blond.

Tuesday, August 5, 1:00 P.M.
Fun Is Good

Garry South, Gray Davis's longtime guru, is at a table in the Four Seasons in Beverly Hills, trying to explain his guy. More than a few people have described South as Gray's closest friend. "Well . . . I wouldn't put it in 'friendship' terms," he says. "I mean, it's not unusual for politicians not to have friends. These people are not normal. I don't say that pejoratively. You know the old saying, No man is a hero to his valet?"

South has worked for Davis for the past ten years. He knows and respects him. He swears there's an emotional side to Gray Davis. He hardly ever shows it, but it's there.

"At his inaugural lunch in 1999, he broke down and cried," says South. "He couldn't finish his speech. He was talking about how important his mother had been in his whole development and life, and how without her he would not be standing here today. And he broke down and cried. Sobbed. Hey, should I introduce myself to Larry Flynt?"

The porn king, who often lunches here, is rolling through the dining room in his golden wheelchair. Garry runs over and stops him midroll.

"Hi, I'm Garry South."

No recognition.

"The governor's campaign manager?"

Larry seems to be at a loss for words.

"I hear you're running for governor."

"Welllll," says Flynt. "I'm havin' a little fun."

"Fun is *good*," South barks. "You'll have a little competition, 300 or so people, but fun is good."

He does have one friend.

Gray Davis met his wife, a former Miss Santee, twenty-five years ago on an airplane when she was a stewardess in red hot pants and a little red hat. He was the chief of staff for Jerry Brown and had just missed his flight. So he got the airline to stop the plane as it was taxiing down the runway. "They literally drove him out to the runway, let down the stairs and put him on the plane," says Sharon. "And he just sits down, like this happens every day." So Sharon went up to her passenger and said, " 'Who do you think you *are*? You just made 120 people late.' And he just looked at me, shocked, like people do who are not used to being spoken to in that manner. And he said, 'Black coffee.' I said, 'I can't hear you because the engines are so loud, but I think what you just said is you want a cup of black coffee, *please*.' And by now the veins are sticking up in his neck."

"I just wanted to get rid of her," says the governor. "Because she was drawing so much attention to me."

After five more awkward flights over the course of six months, he got up the courage to ask Sharon to lunch, and they dated for the next five years. They married only after Sharon gave him a shit-or-get-off-the-pot speech as he was leaving on a trip. "He said, 'I can't talk about this. I've got to go to Israel.' I said, 'Fine. If we're not engaged when you come back from Israel, then just send somebody for your things, but I won't be talking to you, because we'll have nothing to say.' "

"She is a gift from God," the governor says.

The Gray Davis that Sharon sees is not the stiff the world has come to know. "He's lovey-dovey," she says. "At home he's the kind of guy, you don't walk by him without him giving you a kiss or a hug. *All day*. I mean, every time we're in the house, all day long. It's so *cute*. He's kind of the perfect husband."

Telegraphing this Inner Lovable Gray to the public is something that his strategists have sort of given up on. Garry South remembers the time in '96 when they hired Michael Eisner's speech coach in an effort to get Gray to be more animated and forceful, to step up his style a little bit. "It didn't work out very well," says South. "Gray felt the guy was very derisive. It was demeaning to him." Gray's strategists finally realized that "you can't make a chicken bark," says South, and besides, "to make him something he isn't would be worse. People can smell phony." In other words, he may be bland in public, but he's *genuinely* bland.

"I try to remind him to smile more," Sharon says. "I love being around people. And I think because I love it so much, people like to be around me. And so I always try to impart that on him. I always try to tell him, 'You have to enjoy being there so people will enjoy being with you.' "

It is indeed an odd characteristic in a politician to not like being around people. But this is part of the mystery of Gray Davis—who is, at once, as boring as he seems and more complicated than you'd think.

Wednesday, August 6, 10:30 A.M.
Big Brain, Fabulous Clothes *and* a Gay Husband

The show moves to South Central, where Arianna Huffington is announcing her candidacy at a children's shelter named A Place Called Home. *Jesus*, a few reporters bitch as they try to find parking in a hood that could use a few more of Darrell Issa's car alarms, *couldn't she do it at the place she calls her home? That nice $7 million spread in Brentwood that looks like Versailles?*

Arianna is on fire this morning. To a pumped-up crowd in the sweltering hot playground of the school, she razzles them with her plans to "totally reform government!" She promises an unconventional campaign: no polls, no attack ads, "and we'll only be driving in hybrid cars." Most important, she promises to make the rich pay more taxes. Those fat-cat elites who exploit all the loopholes? While the poor people suffer? Not when Arianna is governor! (A week later, she would be outed for paying only $771 in federal taxes—and zero in state—in the past two years. *Zhere ees a difference between loopholes and write-offs, dahlink!*)

It's hard not to like Arianna. She's entertaining and smart and her clothes are fabulous. Plus, what woman could be so cool when her multimillionaire ex-husband came out of the closet? Arianna is the kind of broad who didn't miss a beat when asked, at a gathering of progressives in the early days of the recall, how she feels about gay rights. "My *husband* is!"

Wednesday, August 6, 4:00 P.M.
Finally, a Reason to Watch Jay Leno

The cops have closed off much of Bob Hope Drive in Burbank to accommodate the fleet of satellite trucks that have shown up for the publicity stunt that is the taping of Arnold's Leno appearance. Inside, NBC sets up two cavernous rooms—fully equipped with phone lines at every chair—so the press can get the breaking news to their editors in time for tomorrow's newspapers. A statement in advance of the taping, which the East Coast reporters need to hit their deadlines, has been promised by Team Arnold. But shortly before the taping, Sean Walsh, Arnold's campaign spokesman, interrupts the important goings-on in the pressroom—reporters killing time by doing Arnold impressions ("I am so Vunderble!" "I luff Colleyfornya!")—to announce, with his arms folded across his chest, "We are not releasing a statement in advance of the program." No details. The reporters whine. No details? Well, they ask, will Arnold at least come back into the room afterward and speak with us? "Arnold is his own man and makes his own decisions," says Walsh. And fuck you and thank you for coming.

More misery ensues when a flack from NBC follows on Sean's heels to deliver the "rules." She would like very much if the press would please "embargo" the details of Arnold's announcement until 11:30 EST, the actual airtime of the show. "I don't want this on the Internet in 15 minutes." In fact, she would like everyone to "hold it" until their morning papers come out.

Is she *insane?*

"I'm with AP," says one of the scribes. "And I can*not* agree to that."

The flack tries to explain. What she really means is that they not give "detailed accounts" of everything said on the *Tonight Show*, because then no one will tune in to the *Tonight Show*. "This is an *entertainment* show," she explains.

"Well, it's news to us," says one of the reporters.

After the big shocker—and yes, there are audible gasps in the pressroom—Sean Walsh announces that Arnold will in fact come back and meet the ink-stained wretches. "Grab your seats," he instructs. "Arnold will be here in a few minutes."

And sure enough, here he comes, a blur of stage makeup and overgrown pectorals, security guards at his side, his big clammy paw shaking hands and clapping backs. "Fahntahstik," he says when he makes his way to the front of the room, looks out at the mass of reporters and holds forth.

"Arnold! Arnold! What turned the tide?"

"It was just that—it was just—the tide—I would say for me was my wife. . . . She said, 'I support you no matter what you do, because I know you're passionate. I know that you would help the people in California. I know you will reach out to everyone, Democrats and Republicans alike. . . . ' "

"Was Maria concerned about what you mentioned on the show, about womanizing charges coming out?"

"We talked about all the negative things. . . . People should stick to the issues. And they really should think about it. Each one of *you* should think about that. . . . What's really good for the state?"

By the time Arnold Schwarzenegger—gubernatorial candidate Arnold Schwarzenegger—leaves the NBC studio in his Hummer, a mob has already gathered on the Burbank streets.

Thursday, August 7, 8 A.M.
Time to Gloat

"There are only four words to describe Gray Davis now," chortles H. D. Palmer, the spokesman for the Republican caucus. *"In lieu of flowers."*

Friday, August 8, 8 P.M.
The Counteroffensive

A large pressroom with food and drinks has been set up by the people at HBO to accommodate the media turnout for tonight's big event. Gray Davis is appearing on *Real Time with Bill Maher*!

Four reporters show up.

He tears up at once.

We're back in the bunker, and I've asked him to talk about his father. Gray Davis was a sophomore at Stanford when he got a letter in the mail from his mother, telling him his father had left. "I remember being stunned by it," says Davis.

Gray's father, whom he was named for, was a gregarious, charismatic back-slapping rogue who'd inherited a fortune (his father was an heir to Conaco Oil) and had a schmoozy, cushy job on the business side at *Sports Illustrated*. His father bought him Porsches, introduced him to the Bel-Air Country Club . . . and then pissed it all away. "Gray lived a very comfortable life," says Garry South, "until his dad drank, gambled and womanized away all the money. And then left his mom with five kids [Gray was the eldest] and went off and married somebody else, who was thirty years younger."

Gray made a decision then. "I decided I did not want my life to turn out like his," he says. From that point forward, he would deliberately, stubbornly, do everything he could *not* to be his father. ROTC, the military, law school, church. "What sort of shaped my existence was structure and service," he says. "And then obviously my father just sort of reinforced the importance of discipline and frugality. And not creating pain to the people you love. I mean, he had a wonderful time. But he created a lot of pain for people who loved him dearly. Including me."

For thirty years, they were estranged. Then, in '96, as Gray was gearing up for his first run for governor, he made peace with his father. "And then three months later," says South, "his dad drops over dead of a heart attack on a golf course in Fort Lauderdale. It was traumatic, because they had just reconciled and he was talking about how kind of reassuring it was, and it was still his namesake, it was still his flesh and blood. So his dad's death was pretty traumatic for him. I mean, not that Gray was *emotional* about it."

Saturday, August 9, 8:30 A.M.
Look At Me! Look At Me!

The Arnold fans have been here since dawn. One has a collector's issue of *Flex* for Arnold to sign. "I *will* get his autograph," he says. "I've been supporting him since 1975." Supporting him? "I have books, magazines . . . " Another, in a muscle shirt, has a "limited edition" plastic Arnold drinking cup from Universal Studios. "If I could get him to sign it," he says, "I'd be the richest guy in the world!"

The media are here too, of course, in O.J. numbers, jockeying for position on the steps of the Los Angeles County registrar-recorders' office to document Arnold's arrival—and whatever other freaks show up with the requisite $3,500 filing fee and sixty-five signatures that allow you to run for governor of California.

At nine o'clock, one of the gubernatorial contenders shows up, a guy in a Statue of Liberty tie. He says his platform is to hold *constant* recall elections and use the entry money to pay off the California deficit. It will be the most sensible thing that happens today.

As the countdown to the arrival begins, Team Arnold fields the most important question: Is Maria coming today? "You'll see her when she comes. Or not," an aide replies.

Finally, at ten-forty, hysteria. Screams. Arnold has arrived. *With Maria!*

"Ar-nold! Ar-nold! Ar-nold!"

"Maria!" someone shouts. "Thank you for letting your husband run!"

But who is the other woman? Somehow, Arianna Huffington has suddenly elbowed her way between Arnold and Maria. Who knew that she has been lying in wait in her Toyota Prius to time her arrival with Arnold's and fling her red-headed ass into the photo op?

Which of course works out perfectly when she and the Schwarzeneggers land on the front page of *The New York Times* the next day.

"Nice timing, Arianna!" a reporter yells.

But then she has to push it, as she tends to do, segueing from shrewd to shameless. After Arnold files his papers and emerges from the office, ready to address the screaming crowd, she once again runs to get back into the picture, tripping over the bank of microphones and knocking them all down.

Even the "legitimate" candidates have lost their minds.

By late August, the Davis campaign was in free fall. He'd given a speech that he'd hoped would galvanize his old base and turn the election around. Instead, it got panned in the press. The next day, Arnold Schwarzenegger's first speech got raves from Sacramento to L.A. Meanwhile, Davis's lieutenant governor, Cruz Bustamante, whom he no doubt regrets having spoken to only two or three times, was emerging as an even bigger threat, despite being known mostly as the one who looks like Danny DeVito. "Cruz is my friend," said an ever clueless Davis on CNN. His approval rating was sinking even lower—below 22 percent and dropping. Even Cybill Shepherd's delicious revelation that in 1967 she made out with Gray Davis on a beach in Hawaii and that he was a "good kisser" (is there anyone Cybill Shepherd *hasn't* kissed?) may not be enough to save him. But in this campaign, you never know.

"When I grew up," Gray Davis says, "people were told and taught to keep their emotions inside, not to wear their heart on their sleeve. But now, out here, you know—" he laughs—"it's like you gotta go through some public *drama*, like *Jerry Springer*. That's the standard today. And I've grown up the direct opposite. You got a 1950s guy, with a Catholic and military influence, in a Jerry Springer world."

Welcome to California, Governor.

Protester=Criminal?
Matthew Rothschild

The Progressive | February 2004

The right to protest peacefully against government policies is one of the key liberties of any democracy. Of course, standards change in wartime—and with the war on terror, apparently it will always be wartime, at least for the forseeable future. In this article, Matthew Rothschild, the Progressive's *editor, reports on how law enforcement officers across the country are cracking down on the freedom of U.S. citizens to express their dissenting views in public. . . .*

In many places across George Bush's America, you may be losing your ability to exercise your lawful First Amendment rights of speech and assembly. Increasingly, some police departments, the FBI, and the Secret Service are engaging in the criminalization—or, at the very least, the marginalization—of dissent.

"We have not seen such a crackdown on First Amendment activities since the Vietnam War," says Anthony Romero, executive director of the American Civil Liberties Union (ACLU).

This crackdown took a violent turn in late November [2003] at the Miami protests against the Free Trade Area of the Americas and at an anti-war protest at the Port of Oakland last April. In both cases, the police used astonishing force to break up protests. But even when the police do not engage in violence, they sometimes blatantly interfere with the right to dissent by preemptively arresting people on specious grounds.

Sarah Bantz is a member of the Missouri Resistance Against Genetic Engineering. Last May, she and several hundred others were gathering in St. Louis to protest against Monsanto and the World Agricultural Forum, which was meeting there.

On May 16, the first day of the protest weekend, Bantz and a small group of other activists went to the Regional Chamber and Growth Association to give their pitch on how biotech was hurting local farmers. After that meeting, she and her fellow activists piled into her van, but they were able to get only about a mile down the road when something unusual happened.

"All of a sudden there was one police car and then another, and I was pulled over," she recalls. "One officer came around and asked me to get out of the vehicle, which I did. The cop started to look through the van without permission. I had some Vitamin C pills sitting out, so they decided that was a drug and they were going to arrest me. They put me in cuffs and put me in the back of the car. They really had no grounds for arresting me, but I spent ten hours in jail." One reason they cited, along with the vitamins, was her failure to wear a seatbelt.

Bantz was scheduled to deliver three speeches at what organizers called their Biodevastation 7 Conference. "I gave none of them," she says. "For one, I was in jail, and for another I was talking to the police about why they detained me. And I was too frazzled to give the third. It was all unbelievable."

That same day, the Flying Rutabaga Bicycle Circus expected to take part in the protests. "We are a group of concerned bicyclists, puppeteers, musicians, farmhands, clowns, cheerleaders, activists, eaters of food, and drinkers of water," the circus says on its web page. "We are united in a quest to seek out food (that's our fuel) that is not tampered with by biotechnology companies. We ride for diversity, organic farming, and biojustice everywhere."

But they weren't allowed to ride in St. Louis.

"We set off on our bicycles for our first performance, a small skit, to let the protesters know about our Caravan Across the Corn Belt tour," says Erik Gillard, one of the Flying Rutabagas, who was riding with eight others. "We were following traffic rules when a big police paddy wagon pulled up with its light on. Gradually, more police officers arrived, and they told us we had to leave our bicycles. We were all arrested for operating our bicycles without a license."

There is no such offense in St. Louis, the ACLU of Eastern Missouri says. Afterward, Police Chief Joe Mokwa said the arresting officer was "overenthusiastic," according to the *St. Louis Post-Dispatch*.

After a while, the police changed the charge to "impeding the flow of traffic on a bicycle," Gillard says. "It was written up for some intersection ten blocks from where we were all picked up." He says the police detained the group for six or seven hours. "All of our journals that contained phone directories or e-mail lists or information about where we were going to stay were taken and never returned," he says.

Also on the same day, the police raided the Bolozone, an activist group home where many of the cyclists were staying. Reminiscent of police raids in Washington, D.C., during the 2000 World Bank-IMF protests, this one succeeded in detaining people prior to the demonstration.

One of the residents of the Bolozone, Kelley Meister, a political activist and artist who identifies herself as an anarchist, was there the morning of that raid.

"I was out in the alley painting a sign," says Meister, "and one cop car drove up and then four more. Two officers came toward me, and I said, 'Hi, can I help you? I live here.'

"And they said, 'This building is condemned.' And they started to walk past me.

"I said, 'Do you have a warrant? I don't give you permission to enter my house.'

"The reply was, 'We don't need a warrant. This building is condemned.'" The St. Louis housing inspector, who came with the police, brought a condemnation notice with him, she says.

The owner of the building, Dan Green, had been working cooperatively with the city for months while rehabbing it, according to Denise Lieberman, legal director of the ACLU of Eastern Missouri. The timing of the raid makes it clear that the police used a "bogus housing inspection to conduct a criminal search without a warrant," she says.

"They arrested me and two of the cyclists, and charged us with occupying a condemned building," Meister says. "They put us in handcuffs, and placed us in a police van. I could see them carrying things out of the house, such as art from my room and bags of stuff. I was taken to the station and held for fifteen hours. Some of the others were held for twenty hours."

The police did not let Meister back in her home for five days. "When we finally got inside, we realized that they had ransacked the house from top to bottom," she says. The police also confiscated the bikes, puppets, props, posters, and banners of the Rutabaga Circus cyclists who had been staying at the Bolozone. When they got their bikes back after the weekend was over, many of their tires were slashed, Gillard says.

Meister says she's considering suing the police. And so is the ACLU of Eastern Missouri.

Richard Wilkes, public relations officer for the St. Louis Police Department, says "the department really doesn't have a response" to the allegations about raiding the house or detaining protesters or cyclists. "None of those things had anything to do with preventing people from protesting," he says.

It's not every day that a sitting judge will allege he saw the police commit felonies. But that's what Judge Richard Margolius said on December 11 in regard to police misconduct in Miami during the protests against the Free Trade Area of the Americas (FTAA) in late November.

Judge Margolius was presiding over a case that the protesters brought against the city. In court, he said he saw the police commit at least twenty felonies, Amy Driscoll of the *Miami Herald* reported. "Pretty disgraceful what I saw with my own eyes," he said, according to the paper. "This was a real eye-opener. A disgrace for the community."

Police used tasers, shock batons, rubber bullets, beanbags filled with chemicals, large sticks, and concussion grenades against lawful protesters. (Just prior to the FTAA protests, the city of Miami passed an ordinance requiring a permit for any gathering of more than six people for longer than twenty-nine minutes.) They took the offensive, wading into crowds and driving after the demonstrators. Police arrested more than 250 protesters. Almost all of them were simply exercising their First Amendment rights. Police also seized protest material and destroyed it, and they confiscated personal property, demonstrators say.

"How many police officers have been charged by the state attorney so far for what happened out there during the FTAA?" the judge asked in court, according to the *Herald*. The prosecutor said none. "Pretty sad commentary, at least from what I saw," the judge retorted.

Even for veterans of protests, the police actions in Miami were unlike any they had encountered before. "I've been to a number of the anti-globalization protests—Seattle, Cancún, D.C.—and this was different," says Norm Stockwell, operations coordinator for WORT, the community radio station in Madison, Wisconsin. "At previous events, the police force was defensive, with heavy armor hoping to hold back protests. In Miami, police were in light armor and were poised to go after the protesters, and that's what they did. They actually went into the crowds to divide the protesters, then chased them into different neighborhoods."

Stockwell says some reporters were mistreated, especially if they were not "embedded" with the Miami police.

"I got shot twice [with rubber projectiles], once in the back, another time in the leg," reported Jeremy Scahill of *Democracy Now!* "John Hamilton from the Workers Independent News Service was shot in the neck by a pepper-spray pellet." Ana Nogueira, Scahill's colleague from *Democracy Now!*, was video-taping some of the police mayhem when she was arrested, Scahill said. "In police custody, the authorities made Ana remove her clothes because they were pepper sprayed. The police forced her to strip naked in front of male officers."

John Heckenlively, former head of the Racine County Democratic Party in Wisconsin, says he was cornered by the police late in the afternoon of November 20. Heckenlively and a few companions were trying to move away from the protest area when "a large cordon of police, filling the entire block edge to edge, was moving up the street," he says. "As they approached, an officer told us that we should leave the area. We informed him that was precisely what we were attempting to do, and seconds later, he placed us under arrest."

Police kept Heckenlively in tight handcuffs behind his back for more than six hours, he says, adding that he was held for a total of sixty hours.

Trade unionists were particularly outraged at the treatment they received in Miami. John Sweeney, head of the AFL-CIO, wrote Attorney General John Ashcroft on December 3 to urge the Justice Department to investigate "the massive and unwarranted repression of constitutional rights and civil liberties that took place in Miami."

Sweeney wrote that on November 20, police interfered with the federation's demonstration "by denying access to buses, blocking access to the amphitheater where the rally was occurring, and deploying armored personnel carriers, water cannons, and scores of police in riot gear with clubs in front of the amphitheater entrance. Some union retirees had their buses turned away from Miami altogether by the police, and were sent back home."

Blocking access to the rally was the least of it. After the march, "police advanced on groups of peaceful protesters without provocation," Sweeney wrote. "The police failed to provide those in the crowd with a safe route to disperse, and then deployed pepper spray and rubber bullets against protesters as they tried to leave the scene. Along with the other peaceful protesters, AFL-CIO staff, union peacekeepers, and retirees were trapped in the police advance. One retiree sitting on a chair was sprayed directly in the face with pepper spray. An AFL-CIO staff member was hit by a rubber bullet while trying to leave the scene. When the wife of a retired steelworker verbally protested police tactics, she was thrown to the ground on her face and a gun was pointed to her head."

The ACLU of Greater Miami is planning on filing several suits against the Miami Police Department, says Lida Rodriguez-Taseff, president of the group. "This was a clear abuse of power by the police, and an indiscriminate use of force," she says. "People who were retreating were being shot in the back with rubber bullets. One photojournalist, Carl Kesser, was filming the police, and he was hit in the head with a beanbag above his eye socket. If it had hit him a little bit lower, he could have lost his eye. The police were using tasers on people who were down, who were already restrained. These police officers were using these weapons as if they were Pez dispensers. They acted like as long as it wasn't a firearm, they could use the weapons to their hearts' content."

"We did what we had to do based on the situation at the time," says Miami Police Officer Herminia Salas-Jacobson. "If anyone has any concerns or questions, we've asked them to come forward, and we will address each one on an individual basis."

The police used $8.5 million of the $87 billion Congress appropriated for the Iraq War to patrol the streets of Miami. Police Chief John Timoney thanked his officers for their "remarkable restraint." And he won praise in some law enforcement quarters for what is being called the Miami Model.

By the way, Timoney was the police commissioner in Philadelphia during the 2000 Republican Convention, and his tactics then raised questions about the violation of protesters' civil liberties. Nonetheless, Timoney has consulted with the Democratic National Committee on security issues for the Democratic Convention in Boston this summer.

Seven months before the FTAA in Miami, police used brutal force on the West Coast. At the Port of Oakland on the morning of April 7, more than 500 anti-war demonstrators gathered to protest against two shipping companies that were involved in George Bush's Iraq war.

The police responded by firing rubber bullets, wooden pellets, and tear gas into the crowd. Nine members of Local 10 of the International Longshore and Warehouse Union were injured, as were at least thirty-one demonstrators. These forty individuals have filed a class action lawsuit against the city of Oakland and several Oakland police officers.

"I was hit on the back of the right calf as I attempted to run away from the police fire," wrote Willow Rosenthal, one of the plaintiffs, in her statement. "The entire back of my calf was blood red and swollen with a circular mark of broken skin about three quarters of an inch across in the center. The calf was numb about three inches around the point of impact, and I wasn't able to walk without assistance."

Another plaintiff, Scott Fleming, was "shot five times in the back, shoulder, and under his arms with wooden dowels fired directly at him as he fled," the suit says. The police also allegedly attacked at least two legal observers and two people videotaping the event.

"This was the most outrageous incident of unprovoked mass police violence the National Lawyers Guild has seen in our twenty years of providing legal support to Bay Area demonstrations," said National Lawyers Guild attorney Rachel Lederman, one of the lawyers for the plaintiffs, in a press release.

This case hopes "to reestablish the constitutional principle that the police cannot choose to impose the price of serious physical injury on persons engaging in nonviolent protest activities," said Alan Schlosser, legal director of the ACLU of Northern California, which is part of the case, as well.

"Overall, it was peaceful, but a small element began throwing things at the officers, and that's when the command officers decided to deploy less lethal munitions," says Officer Danielle Ashford of the Oakland Police Department. "Our chief has launched an internal review and has reassessed our crowd control policy to minimize injuries to all involved parties."

What happened in St. Louis, Miami, and Oakland "comes on the heels of more than two years of federal actions and policies that are antagonistic to free speech," says the ACLU's Romero.

One of these was Attorney General John Ashcroft's May 30, 2002, lifting of the Justice Department's strict guidelines curtailing domestic spying. Those guidelines dated back to the Ford Administration, but now the FBI is free once again to spy on protesters and to infiltrate their meetings in public places. This has raised fears of a return to the days of COINTELPRO, the FBI's counterintelligence program that spied on Martin Luther King and Malcolm X and infiltrated the Black Panthers and the American Indian Movement.

One of the most disturbing developments, says Romero, is "the easy conflation of dissenters with criminal suspects or even potential terrorists." He points to the FBI Intelligence Bulletin of October 15, 2003. This bulletin, which the *New York Times* exposed, refers to "extremist elements" who engage in "aggressive tactics." But it doesn't limit its attention to lawbreakers. "Even the more peaceful techniques can create a climate of disorder, block access to a site, draw large numbers of police officers to a specific location in order to weaken security at other locations, obstruct traffic, and possibly intimidate people from attending the events being protested," it says. And it does not distinguish between "extremists" and "activists." It says that "activists often communicate with one another using cell phones"—a dazzling insight. They also may use recording equipment "for documenting potential cases of police brutality and for distribution of information over the Internet," it says.

Using cell phones or filming police brutality or disseminating information over the Internet can hardly be construed as illegal activity. But the FBI memo says, "Law enforcement agencies should be alert to these possible indicators of protest activity and report any potentially illegal acts to the nearest FBI Joint Terrorism Task Force."

Equating protesters with terrorists is not confined to FBI headquarters. Mike Van Winkle, spokesman for the California Anti-Terrorism Information Center, told the *Oakland Tribune* last year: "You can make an easy kind of link that, if you have a protest group protesting a war where the cause that's being fought against is international terrorism, you might have terrorism at that protest. You can almost argue that a protest against that is a terrorist act."

On February 8, 2002, Vice President Dick Cheney was visiting Evansville, Indiana, to campaign for Representative John Hostettler at the local civic center.

Environmentalist John Blair was walking on a public sidewalk nearby and was carrying a sign that read: "Cheney: 19th C. Energy Man."

Police ordered him to move to a "protest zone" more than a block away, and Blair refused, so they arrested him.

"I was arrested for nothing more than exercising my rights as a citizen in what I thought was a free country," Blair wrote in an article for *Counterpunch*, which broke the story.

Blair was at first charged with disorderly conduct. Then the prosecutor increased the charge to a Class A misdemeanor of resisting law enforcement, which could have cost him a year in jail.

But the case against Blair was quickly dropped. "I didn't think the evidence established a case that would be successful in court," says Stan Levco, prosecuting attorney for Vanderburgh County, Indiana. But he adds: "I don't think they were wrong to arrest him under the circumstances. They thought it was a safety issue, and I wouldn't second-guess them."

Blair is suing for $50,000 in damages. "They shouldn't even have approached me in the first place," he says. "Carrying a sign isn't an illegal act in America. At least it wasn't before Bush-Cheney."

Blair's experience was hardly unique. Local police, on orders of the Secret Service, have literally been marginalizing critics of the president or vice president into so-called protest zones far out of earshot and eyesight, the ACLU says.

On September 23, 2003, the ACLU sued the Secret Service for engaging in a "pattern and practice" of discriminating against those who disagree with government policies.

On September 2, 2002, in Neville Island, Pennsylvania, "protesters were sent to a 'designated free speech zone' located on a large baseball field one-third of a mile away from where President Bush was speaking," an ACLU fact sheet notes. "Only people carrying signs critical of the president were required to enter and remain. Many people carrying signs supporting the president and his policies were allowed to stand alongside the motorcade route. . . . When retired steelworker Bill Neel refused to enter the protest zone and insisted on being allowed to stand where the president's supporters were standing, he was arrested for disorderly conduct and detained until the president had departed."

Similarly, when President Bush came to St. Louis on January 22, 2003, to tout his economic plan, one woman with a "We Love You President Bush" sign was allowed to stand near the building where the president was speaking. But Andrew Wimmer, who was standing next to her, was arrested for holding a sign saying "Instead of war invest in people."

Ann Roman, spokeswoman for the Secret Service, says, "We don't comment on pending litigation, but we don't make any distinction on the basis of purpose, message, or intent of any particular group or individual."

Eleanor Eisenberg is the executive director of the Arizona ACLU, but that did not stop police from arresting her on September 27, 2002. That day, Bush came to the Civic Center in Phoenix to raise money for two Republican candidates. A crowd of 1,500 protesters gathered across the street. But all of a sudden and for no discernible reason, the police, both on horseback and on foot, charged into the crowd, says Eisenberg.

"Shortly after the police started their charge, I saw them dragging a young man into the street and grinding his face into the pavement and being very abusive," she says. When Eisenberg, in her official capacity, went over to see what was going on, "a police officer whacked me with his horse's flank and sent me flying. And the next thing I know, I was being arrested."

Randy Force of the Phoenix Police Department says, "We stand by the facts in the police report on this case." That report states that the Secret Service ordered the area cleared and that police told Eisenberg "she was standing in a restricted area." It claims "she started taking photographs of other citizens being involved in disorderly conduct." After giving Eisenberg three orders to move, one police officer gave her "a small shove with his horse to move her," the report states.

"When you connect the dots—the FBI bulletin treating protesters as terrorists, the pattern and practice of the Secret Service of corralling protesters in zones far away, the actions in Miami and San Francisco and elsewhere—you see an increasingly hostile environment for groups that are expressing views that are divergent from the Bush administration's," says ACLU Executive Director Romero. "Clearly, the government has put in place key policies and practices that try to shut down those that disagree with it."

Lieberman of the ACLU of Eastern Missouri puts it this way: "Law enforcement officers are telling people, if you have dissenting views you should think twice about expressing them. And if you don't agree to be invisible, you're going to be liable for criminal prosecution under whatever guise we can think of."

Looking back on her experience with the police in St. Louis at the World Agricultural Forum, Sarah Bantz strikes a philosophical note. "I guess I learned my lesson," she says.

And what is that lesson? "That these issues I keep hearing about—of the increased use of police and military force in this country—are real. They're not happening in the future; they're happening today."

National Conversation:
The Iraq Occupation

How to Get Out of Iraq
Jonathan Schell

The Nation | May 24, 2004

This essay was the opening piece in a collection of opinions published by The Nation *magazine under the headline, "How to Get Out of Iraq—A Forum." The introduction to the collection read, in part: "As the situation in Iraq goes from bad to worse, many Americans who opposed the war . . . understand that the country must find a way to extricate itself from the disaster they predicted. There is, however, no agreement or even clarity about such an exit strategy. Nor is any leadership on this crucial issue coming from the Bush administration or as yet, alas, from the presumptive Democratic candidate, Senator John Kerry. With a sense of obligation and urgency,* The Nation *has asked a range of writers . . . for their ideas on America's way out of Iraq."*

Here, Jonathan Schell—whose 1982 book The Fate of the Earth *became the bible of the anti–nuclear proliferation movement—takes an unambiguously antiwar stance: The U.S. was wrong to invade Iraq in the first place, he says, and we should withdraw our troops as soon as possible. . . .*

In the debate over the Iraq War, a new-minted fragment of conventional wisdom has fixed itself in the minds of mainstream politicians and commentators. Whether or not it was right to go to war, we are told on all sides, the United States must now succeed in achieving its aims. In the words of John Kerry, "Americans differ about whether and how we should have gone to war, but it would be unthinkable now for us to retreat in disarray and leave behind a society deep in strife and dominated by radicals." Or as Senator Richard Lugar has said, "We are in Iraq and so we're going to have to bring stability." Or, as Senator Joseph Biden, among so many others, has said, as if to put an end to all discussion, "Failure is not an option."

The argument is an irritating one for those of us who opposed the war, suggesting, as it does, that we must now sign up for the project ("stay the course") because the very mistake we warned against was made. But the problems are more serious than annoyance. Of course, no one wants to see anarchy or repression in Iraq or any other country. But what can it mean to say that failure is not an option? Has the decision to go to war exhausted our powers of thought and will? Must we surrender now to fate? "Failure" is in truth never an "option." The exercise of an option is a voluntary act; but failure is forced upon you by events. It is what happens when your options run out. To rule out failure is not a policy but a wish—and a wish, indeed, for omnipotence. Yet no one, not even the world's sole superpower, is omnipotent. To imagine otherwise is to set yourself up for a fall even bigger than the failure you imagine you are ruling out.

And so decisions must still be made. It's true that we opponents of the war cannot simply say (as we might like to do), "Please roll history back to March of 2003, and make your disastrous war unhappen." It's also true that when the United States overthrew the Iraqi government it took on new responsibilities. The strongest argument for staying in Iraq is that the United States, having taken over the country, owes its people a better future. But acknowledgment of such a responsibility is only the beginning, not the end, of an argument.

To meet a responsibility to someone, you must have something on offer that they want. Certainly, the people of Iraq want electricity, running water, and other material assistance. The United States should supply it. Perhaps—it's hard to find out—they also want democracy. But democracy cannot be shipped to Iraq on a tanker or a C-5A. It is a homegrown construct, which must flow from the will of the people involved. The expression of that will is, in fact, what democracy is.

But today the United States seeks to impose a government on Iraq in the teeth of an increasingly powerful popular opposition. The result of this policy can be seen in the shameful attacks from the air on the cordoned-off city of Falluja, causing hundreds of casualties. The more the United States tries to force what it insists on calling democracy on Iraq, the more the people of Iraq will hate the United States, and even, perhaps, the name of democracy. There is no definition of an obligation that includes attacking the supposed beneficiaries' cities with F-16s and AC-130 gunships.

President Bush commented recently of the Iraqis, "It's going to take a while for them to understand what freedom is all about." Hachim Hassani, a representative of the Iraqi Islamic Party, a leading Sunni Muslim group represented on the so-called Governing Council, might have been answering him when he commented to the *Los Angeles Times*, "The Iraqi people now equate democracy with bloodshed."

Under these circumstances, staying the course cannot benefit Iraq. On the contrary, each additional day that American troops continue to fight in Iraq can only compound the eventual price of the original mistake—costing more lives, American and Iraqi, disorganizing and pulverizing the society, and reducing, not fostering, any chances for a better future for the country.

There are still many things that the United States can do for the people of Iraq. Continued economic assistance is one. Another is to help international organizations assist (but only to whatever degree is wanted by the local people) in the transition to a new political order. But all combat operations should cease immediately and then, on a fixed and announced timetable, the American forces should withdraw from the country. In short, the United States, working with others, should give Iraqis their best chance to succeed in their own efforts to create their own future.

According to the most recent *Times*/CBS poll, the public, by a margin of 48 percent to 46 percent, has decided, with no encouragement from either of the two major-party presidential candidates or from most media commentators, that the war was a mistake. Forty-six percent have decided that the American troops should be withdrawn. They are right. The United States should never have invaded Iraq. Now it should leave.

Soldier On, Escalate, or Get Out?
Patrick Buchanan

WorldNetDaily.com | April 14, 2004

On April 19, 2004, the New York Times *reported that "The continuing violence and mounting casualties in Iraq have given new strength to the traditional conservative doubts about using American military power to remake other countries and about the potential for Western-style democracy without a Western cultural foundation."*

Former presidential candidate Patrick Buchanan has been one of the most vocal conservative critics of both the Iraq War and the neoconservative doctrine of using military force to promote democracy in the Mideast and elsewhere. In the following column, he doesn't go so far as to call for a U.S. withdrawal from Iraq—but the questions he raises here eloquently sum up the "traditional conservative doubts" the Times *was referring to. . . .*

This is "George Bush's Vietnam," railed Senator Kennedy last week in a charge that angered Senator John McCain.

And by any traditional measure of war, McCain is right.

While Vietnam lasted a decade and took 58,000 U.S. lives, Iraq has lasted a year and cost 650 U.S. dead. Even the Filipino insurrection of 1899-1902 was a far bloodier affair. But one comparison is valid. A U.S. defeat in Iraq would be a far greater strategic disaster than the loss of South Vietnam.

For what is on the line here is not only the Bush presidency, but the myth of American invincibility, the "democratic revolution" the president has been preaching, Tony Blair, the U.S. position in the oil-rich Gulf and Arab world, and our standing as the world's last superpower. For it is the definition of a superpower that when it goes to war, it prevails.

All is now riding on Bush's commitment to create a pro-Western, democratic Iraq and not be forced out in a humiliating retreat and defeat by the burgeoning insurrection. And as in Vietnam around 1963, we have come to a turning point. The critical question before us: Do we go in deeper, or do we cut our losses and look for the nearest exit?

With the battles for Fallujah and Ramadi, the seizure by the Mahdi Army of Sheik al-Sadr of Kut, Karbala and Najaf, the fighting in Sadr City, the recurring attacks on aid workers, the abandonment of their posts by Iraqi police, the refusal to fight of one of four Iraqi battalions we trained, it is clear: We do not have sufficient forces on the ground to crush and snuff out the resistance.

So we must decide. How much blood and treasure are we willing to invest in democracy in Baghdad, and for how long? Is a democratic Iraq vital to our security? What assurances are there that we can win this war?

Finally, how lasting will any victory be? Lest we forget: When U.S. troops and POWs came home from Vietnam in 1973, America appeared to have won the war. Not until the spring of 1975 did a North Vietnamese invasion overrun the South and Saigon.

President Bush faces three options. He can continue to draw down troops and transfer power to the Iraq Governing Council on June 30, and risk a collapse in chaos or civil war. He can hold to present U.S. force levels and accept a war of attrition of indefinite duration, a war on which his countrymen have begun to sour.

Or he can send in more troops and unleash U.S. power to crush all resistance, while declaring our resolve to "pay any price" and fight on to victory, even if it takes two, five or 10 years. The problem with playing Churchill is that, as in Vietnam, it is hard to see the light at the end of the tunnel.

The incidence of attacks on our troops, aid workers and Iraqi allies is rising. The more fiercely we fight back, the higher the casualties we inflict on insurgent and civilian alike, and the greater the hostility grows to our war and our presence. Indeed, if our occupation itself is the cause of the insurgency, how do we win the war by extending and deepening it?

The Shiite regions are now inflamed to a degree they were not just two weeks ago. Where Moqtada Al Sadr was then a thuggish and receding figure, by his killing of U.S. troops he has made himself an adversary to whom our enemies are rallying.

In dealing with him, we have three options. Kill him and make him a dead martyr, which could ignite the Shiite population, compelling even Ayatollah Sistani to condemn us. Arrest him and make him a living martyr. But if arresting his deputy ignited the present uprising, imagine the hell that will break loose if we take the sheik to Baghdad airport.

Or leave him alone. But then he will have shown Iraqis that one can kill U.S. soldiers with impunity, even when Americans control your country. Not a good message to send. Like Vietnam, Iraq, too, has porous borders. There is no way to halt the trickle of foreign fighters slipping in.

Then there are the January elections. If militant Shiites and Sunnis run on a pledge to expel the Americans, what do we do if they win?

Americans supported Bush's war because we were persuaded that the malignancy of Iraq's leader and the horrific nature of the weapons he had or was seeking meant we must destroy his regime or our country was in mortal peril. With that threat gone, what we are fighting for? Democracy in Iraq? Or is it now just to avoid defeat in Iraq?

Generals Weary of Low Troop Levels
Robert Novak

Chicago Sun Times | April 8, 2004

As many readers will recall, syndicated columnist Robert Novak spent part of the past year in the middle of a media firestorm, thanks to his July 14, 2003, op-ed titled "Mission to Niger." The column was devoted to a trip made by diplomat Joseph Wilson to the African nation of Niger in February 2002 at the request of the CIA and Vice President Richard Cheney's office. Wilson's assignment was to investigate evidence that Iraq had tried to purchase yellowcake uranium from Niger—uranium that could be used to make a nuclear bomb. Wilson concluded that the so-called evidence was a forgery, and reported this to Washington.

Ten months later, the following sixteen words appeared in President Bush's 2003 State of the Union Address: "The British government has learned that Saddam Hussein recently sought significant quantities of uranium from Africa." Once Wilson had confirmed that the president was indeed referring to Niger, he penned an explosive op-ed of his own, describing his trip and what he had and had not found there. The following day, the White House admitted that the president's statement had been in error.

A week later came Novak's column, in which he cited "two senior administration officials" who claimed that Wilson had been sent to Niger at the suggestion of his undercover-CIA-agent wife, Valerie Plame. By blowing Plame's cover, Novak's column effectively ended her spy career. It also led the Justice Department to launch an ongoing criminal investigation into who leaked Plame's name to Novak—a probe that included a recent hour-long interview of President Bush himself.

While the dust continues to settle on the Niger saga, Novak has gone on doing what he does best—getting the inside story on the current scuttlebutt in Washington, especially within conservative circles. In the following column, he puts his ear to the wall at the Pentagon, and hears rumblings of serious discontent about the way the Bush administration is prosecuting the military action in Iraq. . . .

The *New York Times Book Review* of last Sunday received unusual attention in the Pentagon's corridors this week. The review of *In the Company of Soldiers* by *Washington Post* war correspondent Rick Atkinson reveals the ridiculously low estimate made by the Pentagon's civilian leadership of troops needed in Iraq. Those words echoed eerily amid news of open fighting in Baghdad between U.S. troops and Shiite militia.

In the afterword following his brilliant account of the actual war, Atkinson wrote: "Pentagon planners in early May had predicted that U.S. troop levels would be down to 30,000 by late summer [of 2003]." That was the first time that prediction had been seen in print by startled readers at the Defense Department. The existing 125,000 troop level (currently at 135,000 because of replacements) is considered inadequate by the generals. General John Abizaid, the regional commander-in-chief, has made clear he will ask for more troops if his subordinate commanders need them.

But Afghanistan also needs more troops. So where will they come from? Nobody knows, and that connotes an overcommitment by the United States and a miscalculation at the Defense Department. The uniformed military does not speak out publicly, but the generals are outraged. A former national security official considers the relationship at the Pentagon between civilians and the military as worse than at any time in his long career.

At the heart of this debate is the original belief by Defense Secretary Donald Rumsfeld's team that conquering U.S. troops would be welcomed by open arms in Iraq. In this highly political season, Democrats are replaying the debate of a year ago. General Eric Shinseki, then about to leave as the Army's chief of staff, said "several hundred thousand soldiers" could be needed in Iraq. "Way off the mark," retorted Deputy Defense Secretary Paul Wolfowitz.

Adhering to the principle of civilian control of the military and unvarying obedience to orders, the generals have not publicly expressed their opinion that Shinseki was much closer to the truth than Wolfowitz. However, Abizaid made clear Monday that he was not going to be the fall guy if conditions in Iraq further deteriorate. If commanders want more troops to fulfill their mission, he will ask for them. That would leave Rumsfeld with no choice. The secretary announced on Tuesday that the generals "will get what they ask."

The problem of where to find these troops is not easily solved. There are simply no large units available and suitable for assignment. The 3rd Infantry Division was sent home early, but is now in the midst of Rumsfeld's "transformation" (from three brigades to five) and so is not ready to be inserted into combat. National Guard brigades could be activated, but the need for full training before going to war means they cannot help resolve the present crisis.

Democrats have demanded the use of foreign troops, but countries that previously refused to help without a UN mandate have not changed their minds. Britain announced Tuesday it was replacing an armored brigade, keeping its contribution at the present level of 8,700 troops but not adding any. Spain's new leftist government wants out. That leaves only Turkey willing to help, but the United States has ruled that out in the face of fierce Kurdish opposition.

Although underestimating troop needs in a less political environment would mean fixing the blame at the Pentagon, every issue today becomes a test of party loyalty. Senators Richard Lugar and Chuck Hagel, the top two Republicans on the Senate Foreign Relations Committee, are assailed by the White House for offering constructive criticism. With Senator Edward M. Kennedy setting the Democratic line by saying that "Iraq is George Bush's Vietnam," sensible dialogue is impossible.

While Democrats roar, the generals are silent—in public. Many confide that they will not cast their normal Republican votes on Nov. 2. They cannot bring themselves to vote for John Kerry, who has been a consistent Senate vote against the military. But they say they are unable to vote for Don Rumsfeld's boss, and so will not vote at all.

Two-Front Insurgency
William Safire

The New York Times | April 7, 2004

In the spring of 2004, with violence in Iraq peaking as the result of both the continuing insurgency in the Sunni triangle and the added military challenge from the young Shiite radical Moktada al-Sadr and his militia, William Safire, one of the wise old men of the right wing, penned this call for a U.S. counterattack. Among other things, the acknowledged champion of alliteration calls on Americans to "cooly confront the quaking quagmirists here at home," and, more ominously, suggests that al-Sadr is getting support from Iraq's Shiite neighbor, Iran. . . .

WASHINGTON—In light of about a dozen American combat deaths yesterday, we should keep in mind our historic bet: that given their freedom from a savage tyrant, the three groups that make up Iraq could, with our help, create a rudimentary democracy that would turn the tide against terror.

In the northern group, we can see success: rival Kurdish parties have come together to work within an Iraqi parliament when elections come. "Kirkuk is our Jerusalem," they say, and that oil-rich area—long the center of Iraqi Kurdistan, before Saddam's ethnic cleansing—should be their regional capital in unified Iraq.

In the center group—the Sunnis, who profited most from Saddam's dictatorship—we see mostly a sullen population, its Baathist diehards allied with an affiliate of Al Qaeda longing for regime restoration. There is where the atrocities of Falluja were committed in the fiercest Sunni challenge to liberation.

In Baghdad and the South, long-oppressed Shiites—60 percent of Iraq's population—have the most to gain from democracy and reconstruction. But they are now split. A minority of terrorists led by the firebrand Moktada al-Sadr, under Iran's influence, are challenging the quietist Ayatollah Ali al-Sistani. That ayatollah is keen to protect his following by complaining about the liberation and wrings his hands about Sadr, who has openly declared alliance with Hamas and Hezbollah and war on the West.

All this means that we are now fighting an active two-front insurgency. That calls for a change in our strategy. Up to now we have tried to hunker down and train Iraqis to handle security, lest we appear to be nasty "occupiers." That only emboldened the Sunni terrorists and Shiite Iranists. One anti-American confidently told another Iraqi with cool nonpartisanship about ousting U.S. presidents: "We'll do to Bush what we did to Carter."

But now that the Saddam restorationists and Islamic fundamentalists have made their terrorist move on both fronts, we can counterattack decisively.

"In war, resolution." Having announced we would pacify rebellious Baathists in Falluja, we must pacify Falluja. Having designated the Shiite Sadr an outlaw, we must answer his bloody-minded challenge with whatever military force is required and with fewer casualties in the long run.

But we must impress on the minds of millions of Shiites that there is no free ride to freedom. We should keep the heat on Shiite ditherers by holding fast to the June 30 deadline for the delivery of sovereignty to Iraq's three groups. It's less about the U.S. election than demanding that Iraqi leaders and UN facilitators live up to their promises.

We should couple this with a temporary increase in troop strength, if necessary: we will pull alongside, not pull out or pull alone. We should take up the Turks on their offer of 10,000 troops to fight on our side against two-front terror. The Kurds, who have patched things up with Ankara and know which side of the two-front war they and we are on, would withdraw their ill-considered earlier objection.

We should break the Iranian-Hezbollah-Sadr connection in ways that our special forces know how to do. Plenty of Iraqi Shiites, who are Arab, distrust the Persian ayatollahs in Iran and can provide actionable intelligence about a Syrian transmission belt.

And we should coolly confront the quaking quagmirists here at home.

Does Ted Kennedy speak for his Massachusetts junior senator, John Kerry, when he calls our effort to turn terror-supporting despotism into nascent liberty in Iraq "Bush's Vietnam"?

Do the apostles of retreat realize how their defeatism, magnified by Arab media, bolsters the morale of the insurgents and increases the nervousness of the waverers?

Does our coulda-woulda-shoulda crowd consider how it dismays the majority of Iraqis wondering if they can count on our continued presence as they feel their way toward freedom?

These are the times that try men's souls, and—as Tom Paine's enlightened acquaintance, Mary Wollstonecraft, would have added—women's, too. This is the crisis; we'll come though it.

Hamstrung Hawks

Richard Wolffe

Newsweek | December 3, 2003

"Unintended consequences" is a phrase that gets thrown around a lot during wartime. Here, Richard Wolffe suggests that the problem-plagued American occupation of Iraq has left the administration with "no appetite—and no resources—to focus on another crisis, no matter how serious or imminent." In particular, Wolffe argues, our Iraq adventure has reduced the ability of the U.S. to deal with what many experts feel is the most pressing danger of our time: the apparently real and growing threats posed by Iran and North Korea's nuclear weapons programs. . . .

It's not easy being a hawk nowadays. Especially if you're hawkish about all the things that took us to war in Iraq: rogue states, weapons of mass destruction, and the weakness of the United Nations. While the Bush administration devotes most of its resources to Iraq, there's precious little time, manpower, or money to fight the bigger battle against the countries that are developing and spreading the lethal firepower we fear so much.

It wasn't meant to be this way. Iraq was supposed to make life easier for the doommongers who spend their lives fretting about the things we would rather forget: nuclear weapons, long-range missiles, and the hostile regimes that try to get their hands on both. Most of the hawks who obsess about weapons of mass destruction—including many inside the Bush administration—believed that Iraq would help them force the world to wake up to the threats they were studying.

Even those who doubted whether Iraq was the most pressing threat facing the United States felt that was good enough reason to support the war. "The best thing you can say about it," one weapons expert told me in the run-up to war, "is that this is the first time we've gotten serious about weapons of mass destruction."

Instead, the hawks are hamstrung by Iraq. Inside the administration, there is no appetite—and no resources—to focus on another crisis, no matter how serious or imminent. Outside the United States, there is even less appetite to invest more political capital in another American adventure. At a time when pro-U.S. officials are getting killed in Iraq, including seven Spanish intelligence officers and two Japanese diplomats over the weekend, there is precious little support for more tough action against other targets.

Those other targets were named by George W. Bush almost two years ago. Iran and North Korea, the remaining members of the administration's axis of evil, reacted to the president's post-9/11 warnings with horror, fearing they would become the next in the firing line after Saddam's regime. In fact, both countries have found Washington a relatively easy-going enemy when it comes to nuclear weapons—the only weapons that really matter. The North Koreans have reprocessed some, perhaps all, of their spent fuel rods to produce weapons-grade plutonium. And the Iranians have lifted the veil on their ambitious plans to enrich uranium and establish a nuclear fuel cycle. Yet the Bush administration has been content to go slow. In Iran's case, the White House seems happy to move at the glacial pace of the UN's internal negotiations. And in North Korea's case, it has effectively handed over the initiative to the untested diplomats of the Chinese government.

For the doves inside the administration, this is welcome news—a sign of lessons learned after Iraq, and a chance to rebuild their internationalist credentials. But for the hawks, it's a maddening sight, a frustrating exercise in sitting on their hands. With far more evidence against Iran and North Korea than they ever had against Iraq, the hawks are being forced to accept far, far less in terms of U.S. policy.

It took John Bolton, the hyperhawkish undersecretary of state for arms control, to hint at those frustrations this week. Bolton, who is close to Vice President Dick Cheney, was famously condemned as "human scum" and a "bloodsucker" by the North Korean foreign ministry after he dared to describe Kim Jong Il as a "tyrannical dictator." Such insults are worn as a badge of honor among the hawks. But they are markedly less proud of their administration's handling of the Stalinist North.

In a speech to the Institute for Foreign Policy Analysis on Tuesday, Bolton warned that North Korea's nukes were "a profound challenge to regional stability." Yet the only way the United States is dealing with that challenge right now are the six-nation talks hosted by the Chinese. The next round of those talks has stalled because Beijing is curiously trying to negotiate a deal before anyone gets together in the Chinese capital. Not surprisingly, they are failing to agree on a final statement in advance of the talks themselves.

So it's also no surprise to find hawks like Bolton pushing for something more than Chinese diplomacy. In his speech, Bolton politely suggests that it might be "logical" for the Security Council to take up the issue of North Korea. After all, the North has withdrawn from the nuclear nonproliferation treaty and ejected UN nuclear inspectors. He also suggests the Security Council might want to look at the case of Iran, and the damning findings of the inspectors about its nuclear program.

It all sounds so polite, so unhawkish. Until you realize that it's also U.S. policy to hang back from the Security Council. As Bolton notes tartly, the other permanent members of the Security Council—Russia, China, France, and Britain—have all wanted to avoid another showdown at the UN "And we have agreed," Bolton concedes. "Of course, we hope that the other four permanent members of the Security Council are aware of the long-term implications of these decisions, as we are. Policies intended to bring about the termination of the Iranian and [North Korean] nuclear weapons programs, which result in reducing the council's role under the [UN] Charter, would be truly unfortunate and ironic."

It is indeed unfortunate and ironic. The hawks have plenty of red meat to tear into when it comes to Iran and North Korea. But like the UN itself, they have been sidelined and are in danger of appearing ignored and unloved. The war in Iraq was not supposed to heighten the world's sense of irony. It was supposed to awaken the world to the spread of the worst weapons known to mankind. In that sense, the hawks won the battle to invade Iraq—but have lost the war they wanted to fight.

A President Beyond the Law
Anthony Lewis

The New York Times | May 7, 2004

When CBS and The New Yorker *magazine broke the Abu Ghraib prisoner-abuse story in late April 2004, the Pentagon's first reponse was to blame the harsh interrogation techniques depicted in photo after photo—naked prisoners forced into human pyramids, threatened with snarling dogs, hung over bunk railings, and worse—on the handiwork of a few misguided "bad apples" in the ranks. Since then, however, a picture has been steadily emerging that suggests Iraq is simply the latest example of a widespread and systematic application of questionable U.S. interrogation techniques— a shift in tactics that began in the early days of the war in Afghanistan, and that extended to the military prison in Guantanamo Bay as well as clandestine CIA detention centers around the world.*

How did the U.S. suddenly turn into a country that tortures? In the following examination of how the abuse was permitted to happen, Anthony Lewis returns to a theme he's sounded often over the past few years—namely, that the Bush administration has an inherent "low regard" for the rule of law. . . .

CAMBRIDGE, Mass.

The question tears at all of us, regardless of party or ideology: How could American men and women treat Iraqi prisoners with such cruelty—and laugh at their humiliation? We are told that there was a failure of military leadership. Officers in the field were lax. Pentagon officials didn't care. So the worst in human nature was allowed to flourish.

But something much more profound underlies this terrible episode. It is a culture of low regard for the law, of respecting the law only when it is convenient.

Again and again, over these last years, President Bush has made clear his view that law must bend to what he regards as necessity. National security as he defines it trumps our commitments to international law. The Constitution must yield to novel infringements on American freedom.

One clear example is the treatment of the prisoners at Guantanamo Bay, Cuba. The Third Geneva Convention requires that any dispute about a prisoner's status be decided by a "competent tribunal." American forces provided many such tribunals for prisoners taken in the Persian Gulf war in 1991. But Mr. Bush has refused to comply with the Geneva Convention. He decided that all the Guantanamo prisoners were "unlawful combatants"—that is, not regular soldiers but spies, terrorists or the like.

The Supreme Court is now considering whether the prisoners can use American courts to challenge their designation as unlawful. The administration's brief could not be blunter in its argument that the president is the law on this issue: "The president, in his capacity as commander in chief, has conclusively determined that the Guantanamo detainees . . . are not entitled to prisoner-of-war status under the Geneva Convention."

The violation of the Geneva Convention and that refusal to let the courts consider the issue have cost the United States dearly in the world legal community—the judges and lawyers in societies that, historically, have looked to the United States as the exemplar of a country committed to law. Lord Steyn, a judge on Britain's highest court, condemned the administration's position on Guantanamo in an address last fall—pointing out that American courts would refuse even to hear claims of torture from prisoners. At the time, the idea of torture at Guantanamo seemed far-fetched to me. After the disclosures of the last 10 days, can we be sure?

Instead of a country committed to law, the United States is now seen as a country that proclaims high legal ideals and then says that they should apply to all others but not to itself. That view has been worsened by the Bush administration's determination that Americans not be subject to the new International Criminal Court, which is supposed to punish genocide and war crimes.

Fear of terrorism—a quite understandable fear after 9/11—has led to harsh departures from normal legal practice at home. Aliens swept off the streets by the Justice Department as possible terrorists after 9/11 were subjected to physical abuse and humiliation by prison guards, the department's inspector general found. Attorney General John Ashcroft did not apologize— a posture that sent a message.

Inside the United States, the most radical departure from law as we have known it is President Bush's claim that he can designate any American citizen an "enemy combatant"—and thereupon detain that person in solitary confinement indefinitely, without charges, without a trial, without a right to counsel. Again, the president's lawyers have argued determinedly that he must have the last word, with little or no scrutiny from lawyers and judges.

There was a stunning moment in President Bush's 2003 State of the Union address when he said that more than 3,000 suspected terrorists "have been arrested in many countries. And many others have met a different fate. Let's put it this way: They are no longer a problem for the United States."

In all these matters, there is a pervasive attitude: that to follow the law is to be weak in the face of terrorism. But commitment to law is not a weakness. It has been the great strength of the United States from the beginning. Our leaders depart from that commitment at their peril, and ours, for a reason that Justice Louis D. Brandeis memorably expressed 75 years ago.

"Our government is the potent, the omnipresent teacher," he wrote. "For good or ill, it teaches the whole people by its example. Crime is contagious. If the government becomes a lawbreaker, it breeds contempt for the law; it invites every man to become a law unto himself."

Bipolar Iraq
Michael Wolff

New York magazine | Nov. 17, 2003

One of the confusing aspects of the Iraq conflict is the difficulty of knowing whether things are getting better or worse. Reconstruction continues, but so do the bombings—and the bombings typically get a lot more coverage by the media. As a result, administration officials have repeatedly criticized the media for indulging in biased, negative reporting on the war and its aftermath. In this column, media critic Michael Wolff examines the struggle to control the conflict's storyline, including the White House's suggestion that bad PR is the single biggest obstacle to achieving military and political success in Iraq. As Wolff notes, it's an argument that sounds eerily familiar. . . .

Here are the two opposite story lines:

(1) It's working.
(2) It's a quagmire.

Let's fill them out a little more:

(1) Iraqis are back in the markets and on the street; schools are opening, businesses getting going again, institutions returning to life. By virtually every happiness-quotient measure, the state of being among the vast majority of Iraqis is more positive now than it was during the reign of Saddam Hussein—and it will be even more positive in the near future. As social experiments go—revivifying a materially and psychologically broken nation—there is every reason to be optimistic (and even proud) about this one.

(2) We've gotten ourselves into an ever-expanding war with a fanatical and well-armed resistance. What's more, growing numbers of ideological defenders are traveling to this battlefield, which threatens to turn Iraq, along with Israel and the Palestinian territories, into a permanent Muslim versus non-Muslim front and international tripwire. We're stuck in a situation with consequences and financial burdens that we cannot estimate. This is the definition of quagmire. And by the logic of quagmire, the situation only ever becomes more intractable and the consequences more fearful and destabilizing.

As you read those quick précis, your inclination is, invariably, to pick one. They can't, after all, really exist together. Or, if perchance they do exist together now, one will inevitably come to overshadow the other. Obviously, if you're a Bush person, you choose the former, and if you're an anti-Bush person, you choose the latter. In some sense, in fact, these are not even alternative views of the reality in Iraq as much as opposite worldviews applicable to almost any situation.

(1) There is, quite simply, the patent superiority of the American way. When people are exposed to it, it spreads like a virus. We have not only righteousness on our side but modernity and economic reality. Eighty-seven billion dollars changes any equation. Everything seems messy, inchoate, ugly, fraught, without organization; but at some point in the

organizational process, rationality and benefit will begin to become clear. Upside will outweigh downside. Ambivalence and self-doubt are the real killers here. Long-term investment and staying the course are the solutions and the way to get a big return.

(2) An incredible arrogance chronically pervades the American mind-set. Our lack of self-doubt makes us stupid. We're blinded to the intractable problems set against us: not just to a deep cultural antipathy but to a million details on the ground that the guys at the Pentagon or at Centcom HQ in Florida don't have the patience or the language skills or the in-country intelligence to think through. What's more, because we pride ourselves on "can-do" and turn up our noses at intellectual and abstract analysis, we never really or accurately appreciate cause and effect. We're always the victims of the law of unintended consequences. Because we're too big and too quick, we necessarily upset the ecology in ways that will certainly come back to haunt and terrorize us.

(1) Essentially good news.
(2) Inevitably bad news.

Which brings us to the Chinook helicopter—and before that the attack on the Al Rashid Hotel, and before that the UN attack.

The fervent bad-news-ites seem to believe that the Bushies understand the kind of mess they're (we're) in and are doing everything they can to disguise (spin) it and to blame someone else for it. But the more interesting and complex and difficult possibility is that they don't see it as a mess at all.

For them, these bad-news incidents represent an illusion created by the small resistance, the leftover Baathists. These thugs and irregulars. What we have here are isolated acts meant to sow widespread fear—it's just, well, terrorism. The odd thing, of course, is that such terrorism is exactly why we went to war—so it's rather disorienting to have it dismissed now as somehow inconsequential in relation to the bigger picture.

It's not bad news, the Bushies seem to be saying, as much as bad PR—or the other side's good PR. The bad guys have effectively influenced the media coverage without, the Bushies seem genuinely convinced, affecting the reality. Life in Iraq gets better and better—except for the fact that these scumballs know how to generate bad press for the Americans who are making life in Iraq better and better.

Hence the Bushies have countered with a campaign to generate good news.

There is even the sense—again, a reality inversion—that the best way to deal with terrorism is in the court of public opinion rather than on the battlefield.

So the good-news offensive. The mainstream media—because it is overly liberal and crassly superficial—is emphasizing the (minimal) bloodshed and ignoring the story of a liberated nation. And there has been the careful parsing of the story: carving the Sunni triangle from the rest of a (largely) pacified country; rushing in American pollsters (and then parsing those results); separating good imams from bad imams.

And, indeed, there has been a sudden rush of not unconvincing good-news accounts. Life was terrible. Life is better. Nothing worked. Now many things are working. Average Iraqis may not be embracing the American occupation, but they are sure grateful not to have Saddam around (cue the torture tapes that the Pentagon released to Fox News). Life, as seen by in-country reporters, is returning to normal.

But there are the bodies.

The Bush people, as they argue their story line, have to distract people's attention from the dead. The president doesn't mention the bodies; doesn't attend funerals. Body-bag shots are on the media proscribed list. You can sense their frustration in this regard—that the bodies are always, annoyingly, the story. This is partly a military-civilian disconnect. Our job, you can hear Rumsfeld saying, is to minimize casualties, not to eliminate them. In sheer military terms—troops deployed versus casualties sustained—it's not even that bad. Arguably (although it's an argument you lose by making it), the kill ratio indicates a big success. I mean, you can't really fight a war if everybody is precious—if nobody is expendable.

And yet, the great nonmilitary sensibility of the country, and of the media, sees each body as a story, and multiple bodies as a bigger story, and the aggregate of bodies as a really damning piece of evidence.

There is a socio-military calculation on the part of reporters and politicians (both Democrats and Republicans) and, one would assume, military people as well, as to how much is too much. What's sustainable and what's a big problem?

When the number of soldiers killed in the aftermath exceeded the number of people killed in the actual war, that was seen as a problematic milestone.

When the total number of people killed in Iraq II surpassed the total number killed in Iraq I, that got serious.

Oh yes, and significant multi-casualty incidents are major bad news. Mogadishu levels would be very dicey. Beirut levels in the Reagan era might well put the whole proposition over the top.

Now, what the Bush administration is arguing is, in effect, that our enemies know these numbers. That they cannot damage us enough to truly harm us or even to actually hamper our mission, but they can inflict enough damage to frighten us (or frighten you—or frighten the media)—precisely because our tolerance for damage has been set artificially low.

Not least of all by Democrats and by the biased media!

And so we move from a military war to a political one.

This is the exact opposite of the wars of the last generation—of the Clinton approach or even of the first Bush administration—that constant and obsessive cost-reward analysis.

Of not being caught out there without a way back. Retreating from Mogadishu. Not following Saddam into Baghdad. Of always making the calculation about when the consensus might divide. Of not making people choose sides. Of not letting there be two stories told at once.

The Bush people don't believe there are two sides. Not two right sides, anyway. This mission is sacrosanct. The WMD canard and the sexing of intelligence reports happened, not least of all, to protect the mission. Nobody is going to go for broke in an elective war—it had to be a necessary war.

There's no debate. There's polling (of course) but no interest in consensus. Stubbornness (Rumsfeldness) is both virtue and strategy. If you refuse to engage in any back-and-forth but just say what you believe relentlessly, repetition eventually changes perceptions.

Righteousness went out of favor in the post–cold war world (incrementalism, globalism, complex systems analysis came in). But righteousness is surely back. The righteous don't compromise, don't negotiate, don't wimp out. The righteous (even if they had planned not to have to) take casualties (unlike that thoroughly nonrighteous Clinton, who hated to take casualties).

There's no longer even a pretense that this is about conventional success measures (indeed, failure suddenly seems part—even a necessary part—of the great ultimate success). The *we're-not-quitters* stance of the Bushies (and that the Democrats are, ipso facto, quitters) is explicitly disconnected from any talk about how we're actually going to win.

The arguable merit of the Bush position—life is certainly better in Iraq—is subsumed by its larger, relentless, messianic, and fatalistic ambitions.

We're at the bear-any-burden stage. That is, in most political terms, a wildly unpopular place to be. We are, after all, selfish, self-obsessed Americans.

So the only way they're going to sell this is to turn it from a problem-solving issue into an ideological one. "We are fighting that enemy in Iraq, in Afghanistan today so that we do not meet him again on our own streets, in our own cities," said the president.

It's a setup. We're going to have to choose position (1) or position (2).

The Democrats and Howard Dean play into that hand (Bush-bashing is probably good for the Bushies).

It's them or us.

Winners or losers.

Lefties or real Americans.

We've been here before, and we know how badly it turns out.

Part Five:
Iraq and the War on Terror

From: *Plan of Attack*
Bob Woodward

In his book Plan of Attack, *published in April 2004, Bob Woodward returned to the subject of his 2002 book,* Bush at War—*the inner workings of the Bush administration, and the decisions that led to the American military actions in Aghanistan and Iraq. President Bush, who was reportedly pleased with* Bush at War, *granted Woodward extensive interview time for his new project, and encouraged other members of the administration to do the same. Woodward eventually talked with seventy-five top officials; the result is a fascinating, highly-detailed account of the months preceding the Iraq invasion.*

This selection contains four excerpts from Plan of Attack. *Each one describes a key moment in the decision-making process during the runup to the Iraq War. The first, taken from the opening pages of the book's prologue, depicts a November 21, 2001, conversation between Bush and Secretary of Defense Donald Rumsfeld, in which the first serious steps are taken towards planning an invasion. The second jumps back two months in time, to the post-9/11 discussions in which the issue of Iraq was first raised and then temporarily put aside. The third excerpt describes a fateful conversation in the Oval Office on December 21, 2002, in which then–CIA Director George Tenet and his deputy director, John McLaughlin, laid out the intelligence indicating that Saddam Hussein possessed weapons of mass destruction—including Bush's famous line, "I've been told all this intelligence about having WMD and this is the best we've got?" and Tenet's equally famous response: "[I]t's a slam dunk!"*

The final excerpt covers another Oval Office meeting several weeks later, in January 2003, between Bush and Secretary of State Colin Powell, in which the president hears out Powell's reservations about the upcoming war—then tells him, "I want you with me." . . .

President George W. Bush clamped his arm on his secretary of defense, Donald H. Rumsfeld, as a National Security Council meeting in the White House Situation Room was just finishing on Wednesday, November 21, 2001. It was the day before Thanksgiving, just 72 days after the 9/11 terrorist attacks and the beginning of the eleventh month of Bush's presidency.

"I need to see you," the president said to Rumsfeld. The affectionate gesture sent a message that important presidential business needed to be discussed in the utmost privacy. Bush knew it was dramatic for him to call the secretary of defense aside. The two men went into one of the small cubby-hole offices adjacent to the Situation Room, closed the door and sat down.

"I want you . . ." the president began, and as is often the case he restarted the sentence. "What kind of a war plan do you have for Iraq? How do you feel about the war plan for Iraq?"

Rumsfeld said he didn't think the Iraq war plan was current. It didn't represent the thinking of General Tommy Franks, the combatant commander for the region, and it certainly didn't represent his own thinking. The plan was basically Desert Storm II Plus, he explained, meaning it was a slightly enhanced version of the massive invasion force employed by Bush's father in the 1991 Gulf War. "I am concerned about all of our war plans," the secretary added. He poured out some of his accumulated frustrations and consternation. He was reviewing all 68 of the department's secret war and other contingency plans worldwide and had been for months.

Bush and Rumsfeld are a contrasting pair. Large and physical with a deep stare from small brown eyes, Bush, 55, has a quick, joshing manner which at time borders on the impulsive. Focused, direct, practical but not naturally articulate, he had been elected to his first political office as governor of Texas only nine years earlier, a novice thrust into the presidency. Rumsfeld, 69, had been elected to his first political office, congressman from the 13th District of Illinois in the Chicago suburbs, 39 years earlier. Small, almost boyishly dashing, with thinning combed-back hair, Rumsfeld was intense and also focused as he squinted through his trifocals. He is capable of a large, infectious smile that can overwhelm his face or alternatively convey impatience, even condescension, though he is deferential and respectful to the president.

In his semi-professional voice Rumsfeld explained to Bush that the process of drafting war plans was so complex that it took years. The present war plans tended to hold assumptions that were stale, he told the president, and they failed to account for the fact that a new administration with different goals had taken over. The war planning process was woefully broken and maddening. He was working to fix it.

"Let's get started on this," Bush recalled saying. "And get Tommy Franks looking at what it would take to protect America by removing Saddam Hussein if we have to." He also asked, Could this be done on a basis that would not be terribly noticeable?

"Sure, because I'm doing all of them," Rumsfeld replied. His worldwide review would provide perfect cover. "There isn't a combatant commander that doesn't know how I feel and that I'm getting them refreshed." He had spoken with all the main regional commanders, the four-star generals and admirals for the Pacific, Europe, Latin America, as well as Frank's Central Command (CENTCOM), which encompassed the Middle East, South-Central Asia, and the Horn of Africa.

The president had another request. Don't talk about what you are doing with others.

Yes, sir, Rumsfeld said. But it would be helpful to be able to know to whom he could talk when the president had brought others into this thinking. "It's particularly important that I talk to George Tenet," the secretary said. CIA Director Tenet would be critical to intelligence gathering and any coordinated covert efforts in Iraq.

"Fine," the president said, indicating that at a later date Tenet and others could become involved. But not now.

Two years later in interviews, Bush said he did not want others in on the secret because a leak would trigger "enormous international angst and domestic speculation. I knew what would happen if people thought we were developing a potential or a war plan for Iraq."

The Bush-Rumsfeld-Franks work remained secret for months and when partial disclosures made their way into the media the next year, the president, Rumsfeld, and others in the administration, attempting to defuse any sense of immediacy, spoke of contingency planning and insisted that war plans were not on the president's desk.

Knowledge of this work would have ignited a firestorm, the president knew. "It was such a high-stakes moment and when people had this sense of war followed, the heels of the Afghan decision," Bush's order for a military operation into Afghanistan in response to 9/11, "it would look like that I was anxious to go to war. And I'm not anxious to go to war." He insisted, "War is my absolute last option."

At the same time, Bush said, he realized that the simple act of setting Rumsfeld in motion on Iraq war plans might be the first step in taking the nation to a war with Saddam Hussein. "Absolutely," Bush recalled.

What he perhaps had not realized was that war plans and the process of war planning become policy by their own momentum, especially with the intimate involvement of both the secretary of defense and the president.

The story of Bush's decisions leading up to the Iraq War is a chronicle of continual dilemmas, since the president was pursuing two simultaneous policies. He was planning for war, and he was conducting diplomacy; aiming to avoid war. At times, the war planning aided the diplomacy, at many other points it contradicted it.

From the conversation in the cubbyhole off the Situation Room that day, Rumsfeld realized how focused Bush was about Iraq. "He should have, " the president called. "Because he knew how serious I was."

Rumsfeld was left with the impression that Bush had not spoken to anyone else. That was not so. That same morning the president had told Condoleezza Rice, his national security adviser, that he was planning to get Rumsfeld to work on Iraq. For Rice, 9/11 had put Iraq on the back burner. The president did not explain to her why he was returning to it now, or what triggered his orders to Rumsfeld.

In the interviews the president said he could not recall if he had talked to Vice President Dick Cheney before he took Rumsfeld aside. But he was certainly aware of Cheney's own position. "The vice president, after 9/11, clearly saw Saddam Hussein as a threat to peace," he said. "And was unwavering in his view that Saddam was a real danger. And again—I see Dick all the time and my relationship—remember since he is not campaigning for office or his own future, he is around. And so I see him quite a bit. And we meet all the time as a matter of fact. And so I can't remember the timing of a particular meeting with him or not."

On the long walk-up to war in Iraq, Dick Cheney was a powerful, steamrolling force. Since the terrorist attacks, he had developed an intense focus on the threats posed by Saddam and by Osama bin Laden's Al Qaeda network, the group responsible for 9/11. It was seen as "fever" by some of his colleagues, even a disquieting obsession. For Cheney, taking care of Saddam was high necessity.

—

The September 11, 2001, terrorist attacks in New York and Washington that killed nearly 3,000 altered and defined the Bush presidency. It was not an exaggeration when Bush dictated to his daily diary that night that, "The Pearl Harbor of the 21st century took place today." In some respects the attacks were more devastating. Instead of 1941 Hawaii, which was not then a state, the targets were the power centers of the homeland. Instead of Japan, the attacks were conducted by a shadowy enemy that had no country or visible army. Worse for Bush, CIA Director Tenet had explicitly warned him about the immediacy and seriousness of the bin Laden threat. Focusing on domestic issues and a giant tax cut, Bush had largely ignored the terrorism problem. "I didn't feel that sense of urgency," the president acknowledged later in an interview. "My blood was not nearly as boiling."

The terrorists who struck the Pentagon flew their plane into the building on the opposite side of Rumsfeld's office, tearing a gaping hole and killing 184 people. At 2:40 P.M. that day, with dust and smoke filling the operations center as he was trying to figure out what had happened, Rumsfeld raised with his staff the possibility of going after Iraq as a response to the terrorist attacks, according to an aide's notes. Saddam Hussein is S.H. in these notes, and UBL is Usama bin Laden. The notes show that Rumsfeld had mused about whether to "hit S.H. @ same time—not only UBL" and asked the Pentagon lawyer to talk to Paul Wolfowitz about the Iraq "connection with UBL." The next day in the inner circle of Bush's war cabinet, Rumsfeld asked if the terrorist attacks did not present an "opportunity" to launch against Iraq.

Four days later in an exhaustive debate at Camp David, none of the president's top advisers recommended attacking Iraq as a first step in the terrorism war—not even Vice President Cheney, who probably read where Bush was headed and said, "If we go after Saddam Hussein, we lose our rightful place as good guy." Cheney, however, voiced deep concerns about Saddam and said he would not rule out going after him at some point. Colin Powell was adamantly opposed to attacking Iraq as a response to September 11. He saw no real linkage between Saddam and 9/11. Members of a rapidly forming international coalition of other nations would jump off the bandwagon, Powell said. "They'll view it as bait and switch—it's not what they signed up to do," the secretary of state said bluntly. He was pumping the brakes.

White House Chief of Staff Andrew H. Card said Iraq should not be a principal, initial target. Tenet also recommended that the initial terrorist target for the military should be Afghanistan, not Iraq.

A tally would show that it was 4 to 0 against hitting Iraq initially, with Rumsfeld abstaining, making it 4 to 0 to 1. Powell found Rumsfeld's abstention most interesting. What did it mean? he wondered. Rumsfeld had this way of asking questions—questions, questions, questions!—and not revealing his own position.

As a former chairman of the Joint Chiefs of Staff, Powell was direct with one of his successors, Army General Hugh Shelton, in a private discussion after an NSC meeting. Powell had rolled his eyes at Shelton after Rumsfeld had raised Iraq as an "opportunity."

"What the hell! What are these guys thinking about?" Powell had asked Shelton. "Can't you get these guys back in the box?"

Shelton promised he was trying. The only strong advocate for attacking Iraq at that point was Wolfowitz, who thought war in Afghanistan would be dicey and uncertain. Wolfowitz worried about 100,000 American troops bogged down in the notoriously treacherous mountains six months from then. In contrast, Iraq was a brittle, oppressive regime that might break easily with an opposition yearning to topple Saddam. He estimated that there was a 10 to 50 percent chance Saddam was involved in the 9/11 attacks—an odd conclusion that reflected deep suspicion but no real evidence.

The next afternoon, Sunday, September 16, Bush told Rice that the first target of the war on terrorism was going to be Afghanistan. "We won't do Iraq now," the president said, "we're putting Iraq off. But eventually we'll have to return to that question."

On September 17, the president signed the Top Secret/Pearl order for new CIA and military operations against terrorists worldwide. Afghanistan was the first priority. Rumsfeld was directed to continue working on Iraq war plans but it was not to be a top priority.

In an interview nearly one year later, President Bush said that in the immediate aftermath of September 11, "There were some who discussed Iraq. That's out of the question at this point. I mean, I didn't need any briefings." He added, "Don, wisely—and I agreed with this—was looking for other places where we could show that the war on terror was global." Rumsfeld also wanted ground forces in Afghanistan, not just cruise missiles and bombers launched from afar. "He was the man who was insistent upon boots on the ground to change the psychology of how Americans viewed war," the president said.

Bush believed Clinton had been risk-averse. He had used cruise missiles to attack bin Laden in Afghanistan in 1998 after Al Qaeda had bombed two American embassies in East Africa. During the Kosovo War, he had limited U.S. involvement to an air campaign, still spooked by the disastrous mission in Somalia in 1993 when eighteen U.S. soldiers died in a fierce urban firefight.

President Bush said, "And Rumsfeld wanted to make sure that the military was active in other regions. My point was that the degree of difficulty had to be relatively small in order to make sure that we continued to succeed in the first battle."

• • •

Two years after 9/11, during an interview in his office in the White House residence, President Bush said, "September the 11th obviously changed my thinking a lot about my responsibility as president. Because September the 11th made the security of the American people the priority . . . a sacred duty for the president. It is the most necessary duty for the president, because if the president doesn't take on that duty, who else is going to?"

It changed his attitude toward "Saddam Hussein's capacity to create harm," he said, adding that "all his terrible features became much more threatening. Keeping Saddam in a box looked less and less feasible to me." Saddam was a "madman," the president said. "He had used weapons of mass destruction in the past. He has created incredible instability in the neighborhood." Saddam had invaded Iran in the 1980s and Kuwait in the 1990s.

Bush added, "The options in Iraq were relatively limited when you are playing the containment game."

—

Tenet and [John] McLaughlin went to the Oval Office the morning of Saturday, December 21 [2003]. The meeting was for presenting "The Case" on WMD as it might be presented to a jury with Top Secret security clearances. There was great expectation. In addition to the president, Cheney, Rice, and Andy Card attended.

With some fanfare, McLaughlin stepped up to brief with a series of flip charts. This was the rough cut, he indicated, still highly classified and not cleared for public release. The CIA wanted to reserve on what would be revealed so as to protect sources and detection methods if there was no military conflict.

McLaughlin pointed out that components for biological weapons were unaccounted for, as were 3,200 tons of precursor for chemical weapons. Some 6,000 shells were unaccounted for going back to the Iran-Iraq War in the 1980s.

He flipped to a large satellite photo of a test stand for rocket engines. The stand, as they could see, was clearly larger than would be needed for the small engines of missiles with the permitted maximum range of 150 kilometers.

Another overhead photo showed scarring of the earth at a facility that had been documented as a chemical weapons facility. The scarring "appeared" to be an effort to clean up after a transfer or a spill of chemicals, McLaughlin said.

He flipped to a graphic of a UAV [unmanned aerial vehicle] flying a racetrack pattern. Technical collection had established with "absolute certainty," a phrase he did not often use, that the drone had flown in the red circles indicated in the graphic a total of 500 kilometers. In their weapons declaration, two weeks earlier, Iraq had said its UAV had a range of 80 kilometers. The United Nations had limited Iraq to 150 kilometers. The UAV was launched from the back of a truck and had an autopilot. The 500-kilometer range was enough to reach neighboring countries.

McLaughlin was aware that it was probably a rather confusing graphic but one that was quite exciting to intelligence analysts because the flight path could be determined down to the kilometer. The length of time in flight also suggested that the Iraqis had a good deal of confidence in their automated guidance system.

This was a clear weapons violation. The question was why they would be so interested in such a drone. Its delivery capabilities were ominous, but there was no proof of what they intended.

Next McLaughlin presented accounts from several human sources and defectors about large mobile trailers that these sources said were biological weapons production facilities that could move around to evade inspectors.

In his most dramatic example, McLaughlin presented the transcript of an intercepted radio conversation between two Republican Guard officers that he showed on his flip charts.

"Remove," the first officer said.

"Remove," repeated the second.

"Nerve agents."

"Nerve agents."

"Whenever it comes up."

McLaughlin explained that the first officer wanted to make sure any reference to "nerve agents" in radio instructions was eliminated. If Iraq had no biological material, weapons or nerve agents, why were these Republican Guard officers discussing it?

On nuclear weapons, McLaughlin mentioned that Saddam convened a group of Iraq's main atomic scientists, dubbed the "nuclear mafia," quite often and spoke to them in terms that "implied" preparations to resume nuclear weapons research.

He presented yet another intercept in which officers had talked about the concealment of a modified vehicle at the al-Kindi company, a known WMD facility, that was clearly a matter of concern since inspectors were about to arrive there.

When McLaughlin concluded, there was a look on the president's face of, What's this? And then a brief moment of silence.

"Nice try," Bush said. "I don't think this is quite—it's not something that Joe Public would understand or would gain a lot of confidence from."

Card was also underwhelmed. The presentation was a flop. In terms of marketing, the examples didn't work, the charts didn't work, the photos were not gripping, the intercepts were less than compelling.

Bush turned to Tenet. "I've been told all this intelligence about having WMD and this is the best we've got?"

From the end of one of the couches in the Oval Office, Tenet rose up, threw his arms in the air. "It's a slam dunk case!" the DCI said.

Bush pressed. "George, how confident are you?"

Tenet, a basketball fan who attended as many home games of his alma mater Georgetown as possible, leaned forward and threw his arms up again. "Don't worry, it's a slam dunk!"

It was unusual for Tenet to be so certain. From McLaughlin's presentation, Card was worried that there might be no "there there," but Tenet's double reassurance on the slam dunk was both memorable and comforting. Cheney could think of no reason to question Tenet's assertion. He was, after all, the head of the CIA and would know the most. The president later recalled that McLaughlin's presentation "wouldn't have stood the test of time," but Tenet's reassurance, "That was very important."

"Needs a lot more work," Bush told Card and Rice. "Let's get some people who've actually put together a case for a jury." He wanted some lawyers, prosecutors if need be. They were going to have to go public with something.

The president told Tenet several times, "Make sure no one stretches to make our case."

—

One of Rice's jobs was, as she called it, "to read the secretaries"—Powell and Rumsfeld. Since the president had told Rumsfeld about his decision to go to war, he had better tell Powell, and fast. Powell was close to Prince Bandar, who now was informed of the decision.

"Mr. President," Rice said, "if you're getting to a place that you really think this might happen, you need to call Colin in and talk to him." Powell had the most difficult job of keeping the diplomatic track alive.

So that Monday, January 13 [2003], Powell and Bush met in the Oval Office.

The president was sitting in his regular chair in front of the fireplace and the secretary was in the chair reserved for the visiting leader or most senior U.S. official. For once, neither Cheney nor Rice was hovering.

Bush complimented Powell for his hard work on the diplomatic front. "The inspections are not getting us there," the president said, getting down to business. The UN inspectors were just sort of stumbling around, and Saddam was showing no intention of real compliance. "I really think I'm going to have to do this." The president said he had made up his mind on war. The U.S. should go to war.

"You're sure?" Powell said.

Yes. It was the assured Bush. His tight, forward-leaning, muscular body language verified his words. It was the Bush of the days following 9/11.

"You understand the consequences," Powell said in a half-question. For nearly six months, he had been hammering on this theme—that the United States would be taking down a regime, would have to govern Iraq, and the ripple effect in the Middle East and the world could not be predicted. The run-up to war had sucked nearly all the oxygen from every other issue in foreign relations. War would surely get all the air and attention.

Yeah, I do, the president answered.

"You know that you're going to be owning this place?" Powell said, reminding Bush of what he had told him at their August 5 dinner. An invasion would mean assuming the hopes, aspirations and all the troubles of Iraq. Powell wasn't sure whether Bush had fully understood the meaning and consequences of total ownership.

But I think I have to do this, the president said.

Right, Powell said.

I just want to let you know that, Bush said, making it clear this was not a discussion, but the president informing one of his cabinet members of his decision. The fork in the road had been reached and Bush had chosen war.

As the only one in Bush's inner circle who was seriously and actively pressing the diplomatic track, Powell figured the president wanted to make sure he would support the war. It was in some way a gut check, but Powell didn't feel the president was making a loyalty check. No way on God's earth could he walk away at that point. It would have been an unthinkable act of disloyalty to the president, to Powell's own soldier's code, to the United States military, and mostly to the several hundred thousand who would be going to war. The kids were the ones who fought, Powell often reminded himself.

It had taken Bush a long time to get to this point. It had come after 12 years of Saddam's games after the first Gulf War, more than a year of war planning, four months of grueling United Nations diplomacy. It was more than 15 months since 9/11. So it might look like a study in patience. It had not been easy for Powell to buy that patience. He had had to go in and buy it nearly every day. Buy it with the vast national security apparatus that surrounded a president, particularly Cheney, Rumsfeld and the boys over at Defense.

"Are you with me on this?" the president asked him now. "I think I have to do this. I want you with me."

It was an extraordinary moment. The president was asking, almost imploring his secretary of state, his most senior cabinet officer and the most visible administration figure other than himself. There was no salesmanship, just a question: yes or no, up or down.

"I'll do the best I can," Powell answered. "Yes, sir, I will support you. I'm with you, Mr. President."

"Time to put your war uniform on," the president said to the former general. He could wear his diplomatic hat, that was fine, but things had changed.

"He's going to do it," Powell told himself as he left. It was momentous. He had come to realize that this president wasn't one to second-guess himself. He didn't know when Bush reconsidered his decisions, replayed the debates, weighed the arguments. He must, he thought. Powell did it all the time. Maybe late at night, Powell thought. And maybe never? Was it possible? The president spoke so confidently.

Powell figured his job was to continue and finish out the diplomatic track. That might be the answer. The president's conclusion was clear—there was no way to avoid war—but the basis for that was Bush's belief that the UN negotiations and inspections were going south. "There may be a way to avoid this," Powell said to himself, imagining he still had time, even though Bush had crossed the river. Powell knew diplomatic efforts could give the president a problem because they could make him walk back across the river. His rationalization went as follows: His goal was not to "unscrew" the presidential decision, it was to play out the diplomatic hand he held. In his mind, he was not doing this against the wishes of his boss, only against his instincts that diplomacy would not work.

This distinction between wishes and instincts was a delicate and dangerous game. Yet in all the discussions, meetings, chats and back-and-forth, the president had never once asked Powell, Would you do this? What's your overall advice? The bottom line?

Perhaps the president feared the answer. Perhaps Powell feared giving it.

It would, after all, have been an opportunity to say he disagreed. But they had not gotten to that core question, and Powell would not push. He would not intrude on that most private of presidential space—where a president made decisions of war and peace—unless he was invited. He had not been invited.

Powell thought Saddam could be contained and would eventually wither. Under the sustained pressure—diplomatic, economic, military and CIA— he might wither faster. Perhaps, contrary to what the president was saying, time was on their side. Saddam had been fully isolated and left friendless in the international community after the passage of UN Resolution 1441 in November. It had been a moment of maximum pressure, but the diplomatic pressure was subsiding.

At times, with his closest friends, Powell was semidespondent. His president and his country were headed for a war that he thought might just be avoided, though he himself would not walk away. He had known it would be what he called "a long patrol" when the president had challenged Saddam at the United Nations on September 12, 2002. Powell wouldn't leave the president at the cross-roads. He would do so only if he thought all the arguments for war were 100 percent wrong. And they weren't. He wanted the bastard gone as much as anyone.

Another consideration was if the war would be immoral. And Powell couldn't say that either. It was clear that the president was convinced it was both 100 percent correct and moral.

He had not been told to halt the diplomatic track. It was still possible, Powell reasoned, that he could pull a rabbit out of the hat at the UN That, he concluded, would leave Bush relieved but unhappy—relieved that all the things Powell had warned him about would not take place but unhappy that the bastard was still there.

Now diplomacy would take on the characteristics of a charade—or the for-malized pantomime of the Japanese Kabuki dance to which Powell often referred.

He had not underestimated the extent to which the president had decided that letting the bastard remain was no longer an option. But he probably had underestimated his own usefulness to a president and vice president deter-mined on war.

After his meeting with Powell, the president reported the outcome to Andy Card. "I told Powell that it looks like we're going to have to do this, and I was going to do it," Bush said. "And he said that he would be with me."

Card believed that others, particularly Powell, nurtured a false hope that a diplomatic solution might be found. But not the president, who was now forced to tell others that they were going to have to let it go.

On the other hand—and the chief of staff had to always consider the alternative, that was his job—the meeting might cause Powell to be a little more creative and energetic in trying to find a way back to the road of diplomacy.

At times, Card thought of the president as a circus-horse rider with one foot on a "diplomacy" steed and the other on the "war" steed, both reins in his hands, leading down a path to regime change. Each horse had blinders on. It was now clear that diplomacy would not get him to his goal, so Bush had let go of that horse and was standing only on the war steed.

About a year later, I spent nearly ten minutes reviewing with the president his conversation with Powell, trying to sort out the various recollections. He finally said, "It sounds like you got it right." It was a time of stress, he said, adding, "It was a very cordial conversation. I would describe as cordial. I was here," he said, lightly tapping his own chair in the Oval Office, "he was here," pointing to the main dignitary's chair. "It wasn't a long conversation. I think the log will show it was relatively short." The president was correct. White House records show it had been a 12-minute meeting. "There wasn't much debate: It looks like we're headed to war."

President Bush also stated emphatically that though he had asked Powell to be with him and support him in a war, "I didn't need his permission."

The War After the War: The Captain
George Packer

from *The New Yorker* | November 24, 2003

Television may rule the media world, but a reporter's eyes and prose can still capture details and insights that TV cameras can't. In this excerpt from Packer's 20,000-word New Yorker *opus, he accompanies a young captain stationed in Baghdad, as he and his men struggle to put a fractured country back together again. . . .*

In April, CNN aired footage of a marine in Baghdad who is confronted with a crowd of angry Iraqis. He shouts back in frustration, "We're here for your fucking freedom!"

In the months following the overthrow of Saddam, tens of thousands of soldiers who thought they would be home by June saw their departures postponed again and again. They are now the occupation's most visible face. Combat engineers trained to blow up minefields sit through meetings of the Baghdad water department; airborne troops who jump in and out of missions spend months setting up the Kirkuk police department; soldiers of the 3rd Infantry Division who spearheaded the invasion pass out textbooks in a Baghdad girls' school. The peacekeeping missions in the Balkans gave some of them a certain amount of preparation, but there was little training for the concerted effort now required of soldiers in Iraq. Ray Jennings, a policy consultant who spent several months in Iraq, told me that he encountered officers running midsized cities who said, "I'm doing the best I can, but I don't know how to do this, I don't have a manual. You got a manual?" A civil-affairs captain asked Albert Cevallos for training in "Robert's Rules of Order 101." Rumsfeld's nightmare of an army of nation-builders has come to pass in Iraq.

The captain who showed me his war log was a company commander named John Prior. He is a twenty-nine-year-old from Indiana, six feet tall and stringy. His youthful face, deadpan sarcasm, and bouncy slew-footed stride do not prepare you for his toughness.

"Some people are just born to do something," Prior said. By his own account, he loves Army life, the taking and giving of orders. "The sappy reasons people say they're in the military—those are the reasons I'm in," he said. "When the Peace Corps can't quite get it done and diplomacy fails and McDonald's can't build enough franchises to win Baghdad over, that's when the military comes in."

His unit, Charlie Company of the 2nd Battalion, 6th Infantry Regiment, is now based at the Iraqi military academy in south Baghdad. (His soldiers' sleeping quarters are festooned with crêpe-paper decorations from the last Ramadan.) The academy is next to the bombed ruins of a vast military camp and airfield that have become home to five thousand displaced people, looters, and petty criminals. After the fall of Baghdad, it took two and a half months for Prior's company to arrive at its current location. During their odyssey in central Iraq, Prior and his men came to realize that what President Bush, on May 1, [2003,] had called the end of "major combat operations" was just the beginning.

Charlie Company's first mission after the fall of Baghdad sent Prior west to the town of Ramadi, to retrieve the body of Veronica Cabrera, an Argentine journalist who had been killed in a highway accident. Prior and his soldiers were the first conventional forces to enter Ramadi, which was becoming a center of Baathist resistance. The company was asked by Special Forces and the CIA to stay on for a few days and help patrol the town. They promptly found themselves in the middle of an anti-American riot, with insults, fruit, shoes, two-by-fours, rocks, and, finally, chunks of concrete flying at them. The Americans didn't shoot and no one was seriously injured; in his log Prior commends his soldiers for their restraint. In the following days in Ramadi, and then in the nearby town of Fallujah, Prior records a series of successful raids on houses and weapons markets. He expresses pride in his soldiers' resourcefulness. Then something new and strange enters the margins of his account: Iraqis.

In Ramadi, a man who speaks broken English around other Iraqis suddenly pulls Prior aside and whispers in flawless English, "I am an American, take me with you." When Prior tries to learn more, the man reverts to broken English and then clams up. Another man on another day approaches a soldier and, speaking perfect English, warns him not to trust Iraqis—that things are not what they seem. He disappears before the soldier can get more information. Prior and his first sergeant, Mark Lahan, track down the man at home with his family. Now using broken English, the man tells them that everything is fine.

In another mysterious incident, an Iraqi approaches Lahan and abruptly asks, "How are things in Baghdad? Have there been any suicide bombings? Have any Americans been killed?" Soon afterward, the guerrilla war starts.

"The entire situation seemed very weird," Prior writes on April 26, after five days in Ramadi. "It is clear now that they are not as happy as they say that we are here. For the first time in a while, I felt extremely nervous being in such close proximity to Iraqi nationals." In another entry, from Fallujah, he writes, "The Iraqis are an interesting people. None of them have weapons, none of them know where weapons are, all the bad people have left Fallujah, and they only want life to be normal again. Unfortunately, our compound was hit by R.P.G."—rocket-propelled-grenade—"fire today, so I am not inclined to believe them."

Prior was among the first soldiers to encounter the hidden nature of things in an Iraq that was neither at war nor at peace. Firepower and good intentions would be less important than learning to read the signs. Iraqis, no longer

forming the cheering crowds that had greeted the company on its way up to
Baghdad, were now going to play an intimate role in Prior's life.

The raids in Ramadi and Fallujah lasted almost a month; then Charlie Company was recalled to Baghdad. There Captain Prior's log ends. "We put trouble
down, we left," he told me. "Trouble came again."

Charlie Company spent its first month back in Baghdad billeted at the zoo.
The soldiers had been there in mid-April, on a mission to escort a truckload
of produce and frozen meat ("A gift from the Kuwaiti people to the Iraqi
people") for the few animals that had survived firefights and were too dangerous or worthless to steal. I visited the zoo several times, and the experience was always upsetting. It was the one place in Iraq where Saddam's regime
seemed still to exist. "It was not a zoo, but more of an animal prison," Prior
notes in his log. "Small cages, closely packed, no attempt to give the animals
any sense of natural setting." Dogs and puppies, favorites of Saddam, lay
panting in sweltering cells next to a catatonic blind bear that had mutilated
its own chest. (Some of the dogs had been fed to the lions during the war,
when food supplies ran out.) The soldiers who took control of the zoo in April
found a baboon loose on the grounds; it proved harmless to them, but when
one of the zookeepers, who had been hiding in his office, was brought out
the animal flew into a rage and attacked him, so that the soldiers had to shoot
the baboon to save the Baathist.

Bremer's C.P.A., needing a public-relations victory, refurbished the zoo and
reopened it to the public in July, with great fanfare; the cost was close to a
half million dollars. On a subsequent visit, I found the place, which had been
popular before the war, desolate and nearly abandoned. It was surrounded
by American checkpoints, which discouraged families from visiting. In September, a group of soldiers at the zoo got drunk after hours, and one of them
reached into the cage of a Bengal tiger with a piece of meat; when his hand
started to disappear into the tiger's mouth, one of his buddies shot the animal.
The Baghdad Zoo seemed to combine the cruelty and injustice of the old
regime with some of the stupidity and carelessness of the new.

Charlie Company spent a month establishing security in the area near the
zoo and setting up a neighborhood council. Then, in late June, the company
was moved again—to the military academy in south Baghdad—because its
zone of control did not coincide with Baghdad's administrative districts. "We'd
made friends there," Prior recalled. Packing up again, he said, "was not that

cool." He added dryly, "We'd been planning this war since freaking 12 September, and it might have helped if someone had drawn a map before the war and figured out where everyone went."

According to the brigade's original calendar, Baghdad's infrastructure would be rebuilt in August, elections would take place in September, and the soldiers would leave the city in October. This brisk forecast was soon abandoned, of course. Because of confused planning, it wasn't until August that Charlie Company's activities began to yield tangible benefits for Iraqis. And there was no time to lose. Throughout the summer, electric power operated sporadically, violence of all kinds kept rising, and Iraqis who could have been won over to the American side were steadily lost.

One morning, I sat in the base-camp canteen with Prior, First Sergeant Lahan, and their translator, Numan Al-Nima, a gray-haired former engineer with Iraqi Airways. Prior opened a coalition map of Baghdad's security zones and showed me the piece of the city he "owns": a rectangle of Zafaraniya, a largely Shiite slum in south Baghdad. Roughly two hundred and fifty thousand people live in the area. Prior chairs the new neighborhood council and is in charge of small reconstruction projects such as renovating schools; he's also responsible for sewage and trash disposal in his battalion's zone, which contains half a million people.

"Infrastructure is the key now," Prior said more than once. "If these people have electricity, water, food, the basics of life, they're less likely to attack." Sewage, Prior realized, was the front line of nation-building. When I met him, in early August, Prior was trying to get two hundred thousand dollars into the hands of Iraqi contractors as fast as he could.

"Show us something," the translator urged Prior. "People are hungry, starving. They don't believe they got rid of Saddam. If they got rid of Saddam, give me something to eat. That's why people hate Americans. We don't hate them because they are Americans. It is because they are the superpower, but where is the super power?"

We went out into the streets of Zafaraniya, travelling in the usual two-Humvee convoy, complete with gunners. Captain Prior's mission that morning was to visit nine pumping stations, which directed the district's untreated sewage into the Tigris and the Diala Rivers. To study a Shiite slum's sewage is to understand that Saddam reduced those parts of Iraq he didn't favor to the level of Kinshasa or Manila. Green ponds of raw waste, eighteen inches deep, blocked the roads between apartment houses where children played. The open ditches that were the area's drainage system were overflowing.

"How foolish of me not to realize that the open sludge flowing past the children is the way the system is supposed to work," Prior remarked. A complete overhaul of the system was not his immediate priority. "I'm going to support their open-sewage sludge line and get it flowing," he said. The heat rose, the streets stank, and Prior moved in battle gear at such a businesslike pace that two engineers from another battalion struggled to keep up. Each of the pumping stations, in various states of disrepair, was maintained and guarded by an Iraqi family that lived in a hovel on the premises, tended a lush vegetable garden, and kept an AK-47. Prior had never studied civil engineering—and he reminded me that his unit contained no city planners—but he already seemed to have mastered the inner workings of the Zafaraniya sewer system. Lahan told me, "People have said the Army's done this before, in '45 with Japan and Germany. Unfortunately, none of those people are in the Army anymore, so we have to figure it out ourselves."

With Prior, there were no earnest attempts to win hearts and minds over multiple cups of tea. He was all brisk practicality, and the Iraqis he worked with, who always had more to say than Prior gave them time for, seemed to respect him. "I will get you the money," he told a grizzled old man who was explaining at length that his pump was broken. "Six thousand U.S.? Yeah, yeah, great. Get started."

Later, we visited Zafaraniya's gas station, another of Prior's responsibilities. Initially, he had devoted his energy to getting customers to wait in orderly lines. "In a lot of ways, you're trying to teach them a new way of doing things," he said. " 'Teach' might be the wrong word—they're capable, competent, intelligent people. We're just giving them a different way to solve certain problems."

Prior's mission that day was to settle a price dispute between the gas-station managers and the community, which was represented by several neighborhood council members. A meeting took place in the gas-station managers' cramped back office, equipped with an underperforming air-conditioner. The council members wanted three hundred litres of diesel set aside every week for neighborhood generators. The managers wanted written permission from the Ministry of Oil.

The council members pulled out authorizations signed by various American officers. Prior tried to move the discussion along, but the Iraqis kept arguing, until it became clear that the problem went beyond a dispute over diesel. One of the most hierarchical, top-down state systems on earth had been wiped out almost overnight, and no new system had yet taken its place. The neighborhood councils are imperfect embryos of local democracy. Confused, frustrated Iraqis turn to the Americans, who seem to have all the power and money; the Americans, who don't see themselves as occupiers, try to force the Iraqis to work within their own institutions, but those institutions have been largely dismantled.

Flies were landing on Prior's brush cut. "Guys, we've been talking about this for twenty minutes," he said to the council members. "Do what I say. Go to the Oil Ministry. Just do it—just be done with it. Then you won't have to have slips of paper and we won't have to have this conversation."

Everyone was getting irritated. One of the council members told Prior that other Iraqis suspected them of making millions of dinars off public service. They were considered collaborators; their lives had been threatened.

Prior changed his tone and lowered the pressure. "I would tell all of you candidly that you have a very tough job," he said. "We are not paying you, your people are angry and frustrated, and I know they take out their anger on you, and I really thank you for what you're doing. They may not understand or appreciate it now, but I'm telling you, your efforts, they're what are going to transform this country."

There was a commotion outside the office—loud, accusatory voices. Prior put on his helmet and flak vest, grabbed his rifle, and went out to the pumps. Customers had left their vehicles, a crowd had formed, and it was getting ugly enough that the soldiers who had been waiting by the Humvees were trying to intervene. Amid the shouting, Prior established that an employee of the Oil Ministry had come to collect diesel samples from each of the pumps for routine testing. One of the council members was accusing him of stealing benzene.

"No accusations!" Prior said. "Let's go see."

The crowd followed him under the blinding sun to the ministry employee's truck. Five metal jerricans stood in back. Prior opened the first can with the air of making a point and sniffed: "Diesel." He opened the second: "Diesel." As he unscrewed the cap on the third jerrican and bent over to smell it, hot diesel fuel sprayed in his face.

Everyone fell silent. Prior stood motionless with the effort to control himself. He squeezed his eyes shut and pressed them with his fingers. The fuel was on his helmet, his flak vest. A sergeant rushed over with bottled water. Then the chorus of shouts rose again.

"Everybody shut up!" Prior yelled. "I'm going to solve this. What is the problem? No accusations." His face wet, he began to interrogate the accusing council member, who now looked sheepish.

"How do you know someone gave him benzene? This is a great object lesson, everybody!" Prior was speaking to the crowd now, as his translator frantically rendered the lesson in Arabic. "You came out here and said this guy's a thief, and everybody's angry and he's going to get fired—and now you're backing down."

"It wasn't just an accusation," the council member said. "The guy drove up on the wrong side—"

"But what proof do you have that he did it? Wait! Hold on! I'm trying to make a point here. How would you like it if my soldiers broke into your house because your neighbors said you have rocket-propelled grenades, and I didn't see them but I broke into your house—how would you feel? Stop accusing people, for the love of God!"

"I caught him red-handed," the council member insisted.

"No, you didn't."

"O.K., no problem."

Prior wasn't letting it go. "There is a problem: the problem is that you people accuse each other without proof! *That's* the problem."

Prior's treatise on evidence-gathering and due process ended. The crowd dispersed, and the meeting resumed inside. Prior tried to laugh off the incident. "Who doesn't like diesel in their eyes?" he joked. Later, he told me, "I wish I hadn't lost my temper. It wasn't the diesel—it was the way they kept bickering."

That afternoon, two of the council members, Ahmed Ogali and Abdul Jabbar Doweich, invited me for lunch. Both men were poor, and neither had a home he was proud of, so we ate chicken and rice in the living room of Ogali's brother-in-law. Ogali, a thirty-three-year-old gym teacher, said, "Today was a small problem. If I told you about our problems, you wouldn't believe it. They exhaust us." Both men were working without pay—they couldn't even get cell phones or travel money from the C.P.A. "Prior is doing more than his best," Ogali said. "But he's also controlled by his leaders."

Doweich, an unemployed father of four, had spent eight years in prison under Saddam for belonging to an Islamist political party. He still hoped for an Islamic state in the future—as did eighty per cent of Iraqis, he added.

"That's his personal opinion," Ogali interrupted. "It's not eighty per cent."

For now, Doweich saw working with Captain Prior on the neighborhood council as the best way to serve his country. The expectations of Iraqis were falling on the council members' heads, and Doweich believed that, at levels well above Prior, American officials had no interest in solving problems.

"The people are watching," Ogali said. "When I come back at night, they're waiting. They want to know what we're doing. Last week, I told them about the schools, the sewer projects. They were happy—but these are very old projects, they were promised for a long time."

Doweich suggested that the Americans give a hundred dollars to every Iraqi family. That would take the edge off people's frustration. "I can't say why the Americans don't do these things," he said. "Iraqis have trouble understanding Americans."

Ogali said that, sadly, the reverse was also true. The Americans, he told me, "came here to do a job, and that's what they'll do. Iraqis work closely with them, but they don't try to understand us."

American soldiers have a phrase for the Iraqis' habit of turning one another in. Prior once used it: "These people dime each other out like there's no tomorrow." With these betrayals, Iraqis play on soldiers' fears and ignorance, pulling them into private feuds that the Americans have no way of adjudicating.

The night after the meeting at the gas station, Prior and a few dozen soldiers from Charlie Company went out in two Humvees and two Bradleys to look for a suspected fedayeen militiaman. For such missions, Prior used a different translator: a strapping young guy with an aggressive manner. I expected to see the rougher side of Prior and Charlie Company that night—these were soldiers, after all, not civil engineers.

The suspected fedayeen happened to be named Saddam Hussein, and he was High Value Target No. 497. It would be the Americans' second visit to his house. The tip had come from a plump informant whom Prior called Operative Chunky Love, and whose intelligence had already tagged three men in the neighborhood, including his brother-in-law. Tonight, Chunky Love was supposed to show up at his sister's house, near Saddam Hussein's, in an orange garbage truck loaded with weapons—a sting operation. Lahan warned me, "Out of a hundred tips we've gotten from Iraqi intelligence, one has worked out."

Recently, Prior had experienced what he called an epiphany. He and his soldiers were searching a man's house on what turned out to be a false accusation. "And I just realized—we're on top," he said. "Rome fell, and Greece fell, and I thought, I like being an American. I like being on top, and you don't stay on top unless there's people willing to defend it." It was a feeling not of triumph but of clarity—and a limited kind of empathy. "I thought, What if someone did this to my family? I'd be pissed. And what if I couldn't do anything about it?

And I thought, I don't want this to happen to me or my family, and we need to maintain superiority as the No. 1 superpower."

Tonight's target was a village along a dirt road, on a peninsula where the Diala River doubles back on itself. At sunset, Prior pulled up before a yard where a cow was grazing. A middle-aged woman came to the gate. She was the sister of Saddam Hussein and the wife of one of the men picked up on Prior's last visit.

"Saddam Hussein?" she said. "The President? He's not here." She laughed nervously. Prior did not; his dry humor was not in evidence tonight. "Saddam Hussein moved out with his wife and children," she said. "I don't know where they went."

"She's lying," the translator told Prior, in a thuggish tone. Prior told the woman that he wanted to search the house. A younger woman who looked ill was trying to calm a crying baby.

The search of the bedroom turned up nothing: pictures of a young man with his girlfriend, love notes, Arab girlie photographs.

I went back into the living room, which was nearly bare except for a television. An old Egyptian movie was on, without sound. The woman with the baby was retching in the doorway. Speaking Arabic, the middle-aged woman exclaimed, "We were happy when you Americans came to get rid of the dictator—and now here you are searching our house." Her two sons, about six and ten, were standing against a wall and staring at the soldiers. They would never forget this, I thought—big strangers in uniforms, with guns, who had already come once and taken away their father, speaking a strange language, walking through their home, removing things from closets.

The bedroom that Prior had searched turned out to be the wrong one. Saddam Hussein's bedroom was locked, and the woman couldn't produce a key. A soldier arrived with an axe; three blows with the blunt end broke open the door. The younger woman's retching grew louder. This search, too, was fruitless. Saddam Hussein was long gone.

Night had fallen while we were inside. As we left, the translator taunted the woman: he said her brother was wanted because his name was Saddam Hussein. When Prior heard this, he snapped, "Tell her the truth—he's wanted for being fedayeen." By morning, I was sure, the translator's remark would have made its way around the neighborhood as an example of American justice—baseless arrest, accusation without proof.

The woman brought up her husband's case. Why had he been taken away? "Because he's fedayeen," Prior said. "He's Baath Party."

"No! No! No!"

"Tell her he's in detention," Prior instructed the translator. "That if he's guilty he'll be kept there. If he's not, he'll be processed and released." (A few days later, he was let go.)

Out on the road, Prior shone his flashlight on an old man sitting on the ground. "Why did you lie to me last time we were here and say he was just gone for the day? Tell Saddam Hussein that he's a fugitive from coalition justice, and when he returns he should turn himself in to coalition forces immediately. Let's go, we're out of here."

We drove farther down the road and parked in front of a tall hedge. The house behind the hedge was owned by Chunky Love's sister. Prior and another soldier moved along the hedge under the palm trees and a full moon. Prior called out into the silence, "Salaam alaikum"—"Peace be with you."

The translator turned to me. "Like Vietnam."

I was having the same thought. I knew that it was a limited analogy, more useful for polemic than for insight, but at the moment Iraq *did* feel like Vietnam. The Americans were moving half blind in an alien landscape, missing their quarry and leaving behind frightened women and boys with memories.

There was no sign of Chunky Love or his orange garbage truck full of weapons. His sister hadn't seen him in a month; when she did, she told the translator, she would kill him for turning in her husband.

Prior realized that he'd been pulled into a family feud. The sister was told that her husband would be released. Prior called this the "hearts and minds moment," but the sister did not look grateful.

"What do you think, First Sergeant?" Prior asked Lahan on the way back to the base.

"I think we should disassociate ourselves from any information from Chunky Love," Lahan said. Operative Chunky Love had gone from informant to fugitive.

Prior marvelled over how many flatly contradictory stories he had heard from the same people during his two visits to the neighborhood. He admitted that he would never get to the bottom of them all. "I'm not freaking Sherlock Holmes," he said. Then he deadpanned, "I'm just an average guy, trying to get by."

Later, I asked Prior whether his night work threatened to undo the good accomplished by his day work. He didn't think so: as the sewage started to flow and the schools got fixed up, Iraqis would view Americans the way the Americans see themselves—as people trying to help.

Others at Prior's base are less sanguine. His battalion is under serious strain: In their first six months of deployment, some soldiers had only three days off. Others are stretched so thin that, one soldier told me, they've been reporting "ghost patrols" back to headquarters—logging in scheduled patrols that didn't actually take place. Prior wants to make a career in the Army, but many other junior officers plan to quit after their current tour. Alcohol use, which is illegal for soldiers stationed in Iraq, has become widespread, and there have been three suicides in other battalions at the base.

At the end of a four-day patrol rotation, relations between young Americans and the Iraqis tend to deteriorate, according to one officer, into "guys kicking dogs, yelling at grown men twenty years older than they are, and pushing kids into parked cars to keep them from following and bothering them." In September, soldiers in a platoon from Charlie Company were accused of beating up Iraqi prisoners. All the soldiers suffer from the stress of heat, long days, lack of sleep, homesickness, the constant threat of attack (about which they are fundamentally fatalistic), and the simple fact that there are nowhere near enough of them to do the tasks they've been given.

For some reason, this last point continues to be controversial in Washington. Rumsfeld echoes his generals' assurances that no additional American divisions are needed. Meanwhile, Iraq's borders remain basically undefended and its highways unpatrolled; tons of munitions lie around the country unguarded. Overburdened soldiers have begun to lose hope even as their work begins to show results.

One soldier at Prior's base recently wrote me a lengthy e-mail:

> The reason why morale sucks is because of the senior leadership, the brigade and division commanders, and probably the generals at the Pentagon and Central Command too, all of whom seem to be insulated from what is going on at the ground level. Either that or they are unwilling to hear the truth of things, or (and this is the most likely), they do know what is going on, but they want to get promoted so badly that they're willing to screw over soldiers by being unwilling to face the problem of morale, so they continue pushing the soldiers to do more with less because Rummy wants them to get us out of here quickly. These people are like serious alcoholics unwilling to admit there even is a problem.

His letter concluded:

There are great things we're doing here, much has already been done, yet much more remains to be accomplished, and what we need now is the money, people, and most importantly, time to do it. We'll win, that's for sure, and this won't be another Vietnam; I truly believe that.

In early November, Captain Prior spoke with me on the phone from Baghdad. The sewage ponds have been cleaned up, and security in his sector has improved with better intelligence. The council members are now being paid sixty dollars a month and run their own meetings. Abdul Jabbar Doweich has a job as a security guard. But, for various reasons, Prior's division has stopped paying for new reconstruction projects, and current projects are running out of funds. Hearing this, I remembered something Prior had said as we were driving into Saddam Hussein's village: "The most frustrating thing is we can't do more for them. My hands are tied—everyone's are."

The Right War for the Right Reasons
Robert Kagan and William Kristol

The Weekly Standard | February 23, 2004

As the U.S. and their allies struggles to secure Iraq, the failure to find evidence of any significant nuclear, biological, or chemical weapons programs in the country continues to be a political bone of contention. In mid-December 2003, following the capture of Saddam Hussein, President Bush was confident enough to respond "So what's the difference?" when Diane Sawyer pressed him on the missing weapons of mass destruction in a televised interview. The issue was brought to the forefront again in January 2004, however, when David Kay, former director of the Iraq Survey Group (the organization tasked with finding the WMDs), told a Senate committee "we were almost all wrong" in assuming that Hussein possessed such weapons.

Clearly, Robert Kagan and William Kristol saw this as a good time to weigh in with the following article, which lays out in updated detail the case for invading Iraq. They and other neoconservatives have made the argument for overthrowing Hussein repeatedly over the past decade—an effort that included frequent calls for action in The

Weekly Standard, which Kristol edits and where Kagan is a contributing editor. In their view, Hussein had to go for many, related reasons, only one of which was his suspected WMD stockpile. . . .

With all the turmoil surrounding David Kay's comments on the failure to find stockpiles of biological and chemical weapons in Iraq, it is time to return to first principles, and to ask the question: Was it right to go to war?

Critics of the war, and of the Bush administration, have seized on the failure to find stockpiles of weapons of mass destruction in Iraq. But while his weapons were a key part of the case for removing Saddam, that case was always broader. Saddam's pursuit of weapons of mass destruction was inextricably intertwined with the nature of his tyrannical rule, his serial aggression, his defiance of international obligations, and his undeniable ties to a variety of terrorists, from Abu Nidal to Al Qaeda (a topic we will not cover in detail here, rather referring readers to Stephen F. Hayes's reporting in this magazine over the past year). Together, this pattern of behavior made the removal of Saddam desirable and necessary, in the judgment of both the Clinton and Bush administrations. That judgment was and remains correct.

I

It is fashionable to sneer at the moral case for liberating an Iraqi people long brutalized by Saddam's rule. Critics insist mere oppression was not sufficient reason for war, and in any case that it was not Bush's reason. In fact, of course, it was one of Bush's reasons, and the moral and humanitarian purpose provided a compelling reason for a war to remove Saddam. It should certainly have been compelling to those (like us) who supported the war on Slobodan Milosevic a few years ago. In our view—and here we disagree with what Paul Wolfowitz said to *Vanity Fair* a few months ago—liberating the Iraqi people from Saddam's brutal, totalitarian dictatorship would by itself have been sufficient reason to remove Saddam.

Such a rationale is not "merely" moral. As is so often the case in international affairs, there was no separating the nature of Saddam's rule at home from the kinds of policies he conducted abroad. Saddam's regime terrorized his own people, but it also posed a threat to the region, and to us. The moral case for war was linked to strategic considerations related to the peace and security of the Middle East.

Saddam was not a "madman." He was a predator and an aggressor. He achieved through brute force total dominance at home, and it was through force and the threat of force that he sought dominance in his region, as well. He waged war against Iran throughout the 1980s. He invaded Kuwait in 1990. He spent tens of billions of dollars on weapons, both conventional and unconventional. His clear and unwavering ambition, an ambition nurtured and acted upon across three decades, was to dominate the Middle East, both economically and militarily, by attempting to acquire the lion's share of the region's oil and by intimidating or destroying anyone who stood in his way. This, too, was a sufficient reason to remove him from power.

The last time we restated the case for war in Iraq (in October 2003), we quoted extensively from a speech delivered by President Clinton in February 1998. This time we quote extensively from another speech, delivered ten months later, in December 1998, by President Clinton's national security adviser, Sandy Berger. Like President Clinton, Berger did a masterful job of laying out the case for removing Saddam Hussein. And Berger's argument extended beyond the issue of weapons.

Yes, Berger acknowledged, America's "most vital national interest in dealing with Iraq" was to "prevent Saddam from rebuilding his military capability, including weapons of mass destruction, and from using that arsenal to move against his neighbors or his own people." But the threat Saddam posed, by his "continued reign of terror inside Iraq and intimidation outside Iraq," was broader than that. The future course of the Middle East and the Arab world were at stake in Iraq.

"The future of Iraq," Berger argued, "will affect the way in which the Middle East and the Arab world in particular evolve in the next decade and beyond." Those peoples were engaged in a "struggle between two broad visions of the future." One vision was of "political pluralism" and "economic openness." The other vision fed on discontent and fear; it stood for "violent opposition to liberalizing forces." So long as Saddam remained "in power and in confrontation with the world," Berger argued, Iraq would remain "a source of potential conflict in the region," and perhaps more important, "a source of inspiration for those who equate violence with power and compromise with surrender."

In the end, Berger explained, containment of Saddam would not be enough. The "immediate military threat" might be held at bay for the moment. "But even a contained Saddam" was "harmful to stability and to positive change in the region." And in fact, containment was probably not "sustainable over the long run." It was "a costly policy, in economic and strategic terms." The pattern of the previous years—"Iraqi defiance, followed by force mobilization on our part, followed by Iraqi capitulation"—had left "the international community vulnerable to manipulation by Saddam." The longer the standoff continued, Berger warned, "the harder it will be to maintain" international support. Nor was there any question what Saddam would do if and when containment collapsed. "Saddam's history of aggression, and his recent record of deception and defiance, leave no doubt that he would resume his drive for regional domination if he had the chance. Year after year, in conflict after conflict, Saddam has proven that he seeks weapons, including weapons of mass destruction, in order to use them."

For this reason, Berger continued, the Clinton administration had concluded it would be necessary at some point to move beyond containment to regime change. At stake was "our ability to fight terror, avert regional conflict, promote peace, and protect the security of our friends and allies." Quoting President Clinton, Berger suggested "the best way to address the challenge Iraq poses is 'through a government in Baghdad—a new government— that is committed to represent and respect its people, not repress them; that is committed to peace in the region.' "

We made substantially the same argument in a January 1998 letter to President Clinton, a letter whose signatories included Donald Rumsfeld, Paul Wolfowitz, Richard Armitage, and Robert Zoellick. In our letter, we argued that

The policy of "containment" of Saddam Hussein has been steadily eroding over the past several months. As recent events have demonstrated, we can no longer depend on our partners in the Gulf War coalition to continue to uphold the sanctions or to punish Saddam when he blocks or evades UN inspections. Our ability to ensure that Saddam Hussein is not producing weapons of mass destruction, therefore, has substantially diminished. Even if full inspections were eventually to resume, which now seems highly unlikely, experience has shown that it is difficult if not impossible to monitor Iraq's chemical and biological weapons production. The lengthy period during which the inspectors will have been unable to enter many Iraqi facilities has made it even less likely that they will be able to uncover all of Saddam's secrets. As a result, in the not-too-distant future we will be unable to determine with any reasonable level of confidence whether Iraq does or does not possess such weapons.

That last prediction turned out to be better than we knew at the time. But we did note that uncertainty itself was a danger, because it meant that the United States would have difficulty knowing whether or how fast the risk from

Saddam was increasing. The uncertainty of the situation would, we argued, "have a seriously destabilizing effect on the entire Middle East." It now appears that this uncertainty about Iraq's actual capabilities was perhaps what Saddam aimed to achieve.

II

So the threat of Saddam's weapons of mass destruction was related to the overall political and strategic threat his regime posed to the Middle East. Still, there is no question that Saddam's history with and interest in weapons of mass destruction made his threat distinctive. The danger was not, however, that Iraq would present a direct threat to the physical security of the United States or, in the current popular phrase, pose an "imminent" threat to the American homeland. Our chief concern in 1998, like Berger's, was the threat Saddam posed to regional security and stability, the maintenance of which was in large part the responsibility of the United States. If Saddam "does acquire the capability to deliver weapons of mass destruction," we argued, which eventually he was "almost certain to do if we continue along the present course," American troops in the region, American allies, the stability of the Middle East, and the world's supply of oil would all be put at risk. The threat to the United States was that we would be compelled to defend our allies and our interests in circumstances made much more difficult and dangerous by Saddam's increasingly lethal arsenal.

That was why Saddam's weapons of mass destruction programs, both what we knew about them and what we did not know about them, gave the situation a special urgency. It was urgent in 1998, and it was urgent four years later. There was no doubt in 1998—and there is no doubt today, based on David Kay's findings—that Saddam was seeking both to pursue WMD programs and to conceal his efforts from UN weapons inspectors. After 1995, when the defection of Saddam Hussein's son-in-law and chief organizer of the weapons programs, Hussein Kamal, produced a wealth of new information about Iraqi weapons programs and stockpiles—information the Iraqis were forced to acknowledge was accurate—the UN weapons inspections process had become an elaborate cat-and-mouse game. As President Clinton recalled in his speech three years later, Kamal had "revealed that Iraq was continuing to conceal weapons and missiles and the capacity to build many more." The inspectors intensified their search. And they must have been having some success, for as they drew closer to uncovering what the Iraqis were hiding, Saddam grew less and less cooperative and began to block their access to certain facilities.

Finally, there was the famous confrontation over the so-called "presidential palaces"—actually vast complexes of buildings and warehouses that Saddam simply declared off-limits to inspectors. Clinton intelligence officials observed the Iraqis moving equipment that could be used to manufacture weapons out of the range of video cameras that had been installed by UN inspectors. By the end of 1997, the *New York Times* reported, the UN inspection team could "no longer verify that Iraq is not making weapons of mass destruction" and specifically could not monitor "equipment that could grow seed stocks of biological agents in a matter of hours."

President Clinton declared in early 1998 that Saddam was clearly attempting "to protect whatever remains of his capacity to produce weapons of mass destruction, the missiles to deliver them, and the feed stocks necessary to produce them." The UN inspectors believed, Clinton continued, that "Iraq still has stockpiles of chemical and biological munitions . . . and the capacity to restart quickly its production program and build many, many more weapons." Meanwhile, a February 13, 1998, U.S. government White Paper on Iraq's weapons of mass destruction stated that "in the absence of UNSCOM inspectors, Iraq could restart limited mustard agent production within a few weeks, full-production of sarin within a few months, and pre–Gulf War production levels—including VX—within two or three years."

It was President Clinton who, in February 1998, posed the critical question: "What if [Saddam] fails to comply and we fail to act, or we take some ambiguous third route, which gives him yet more opportunities to develop this program of weapons of mass destruction? . . . Well, he will conclude that the international community has lost its will. He will then conclude that he can go right on and do more to rebuild an arsenal of devastating destruction. And some day, some way, I guarantee you he'll use this arsenal." "In the next century," Clinton predicted, "the community of nations may see more and more of the very kind of threat Iraq poses now—a rogue state with weapons of mass destruction, ready to use them or provide them to terrorists . . . who travel the world among us unnoticed."

Over the course of 1998, the UN inspections process collapsed. Attempts to break the stalemate with Saddam and allow the UN inspectors access to the prohibited sites came to naught. About a week after Berger gave his speech warning of the limitations of containment, the Clinton administration launched Operation Desert Fox, a four-day missile and bombing strike on Iraq aimed at destroying as much of Saddam's weapons capabilities as possible. Based on American intelligence, the Clinton administration targeted suspected weapons production facilities throughout Iraq. The Air Force and intelligence agencies believed the bombing had destroyed or degraded a number of Iraqi weapons of mass destruction facilities, but they never knew the extent of the damage, because, of course, there were no inspectors left to investigate.

Saddam expelled the UN inspectors in response to the attack, and they did not return until November 2002. As Clinton this past summer recalled, "We might have gotten it all; we might have gotten half of it; we might have gotten none of it. But we didn't know." Clinton went on to say about President Bush's actions in the fall of 2002, "So I thought it was prudent for the president to go to the UN and for the UN to say you got to let these inspectors in, and this time if you don't cooperate the penalty could be regime change, not just continued sanctions."

The situation as it stood at the beginning of 1999 was troubling to all concerned, and not just to American officials. A report to the UN Security Council in January 1999 by Richard Butler, head of the UN weapons inspections team, warned that much was not known about the Iraqi program but that there was ample reason to believe a significant weapons of mass destruction program still existed in Iraq. Butler recounted a seven-year history of Iraqi deception and concealment of proscribed weapons and activities. During the first four years of inspections, Butler noted, the inspectors "had been very substantially misled by Iraq both in terms of its understanding of Iraq's proscribed weapons programs and the continuation of prohibited activities, even under the [UN's] monitoring." Only the defection of Hussein Kamal had revealed that the inspectors had been wrong in their "positive conclusions on Iraq's compliance." But even after Kamal's defection, the Iraqis had continued to conceal programs and mislead the inspectors. The Iraqis were caught lying about whether they had ever put VX nerve agent in so-called "special warheads." Scientific examinations proved that they had.

The Iraqis were also caught lying about their biological weapons program. First they denied having one; then, when that falsehood was exposed, they denied weaponizing their biological weapons agents. Eventually they were forced to admit that they "had weaponized BW agents and deployed biological weapons for combat use." The UN inspectors reported that hundreds of shells filled with mustard agent had been declared "lost" by Iraq and remained unaccounted for. There were some 6,000 aerial bombs filled with chemical agent that were unaccounted for. There were also some "special warheads" with biological weapons agent unaccounted for. Butler's report concluded that, in addition, "it needs to be recognized that Iraq possesses an industrial capacity and knowledge base, through which biological warfare agents could be produced quickly and in volume, if the government of Iraq decided to do so."

The inspectors left, and for the next four years, Saddam's activities were shrouded in darkness. After all, many prohibited Iraqi activities had escaped detection even while the inspectors were trying to monitor them. Without the inspectors, the task of keeping track of Saddam's programs was well-nigh impossible.

III

When the Bush administration came to office, therefore, it had no less reason to worry about Saddam's potential capabilities than the Clinton administration. And it had no more reason to believe that containment would be sustainable. In the early months of the administration, Bush officials began to contemplate some increased support for Iraqi opposition forces, pursuant to legislation passed overwhelmingly in 1998, which was supported by the Clinton administration. (The Iraq Liberation Act chronicled Saddam's use of chemical weapons and declared that Iraq "has persisted in a pattern of deception and concealment regarding the history of its weapons of mass destruction programs." It continued: "It should be the policy of the United States to support efforts to remove the regime headed by Saddam Hussein from power in Iraq and to promote the emergence of a democratic government to replace that regime.") Meanwhile, Secretary of State Colin Powell was trying to prevent the collapse of the international sanctions regime and to staunch the hemorrhaging of consensus at the UN Security Council by instituting a more streamlined effort, the so-called "smart sanctions."

Then came the terrorist attacks of September 11, 2001. September 11 shocked the nation, and it shocked the president. Its effect was to make many both inside and outside the administration take a closer look at international threats, because it was clear that all of us had been too sanguine about such threats prior to September 11. Nor was it in the least surprising that the issue of Iraq arose immediately. True, neither candidate in the 2000 election had talked much about Iraq. But that was not because anyone believed it had ceased to be an urgent and growing problem. The Clinton administration didn't want to talk about it because it felt it had run out of options. The Bush campaign didn't talk about it because Bush was running a campaign, ironic in retrospect, which promised a less active, more restrained American role in the world. But that did not mean the Iraq issue had gone away, and after

September 11, it returned to the fore. After all, we had a decade-long history of confrontation with Iraq, we were flying military missions in Iraqi air space, President Clinton had declared Saddam the greatest threat to our security in the 21st century, Clinton officials like Sandy Berger and Madeleine Albright had concluded that Saddam must eventually be removed, and UN weapons inspectors had written one alarming report after another about Saddam's current and potential weapons capabilities.

So the Bush administration concluded that it had to remove the Saddam Hussein regime once and for all, just as Clinton and Berger had suggested might someday be necessary. For all the reasons that Berger had outlined, Saddam's regime itself was the problem, above and beyond his weapons capabilities. It was an obstacle to progress in the Middle East and the Arab world. It was a threat to the Iraqi people and to Iraq's neighbors. But a big part of the threat involved Saddam's absolute determination to arm himself with both conventional and unconventional weapons.

September 11 had added new dimensions to the danger. For as Bush and many others argued, what if Saddam allowed his weapons capabilities to be shared with terrorists? What if, someday in the future, terrorists like those who crashed airplanes into the World Trade Center and the Pentagon had nuclear, chemical, or biological weapons? Would they hesitate to use them? The possible nexus between terrorism and Iraq's weapons program made Iraq an even more urgent issue. Was this concern far-fetched? If so, it was exactly the same far-fetched concern that had preoccupied President Clinton in 1998, when he warned, in his speech on Iraq, about a "rogue state with weapons of mass destruction, ready to use them or provide them to terrorists," and when he had spoken of an "unholy axis" of international terrorists and outlaw states as one of the greatest threats Americans faced.

Nor was it surprising that as President Bush began to move toward war with Iraq in the fall and winter of 2002, he mustered substantial support among Democrats as well as Republicans. A majority of Democratic senators—including, of course, John Kerry and John Edwards—voted for the resolution authorizing the president to use force against Iraq. And why not? The Bush administration's approach to Iraq was fundamentally in keeping with that of the Clinton administration, except that after September 11, inaction seemed even less acceptable. The majority of the Democratic party foreign policy establishment supported the war, and not because they were misled by the Bush administration's rhetorical hype leading up to the war. (Its hype was appreciably less than that of Clinton secretary of defense William Cohen, who appeared on national television in late 1997 holding a bag of sugar and noting that the same amount of anthrax "would destroy at least half the population" of Washington, D.C. At a Pentagon press briefing on Iraq's WMD, Cohen also noted that if Saddam had "as much VX in storage as the UN suspects," he would "be able to kill every human being on the face of the planet.") Nor did they support the war because they were fundamentally misled by American intelligence about the nature and extent of Saddam's weapons programs. Most of what they and everyone else knew about those programs we had learned from the UN inspectors, not from U.S. intelligence.

IV

Some of that intelligence has now turned out to be wrong. Some of it has turned out to be right. And it is simply too soon to tell about the rest. The press has focused attention almost entirely on David Kay's assertion that there were no stockpiles of chemical and biological weapons when the United States and its allies invaded Iraq last March. We'll address that assertion in a moment. But what about the rest of Kay's testimony?

The key question for more than a decade, for both the Clinton and the Bush administrations, was not only what weapons Saddam had but what weapons he was trying to obtain, and how long it might be before containment failed and he was able to obtain them. The goal of American policy, and indeed of the UN Security Council over the course of the dozen years after the end of the Gulf War in 1991, was not primarily to find Saddam's existing stockpiles. That was subsidiary to the larger goal, which was to achieve Iraq's disarmament, including the elimination not only of existing prohibited weapons but of all such weapons programs, to ensure that Iraq would not possess weapons of mass destruction now or in the future. As Richard Butler and other weapons inspectors have argued, this task proved all but impossible once it became clear that Saddam was determined to acquire such weapons at some point. As Butler repeated time and again in his reports to the Security Council, the whole inspections regime was premised on Saddam's cooperation. But Saddam never cooperated, not in the 1990s and not in 2003.

It is important to recall that the primary purpose of Security Council Resolution 1441, passed on November 8, 2002, was not to discover whether Saddam had weapons and programs. There was little doubt that Saddam had them. The real question was whether he was ready to make a clean breast of everything and give up not only his forbidden weapons but also his efforts to acquire them once and for all. The purpose was to give Saddam "one final chance" to change his stripes, to offer full cooperation by revealing and dismantling all his programs and to forswear all such efforts in the future.

After all, what would be accomplished if Saddam turned over stockpiles and dismantled programs, only to restart them the minute the international community turned its back? Saddam might be slowed, but he would not be stopped. This was the logic that had led the Clinton administration to conclude that someday, somehow, the only answer to the problem would be Saddam's removal from power. Not surprisingly, the Bush administration was even more convinced that Saddam's removal was the only answer. That the administration went along with the inspections process embodied in Resolution 1441 was a concession to international and domestic pressure. No senior official, including Secretary Powell, believed there was any but the smallest chance Saddam would comply with the terms of Resolution 1441.

Resolution 1441 demanded that, within 30 days, Iraq provide "a currently accurate, full, and complete declaration of all aspects of its programs to develop chemical, biological, and nuclear weapons, ballistic missiles, and other delivery systems such as unmanned aerial vehicles and dispersal systems designed for use on aircraft, including any holdings and precise locations of such weapons, components, sub-components, stocks of agents, and related material and equipment, the locations and work of its research, development and production facilities, as well as all other chemical, biological, and nuclear programs, including any which it claims are for purposes not related to weapon production or material." Administration officials doubted Saddam would do this. They hoped only that, once Saddam's noncompliance became clear, they would win unanimous support for war at the UN Security Council.

And it was pretty clear at the time that Saddam was not complying. In his May 30, 2003, report to the Security Council, Hans Blix reported that the declared stocks of anthrax and VX remained unaccounted for. And he elaborated: "Little progress was made in the solution of outstanding issues. . . . The long list of proscribed items unaccounted for and as such resulting in unresolved disarmament issues was not shortened either by the inspections or by Iraqi declarations and documentation."

Now, of course, we know more definitively that Saddam did not comply with Resolution 1441. That is a part of Kay's testimony that has been widely ignored. What Kay discovered in the course of his eight-month-long investigation was that Iraq had failed to answer outstanding questions about its arsenal and programs. Indeed, it had continued to engage in an elaborate campaign of deception and concealment of weapons activities throughout the time when Hans Blix and the UNMOVIC inspectors were in the country, and right up until the day of the invasion, and beyond.

As Kay told the Senate Armed Services Committee last month, the Iraq Survey Group "discovered hundreds of cases, based on both documents, physical evidence and the testimony of Iraqis, of activities that were prohibited under the initial UN Resolution 687 and that should have been reported under 1441, with Iraqi testimony that not only did they not tell the UN about this, they were instructed not to do it and they hid material." Kay reported, "We have had a number of Iraqis who have come forward and said, 'We did not tell the UN about what we were hiding, nor would we have told the UN,' " because the risks were too great. And what were the Iraqis hiding? As Kay reports, "They maintained programs and activities, and they certainly had the intentions at a point to resume their programs. So there was a lot they wanted to hide because it showed what they were doing was illegal." As Kay reported last October, his survey team uncovered "dozens of WMD-related program activities and significant amounts of equipment that Iraq concealed from the UN during the inspections that began in late 2002." Specifically, Kay reported:

- A clandestine network of laboratories and safehouses within the Iraqi Intelligence Service that contained equipment suitable for research in the production of chemical and biological weapons. This kind of equipment was explicitly mentioned in Hans Blix's requests for information, but was instead concealed from Blix throughout his investigations.
- A prison laboratory complex, which may have been used in human testing of biological weapons agents. Iraqi officials working to prepare for UN inspections in 2002 and 2003 were explicitly ordered not to acknowledge the existence of the prison complex.
- So-called "reference strains" of biological organisms, which can be used to produce biological weapons. The strains were found in a scientist's home.
- New research on agents applicable to biological weapons, including Congo Crimean Hemorrhagic Fever, and continuing research on ricin and aflatoxin—all of which was, again, concealed from Hans Blix despite his specific request for any such information.
- Plans and advanced design work on new missiles with ranges up to at least 1,000 kilometers—well beyond the 150-kilometer limit imposed

on Iraq by the UN Security Council. These missiles would have allowed Saddam to threaten targets from Ankara to Cairo.

Last month Kay also reported that Iraq "was in the early stages of renovating the [nuclear] program, building new buildings."

As Kay has testified repeatedly, Iraq was "in clear material violation of 1441." So if the world had known in February 2003 what Kay says we know now—that there were no large stockpiles of weapons, but that Iraq continued to pursue weapons of mass destruction programs and to deceive and conceal these efforts from the UN inspectors led by Blix during the time allocated by Resolution 1441—wouldn't there have been at least as much, and probably more, support for the war? For Saddam would have been in flagrant violation of yet another set of commitments to disarm. He would have demonstrated once again that he was unwilling to abandon these programs, that he was unwilling to avail himself of this "last chance" and disarm once and for all. Had the world discovered unambiguously in February 2003 that Saddam was cheating on its commitments in Resolution 1441, surely even the French would have found it difficult to block a UN resolution authorizing war. As Dominique de Villepin acknowledged in the contentious months before the war, "We all realize that success in the inspections presupposes that we get full and complete cooperation from Iraq." What if it were as clear then as it is now that Saddam was engaged in another round of deceit and concealment?

If Kay is right, Saddam had learned a lesson at some point in the 1990s, perhaps after the Kamal defection, perhaps before or after Operation Desert Fox in 1998. But it was not the lesson the United States or the rest of the world wanted him to learn. At some point, Saddam may have decided that instead of building up large stockpiles of weapons, the safer thing would be to advance his covert programs for producing weapons but wait until the pressure was off to produce the weapons themselves. By the time inspectors returned to Iraq in 2002, Saddam was ready to be a little more forthcoming, because he had rejiggered his program to withstand somewhat greater scrutiny. He had scaled back to a skeletal program, awaiting the moment when he could breathe life back into it. Nevertheless, even then he could not let the inspectors see everything. Undoubtedly he hoped that if he could get through that last round, he would be home free, eventually without sanctions or further inspections. We now know that in early 2003, Saddam assumed that the United States would once again launch a bombing campaign, but not a full scale invasion. So he figured he would survive, and, as Kay concluded, "They maintained programs and activities, and they certainly had the intentions at a point to resume their programs."

Was this a satisfactory outcome? If this much had been accomplished, if we had succeeded in getting Saddam to scale back his programs in the hope of eventually turning them on again, was that a reason not to go to war? Kay does not believe so. Nor do we. If the United States had pulled back last year, we would have placed ourselves in the trap that Berger had warned about five years earlier. We would have returned to the old pattern of "Iraqi defiance, followed by force mobilization on our part, followed by Iraqi capitulation," followed by a new round of Iraqi defiance—and the wearing down of both the international community and the United States.

There was an argument against going to war last year. But let's remember what that argument was. It had nothing to do with whether or not Saddam had weapons of mass destruction and WMD programs. Everyone from Howard Dean to the *New York Times* editorial board to Dominique de Villepin and Jacques Chirac assumed that he had both. Most of the arguments against the war concerned timing. The most frequent complaint was that Bush was rushing to war. Why not give Blix and his inspectors another three months or six months?

We now know, however, that giving Blix a few more months would not have made a difference. Last month Kay was asked what would have happened if Blix and his team had been allowed to continue their mission. Kay responded, "All I can say is that among an extensive body of Iraqi scientists who are talking to us, they have said: The UN interviewed us; we did not tell them the truth, we did not show them this equipment, we did not talk about these programs; we couldn't do it as long as Saddam was in power. I suspect regardless of how long they had stayed, that attitude would have been the same." Given the "terror regime of Saddam," Kay concluded, he and his team learned things after the war "that no UN inspector would have ever learned" while Saddam was still in power.

So it is very unlikely that, given another three months or six months, the Blix team would have come to any definitive conclusion one way or another. Nor, therefore, would there have been a much greater probability of winning a unanimous vote at the Security Council for war once those additional six months had passed. Whether the United States could have kept 200,000 troops on a permanent war footing in the Persian Gulf for another six months is even more doubtful.

V

Did the administration claim the Iraqi threat was imminent, in the sense that Iraq possessed weapons that were about to be used against the United States? That is the big charge leveled by the Bush administration's critics these days. It is rather surprising, given the certainty with which this charge is thrown around, how little the critics have in the way of quotations from administration officials to back it up. Saying that action is urgent is not the same thing as saying the threat is imminent. In fact, the president said the threat was not imminent, and that we had to act (urgently) before the threat became imminent. This was well understood. As Senate Democratic leader Tom Daschle said on October 10, 2002, explaining his support for the legislation authorizing the president to go to war, "The threat posed by Saddam Hussein may not be imminent, but it is real, it is growing and it cannot be ignored."

One reason critics have been insisting that the administration claimed the threat from Iraq was imminent, we believe, is that it is fairly easy to prove that the danger to the United States was not imminent. But the central thesis of the antiwar argument as it was advanced before the war asserted that the threat from Iraq would not have been imminent even if Saddam had possessed every conceivable weapon in his arsenal. Remember, the vast majority of arguments against the war assumed that he did have these weapons. But those weapons, it was argued, did not pose an imminent threat to the nation because Saddam, like the Soviet Union, could be deterred. Indeed, the fact that he had the weapons, some argued, was all the more reason why the United States should not go to war. After all, it was argued, the likeliest scenario for Saddam's actually using the weapons he had was in the event of an American invasion. The current debate over "imminence" is an ex post facto attempt to relitigate the old argument over the war. The non-discovery of weapons stockpiles has not changed the contours of that debate.

VI

On *Meet the Press* on February 8, [2004], Tim Russert asked the president whether the war in Iraq was "a war of choice or a war of necessity." The president paused before responding, asking Russert to elaborate, as if unwilling to accept the dichotomy. He was right.

After all, fighting a "war of choice" sounds problematic. But how many of our wars have been, strictly speaking, wars of necessity? How often did the country face immediate peril and destruction unless war was launched?

Was World War I a war of necessity? Was World War II before the attack on Pearl Harbor, or afterwards with respect to fighting Germany in Europe? Was the Spanish-American War a war of necessity? Was the Korean War? Never mind Vietnam, the Dominican Republic, Grenada, Panama, Somalia, Haiti, Bosnia, and Kosovo. And what about the first Gulf War? Many argued that Saddam could be (indeed, was) contained in Kuwait, and that he could eventually have been forced to retreat by economic sanctions.

In some sense all of these wars were wars of choice. But when viewed in the context of history and international circumstances, they were all based on judgments about the costs of inaction, the benefits of action, and on strategic calculations that action then would be far preferable to action later in less favorable circumstances. In other words, war was necessary to our national interest, if not absolutely necessary to the immediate protection of the homeland.

In this case, we believe that war would have come eventually because of the trajectory that Saddam was on—assuming the United States intended to continue to play its role as guarantor of peace and security in the Middle East. The question was whether it was safer to act sooner or later. The president argued, convincingly, that it was safer—it was necessary—to act sooner. Sanctions could not have been maintained; containment, already dubious, was far less persuasive after September 11; and so the war to remove Saddam was, in the broad strategic sense, in the sense relevant to serious international politics, necessary. This is of course a legitimate subject of debate—but it would be almost as much so even if large stockpiles of weapons had already been recovered.

VII

So what about those stockpiles? The failure to find them, and now David Kay's claim that they did not exist at the time of the invasion last year (a claim reported by an astonishing number of journalists as meaning they never existed at all), has led many to maintain that the entire war was fought on false pretenses. We have addressed that claim. But we also want to address Kay's assertion.

We are prepared to believe that the large stockpiles of anthrax, ricin, VX, and other biological and chemical weapons that once existed were at some point destroyed by the Iraqis. But we do not understand why Kay is so confident he knows what happened to those stockpiles, or to other parts of Saddam's weapons programs that have not been found.

According to Kay's testimony before the Senate (and since he has provided no written report and no documentation to support his recent claims, this is all anyone has to go on), Kay and his team "went after this not in the way of trying to find where the weapons are hidden." When the Survey Group did not find the weapons in "the obvious places," presumably meaning the places that had been identified by intelligence and other sources, Kay explains, he tried other means of discovering the truth. His principal method appears to have been interviews with scientists who would have known what was produced and where it might be stored, as well as a search through a portion of the documents uncovered after the war. Kay acknowledges that stockpiles may, in fact, still be hidden somewhere. But he does not believe they are.

Under questioning from the senators, however, Kay admitted a few areas of uncertainty. The first concerns his interviews with Iraqi scientists. On some occasions Kay has claimed that, with Saddam out of power, it could be assumed that scientists once fearful of telling the truth would now be willing to speak. Therefore, their testimony that no weapons stockpiles exist could be trusted. But when asked whether people involved in Iraqi weapons programs might now fear prosecution for war crimes, Kay said, "Absolutely. And a number of those in custody are worried about that greatly," which is "one reason they're not talking." So it turns out there are scientists who are not talking. This produces, Kay suggests, "a level of unresolvable ambiguity" about Saddam's weapons programs. But is the ambiguity truly "unresolvable," or was it just unresolvable within the limited time of Kay's investigation? Is it possible that when all the scientists feel safe enough to talk, we may learn more?

The same question might be asked about the physical searches Kay did not conduct. When Kay delivered his interim report in October 2003, he noted that there were approximately 130 ammunition storage areas in Iraq, some of them spanning an area of about 50 square miles, and including some 600,000 tons of artillery shells, rockets, aviation bombs, and other ordnance. In the 1990s, UN inspectors learned that the Iraqi military stored chemical ordnance at the same ammunition depots where the conventional rounds were stored. As of October [2003], only 10 of these ammunition depots had been searched by U.S. teams. Kay has not said how many were searched in the succeeding four months, but one suspects a great many still have not been examined. Surely this creates another level of ambiguity, which, in time, may be resolved.

Finally there is the question of Iraqi documents. We understand that thousands of pages of documents seized at the end of the war have still not been read. During the 1990s, UN inspectors frequently opened treasure troves of information simply with the discovery of a single document in a mountain of paper. Is it possible that some of the unread documents contain useful information? In addition, according to Kay's October report and his most recent testimony, Iraqi officials undertook a massive effort to destroy evidence, burning documents and destroying computer hard-drives. The result, Kay acknowledged, is that "we're really not going to be able to prove . . . some of the positive conclusions that we're going to come to." Yet another level of ambiguity.

The truth is, neither Kay nor anyone else knows what happened to the weapons stockpiles that we know Iraq once had—because the Iraqis admitted having them. Again, we are willing to be persuaded that Saddam had no weapons stockpiles last year when the war began. But it is too soon, we believe, to come firmly to that conclusion. Nor do we find particularly persuasive the argument that Saddam was only pretending to have weapons of mass destruction, or that he was delusional and being deceived by all around him. These hypotheses are possible. It is also possible we will find stockpiles of weapons, or evidence of their destruction or removal just before the war.

Kay, oddly, has himself suggested in one press interview that the stockpiles or some portion of them may have been transferred to Syria before the war. If that were true, then it would not be the case, *pace* Kay, that "we were all wrong." This past week, moreover, another U.S. government report concerning Iraq's weapons surfaced in the press. Although widely misreported as confirming Kay's claim regarding the stockpiles, in fact the report casts doubt on it. In December 2002, according to *USA Today*, a team of U.S. intelligence analysts predicted it would be extremely difficult to find weapons of mass destruction in the aftermath of an invasion. The study had "considered but rejected the possibility that Iraq had no banned weapons." But it predicted that "locating a program that . . . has been driven by denial and deception imperatives is no small task." Efforts to find the arms after the war would be like "trying to find multiple needles in a haystack . . . against the background of not knowing how many needles may have been hidden."

It remains possible that new evidence will be found. We understand why some now want to declare the search over. But we can hardly see how it benefits the people of the United States or the world to declare it over prematurely.

VIII

Whatever the results of that search, it will continue to be the case that the war was worth fighting, and that it was necessary. For the people of Iraq, the war put an end to three decades of terror and suffering. The mass graves uncovered since the end of the war are alone sufficient justification for it. Assuming the

United States remains committed to helping establish a democratic government in Iraq, that will be a blessing both to the Iraqi people and to their neighbors. As for those neighbors, the threat of Saddam's aggression, which hung over the region for more than two decades, has finally been eliminated. The prospects for war in the region have been substantially diminished by our action.

It is also becoming clear that the battle of Iraq has been an important victory in the broader war in which we are engaged, a war against terror, against weapons proliferation, and for a new Middle East. Already, other terror-implicated regimes in the region that were developing weapons of mass destruction are feeling pressure, and some are beginning to move in the right direction. Libya has given up its weapons of mass destruction program. Iran has at least gestured toward opening its nuclear program to inspection. The clandestine international network organized by Pakistan's A.Q. Khan that has been so central to nuclear proliferation to rogue states has been exposed. From Iran to Saudi Arabia, liberal forces seem to have been encouraged. We are paying a real price in blood and treasure in Iraq. But we believe that it is already clear—as clear as such things get in the real world—that the price of the liberation of Iraq has been worth it.

Blueprint for a Mess
David Rieff

The New York Times Magazine | November 2, 2003

By late autumn of 2003, it had become clear the Iraqi insurgency that had begun in August was not going to end anytime soon—and that the military, political, and logistical challenges of rebuilding Iraq were going to be much greater than originally anticipated. In this article, David Rieff, a writer who specializes in reporting on humanitarian crises, analyzes where the United States went off track. He identifies a number of key factors, including too much initial reliance on Ahmad Chalabi, founder of the London-based opposition group the Iraqi National Congress (whose offices were raided by American and Iraqi forces in the spring of 2004, reportedly for sharing top-secret information with Iran); a bitter feud between the Pentagon and the State Department, which led Defense to shun the expertise of the diplomatic community; and a woefully late start in actually planning for the post-invasion occupation. . . .

In the streets of Baghdad today, Americans do not feel welcome. United States military personnel in the city are hunkered down behind acres of fencing and razor wire inside what was once Saddam Hussein's Republican Palace. When L. Paul Bremer III, head of the Coalition Provisional Authority, leaves the compound, he is always surrounded by bodyguards, carbines at the ready, and G.I.s on patrol in the city's streets never let their hands stray far from the triggers of their machine guns or M-16 rifles. The official line from the White House and the Pentagon is that things in Baghdad and throughout Iraq are improving. But an average of thirty-five attacks are mounted each day on American forces inside Iraq by armed resisters of one kind or another, whom American commanders concede are operating with greater and greater sophistication. In the back streets of Sadr City, the impoverished Baghdad suburb where almost two million Shiites live—and where Bush administration officials and Iraqi exiles once imagined American troops would be welcomed with sweets and flowers—the mood, when I visited in September [2003], was angry and resentful. In October, the 24-member American-appointed Iraqi Governing Council warned of a deteriorating security situation.

Historically, it is rare that a warm welcome is extended to an occupying military force for very long, unless, that is, the postwar goes very smoothly. And in Iraq, the postwar occupation has not gone smoothly.

I have made two trips to Iraq since the end of the war and interviewed dozens of sources in Iraq and in the United States who were involved in the planning and execution of the war and its aftermath. It is becoming painfully clear that the American plan (if it can even be dignified with the name) for dealing with postwar Iraq was flawed in its conception and ineptly carried out. At the very least, the bulk of the evidence suggests that what was probably bound to be a difficult aftermath to the war was made far more difficult by blinkered vision and overoptimistic assumptions on the part of the war's greatest partisans within the Bush administration. The lack of security and order on the ground in Iraq today is in large measure a result of decisions made and not made in Washington before the war started, and of the specific approaches toward coping with postwar Iraq undertaken by American civilian officials and military commanders in the immediate aftermath of the war.

Despite administration claims, it is simply not true that no one could have predicted the chaos that ensued after the fall of Saddam Hussein. In fact, many officials in the United States, both military and civilian, as well as many Iraqi exiles, predicted quite accurately the perilous state of things that exists in Iraq today. There was ample warning, both on the basis of the specifics of Iraq and the precedent of other postwar deployments—in Panama, Kosovo and elsewhere—that the situation in postwar Iraq was going to be difficult and might become unmanageable. What went wrong was not that no one could know or that no one spoke out. What went wrong is that the voices of Iraq experts, of the State Department almost in its entirety and, indeed, of important segments of the uniformed military were ignored. As much as the invasion of Iraq and the rout of Saddam Hussein and his army was a triumph of planning and implementation, the mess that is postwar Iraq is a failure of planning and implementation.

1. Getting In Too Deep With Chalabi

In the minds of the top officials of the Department of Defense during the run-up to the war, Iraq by the end of this year would have enough oil flowing to help pay for the country's reconstruction, a constitution nearly written and set for ratification and, perhaps most important, a popular new leader who shared America's vision not only for Iraq's future but also for the Middle East's.

Ahmad Chalabi may on the face of it seem an odd figure to count on to unify and lead a fractious postwar nation that had endured decades of tyrannical rule. His background is in mathematics and banking, he is a secular Shiite Muslim and he had not been in Baghdad since the late 1950s. But in the early 90s he became close to Richard Perle, who was an assistant secretary of defense in the Reagan administration, and in 1992, in the wake of the first gulf war, he founded the Iraqi National Congress, an umbrella organization of Iraqi opposition groups in exile.

In the mid-90s, Chalabi attended conferences on a post-Hussein Iraq organized by Perle and sponsored by the American Enterprise Institute. There he met a group of neoconservative and conservative intellectuals who had served in the administrations of Ronald Reagan and George H.W. Bush, including Dick Cheney, Donald Rumsfeld, and Paul Wolfowitz, who later formed the core group that would persuade President George W. Bush to go to war with Iraq. As a number of Iraqi exiles have since related, Wolfowitz, then the dean of the Nitze School of Advanced International Studies at Johns Hopkins University, was particularly appalled and shamed by the first Bush administration's failure to help the Kurds and the southern Shiites in the aftermath of the first gulf war. Encouraged by President Bush to "take matters into their own hands," these groups had risen against Saddam Hussein, only to be crushed by his forces while America did nothing. Wolfowitz and his colleagues believed that removing Saddam Hussein would have been the right way to end the first gulf war, and during their years out of power they lobbied the Clinton administration both publicly and privately to make the overthrow of Saddam Hussein a priority.

In the mid-90s Chalabi fell out of favor with the CIA and the State Department, which questioned his popular support in Iraq and accused him of misappropriating American government funds earmarked for armed resistance by Iraqi exile groups against Saddam Hussein. He remained close with Perle and Wolfowitz, however, as well as with other neoconservative figures in Washington, including Douglas Feith, a former aide to Perle, and regularly appeared with them on panels at conservative policy institutes like the Heritage Foundation and the American Enterprise Institute. Chalabi lobbied senators and congressmen to support action against Saddam Hussein, and a coalition of neoconservatives, including Rumsfeld, Wolfowitz, and Perle, sent a letter to President Clinton calling for a tougher Iraq policy. Together they succeeded in persuading the Republican-controlled Congress in 1998 to pass the Iraq Liberation Act, signed into law by President Clinton, a piece of legislation that made regime change in Iraq the official policy of the United States.

After George W. Bush assumed the presidency, Chalabi's Washington allies were appointed to senior positions in the defense establishment. Wolfowitz became deputy defense secretary, Feith under secretary of defense for policy, and Perle head of the Defense Policy Board. Chalabi and the neoconservatives in the Pentagon were united by a shared vision of a radically reshaped Middle East and a belief that the overthrow of Saddam Hussein was the essential first step in the realization of that vision. The Iraq Chalabi envisioned—one that would make peace with Israel, have adversarial relations with Iran and become a democratic model for (or, seen another way, a threat to) Saudi Arabia—coincided neatly with the plan of the administration neoconservatives, who saw post-Hussein Iraq as a launching pad for what they described as the democratization of the Middle East. (Wolfowitz, Perle and Chalabi all refused or did not respond to requests to be interviewed for this article.)

Bush had come into office strenuously opposing "nation building," and in the early months of his presidency the neoconservatives' interventionist view was by no means dominant. But the attacks of September 11, 2001, gave the movement new energy. Within days of the attacks, Wolfowitz was spearheading efforts to put on the table a plan to overthrow Saddam Hussein.

Initially these efforts seemed to go nowhere. There was the war in Afghanistan to fight first, and many senior officers within the military feared that a war in Iraq would stretch American military capabilities beyond their limit at a time when the threat of war loomed on the Korean Peninsula. But the war in Afghanistan was a quick success, and in early 2002 a vigorous lobbying effort by the neoconservatives, both in public and inside the White House, succeeded in moving the idea of Hussein's overthrow to the center of the administration's foreign policy agenda.

Planning began not only for the war itself but also for its aftermath, and various government departments and agencies initiated projects and study groups to consider the questions of postwar Iraq. As Secretary of Defense Rumsfeld would put it later, planning "began well before there was a decision to go to war. It was extensive."

Chief among these agencies was the so-called Office of Special Plans, set up after September 11, 2001, reporting to Douglas Feith in the Pentagon. It was given such a vague name, by Feith's own admission, because the administration did not want to have it widely known that there was a special unit in the Pentagon doing its own assessments of intelligence on Iraq. "We didn't think it was wise to create a brand-new office and label it an office of Iraq policy," Feith told the BBC in July.

The office's main purpose was to evaluate the threat of Saddam Hussein's nuclear, chemical and biological warfare capabilities; its mission reflected the Department of Defense's dissatisfaction with the CIA's conservative estimates of Saddam Hussein's suspected weapons of mass destruction. Chalabi provided the Office of Special Plans with information from defectors ostensibly from Saddam Hussein's weapons programs—defectors who claimed to be able to establish that the Iraqi dictator was actively developing weapons of mass destruction.

Through such efforts, Chalabi grew even closer to those planning the war and what would follow. To the war planners, the Iraqi National Congress became not simply an Iraqi exile group of which Chalabi was a leader, but a kind of government-in-waiting with Chalabi at its head. The Pentagon's plan for postwar Iraq seems to have hinged, until the war itself, on the idea that Chalabi could be dropped into Baghdad and, once there, effect a smooth transition to a new administration.

At the insistence of the civilian administrators in the Pentagon, Chalabi and 500 of his fighters in the Free Iraqi Forces were flown to Nasiriya in southern Iraq in April [2003], in the first weeks of the war. At the time, American military officials were continuing to stress the importance of Chalabi and the Free Iraqi Forces. General Peter Pace, then the vice chairman of the Joint Chiefs of Staff, described them as the "core of the new Iraqi Army." But to the surprise and disappointment of American military leaders on the ground, Chalabi failed to make much of an impression on the people he tried to mobilize.

Timothy Carney, a former American ambassador to Sudan and Haiti who served in the reconstruction team in Iraq just after the war, says that there was, in the Pentagon, "a complete lack of grasp of Chalabi's lack of appeal for ordinary Iraqis." In the end, Chalabi sat out the war in the Iraqi desert and was taken to Baghdad only after the city had fallen and the Americans had moved in.

Many Iraqis outside the Iraqi National Congress felt marginalized by the Pentagon's devotion to Chalabi. According to Isam Al Khafaji, a moderate Iraqi academic who worked with the State Department on prewar planning and later with the American reconstruction office in Baghdad, "What I had originally envisioned—working with allies in a democratic fashion"—soon turned into "collaborating with occupying forces," not what he and other Iraqi exiles had had in mind at all.

Carney agrees. "There was so much reliance on Chalabi in those early days," he says.

2. Shutting Out State

In the spring of 2002, as support for a war to oust Saddam Hussein took root within the Bush administration, the State Department began to gather information and draw up its own set of plans for postwar Iraq under the leadership of Thomas Warrick, a longtime State Department official who was then special adviser to the department's Office of Northern Gulf Affairs. This effort involved a great number of Iraqi exiles from across the political spectrum, from monarchists to communists and including the Iraqi National Congress.

Warrick's Future of Iraq Project, as it was called, was an effort to consider almost every question likely to confront a post-Hussein Iraq: the rebuilding of infrastructure, the shape Iraqi democracy might take, the carrying out of transitional justice and the spurring of economic development. Warrick called on the talents of many of the best Middle Eastern specialists at State and at the CIA He divided his team into working groups, each of which took on one aspect of the reconstruction.

David L. Phillips, an American conflict-prevention specialist at the Council on Foreign Relations in New York and a former adviser to the State Department, served on the project's "democratic principles" group. In his view of the project, "Iraqis did a lot of important work together looking at the future." But however useful the work itself was, Phillips says, the very process of holding the discussions was even more valuable. "It involved Iraqis coming together, in many cases for the first time, to discuss and try to forge a common vision of Iraq's future," Phillips says.

There were a number of key policy disagreements between State and Defense. The first was over Chalabi. While the Pentagon said that a "government in exile" should be established, presumably led by Chalabi, to be quickly installed in Baghdad following the war, other Iraqis, including the elder statesman of the exile leaders, Adnan Pachaci, insisted that any government installed by United States fiat would be illegitimate in the eyes of the Iraqi people. And the State Department, still concerned that Chalabi had siphoned off money meant for the Iraqi resistance and that he lacked public support, opposed the idea of a shadow government. The State Department managed to win this particular battle, and no government in exile was set up.

There was also a broader disagreement about whether and how quickly Iraq could become a full-fledged democracy. The State Department itself was of two minds on this question. One prewar State Department report, echoing the conventional wisdom among Arabists, asserted that "liberal democracy would be difficult to achieve" in Iraq and that "electoral democracy, were it to emerge, could well be subject to exploitation by anti-American elements." The CIA agreed with this assessment; in March 2003, the agency issued a report that was widely reported to conclude that prospects for democracy in a post-Hussein Iraq were bleak. In contrast, the neoconservatives within the Bush administration, above all within the Department of Defense, consistently asserted that the CIA and the State Department were wrong and that there was no reason to suppose that Iraq could not become a full-fledged democracy, and relatively quickly and smoothly.

But Thomas Warrick, who has refused to be interviewed since the end of the war, was, according to participants in the project, steadfastly committed to Iraqi democracy. Feisal Istrabadi, an Iraqi-American lawyer who also served on the project's democratic principles group, credits Warrick with making the Future of Iraq Project a genuinely democratic and inclusive venture. Warrick, he says, "was fanatically devoted to the idea that no one should be allowed to dominate the Future of Iraq Project and that all voices should be heard— including moderate Islamist voices. It was a remarkable accomplishment."

In fact, Istrabadi rejects the view that the State Department was a holdout against Iraqi democracy. "From Colin Powell on down," he says, "I've spent hundreds of hours with State Department people, and I've never heard one say democracy was not viable in Iraq. Not one."

Although Istrabadi is an admirer of Wolfowitz, he says that the rivalry between State and Defense was so intense that the Future of Iraq Project became anathema to the Pentagon simply because it was a State Department project. "At the Defense Department," he recalls, "we were seen as part of 'them.' " Istrabadi was so disturbed by the fight between Defense and State that on June 1, 2002, he says, he took the matter up personally with Douglas Feith. "I sat with Feith," he recalls, "and said, 'You've got to decide what your policy is.' "

The Future of Iraq Project did draw up detailed reports, which were eventually released to Congress last month and made available to reporters for the *New York Times*. The 13 volumes, according to the *Times*, warned that "the period immediately after regime change might offer . . . criminals the opportunity to engage in acts of killing, plunder and looting."

But the Defense Department, which came to oversee postwar planning, would pay little heed to the work of the Future of Iraq Project. General Jay Garner, the retired Army officer who was later given the job of leading the reconstruction of Iraq, says he was instructed by Secretary of Defense Rumsfeld to ignore the Future of Iraq Project.

Garner has said that he asked for Warrick to be added to his staff and that he was turned down by his superiors. Judith Yaphe, a former CIA analyst and a leading expert on Iraqi history, says that Warrick was "blacklisted" by the Pentagon. "He did not support their vision," she told me.

And what was this vision?

Yaphe's answer is unhesitant: "Ahmad Chalabi." But it went further than that: "The Pentagon didn't want to touch anything connected to the Department of State."

None of the senior American officials involved in the Future of Iraq Project were taken on board by the Pentagon's planners. And this loss was considerable. "The Office of Special Plans discarded all of the Future of Iraq Project's planning," David Phillips says. "I don't know why."

To say all this is not to claim that the Future of Iraq Project alone would have prevented the postwar situation from deteriorating as it did. Robert Perito, a former State Department official who is one of the world's leading experts on postconflict police work, says of the Future of Iraq Project: "It was a good idea. It brought the exiles together, a lot of smart people, and its reports were very impressive. But the project never got to the point where things were in place that could be implemented."

Nonetheless, Istrabadi points out that "we in the Future of Iraq Project predicted widespread looting. You didn't have to have a degree from a Boston university to figure that one out. Look at what happened in L.A. after the police failed to act quickly after the Rodney King verdict. It was entirely predictable that in the absence of any authority in Baghdad that you'd have chaos and lawlessness."

According to one participant, Iraqi exiles on the project specifically warned of the dangers of policing postwar Iraq: "Adnan Pachaci's first question to U.S. officials was, How would they maintain law and order after the war was over? They told him not to worry, that things would get back to normal very soon."

3. Too Little Planning, Too Late

The Office of Reconstruction and Humanitarian Assistance (ORHA) was established in the Defense Department, under General Garner's supervision, on January 20, 2003, just eight weeks before the invasion of Iraq. Because the Pentagon had insisted on essentially throwing out the work and the personnel of the Future of Iraq Project, Garner and his planners had to start more or less from scratch. Timothy Carney, who served in ORHA under Garner, explains that ORHA lacked critical personnel once it arrived in Baghdad. "There were scarcely any Arabists in ORHA in the beginning" at a senior level, Carney says. "Some of us had served in the Arab world, but we were not experts, or fluent Arabic speakers." According to Carney, Defense officials "said that Arabists weren't welcome because they didn't think Iraq could be democratic."

Because of the battle between Defense and State, ORHA, which Douglas Feith called the "U.S. government nerve center" for postwar planning, lacked not only information and personnel but also time. ORHA had only two months to figure out what to plan for, plan for it, and find the people to implement it. A senior Defense official later admitted that in late January "we only had three or four people"; in mid-February, the office conducted a two-day "rehearsal" of the postwar period at the National Defense University in Washington. Judith Yaphe says that "even the Messiah couldn't have organized a program in that short a time."

Although ORHA simply didn't have the time, resources, or expertise in early 2003 to formulate a coherent postwar plan, Feith and others in the Defense Department were telling a different story to Congress. In testimony before the Senate Foreign Relations Committee on February 11, shortly before the beginning of the war, Feith reassured the assembled senators that ORHA was "staffed by officials detailed from departments and agencies throughout the government." Given the freeze-out of the State Department officials from the Future of Iraq Project, this description hardly encompassed the reality of what was actually taking place bureaucratically.

Much of the postwar planning that did get done before the invasion focused on humanitarian efforts—Garner's area of expertise. Through the U.S. Agency for International Development, Washington was planning for a possible humanitarian emergency akin to the one that occurred after the first gulf war, when hundreds of thousands of Kurds fled their homes in northern Iraq and needed both emergency relief and protection from Saddam Hussein. This operation, led by Garner, had succeeded brilliantly. American planners in 2003 imagined (and planned for) a similar emergency taking place. There were plans drawn up for housing and feeding Iraqi refugees. But there was little thought given to other contingencies—like widespread looting.

Garner told me that while he had expected Iraqis to loot the symbols of the old regime, like Hussein's palaces, he had been utterly unprepared for the systematic looting and destruction of practically every public building in Baghdad. In fairness to Garner, many of the Iraqis I spoke with during my trips were also caught by surprise. One mullah in Sadr City observed to me caustically that he had never seen such wickedness. "People can be weak," he said. "I knew this before, of course, but I did not know how weak. But while I do not say it is the Americans' fault, I simply cannot understand how your soldiers could have stood by and watched. Maybe they are weak, too. Or maybe they are wicked."

One reason for the looting in Baghdad was that there were so many intact buildings to loot. In contrast to their strategy in the first gulf war, American war planners had been careful not to attack Iraqi infrastructure. This was partly because of their understanding of the laws of war and partly because of their desire to get Iraq back up and running as quickly and smoothly as possible. They seem to have imagined that once Hussein fell, things would go back to normal fairly quickly. But on the ground, the looting and the violence went on and on, and for the most part American forces largely did nothing.

Or rather, they did only one thing—station troops to protect the Iraqi Oil Ministry. This decision to protect only the Oil Ministry—not the National Museum, not the National Library, not the Health Ministry—probably did more than anything else to convince Iraqis uneasy with the occupation that the United States was in Iraq only for the oil. "It is not that they could not protect everything, as they say," a leader in the Hawza, the Shiite religious authority, told me. "It's that they protected nothing else. The Oil Ministry is not off by itself. It's surrounded by other ministries, all of which the Americans allowed to be looted. So what else do you want us to think except that you want our oil?"

As Istrabadi, the Iraqi-American lawyer from the Future of Iraq Project, says, "When the Oil Ministry is the only thing you protect, what do you expect people to think?" And, he adds: "It can't be that U.S. troops didn't know where the National Museum was. All you have to do is follow the signs—they're in English!—to Museum Square."

For its part, the Hawza could do little to protect the 17 out of 23 Iraqi ministries that were gutted by looters, or the National Library, or the National Museum (though sheiks repeatedly called on looters to return the stolen artifacts). But it was the Hawza, and not American forces, that protected many of Baghdad's hospitals from looters—which Hawza leaders never fail to point out when asked whether they would concede that the United States is now doing a great deal of good in Iraq. The memory of this looting is like a bone in Iraq's collective throat and has given rise to conspiracy theories about American motives and actions.

"The U.S. thinks of Iraq as a big cake," one young Iraqi journalist told me. "By letting people loot—and don't tell me they couldn't have stopped the looters if they'd wanted to; look at the war!—they were arranging to get more profits for Mr. Cheney, for Bechtel, for all American corporations."

4. The Troops: Too Few, Too Constricted

On February 25, [2003], the Army's chief of staff, General Eric Shinseki, warned Congress that postwar Iraq would require a commitment of "several hundred thousand" U.S. troops. Shinseki's estimate was dismissed out of hand by Rumsfeld, Wolfowitz, and other civilian officials at the Pentagon, where war plans called for a smaller, more agile force than had been used in the first gulf war. Wolfowitz, for example, told Congress on February 27 that Shinseki's number was "wildly off the mark," adding, "It's hard to conceive that it would take more forces to provide stability in post-Saddam Iraq than it would take to conduct the war itself and secure the surrender of Saddam's security force and his army." Shinseki retired soon afterward.

But Shinseki wasn't the only official who thought there were going to be insufficient troops on the ground to police Iraq in the aftermath of the war. The lack of adequate personnel in the military's plan, especially the military police needed for postconflict work, was pointed out by both senior members of the uniformed military and by seasoned peacekeeping officials in the United Nations secretariat.

Former Ambassador Carney, recalling his first days in Iraq with ORHA, puts it this way, with surprising bitterness: The U.S. military "simply did not understand or give enough priority to the transition from their military mission to our political military mission."

The Department of Defense did not lack for military and civilian officials—men and women who supported the war—counseling in private that policing a country militarily would not be easy. As Robert Perito recalls: "The military was warned there would be looting. There has been major looting in every important postconflict situation of the past decade. The looting in Panama City in the aftermath of the U.S. invasion did more damage to the Panamanian economy than the war itself. And there was vast looting and disorder in Kosovo. We know this."

Securing Iraq militarily after victory on the battlefield was, in the Pentagon's parlance, Phase IV of Operation Iraqi Freedom. Phases I through III were the various stages of the invasion itself; Phase IV involved so-called stability and support operations—in other words, the postwar. The military itself, six months into the occupation, is willing to acknowledge—at least to itself—that it did not plan sufficiently for Phase IV. In its secret report "Operation Iraqi Freedom: Strategic Lessons Learned," a draft of which was obtained by the *Washington Times* in August, the Department of Defense concedes that "late formation of Department of Defense [Phase IV] organizations limited time available for the development of detailed plans and pre-deployment coordination."

The planning stages of the invasion itself were marked by detailed preparations and frequent rehearsals. Lt. Colonel Scott Rutter is a highly decorated U.S. battalion commander whose unit, the Second Battalion, Seventh Infantry of the Third Infantry Division, helped take the Baghdad airport. He says that individual units rehearsed their own roles and the contingencies they might face over and over again. By contrast, the lack of postwar planning made the difficulties the United States faced almost inevitable. "We knew what the tactical end state was supposed to be at the end of the war, but we were never told what the end state, the goal was, for the postwar," Rutter said. (Rutter was on active duty when I spoke to him, but he is scheduled to retire this month.)

Rutter's unit controlled a section of Baghdad in the immediate postwar period, and he was forced to make decisions on his own on everything from how to deal with looters to whether to distribute food. When I asked him in

Baghdad in September whether he had rehearsed this or, indeed, whether he received any instructions from up the chain of command, he simply smiled and shook his head.

Rutter's view is confirmed by the "After Action" report of the Third Infantry Division, a document that is available on an Army Web site but that has received little attention. Running 293 pages and marked "official use only," it is a comprehensive evaluation of the division's performance during the war in Iraq, covering every aspect of operations, from the initial invasion to the postwar period. The tone of the report is mostly self-congratulatory. "Operating considerably beyond existing doctrine," it begins, "the Third Infantry Division (Mechanized) proved that a lethal, flexible and disciplined mechanized force could conduct continuous offensive operations over extended distances for 21 days."

If the report contains one pre-eminent lesson, it is that extensive training is what made the division's success possible. "The roots of the division's successful attack to Baghdad," the authors of the report write, "are found on the training fields of Fort Stewart"—the Third Infantry Division's Georgia base. "A direct correlation can be drawn between the division's training cycle prior to crossing the line of departure and the division's successful attack into Iraq."

But as the report makes clear, no such intensive training was undertaken for postwar operations. As the report's authors note: "Higher headquarters did not provide the Third Infantry Division (Mechanized) with a plan for Phase IV. As a result, Third Infantry Division transitioned into Phase IV in the absence of guidance."

The report concludes that "division planners should have drafted detailed plans on Phase IV operations that would have allowed it"—the Third Infantry Division—"to operate independently outside of guidance from higher headquarters. Critical requirements should have been identified prior to" the beginning of the war, the report states. The division also should have had "a plan to execute" a stability-and-support operation "for at least 30 days."

The report says that such an operation should have included "protecting infrastructure, historic sites, administrative buildings, cultural sites, financial institutions, judicial/legal sites and religious sites." It notes, with hindsight, that "protecting these sites must be planned for early in the planning process." But as the report makes clear, no such planning took place.

Without a plan, without meticulous rehearsal, and without orders or, at the very least, guidance from higher up the chain of command, the military is all but paralyzed. And in those crucial first postwar days in Baghdad, American forces (and not only those in the Third Infantry Division) behaved that way, as all around them Baghdad was ransacked and most of the categories of infrastructure named in the report were destroyed or seriously damaged.

Some military analysts go beyond the lack of Phase IV planning and more generally blame the Bush administration's insistence, upon coming into office, that it would no longer commit American armed forces to nation-building missions—a position symbolized by the decision, now being reconsidered, to close the Peacekeeping Institute at the Army War College in Carlisle, Pennsylvania. According to Major General William Nash, now retired from the Army, who commanded U.S. forces in northern Bosnia after the signing of the Dayton peace accords: "This is a democratic army. If the national command authority tells it that it doesn't have to worry about something anymore"—he was talking about peacekeeping—"it stops worrying about it."

It is hardly a secret that within the Army, peacekeeping duty is not the road to career advancement. Civil-affairs officers are not the Army's "high-fliers," Rutter notes.

Nash, understandably proud of his service as commander of U.S. forces in postconflict Bosnia, is chagrined by the way American forces behaved in the immediate aftermath of the fall of Baghdad. "I know they expected to be greeted with flowers and candy," he says, "or at least the civilians in the Pentagon had assured them they would be. But we know from experience that this kind of welcome lasts only a few days at most. You are welcomed with roses—for one day. Then you have to prove yourself, and keep on proving yourself, every succeeding day of the mission. There are no excuses, and few second chances. That was why, when we went into Bosnia, we went in hard. The only way to keep control of the situation, even if people are initially glad to see you, is to take charge immediately and never let go of control. Instead, in postwar Iraq, we just stood around and responded to events, rather than shaping them."

5. Neglecting ORHA

In his Congressional testimony before the war, Douglas Feith described General Garner's mission as head of ORHA as "integrating the work of the three substantive operations" necessary in postwar Iraq. These were humanitarian relief, reconstruction, and civil administration. Garner, Feith said, would ensure that the fledgling ORHA could "plug in smoothly" to the military's command structure on the ground in Iraq. But far from plugging in smoothly to Central Command, ORHA's people found themselves at odds with the military virtually from the start.

Timothy Carney has given the best and most damning account of this dialogue of the deaf between ORHA officials and the U.S. military on the ground in Iraq. "I should have had an inkling of the trouble ahead for our reconstruction team in Iraq," he wrote in a searing op-ed article in the *Washington Post* in late June, "from the hassle we had just trying to get there. About 20 of us from the Organization for Reconstruction and Humanitarian Assistance showed up at a military airport in Kuwait on April 24 for a flight to Baghdad. But some general's plane had broken down, so he had taken ours."

Carney stressed the low priority the military put on ORHA's efforts. "Few in the military understood the urgency of our mission," he wrote, "yet we relied on the military for support. For example, the military commander set rules for transportation: we initially needed a lead military car, followed by the car with civilians and a military vehicle bringing up the rear. But there weren't enough vehicles. One day we had 31 scheduled missions and only nine convoys, so 22 missions were scrubbed."

More substantively, he added that "no lessons seem to have taken hold from the recent nation-building efforts in Bosnia or Kosovo, so we in ORHA felt as though we were reinventing the wheel." And doing so under virtually impossible constraints. Carney quoted an internal ORHA memorandum arguing that the organization "is not being treated seriously enough by the command given what we are supposed to do."

The lack of respect for the civilian officials in ORHA was a source of astonishment to Lieutenant Colonel Rutter. "I was amazed by what I saw," he says. "There would be a meeting called by Ambassador Bodine"—the official on Garner's staff responsible for Baghdad—"and none of the senior officers would show up. I remember thinking, This isn't right, and also thinking that if it had been a commander who had called the meeting, they would have shown up all right."

Carney attributes some of the blame for ORHA's impotence to the fact that it set up shop in Saddam Hussein's Republican Palace, where "nobody knew where anyone was, and, worse, almost no one really knew what was going on outside the palace. Some of us managed to talk to Iraqis, but not many, since the military didn't want you to go out for security reasons unless accompanied by M.P.'s."

Kevin Henry of CARE, a humanitarian organization active in Iraq, says that he still has similar concerns. "One of my biggest worries," he says, "is the isolation of the palace."

Garner disputes these complaints. He is adamant that he managed to talk with many Iraqis and strongly disagrees with claims that officials in the palace were out of touch.

Still, ORHA under Pentagon control was compelled to adhere rigidly to military force-protection rules that were anything but appropriate to the work the civilians at ORHA were trying to do. Larry Hollingworth, a former British colonel and relief specialist who has worked in Sarajevo and Chechnya and who briefly served with ORHA right after Baghdad fell, says that "at the U.S. military's insistence, we traveled out from our fortified headquarters in Saddam's old Republican Palace in armored vehicles, wearing helmets and flak jackets, trying to convince Iraqis that peace was at hand, and that they were safe. It was ridiculous."

And Judith Yaphe adds, "In some ways, we're even more isolated than the British were when they took over Iraq" after World War I.

Kevin Henry has described the Bush administration as peculiarly susceptible to a kind of "liberation theology in which they couldn't get beyond their own rhetoric and see things in Iraq as they really were."

As the spring wore on, administration officials continued to insist publicly that nothing was going seriously wrong in Iraq. But the pressure to do something became too strong to resist. Claiming that it had been a change that had been foreseen all along (though it had not been publicly announced and was news to Garner's staff), President Bush replaced Garner in May with L. Paul Bremer. Glossing over the fact that Bremer had no experience in postwar reconstruction or nation-building, the Pentagon presented Bremer as a good administrator—something, or so Defense Department officials implied on background, Garner was not.

Bremer's first major act was not auspicious. Garner had resisted the kind of complete de-Baathification of Iraqi society that Ahmad Chalabi and some of his allies in Washington had favored. In particular, he had resisted calls to completely disband the Iraqi Army. Instead, he had tried only to fire Baathists and senior military officers against whom real charges of complicity in the regime's crimes could be demonstrated and to use most members of the Iraqi Army as labor battalions for reconstruction projects.

Bremer, however, took the opposite approach. On May 15, [2003], he announced the complete disbanding of the Iraqi Army, some 400,000 strong, and the lustration of 50,000 members of the Baath Party. As one U.S. official remarked to me privately, "That was the week we made 450,000 enemies on the ground in Iraq."

The decision—which many sources say was made not by Bremer but in the White House—was disastrous. In a country like Iraq, where the average family size is six, firing 450,000 people amounts to leaving 2,700,000 people without incomes; in other words, more than 10 percent of Iraq's 23 million people. The order produced such bad feeling on the streets of Baghdad that salaries are being reinstated for all soldiers. It is a slow and complicated process, however, and there have been demonstrations by fired military officers in Iraq over the course of the summer and into the fall.

6. Ignoring the Shiites

It should have been clear from the start that the success or failure of the American project in postwar Iraq depended not just on the temporary acquiescence of Iraq's Shiite majority but also on its support—or at least its tacit acceptance of a prolonged American presence. Before the war, the Pentagon's planners apparently believed that this would not be a great problem. The Shiite tradition in Iraq, they argued, was nowhere near as radical as it was in neighboring Iran. The planners also seem to have assumed that the overwhelming majority of Iraqi Shiites would welcome American forces as liberators—an assumption based on the fact of the Shiite uprisings in southern Iraq in 1991, in the aftermath of the first gulf war. American officials do not seem to have taken seriously enough the possibility that the Shiites might welcome their liberation from Saddam Hussein but still view the Americans as unwelcome occupiers who would need to be persuaded, and if necessary compelled, to leave Iraq as soon as possible.

Again, an overestimation of the role of Ahmad Chalabi may help account for this miscalculation. Chalabi is a Shiite, and based on that fact, the Pentagon's planners initially believed that he would enjoy considerable support from Iraq's Shiite majority. But it rapidly became clear to American commanders on the ground in postwar Iraq that the aristocratic, secular Chalabi enjoyed no huge natural constituency in the country, least of all among the observant Shiite poor.

The Americans gravely underestimated the implications of the intense religious feelings that Iraqi Shiites were suddenly free to manifest after the fall of Saddam Hussein. Making religious freedom possible for the Shiites was one of the great accomplishments of the war, as administration officials rightly claim. But the Shiites soon demonstrated that they were interested in political as well as religious autonomy. And although the Americans provided the latter, their continued presence in Iraq was seen as an obstacle to the former— especially as the occupation dragged on and Secretary Rumsfeld warned of a "long, hard slog ahead."

After the war, American planners thought they might be able to engage with one of the most moderate of the important Shiite ayatollahs, Muhammad Bakr al-Hakim. He was rhetorically anti-American and yet was willing (and urged his followers) to establish a detente with the occupiers. Had he lived, he might have helped the Americans assuage Shiite fears and resentments. But Hakim was assassinated during Friday prayers in the holy city of Najaf on August 29, [2003,] along with more than 80 of his followers. At this point, it is not clear who the current American candidate is, although there are reports that American planners now believe they can work with and through Grand Ayatollah Ali al-Sistani.

Meanwhile, in the streets the anger of ordinary Shiites grows hotter. Every reporter who has been in Iraq has encountered it, even if administration officials think they know better. As Robert Perito argues, "One of the things that has saved the U.S. effort is that the Shiites have decided to cooperate with us, however conditionally." But, he adds, "if the Shiites decide that they can't continue to support us, then our position will become untenable."

Although they are, for the most part, not yet ready to rebel, the Shiites' willingness to tolerate the American occupation authorities is growing dangerously thin. "We're happy the Americans got rid of Saddam Hussein," a young member of the Hawza in Sadr City told me. "But we do not approve of replacing 'the tyrant of the age' "—as he referred to Hussein—"with the Americans. We will wait a little longer, but we will fight if things don't change soon."

Or as his sheik told me later that afternoon at the nearby mosque, so far they "have no orders" from their religious superiors to fight the Americans. Still, he warned, "we have been very nice to them. But the U.S. is not reciprocating." Last month, in the Shiite holy city of Karbala, the first firefights between American forces and Shiite militants took place, suggesting that time may be running out even more quickly than anyone imagined.

The Next Steps

In Iraq today, there is a steadily increasing disconnect between what the architects of the occupation think they are accomplishing and how Iraqis on the street evaluate postwar progress. And as the security situation fails to improve, these perceptions continue to darken.

The Bush administration fiercely denies that this "alarmist" view accurately reflects Iraqi reality. It insists that the positive account it has been putting forward is the real truth and that the largely downbeat account in much of the press is both inaccurate and unduly despairing. The corner has been turned, administration officials repeat.

Whether the United States is eventually successful in Iraq (and saying the mission "has to succeed," as so many people do in Washington, is not a policy but an expression of faith), even supporters of the current approach of the Coalition Provisional Authority concede that the United States is playing catch-up in Iraq. This is largely, though obviously not entirely, because of the lack of postwar planning during the run-up to the war and the mistakes of the first 60 days after the fall of Saddam Hussein. And the more time passes, the clearer it becomes that what happened in the immediate aftermath of what the administration calls Operation Iraqi Freedom was a self-inflicted wound, a morass of our own making.

Call it liberation or occupation, a dominating American presence in Iraq was probably destined to be more difficult, and more costly in money and in blood, than administration officials claimed in the months leading up to the war. But it need not have been this difficult. Had the military been as meticulous in planning its strategy and tactics for the postwar as it was in planning its actions on the battlefield, the looting of Baghdad, with all its disastrous material and institutional and psychological consequences, might have been stopped before it got out of control. Had the collective knowledge embedded in the Future of Iraq Project been seized upon, rather than repudiated by, the Pentagon after it gained effective control of the war and postwar planning a few months before the war began, a genuine collaboration between the American authorities and Iraqis, both within the country and from the exiles, might have evolved. And had the lessons of nation-building—its practice but also its inevitability in the wars of the 21st century—been embraced by the Bush administration, rather than dismissed out of hand, then the opportunities that did exist in postwar Iraq would not have been squandered as, in fact, they were.

The real lesson of the postwar mess is that while occupying and reconstructing Iraq was bound to be difficult, the fact that it may be turning into a quagmire is not a result of fate, but rather (as quagmires usually are) a result of poor planning and wishful thinking. Both have been in evidence to a troubling degree in American policy almost from the moment the decision was made to overthrow Saddam Hussein's bestial dictatorship.

Iraq: Losing the American Way
James Kurth

The American Conservative | March 15, 2004

In this essay, James Kurth, a political science professor at Swarthmore University, looks at the Iraq democracy project from a long-range, military-political perspective—and finds much to be concerned about. "[I]t is increasingly evident," he writes, "that the war policy of the Bush administration represents a radical abandonment of traditional American ways of dealing with the world, ways that overall have served the United States very well."

Kurth cites three main areas where American policy has diverged from its traditional formula for success: The United States' disregard of the need for international consensus; our abandoment of the Weinberger/Powell Doctrine, which calls for using overwhelming force against a clearly defined military opponent; and a lack of realism in thinking that our democratization experiences in Germany and Japan can be extrapolated to the ethnically divided, democracy-starved nation of Iraq. . . .

The Iraq War has been underway for less than a year, but it has already lasted long enough for us to get some sense of its place in American history and particularly in the grand narrative of America's role in the world. The war has a complex relation with the major dimensions of American foreign policy—particularly the diplomatic, military, and political—but it is increasingly evident that the war policy of the Bush administration represents a radical abandonment of traditional American ways of dealing with the world, ways that overall have served the United States very well.

First, the way that the administration prepared for the war—disregarding the objections of every international organization and most of America's traditional allies—was a sharp departure from the long-standing U.S. diplomatic practice of obtaining some form of international approval and legitimization for our wars and military interventions. The Iraq War represents a repudiation of the traditional American way of diplomacy. Second, the way that the administration has fought the war—deploying military forces unusually few in number and now stretched far too thin—has been a sharp departure from the long-standing U.S. military practice of using overwhelming mass not only to defeat an enemy but also to deter any renewed resistance later. The Iraq

War represents a repudiation of the traditional American way of war. Finally, the way that the administration has tried to establish stability and peace—promoting liberal democracy while imposing military occupation—is in some senses an extension of the historic U.S. practice with democratization projects, but it is one carried to such an unrealistic and impractical extreme that the prospects for success are bleak. The Iraq War represents a perversion of the traditional American way of democratization. In sum, the war is a three-dimensional assault on the American way in international affairs. It is reasonable to expect that it will cause serious harm to America's role in the world.

The diplomatic damage has already been much discussed by policy analysts. Certainly, the arrogant posturing and unilateral actions of the Bush administration as it went to war alienated most of our traditional European allies and provoked suspicion, resentment, and even anger in many. However, unexpected difficulties and experienced incapacities can teach even abrasive officials that help from others—even inferior others—can be a good thing. By now, almost one year into the war, the administration has been driven by its hardships in Iraq to solicit the assistance of the very nations, and the United Nations, that it held in such contempt at the beginning of the war. And remarkably, but realistically, these nations and the United Nations are beginning to respond positively and to heal their breach with the United States. Most of the diplomatic damage from the war is likely to prove self-correcting and short-lived, perhaps like the quarrels of Russia and China with the United States regarding the Kosovo War five years ago.

The Iraq War is likely, however, to cause more grave and long-term injury to the U.S. military and to U.S. efforts to promote democracy abroad. This is because of its violations of the traditional American way of war and way of democratization.

The American Way of War

Military strategists and historians have discerned in some nations a distinctive strategic culture or way of war. In the last third of the 20th century, there was a widespread understanding among these professionals that there was a distinctive American way of war and that it was characterized by a reliance upon such advantages as (1) overwhelming mass (a pronounced advantage in men and materiel), (2) wide-ranging mobility (a pronounced advantage in transportation and communication), (3) high-technology weapons systems, and, underlying and sustaining them all, (4) high public support for the war effort. The purest expression of this American way of war was, of course, World War

II. Another excellent example was the Persian Gulf War. However, the origins of the American way of war lie in the greatest American conflict of all, the Civil War. The use of overwhelming mass was crucial to the final victory of the North; it was exemplified by the strategy of Ulysses S. Grant. Conversely, the use of wide-ranging mobility was critical to the initial victories of the South; it was exemplified by the strategy of Robert E. Lee.

The classical American way of war was a product of the distinctive geographical and economic features of the United States. The U.S. possessed a vast continental territory, which was endowed with ample natural resources and with a population larger than that of most European powers. Thus the United States almost always had a pronounced advantage in men and materiel. Only the Soviet Union could surpass the U.S. in this respect. In turn, mass geography and widespread population created a need for a correspondingly extensive transportation and communication network, and the large industry and advanced technology of the U.S. economy provided the means with which to build it. Furthermore, the United States was bordered by two oceans; it was not only a continent but also a continental island. This also created demand for a transportation and communication network that extended to other continents. This meant that the United States always had a pronounced advantage in the rapid movement of people and products in peace and of men and materiel in war. No power has ever surpassed the U.S. in this respect. The conjunction of a pronounced advantage in both mass and mobility made the United States the most successful military power of the 20th century, and thereby made the 20th century the American century. No other military power could excel in both dimensions.

On the rare but important occasions when the United States could not deploy its advantages in both mass and mobility, the U.S. military faced serious problems. Both the Korean War and the Vietnam War degenerated into wars of attrition in which the U.S. military had the advantage in mass firepower but no obvious advantage in the mobility of its ground combat forces. In the last two years of the Korean War, both the U.S. Army and the communist armies were trapped in a static war of position near the 38th Parallel, and the end result was a stalemate. In the Vietnam War, the communist guerrilla forces had the advantage in mobility, and this contributed greatly to the U.S. defeat. Indeed, it is the nature of any guerrilla war that the insurgent forces have the advantage of mobility, and the counterinsurgency forces have the advantage of mass. It seems that the classical American way of war has no obvious answer if the military challenge comes from guerrillas and insurgents.

In the aftermath of its Vietnam debacle, the U.S. Army painfully examined the lessons of that war, and it largely concluded that the classical American way of war was really the only right way of war for the Army. The lessons learned were institutionalized in the curriculum of the Army War College, as well as several other military schools, and in the strategic doctrine, bureaucratic organization, and weapons procurement of the Army itself. Many of the lessons learned were crystallized in what became known as the Weinberger/Powell Doctrine (after Caspar Weinberger, secretary of defense in the Reagan administration and General Colin Powell, chairman of the Joint Chiefs of Staff in the first Bush administration). Central to the classical American way of war and its recapitulation in the Weinberger/Powell Doctrine was the idea that when the United States goes to war, it should do so as a nation defending its vital national interests against another nation, and when the U.S. Army goes to war, it should do so as an army fighting another army. Wars to advance peripheral, imperial interests and wars against insurgent forces were violations of the American way of war.

The Rumsfeld Transformation Project

From the beginning of the second Bush administration, Secretary of Defense Donald Rumsfeld has worked vigorously and systematically to overthrow the classical American way of war and the Weinberger/Powell Doctrine and to replace them with a new program of military "transformation" and a new doctrine of preemptive (really preventive) war. He has moved to reduce the role of heavy weapons systems (armor and artillery) and large combat divisions in the U.S. Army and to increase the role of lighter and smaller forces (airborne and special operations); in effect, he seeks to reduce the role of mass and to accentuate the role of mobility. To implement his transformation project, he has canceled the Crusader heavy-artillery system, and he has appointed a retired Special Forces general to be the new Army Chief of Staff. Most importantly, however, Rumsfeld has seen the Iraq War as the pilot plant and exemplary case of his grand project of transformation. If the U.S. could win a war in Iraq with a transformed military and a transformed doctrine, it would also be a decisive victory in Washington for the thoroughly new American way of war in its bureaucratic struggles with the old one.

The Rumsfeld transformation project gains credibility because there are indeed some serious problems with the classical American way of war—particularly with the idea that the U.S. Army should only fight another army. The most obvious difficulty is that there no longer seems to be any other real army to fight. Indeed, neither the Army, the Navy, nor the Air Force have any equivalent force or "peer competitor" to fight. Although the Chinese nation might become a peer competitor to the American nation in a couple of decades, that is far in the future, and the last peer competitor—the Soviet military—is now far in the past.

The United States still has enemies, however, most obviously in transnational networks of Islamic terrorists but also in rogue states, such as North Korea. These enemies will seek to attack the United States not with conventional military forces or an American-style way of war but with asymmetrical warfare. At the upper end of the war spectrum, this will mean weapons of mass destruction, particularly nuclear ones in the case of North Korea. At the lower end of the spectrum will be terrorist operations like Al Qaeda and guerrilla warfare, with the Iraqi insurgents now becoming the exemplar. Of course, the most ominous threat comes from a diabolical synthesis of the upper end and the lower end—weapons of mass destruction in the hands of transnational terrorist networks.

The Rumsfeld transformation program and preemptive doctrine does not really address the challenge of rogue states that have already acquired nuclear weapons. Hypothetically, some combination of highly accurate intelligence and highly effective weapons, such as nuclear bunker bombs, could destroy an enemy's stock of WMD. However, the failure to find any significant stock of such weapons in Iraq certainly casts doubt on the accuracy of U.S. intelligence. And even highly effective weapons systems would have a hard time destroying widely dispersed stocks of biological weapons. The only way that the Rumsfeld transformation project can deal with the WMD threat is when a rogue state has not yet acquired these weapons and a U.S. military operation can destroy the rogue regime before it does so. But this would really be a preventive war, not a preemptive one. This was the case with Iraq and conceivably could become the case with Iran.

Nor does the Rumsfeld transformation project really address the challenge of transnational terrorist networks, such as Al Qaeda. This threat is better dealt with by a multidimensional array of agencies and instruments (intelligence, security, and financial) working with their counterparts in other countries that face similar threats, particularly those in Europe. The war in Iraq certainly has not helped to enhance these counterterrorist capabilities, and it may have made more difficult the necessary international trust and cooperation.

• • •

The Rumsfeld Army and Counterinsurgency War

The only task that the new Rumsfeld Army, with its lighter, more mobile configuration, can perform better than the old classical Army, with its heavy armor and artillery configuration, will be operations against an enemy that is even more light and mobile, such as guerrillas and insurgents. And here, several ironies are immediately apparent. First, the origins of the Weinberger/Powell Doctrine lie in the lessons learned from the Vietnam War, and its basic impetus was "no more Vietnams." Among other things, this meant that the regular units of the U.S. Army would fight no more counterinsurgency wars. The Rumsfeld transformation project amounts to a radical overthrow of the Weinberger/ Powell Doctrine, and it seeks to return the Army to the period at the beginning of the Vietnam War—the era when Secretary of Defense Robert McNamara was engaged in his own radical program of military transformation and when other political appointees of the Kennedy and Johnson administrations were enthusiastic advocates of some major combination of high-technology and counterinsurgency. More fundamentally, the Rumsfeld project seeks to transform the U.S. Army into an instrument which will fight for peripheral, imperial interests, and not just for vital national ones. As such, the new way of war can be seen as the neoconservative way of war.

Second, it was not until the United States invaded Iraq and imposed a military occupation that the U.S. faced any guerrilla threat that needed to be dealt with by regular U.S. military forces. (Almost everyone agreed that the guerrilla forces in Afghanistan and in Colombia would be better handled by a combination of U.S. Special Forces and local military forces.) The U.S. occupation of Iraq has created, for the first time since the Vietnam War, the very problem that the Rumsfeld transformation project was supposed to solve.

Third, even before Rumsfeld began his construction of his new Army and his deconstruction of the old one, the United States already had a long established, lighter, and more mobile ground force. That was the U.S. Marines. During the first half of the 20th century, the Marines had far more experience and success with light and mobile operations than did the Army. This included operations against insurgents in the Caribbean basin and in Central America. With only minor modifications, and perhaps some expansion, the Marines could perform virtually all of the tasks that Rumsfeld's lighter, more mobile, transformed Army is supposed to perform. But his new Army may not be able to perform some of the tasks that the old army could perform so well, such as quickly overwhelming another peer competitor army, if one should ever come into being and pose a threat to the vital national interests of the United States.

The American Way of Democratization

The 20th century witnessed numerous attempts to bring democracy to countries that hitherto had been ruled by dictatorial or authoritarian regimes. Most of these efforts were promoted by the United States, and many of them were backed by U.S. military intervention and occupation. Because the 20th century was the American century, it was also the century of democratization. Indeed, the century began with the United States engaged in two separate military occupations to bring democracy (albeit of a distinctively American sort and in a somewhat distant future) to colonies of the former Spanish empire, one in the Philippines and one in Cuba; the Philippine occupation and successful repression of the insurgents there was especially bloody and costly. A decade later, President Woodrow Wilson defined the essence of this new century—which indeed might be seen also as the Wilsonian century—when he first sent the U.S. Marines into several Latin American countries and declared that he was going to "teach the South Americans to elect good men," and then sent the entire U.S. military into Europe and declared that the United States was going "to make the world safe for democracy."

The U.S. attempt at the beginning of the 21st century to use military conquest and occupation to bring democracy to Iraq and, by a process vaguely defined, perhaps to its neighbors as well (particularly Syria, Iran, and Saudi Arabia) is thus the latest chapter in a grand American narrative has been underway for more than a hundred years. By now, many countries know what it means to be, in the words of Jean-Jacques Rousseau, "forced to be free."

Indeed, there have been four great theaters where the United States has performed its epic drama of political democratization through military occupation, of ballots through bullets, over the decades. These were (1) the Caribbean basin and Central America from the 1900s-1930s (Cuba, the Dominican Republic, Haiti, and Nicaragua) and again from the 1960s-1990s (the Dominican Republic and Haiti again and also Grenada and Panama); (2) Central Europe from the 1940s-1950s (West Germany, Austria, and Italy); (3) Northeast Asia from the 1940s-1950s (Japan and South Korea); and (4) Southeast Asia from the 1960s-1970s (particularly South Vietnam).

Together, these add up to more than a dozen cases in which the United States has used military occupation to bring about political democratization.

They provide useful precedents and lessons for the current efforts in Iraq. (The Bush administration and neoconservative writers have repeatedly cited the U.S. successes in West Germany and Japan, but they have been notably silent about the large numbers of failures or disappointments elsewhere, particularly in the Caribbean basin and Central America.)

In addition, the 1990s were the decade of numerous attempts to bring democracy to the countries of the former Soviet Union and communist Eastern Europe. With the exception of Bosnia and Kosovo, these democratization projects did not involve military occupation by U.S. forces. However, as we will see, these ex-communist countries (almost two dozen in number) also provide plenty of evidence and lessons relevant to the prospects for democratization in Iraq.

The Bush administration and the neoconservatives promoted the Iraq War and accompanying regime change as the first phase in a grand project that would bring democracy to Iraq's neighbors and perhaps even to the Middle East more generally. Whenever they had to present an historical precedent to show that this kind of radical and ambitious project had succeeded in the past, they pointed to West Germany and Japan.

They never mentioned the many other U.S. efforts to use military force to democratize countries in Latin America, and of course they never mentioned the epic U.S. failure in South Vietnam. (The one exception is Max Boot, especially in his important book, *The Savage Wars of Peace: Small Wars and the Rise of American Power*.) Nor did they mention the most recent, wide-ranging, and numerous efforts with democratization among the countries of the former Soviet Union and communist Eastern Europe. If any honest discussion about the prospects for democratization in Iraq and other countries of the Middle East had included any analysis of a few of these three dozen cases, the discussion would have ended with a general consensus that the prospects were surely bleak.

The German and Japanese Exceptions

The cases of West Germany and Japan certainly demonstrate that military conquest and occupation can bring about a successful and permanent democratization. The U.S. achievement in these countries was all the more impressive since, in the 1940s, the leading American area specialists and professional experts frequently argued that the peculiar features of German and Japanese history and culture made democracy an alien and unlikely system for these nations. When, in the early 2000s, the leading American area specialists and professional experts have made similar arguments about Arab or Muslim history and culture, one can understand why the promoters of the democratization project for the Middle East could dismiss these arguments and why they might do so in good faith. It is important, however, to look at the circumstances of the German and Japanese cases in more detail. There were three crucial ways in which these circumstances differed from those of today's Iraq.

A prior liberal-democratic experience. First, Germany and Japan (as well as Austria and Italy) actually had considerable experience with some version of liberal democracy only a couple of decades before, during the 1920s between the First World War and the Great Depression. The Weimar Republic, with its grand drama of blighted hopes and dark tragedy, is especially well-known, but Japan also experienced liberalization and even democratization in the 1920s. Austria had a political system similar to the Weimar Republic. And Italy had had a functioning liberal democracy for more than two decades before Mussolini put an end to it in 1922. For a time, each of these countries had developed liberal, democratic, and even social-democratic parties. Although these parties were repressed by the later totalitarian or authoritarian regimes, in the late 1940s the experience was still in the memories of substantial portions of the population. Indeed, some of the prominent leaders of the liberal-democratic period were still there—Konrad Adenauer in Germany, Karl Renner in Austria, Alcide de Gasperi in Italy, and Shigeru Yoshida in Japan—and the U.S. occupation authorities soon drew upon them to assume leadership in the new (really re-newed) liberal-democratic systems.

With regard to this feature of prior historical experience, the contrast between West Germany and Japan in the late 1940s and Iraq (as well as Iran, Syria, and Saudi Arabia) today could not be greater. These latter countries have never been liberal democracies. Further, the most liberal (but hardly democratic) regime in Iraqi history was the monarchy of King Faisal II, but that was violently overthrown in 1958, almost half a century ago. In Iraq, there is no historical base whatsoever for the American democratization project.

To get some sense of how successful externally imposed democratization would be in the absence of internally developed historical experience, one would have to look instead at the U.S. efforts to impose democracy upon such countries as Cuba, the Dominican Republic, Haiti, Nicaragua, and Panama. Here, the only cases that can be said to be successful were the slow establishment of a liberal-democratic system in the Dominican Republic during the decade or so after the U.S. military intervention and occupation in 1965-1966 and the quick establishment of such a system in Panama after the U.S. intervention and occupation of 1989-1990. In contrast, each of the U.S. democratization projects of the 1900s-1930s ended in failure, with the liberal-democratic system overthrown and replaced by some kind of dictatorial regime.

A greater foreign threat. Second, and probably more important, West Germany and Japan in the late 1940s each perceived a foreign threat that was even greater than the one posed by the U.S. occupation. As oppressive as the military forces of the United States might have seemed to the West Germans and Japanese, there was the fear of something that would be even worse: the military forces of the Soviet Union. The threat from the Soviet military was especially obvious to the West Germans, who had ample evidence of the reign of pillage, rape, and murder that the Red Army inflicted upon Germans in the East and could be expected to inflict upon Germans in the West, if they ever got the chance. Even the Japanese feared a possible conquest by the Soviet military and revolution by the Japanese communists, particularly after they saw what the Soviets did to the Japanese colonists and soldiers they captured in Manchuria. As bad as the reality of the American occupation was for both nations, the specter of a Soviet occupation was a good deal worse. And it soon became clear to many West Germans and Japanese that only the American military stood in the way of that specter being realized.

With regard to this second feature, that of perceived foreign threat, there is again a great contrast between West Germany and Japan then and Iraq now. Of course, given the memory of the Iran-Iraq War of the 1980s and the close relations between the Shiite regime in Iran and the Shiite majority in Iraq, Iran would appear to pose a potential threat to Iraq. And given the long-standing hostility of the Turks to the Kurds, Turkey might also appear to pose a potential threat to Iraq.

But Iraqis perceive these hypothetical threats in the context of the ethnic hostilities within Iraq itself. For now, the Iraqi Shiites fear and loathe the Iraqi Sunnis more than they do the Iranian Shiites, and it even seems that for now the Iraqi Kurds fear and loathe the Iraqi Sunni Arabs more than they do the Turks. And it is increasingly evident that both the Sunnis and the Shiites loathe the American occupation as much or more.

Again, to get some sense of how acceptable a U.S. military occupation would be in the absence of a still-greater foreign military threat, one would have to look not at West Germany and Japan but instead at the U.S. occupations in Cuba, the Dominican Republic, Haiti, Nicaragua, and Panama. In the cases where the occupation was prolonged beyond a couple of years, there developed substantial local resentment and even resistance. And in the two most successful cases (the Dominican Republic in 1965-1966 and Panama in 1989-1990), the United States withdrew its military forces and ended its occupation in less than a year.

An ethnically homogenous population. Third, and probably most important, West Germany and Japan (and also Austria and Italy) were among the most ethnically homogeneous nations in the world. There were no significant ethnic minorities—they formed less than two percent of the populations—and there were no significant secession movements. Democratization did bring all sorts of political conflicts and cleavages—particularly around issues of economic class—but no ethnic group or territory voted to separate itself from the rest of the nation.

With regard to this third feature, the ethnic homogeneity prevalent in Germany and Japan is manifestly lacking in Iraq. As is well known, Iraq has never been ethnically homogeneous; from its creation in 1920, it has always been divided into three ethnic parts, the Sunni Arabs, the Shiite Arabs, and the Kurds (who are Sunni, but non-Arab), with the Sunni minority imposing an authoritarian and usually brutal regime upon the Shiite majority and the Kurdish minority. Moreover, the three ethnic parts have roughly corresponded to three territorial parts, with the Sunni Arabs in the center, the Shiite Arabs in the south, and the Kurds in the north (with mixed populations in major cities). Iraq was always an unstable equilibrium, a partition waiting to happen, artificially held together by the iron bonds of an authoritarian and brutal regime. In such circumstances, "regime change" would inevitably result in state change or even country change; in particular, democratization would mean that one or more of the three ethnic and territorial parts of Iraq would vote to separate itself from the others. One could have an Iraq, but without democracy. Alternatively, one could have democracy, but without an Iraq. But one could not have both.

To get some sense of how successful democratization would be with such pronounced ethnic heterogeneity, one would have to look not at West Germany and Japan in the late 1940s but instead at the recent and very extensive experience of democratization in the former communist countries. Certainly, one would have to look especially at the Balkans, which were once called the Near East and which is not that far geographically and sociologically from the contemporary Middle East.

Here the evidence is unambiguous. In virtually every country in the communist world where there was ethnic heterogeneity, democratization—which included free elections—was followed immediately by secession and partition. This was largely peaceful in the case of the Slavic and the Baltic republics of the Soviet Union and in the case of the "velvet divorce" between the Czech Republic and the Slovak Republic. It was violent and even genocidal in the Caucasian republics of the Soviet Union and in several of the republics of Yugoslavia. But be the process peaceful or violent, the democratization of multiethnic societies almost always issued in secession and partition. Given these results of democratization in multiethnic countries of the communist world in the 1990s—especially the violent results in the Caucasus and the Balkans, which are so proximate to Iraq both geographically and historically— it is almost incredible that anyone could seriously argue that the most relevant comparisons to Iraq were the homogeneous nations of West Germany and Japan in the 1940s.

The Coming Failure

In summary, ample historical experience with a wide variety of democratization projects predicts that the U.S. effort to bring democracy to Iraq will end in failure. That effort may fail because the Iraqi people do not have the cultural values, social conditions, or historical experience with which to construct a democracy. Or it may fail because the Iraqi people come to associate democracy with the U.S. occupation and with all the disruptions and humiliations that a military administration inevitably brings. Or it may fail because there is actually no Iraqi people at all, only three peoples who will use democracy to break away from each other—at best, this would result in three democracies, rather than one; at worst, it would result in three states engaged in a new war of their very own. Or it may fail because of all of the above. With all these paths leading straight to failure, it will take a miracle for the U.S. democratization project in Iraq to succeed.

The failure of democratization in Iraq will discredit similar U.S. efforts elsewhere. The damage will be greatest in the Middle East and in the Muslim world more broadly, where Islamism will be left as the only valid ideology and Islamization as the only vital political and social project. Elsewhere, the harm will not be as profound, but for a few years at least, other countries will dismiss any U.S. proclamations and promotions of democratization as just another preposterous, feckless, and tiresome American conceit.

The United States might be able to absorb and eventually recover from this failure in Iraq, rather like it absorbed and eventually recovered from its epic failure in Vietnam three decades ago. Indeed, 30 years from now,

Islamism might itself be discredited in the Middle East, rather like communism is discredited in Southeast Asia today. But like that earlier war, at the end of the day virtually all honest and reasonable people will agree that it would have been best if the United States had never gone to war at all.

Blind Into Baghdad
James Fallows

from *The Atlantic Monthly* | January/February 2004

This year's anthology concludes with the following selection, consisting of several excerpts from a much longer Atlantic Monthly *article. Secretary of Defense Donald Rumsfeld has said repeatedly that his commanders in Iraq will get any additional troops they need—all they have to do is ask. Here, James Fallows provides a reality check, as he reports how Rumsfeld, Vice President Dick Cheney, and Deputy Defense Secretary Paul Wolfowitz consistently pushed for smaller force recommendations from the uniformed military in planning for the war in Iraq. . . .*

Four Months Before the War: The Battle in the Pentagon
On November 5, 2002, the Republicans regained control of the Senate and increased their majority in the House in national midterm elections. On November 8 the UN Security Council voted 15-0 in favor of Resolution 1441, threatening Iraq with "serious consequences" if it could not prove that it had abandoned its weapons programs.

Just before 9/11 Donald Rumsfeld had been thought of as standing on a banana peel. The newspapers were full of leaked anonymous complaints from military officials who thought that his efforts to streamline and "transform" the Pentagon were unrealistic and damaging. But with his dramatic metamorphosis from embattled Secretary of Defense to triumphant Secretary of War, Rumsfeld's reputation outside the Administration and his influence within it rose. He was operating from a position of great power when, in November, he decided to "cut the TPFDD."

"Tipfid" is how people in the military pronounce the acronym for "time-phased force and deployment data," but what it really means to the armed forces, in particular the Army, is a way of doing business that is methodical, careful, and sure. The TPFDD for Iraq was an unbelievably complex master plan governing which forces would go where, when, and with what equipment, on which planes or ships, so that everything would be coordinated and ready at the time of attack. One reason it took the military six months to get set for each of its wars against Iraq, a comparatively pitiful foe, was the thoroughness of TPFDD planning. To its supporters, this approach is old-school in the best sense: if you fight, you really fight. To its detractors, this approach is simply old—ponderous, inefficient, and, although they don't dare call it cowardly, risk-averse at the least.

A streamlined approach had proved successful in Afghanistan, at least for a while, as a relatively small U.S. force left much of the ground fighting to the Northern Alliance. In the longer run the American strategy created complications for Afghanistan, because the victorious Northern Alliance leaders were newly legitimized as warlords. Donald Rumsfeld was one member of the Administration who seemed still to share the pre-9/11 suspicion about the risks of nation-building, and so didn't much care about the postwar consequences of a relatively small invasion force. (His deputy, Paul Wolfowitz, was more open to the challenge of rebuilding Iraq, but he would never undercut or disobey Rumsfeld.) In November, Rumsfeld began working through the TPFDD, with the goal of paring the force planned for Iraq to its leanest, lightest acceptable level.

The war games run by the Army and the Pentagon's joint staff had led to very high projected troop levels. The Army's recommendation was for an invasion force 400,000 strong, made up of as many Americans as necessary and as many allied troops as possible. "All the numbers we were coming up with were quite large," Thomas White, a retired general (and former Enron executive) who was the Secretary of the Army during the war, told me recently. But Rumsfeld's idea of the right force size was more like 75,000. The Army and the military's joint leadership moderated their requests in putting together the TPFDD, but Rumsfeld began challenging the force numbers in detail. When combat began, slightly more than 200,000 U.S. soldiers were massed around Iraq.

"In what I came to think of as Secretary Rumsfeld's style," an Army official who was involved in the process told me recently, "he didn't directly say no but asked a lot of hard questions about the plan and sent us away without approval. He would ask questions that delayed the activation of units, because he didn't think the planned flow was right. Our people came back with the understanding that their numbers were far too big and they should be thinking more along the lines of Afghanistan"—that is, plan for a light, mobile attack featuring Special Forces soldiers. Another participant described Rumsfeld as looking line by line at the deployments proposed in the TPFDD and saying, "Can't we do this with one company?" or "Shouldn't we get rid of this unit?" Making detailed, last-minute adjustments to the TPFDD was, in the Army's view, like pulling cogs at random out of a machine. According to an observer, "The generals would say, Sir, these changes will ripple back to every railhead and every company."

The longer-term problem involved what would happen after Baghdad fell, as it inevitably would. This was distinctly an Army rather than a general military concern. "Where's the Air Force now?" an Army officer asked rhetorically last fall. "They're back on their bases—and they're better off, since they don't need to patrol the 'no-fly' zones [in northern and southern Iraq, which U.S. warplanes had patrolled since the end of the Gulf War]. The Navy's gone, and most of the Marines have been pulled back. It's the Army holding the sack of shit." A related concern involved what a long-term commitment to Iraq would do to the Army's "ops tempo," or pace of operations—especially if Reserve and National Guard members, who had no expectations of long-term foreign service when they signed up, were posted in Iraq for months or even years.

The military's fundamental argument for building up what Rumsfeld considered a wastefully large force is that it would be even more useful after Baghdad fell than during actual combat. The first few days or weeks after the fighting, in this view, were crucial in setting long-term expectations. Civilians would see that they could expect a rapid return to order, and would behave accordingly—or they would see the opposite. This was the "shock and awe" that really mattered, in the Army's view: the ability to make clear who was in charge. "Insights from successful occupations suggest that it is best to go in real heavy and then draw down fast," Conrad Crane, of the Army War College, told me. That is, a larger force would be necessary during and immediately after the war, but might mean a much smaller occupation presence six months later.

"We're in Baghdad, the regime is toppled—what's next?" Thomas White told me, recounting discussions before the war. One of the strongest advocates of a larger force was General Eric Shinseki, the Army Chief of Staff. White said, "Guys like Shinseki, who had been in Bosnia [where he supervised the NATO force], been in Kosovo, started running the numbers and said,

'Let's assume the world is linear.' For five million Bosnians we had two hundred thousand people to watch over them. Now we have twenty-five million Iraqis to worry about, spread out over a state the size of California. How many people is this going to take?" The heart of the Army's argument was that with too few soldiers, the United States would win the war only to be trapped in an untenable position during the occupation.

A note of personal rancor complicated these discussions, as it did many disagreements over postwar plans. In our interview [Undersecretary of Defense] Douglas Feith played this down—maintaining that press reports had exaggerated the degree of quarreling and division inside the Administration. These reports, he said, mainly reflected the experience of lower-level officials, who were embroiled in one specific policy area and "might find themselves pretty much always at odds with their counterparts from another agency." Higher up, where one might be "fighting with someone on one issue but allied with them on something else," relations were more collegial. Perhaps so. But there was no concealing the hostility within the Pentagon between most uniformed leaders, especially in the Army, and the civilians in the Office of the Secretary of Defense (OSD).

Donald Rumsfeld viewed Shinseki as a symbol of uncooperative, old-style thinking, and had in the past gone out of his way to humiliate him. In the spring of 2002, fourteen months before the scheduled end of Shinseki's term, Rumsfeld announced who his successor would be; such an announcement, which converts the incumbent into a lame duck, usually comes at the last minute. The action was one of several calculated insults.

From OSD's point of view, Shinseki and many of his colleagues were dragging their feet. From the Army's point of view, OSD was being reckless about the way it was committing troops and high-handed in disregarding the military's professional advice. One man who was then working in the Pentagon told me of walking down a hallway a few months before the war and seeing Army General John Abizaid standing outside a door. Abizaid, who after the war succeeded Tommy Franks as commander of the Central Command, or CENTCOM, was then the director of the Joint Staff—the highest uniformed position in the Pentagon apart from the Joint Chiefs. A planning meeting for Iraq operations was under way. OSD officials told him he could not take part.

The military-civilian difference finally turned on the question of which would be harder: winning the war or maintaining the peace. According to Thomas White and several others, OSD acted as if the war itself would pose the real challenge. As White put it, "The planning assumptions were that the people would realize they were liberated, they would be happy that we were there, so it would take a much smaller force to secure the peace than it did to win the war. The resistance would principally be the remnants of the Baath Party, but they would go away fairly rapidly. And, critically, if we didn't damage the infrastructure in our military operation, as we didn't, the restart of the country could be done fairly rapidly." The first assumption was clearly expressed by Cheney three days before the war began, in an exchange with Tim Russert on *Meet the Press*:

> RUSSERT: If your analysis is not correct, and we're not treated as liberators but as conquerors, and the Iraqis begin to resist, particularly in Baghdad, do you think the American people are prepared for a long, costly, and bloody battle with significant American casualties?

> CHENEY: Well, I don't think it's likely to unfold that way, Tim, because I really do believe that we will be greeted as liberators . . . The read we get on the people of Iraq is there is no question but what they want to get rid of Saddam Hussein and they will welcome as liberators the United States when we come to do that.

Through the 1990s Marine General Anthony Zinni, who preceded Tommy Franks as CENTCOM commander, had done war-gaming for a possible invasion of Iraq. His exercises involved a much larger U.S. force than the one that actually attacked last year. "They were very proud that they didn't have the kind of numbers my plan had called for," Zinni told me, referring to Rumsfeld and Cheney. "The reason we had those two extra divisions was the security situation. Revenge killings, crime, chaos—this was all foreseeable."

Thomas White agrees. Because of reasoning like Cheney's, "we went in with the minimum force to accomplish the military objectives, which was a straightforward task, never really in question," he told me. "And then we immediately found ourselves shorthanded in the aftermath. We sat there and watched people dismantle and run off with the country, basically."

Three Weeks Before the War

As the war drew near, the dispute about how to conduct it became public. On February 25 the Senate Armed Services Committee summoned all four Chiefs of Staff to answer questions about the war—and its aftermath. The crucial exchange began with a question from the ranking Democrat, Carl Levin. He asked Eric Shinseki, the Army Chief of Staff, how many soldiers would be required not to defeat Iraq but to occupy it. Well aware that he was at odds with his civilian superiors at the Pentagon, Shinseki at first deflected the question. "In specific numbers," he said, "I would have to rely on combatant commanders' exact requirements. But I think . . . " and he trailed off.

"How about a range?" Levin asked. Shinseki replied—and recapitulated the argument he had made to Rumsfeld.

> I would say that what's been mobilized to this point, something on the order of several hundred thousand soldiers, are probably, you know, a figure that would be required.
>
> We're talking about post-hostilities control over a piece of geography that's fairly significant, with the kinds of ethnic tensions that could lead to other problems. And so, it takes significant ground force presence to maintain safe and secure environment to ensure that the people are fed, that water is distributed, all the normal responsibilities that go along with administering a situation like this.

Two days later Paul Wolfowitz appeared before the House Budget Committee. He began working through his prepared statement about the Pentagon's budget request and then asked permission to "digress for a moment" and respond to recent commentary, "some of it quite outlandish, about what our postwar requirements might be in Iraq." Everyone knew he meant Shinseki's remarks.

"I am reluctant to try to predict anything about what the cost of a possible conflict in Iraq would be," Wolfowitz said, "or what the possible cost of reconstructing and stabilizing that country afterwards might be." This was more than reluctance—it was the Administration's consistent policy before the war. "But some of the higher-end predictions that we have been hearing recently, such as the notion that it will take several hundred thousand U.S. troops to provide stability in post-Saddam Iraq, are wildly off the mark."

This was as direct a rebuke of a military leader by his civilian superior as the United States had seen in fifty years. Wolfowitz offered a variety of incidental reasons why his views were so different from those he alluded to: "I would expect that even countries like France will have a strong interest in assisting Iraq's reconstruction," and "We can't be sure that the Iraqi people will welcome us as liberators . . . [but] I am reasonably certain that they will greet us as liberators, and that will help us to keep requirements down." His fundamental point was this: "It's hard to conceive that it would take more forces to provide stability in post-Saddam Iraq than it would take to conduct the war itself and to secure the surrender of Saddam's security forces and his army. Hard to imagine."

None of the government working groups that had seriously looked into the question had simply "imagined" that occupying Iraq would be more difficult than defeating it. They had presented years' worth of experience suggesting that this would be the central reality of the undertaking. Wolfowitz either didn't notice this evidence or chose to disbelieve it. What David Halberstam said of Robert McNamara in *The Best and the Brightest* is true of those at OSD as well: they were brilliant, and they were fools.

Afterward

On April 9 U.S. forces took Baghdad. On April 14 the Pentagon announced that most of the fighting was over. On May 1 President Bush declared that combat operations were at an end. By then looting had gone on in Baghdad for several weeks. "When the United States entered Baghdad on April 9, it entered a city largely undamaged by a carefully executed military campaign," Peter Galbraith, a former U.S. ambassador to Croatia, told a congressional committee in June. "However, in the three weeks following the U.S. takeover, unchecked looting effectively gutted every important public institution in the city—with the notable exception of the oil ministry." On April 11, when asked why U.S. soldiers were not stopping the looting, Donald Rumsfeld said, "Freedom's untidy, and free people are free to make mistakes and commit crimes and do bad things. They're also free to live their lives and do wonderful things, and that's what's going to happen here."

This was a moment, as when he tore up the TPFDD, that Rumsfeld crossed a line. His embrace of "uncertainty" became a reckless evasion of responsibility. He had only disdain for "predictions," yes, and no one could have forecast every circumstance of postwar Baghdad. But virtually everyone who had thought about the issue had warned about the risk of looting. U.S. soldiers could have prevented it—and would have, if so instructed.

The looting spread, destroying the infrastructure that had survived the war and creating the expectation of future chaos. "There is this kind of magic moment, which you can't imagine until you see it," an American civilian who was in Baghdad during the looting told me. "People are used to someone being in charge, and when they realize no one is, the fabric rips."

On May 6 the administration announced that Bremer would be the new

U.S. administrator in Iraq. Two weeks into that job Bremer disbanded the Iraqi army and other parts of the Baathist security structure.

If the failure to stop the looting was a major sin of omission, sending the Iraqi soldiers home was, in the view of nearly everyone except those who made the decision, a catastrophic error of commission. There were two arguments for taking this step. First, the army had "already disbanded itself," as Douglas Feith put it to me—soldiers had melted away, with their weapons. Second, the army had been an integral part of the Sunni-dominated Baathist security structure. Leaving it intact would be the wrong symbol for the new Iraq—especially for the Shiites, whom the army had oppressed. "These actions are part of a robust campaign to show the Iraqi people that the Saddam regime is gone, and will never return," a statement from Bremer's office said.

The case against wholesale dissolution of the army, rather than a selective purge at the top, was that it created an instant enemy class: hundreds of thousands of men who still had their weapons but no longer had a paycheck or a place to go each day. Manpower that could have helped on security patrols became part of the security threat. Studies from the Army War College, the Future of Iraq project, and the Center for Strategic and International Studies, to name a few, had all considered exactly this problem and suggested ways of removing the noxious leadership while retaining the ordinary troops. They had all warned strongly against disbanding the Iraqi army. The Army War College, for example, said in its report, "To tear apart the Army in the war's aftermath could lead to the destruction of one of the only forces for unity within the society."

"This is not something that was dreamed up by somebody at the last minute," Walter Slocombe—who held Feith's job, undersecretary of defense for policy, during the Clinton administration, and who is now a security adviser on Bremer's team—told Peter Slevin, of the *Washington Post*, last November. He said that he had discussed the plan with Wolfowitz at least once and with Feith several times, including the day before the order was given. "The critical point," he told Slevin, "was that nobody argued that we shouldn't do this." No one, that is, the administration listened to.

Here is the hardest question: How could the administration have thought that it was safe to proceed in blithe indifference to the warnings of nearly everyone with operational experience in modern military occupations? Saying that the administration considered this a truly urgent "war of necessity" doesn't explain the indifference. Even if it feared that Iraq might give terrorists fearsome weapons at any moment, it could still have thought more carefully about the day after the war. World War II was a war of absolute necessity, and the United States still found time for detailed occupation planning.

The president must have known that however bright the scenarios, the reality of Iraq eighteen months after the war would affect his re-election. The political risk was enormous and obvious. Administration officials must have believed not only that the war was necessary but also that a successful occupation would not require any more forethought than they gave it.

It will be years before we fully understand how intelligent people convinced themselves of this. My guess is that three factors will be important parts of the explanation.

One is the panache of Donald Rumsfeld. He was near the zenith of his influence as the war was planned. His emphasis on the vagaries of life was all the more appealing within his circle because of his jauntiness and verve. But he was not careful about remembering his practical obligations. Precisely because he could not foresee all hazards, he should have been more zealous about avoiding the ones that were evident—the big and obvious ones the rest of the government tried to point out to him.

A second is the triumphalism of the administration. In the twenty-five years since Ronald Reagan's rise, political conservatives have changed position in a way they have not fully recognized. Reagan's arrival marked the end of a half century of Democrat-dominated government in Washington. Yes, there has been one Democratic president since Reagan, and eventually there will be others. But as a rule the Republicans are now in command. Older Republicans—those who came of age in the 1960s and 1970s, those who are now in power in the administration—have not fully adjusted to this reality. They still feel like embattled insurgents, as if the liberals were in the driver's seat. They recognize their electoral strength but feel that in the battle of ideology their main task is to puncture fatuous liberal ideas.

The consequence is that Republicans are less used to exposing their own ideas to challenges than they should be. Today's liberals know there is a challenge to every aspect of their world view. All they have to do is turn on the radio. Today's conservatives are more likely to think that any contrary ideas are leftovers from the tired 1960s, much as liberals of the Kennedy era thought that conservatives were in thrall to Herbert Hoover. In addition, the conservatives' understanding of modern history makes them think that their instincts are likely to be right and that their critics will be proved wrong. Europeans scorned Ronald Reagan, and the United Nations feared him, but in the end the Soviet Union was gone. So for reasons of personal, political, and intellectual history, it is understandable that members of this administration could proceed down one path in defiance of mounting evidence of its perils. The Democrats had similar destructive self-confidence in the 1960s, when they did their most grandiose Great Society thinking.

The third factor is the nature of the president himself. Leadership is always a balance between making large choices and being aware of details. George W. Bush has an obvious preference for large choices. This gave him his chance for greatness after the September 11 attacks. But his lack of curiosity about significant details may be his fatal weakness. When the decisions of the past eighteen months are assessed and judged, the administration will be found wanting for its carelessness. Because of warnings it chose to ignore, it squandered American prestige, fortune, and lives.

Contributors

Spencer Ackerman is an assistant editor at *The New Republic*.

David Brooks is an op-ed columnist for the *New York Times*, a senior editor at *The Weekly Standard*, a contributing editor at *Newsweek* and the *Atlantic Monthly*, and a political commentator for *The News Hour with Jim Lehrer*. His most recent book is *On Paradise Drive: How We Live Now (and Always Have) in the Future Tense*.

Tina Brown is a columnist for the *Washington Post*, the *London Times* and *Salon.com*. She is the former editor of *The New Yorker* and *Vanity Fair*, and former publisher of *Talk* magazine.

Patrick Buchanan is the founder and editor of *The American Conservative* magazine, and is a columnist for *WorldNetDaily.com*. He is the host of a daily news program, *Buchanan and the Press*, and is a regular panelist on *The McLaughlin Group*. A former presidential candidate, he is the author of numerous books, including *The Death of the West*.

Jonathan Chait is a senior editor at *The New Republic*.

Eleanor Clift is a contributing editor and columnist at *Newsweek*, and a regular panelist on *The McLaughlin Group*. She is the author of several books including, most recently, *Founding Sisters and the Nineteenth Amendment*.

Michael Crowley is an associate editor at *The New Republic*.

Veronique de Rugy is an adjunct scholar specializing in fiscal policy analysis at the Cato Institute. She is the author of the book *Action ou Taxation* (published in Switzerland).

Tad DeHaven is a policy researcher at the Cato Institute.

Lisa DePaulo writes regularly on political subjects in *GQ*, *New York* magazine, and other publications.

E. J. Dionne Jr. is an op-ed columnist for the *Washington Post* and a senior fellow in government studies at the Brookings Institution. He is the author of several books, including *Stand Up, Fight Back: Republican Toughs, Democratic Wimps, and the Politics of Revenge.*

Daniel Drezner is an assistant professor of political science at the University of Chicago. He is the author of the book *The Sanctions Paradox* and has his own weblog—www.danieldrezner.com.

James Fallows is a national correspondent for *The Atlantic Monthly*, and has also written for *The New Yorker*, the *New York Times Magazine*, *The American Prospect*, *The New York Review of Books* and other publications. He is the author of numerous books, including *Breaking the News: How the Media Undermine American Democracy.*

Franklin Foer is an associate editor at *The New Republic.*

Thomas Frank is a contributing editor for *Harper's Magazine*. He is the author of several books, including *What's the Matter with Kansas?: How Conservatives Won the Heart of America.*

Philip Gourevitch is a staff writer at *The New Yorker*. He is the author of several books, including *We Wish to Inform You That Tomorrow We Will Be Killed With Our Families: Stories from Rwanda,* which won the 1998 National Book Critics Circle Award for general nonfiction.

Joshua Green is a senior editor at *The Atlantic Monthly* and a contributing editor for *Washington Monthly.*

Hugh Hewitt is the host of *The Hugh Hewitt Show*, a nationally syndicated radio talk show, and a contributing writer to *The Daily Standard*, the online publication of *The Weekly Standard*. He is also the author of the book *In, But Not Of: A Guide to Christian Ambition and the Desire to Influence the World.*

Christopher Hitchens is a contributing editor for *The Atlantic Monthly*, and a columnist for *Vanity Fair* and *Slate.com*. He is the author of numerous books, including *Why Orwell Matters* and *The Trial of Henry Kissinger.*

Robert Kagan is a contributing editor for *The Weekly Standard* and a senior associate at the Carnegie Endowment for International Peace. A former State Department official, he also writes a monthly column on world affairs for the *Washington Post* and is the author of the book *Of Paradise and Power: American and Europe in the New World Order.*

Robert Kennedy Jr. is senior attorney for the Natural Resources Defense Council, chief prosecuting attorney for the Hudson Riverkeeper, and the president of Waterkeeper Alliance.

Michael Kinsley is the founding editor of the webzine *Slate.com*, and a contributing writer to *Time* magazine. He also served for six years as cohost of CNN's *Crossfire* and is the author of several books, including *The Explainer* (co-authored with Bryan Curtis).

Joe Klein is a columnist for *Time* magazine and a contributing writer to *The New Yorker*. He is the author of several books, including *Primary Colors* and *The Natural: Bill Clinton's Misunderstood Presidency.*

William Kristol is editor of *The Weekly Standard.* The former chief of staff for Vice President Dan Quayle, he also appears regularly on *Fox News Sunday* and on the Fox News Channel, and is the coauthor with Lawrence Kaplan of the book *The War Over Iraq: America's Mission and Saddam's Tyranny.*

Paul Krugman is a professor of economics and international affairs at Princeton University, and an op-ed columnist for the *New York Times*. He is the author of numerous books, including *The Great Unraveling: Losing Our Way in the New Century.*

James Kurth is a professor of political science at Swarthmore College, specializing in American foreign policy, defense policy, and international politics. He is the coauthor, with James Petras, of *Mediterranean Paradoxes: Politics and Social Structure of Southern Europe.*

Scot Lehigh writes a regular op-ed column on Massachusetts politics for the *Boston Globe*.

Nicholas Lemann is the dean of the Columbia School of Journalism. He has worked as a staff writer for *The New Yorker*, national correspondent for *The Atlantic*, and managing editor of *Washington Monthly*, and is the author of several books, including *The Big Test: The Secret History of the American Meritocracy*.

Anthony Lewis is a former *New York Times* columnist and a regular contributor to *The New York Review of Books*. He won the Pulitzer Prize for national reporting in 1955 and again in 1963, and is the author of several books, including *Gideon's Trumpet*.

Ryan Lizza is an associate editor at *The New Republic*.

Harold Meyerson is editor at large for *The American Prospect*, political editor of *L.A. Weekly*, and a weekly op-ed columnist for the *Washington Post*.

Charles Morris is the author of numerous books, including *Money, Greed and Risk: Why Financial Crises and Crashes Happen*.

Terry Neal is the chief political correspondent and a regular columnist for *WashingtonPost.com*.

Robert Novak is a nationally syndicated columnist. He is a regular panelist and co-executive producer for CNN's *Capital Gang*, and has coauthored several books with Rowland Evans, including *The Reagan Revolution*.

Bruce Nussbaum is the editorial page editor at *Business Week*, and author of the book *Good Intentions: How Big Business and the Medical Establishment Are Corrupting the Fight Against AIDS*.

George Packer is a staff writer for *The New Yorker* and a columnist for *Mother Jones*. His work has also appeared in *The Nation, Harper's,* and the *New York Times Magazine*. He is the author of numerous books including, most recently, *The Fight is For Democracy: Winning the War of Ideas in America and the World*.

Katha Pollitt is a columnist for *The Nation*. She is the author of several books, including *Antarctic Traveller*, winner of the 1982 National Book Critics Circle

Award for Poetry, and *Subject to Debate: Sense and Dissents on Women, Politics, and Culture.*

Edward Pound is assistant managing editor for investigative projects at *U.S. News & World Report*.

Bruce Reed is president of the Democratic Leadership Council, and a former domestic policy adviser for the Clinton administration.

David Rieff is a senior fellow at the World Policy Institute at the New School in New York City and a fellow at the New York Institute for the Humanities at New York University. He is the author of several books including, most recently, *A Bed for the Night: Humanitarianism in Crisis.*

Ruth Rosen is a columnist for the *San Francisco Chronicle*. She is the author of several books, including *The World Split Open: How the Modern Women's Movement Changed America.*

Matthew Rothschild is editor of *The Progressive.*

William Safire is an op-ed columnist for the *New York Times*, and a recipient of the 1978 Pulitzer Prize for commentary. A former speechwriter for Richard Nixon, he is the author of several books including, most recently, *Scandalmonger.*

David Samuels is a contributing editor for *Harper's Magazine*. He has also written for *The New Yorker* and *Slate.com.*

Jonathan Schell is the peace and disarmament correspondent for *The Nation*, and holds the position of Harold Willens Peace Fellow at The Nation Institute. He is the author of numerous books including, most recently, *The Unconquerable World: Power, Nonviolence, and the Will of the People.*

Christopher Schmitt is a senior writer at *U.S. News & World Report.*

Andrew Sullivan is a senior editor at *The New Republic*. He is the author of several books, including *Virtually Normal: An Argument About Homosexuality.*

Ron Suskind writes for a variety of publications, including *Esquire* and the *New York Times Magazine*. He was a recipient of the Pulitzer Prize for feature writing in 1995, while working for the *Wall Street Journal,* and is the author of *The Price of Loyalty: George W. Bush, the White House and the Education of Paul O'Neill.*

Jeffrey Toobin is a staff writer for *The New Yorker* and a legal analyst for CNN. He is the author of several books, including *Too Close to Call: The 36-Day Battle to Decide the 2000 Election.*

Michael Wolff recently joined *Vanity Fair* as a columnist, after a long stint as media columnist and contributing editor for *New York* magazine. He is the author of numerous books, including *Burn Rate: How I Survived the Gold Rush Years on the Internet.*

Richard Wolffe is *Newsweek's* diplomatic correspondent, and writes a regular column for the magazine's website.

Bob Woodward is an assistant managing editor at the *Washington Post*. He is the author of numerous books, including *Plan of Attack* and *Bush at War*.

Permissions

Excerpt from *The Price of Loyalty: George W. Bush, the White House, and the Education of Paul O'Neill* by Ron Suskind. Copyright © 2004 by Ron Suskind. Reprinted by permission of Simon & Schuster Adult Publishing Group.

"The Radical" by Franklin Foer and Spencer Ackerman. Copyright © 2003 by The New Republic LLC. Reprinted by permission. Originally appeared in *The New Republic*, December 1, 2003.

"The Controller" by Nicholas Lemann. Copyright © 2003 by Nicholas Lemann. Used by permission of International Creative Management Inc. Originally appeared in *The New Yorker*, May 12, 2003.

"Bush's War Against Wonks" by Bruce Reed. Copyright © 2004 by Washington Monthly Publishing LLC, 733 15ᵗʰ St. NW, Suite 520, Washington DC 20005. On the Web at www.washingtonmonthly.com. Reprinted with permission. Originally appeared in *The Washington Monthly*, March 2004.

"Keeping Secrets" by Christopher Schmitt and Edward Pound. Copyright © 2003 by U.S. News & World Report L.P. Reprinted with permission. Originally appeared in *U.S News & World Report*, December 22, 2003.

"Un-American Recovery" by Harold Meyerson. Copyright © 2004 by Harold Meyerson. Used by permission of the author. Originally appeared in the *Washington Post*, December 24, 2003.

"Where Are The Jobs?" by Bruce Nussbaum. Copyright © 2004 by Business-Week. Reprinted with permission. Originally appeared in *BusinessWeek*, March 22, 2004.

"The Mother of All Big Spenders: Bush Spends Like Carter and Panders Like Clinton" by Veronique de Rugy and Tad DeHaven. Copyright © 2003 by the National Review Online / Distributed by United Feature Syndicate Inc. Reprinted with permission. Originally appeared in the *National Review Online*, July 28, 2003.

"The Nixon Recovery" by Charles Morris. Copyright © 2004 by The New York Times Company. Reprinted by permission. Originally appeared in the *New York Times*, February 7, 2004.

"Fighting Big Pharmacy" by Eleanor Clift. Copyright © 2003 by Newsweek Inc. All rights reserved. Reprinted by permission. Originally appeared in the online edition of *Newsweek*, August 1, 2003.